SAP Crystal Reports 2011 For Beginners

By Dr. Indera E. Murphy

Tolana Publishing
Teaneck, New Jersey

SAP Crystal Reports 2011 For Beginners

Published By:
Tolana Publishing
PO Box 719
Teaneck, NJ 07666 USA

Find us online at www.tolanapublishing.com
Inquiries may be sent to the publisher: tolanapub@yahoo.com

Our books are available online at www.barnesandnoble.com. They can also be ordered from Ingram and Baker & Taylor.

Quantity discounts are available for corporations, non-profit organizations and educational institutions for educational purposes, fundraising or resale. www.tolana.com/wholesale.html

ISBN-13: 978-1-935208-15-0
ISBN-10: 1-935208-15-2

Library of Congress Control Number: 2011939873

Printed and bound in the United States Of America

Notice of Liability
The information in this book is distributed on as "as is" basis, without warranty. Every effort has been made to ensure that this book contains accurate and current information. However, the publisher and author shall not be liable to any person or entity with respect to any loss or damage caused or alleged to be caused directly or indirectly, as a result of any information contained herein or by the computer software and hardware products described in it.

Trademarks
All companies and product names are trademarks or registered trademarks of their respective companies. They are used in this book in an editorial fashion only. No use of any trademark is intended to convey endorsement or other affiliation with this book.

Cover by Mary Kramer, owner of Milkweed Graphics, www.milkweedgraphics.com

v1.0

About The No Stress Tech Guide Series

SAP Crystal Reports 2011 For Beginners, is part of the growing series of computer software books that are designed to be used as a self-paced learning tool, in a classroom setting or in an online class. The books in this series contain an abundance of step-by-step instructions and screen shots to help reduce the "stress" often associated with learning new software.

Titles In The Series

	ISBN
ACT! 2007	978-0-9773912-5-7
ACT! 2009	978-1-935208-07-5
ACT! 2010	978-1-935208-09-9
ACT! Pro 2011	978-1-935208-13-6
ACT! Pro 2012	978-1-935208-17-4
Using Crystal Reports 2008 With ACT! 2010 Databases	978-1-935208-10-5
Crystal Reports XI For Beginners (2nd Edition)	978-1-935208-00-6
What's New In Crystal Reports 2008	978-1-935208-01-3
Crystal Reports 2008 For Beginners	978-0-9773912-9-5
Crystal Reports 2011 For Beginners	978-1-935208-15-0
Crystal Reports For Visual Studio 2005	978-0-9773912-6-4
Crystal Reports Basic For Visual Studio 2008	978-0-9773912-8-8
Crystal Reports For Visual Studio 2010	978-1-935208-12-9
Crystal Xcelsius 4.5	978-1-935208-02-0
Xcelsius 2008	978-1-935208-05-1
OpenOffice.org 2 Writer	978-0-9773912-4-0
OpenOffice.org 3 Writer	978-1-935208-08-2
Microsoft Office Starter 2010 (Word & Excel)	978-1-935208-14-3
Microsoft PowerPivot For Excel 2010	978-1-935208-16-7
Microsoft Works 7	978-0-9773912-2-6
Microsoft Works 8 & 8.5	978-0-9773912-1-9
Microsoft Works 9	978-0-9773912-7-1
Windows XP	978-0-9773912-0-2

Coming Soon

| SAP Crystal Dashboard Design 2011 For Beginners | 978-1-935208-11-2 |
| (Formerly known as Xcelsius 2008) | |

About The Author

Dr. Indera E. Murphy is an author, educator and IT professional that has over 20 years of experience in the Information Technology field. She has held a variety of positions including technical writer, programmer, consultant, web designer, course developer and project leader. Indera has designed and developed software applications and web sites, as well as, manage technology driven projects in several industries. In addition to being an Executive Director and consultant, as an online adjunct professor, she has taught courses in a variety of areas including project management, technical writing, information processing, Access, HTML, Windows, Excel, Dreamweaver and critical thinking.

Thank you for purchasing this book!

Why A Book On Crystal Reports 2011?

After reading the Users Guide that comes with Crystal Reports 2011, I felt that users, especially new users would prefer to have more assistance in learning how to get the most out of the software. As a professor and author, I do not feel that flipping between a book and the Help System is the most ideal way to learn how to use a software package.

I know that many books claim to have "step-by-step instructions". If you have tried to follow books that make this claim and you got lost or could not complete a task as instructed, it may not have been your fault. When I decided to write computer books, I vowed to really have step-by-step instructions that actually included every step. This includes steps like which file to open, which menu option to select, when to save a file and more. In my opinion, it is this level of detail that makes a computer book easy to follow. I hope that you feel the same way.

Why I Wrote This Book

There are a few reasons that I decided to write a book for Crystal Reports 2011. They are listed below.

⇒ In general, there are not a lot of beginner level books with hands-on exercises for complex software.
⇒ I felt that users, especially new report writers and designers would prefer to have more assistance in learning how to get the most out of Crystal Reports 2011.

Who This Book Is For

This book is for people that want to learn SAP Crystal Reports 2011. This book does not cover **SAP CRYSTAL REPORTS FOR ENTERPRISE 4.0**.

This book is primarily for beginners and end-users, as well as, report designers and developers that have never used Crystal Reports. Business Intelligence consultants and professionals will find this book helpful in terms of how they can incorporate Crystal Reports into the projects that they work on.

Over the years, I have come to realize that many people only use a small percent of the features that software has to offer. One of my goals in all of the books that I write is to point out as many features as possible. My theory is that if more people knew about more than 10% of the features that a software package has, at the very least, they would try a few of them.

I know that many books claim to have "step-by-step instructions". If you have tried to follow books that make this claim and you got lost or could not complete a task as instructed, it may not have been your fault. When I decided to write computer books, I vowed to really have step-by-step instructions that actually included every step, even though some people claim that it is annoying. This includes steps like which file to open, which option to select, when to save a file and more. In my opinion, it is this level of detail that makes a computer book easy to follow. I hope that you feel the same way. If not, this is probably not the book for you.

CONTENTS

GETTING STARTED WITH SAP CRYSTAL REPORTS 2011 1-1
    How This Book Is Organized 1-3
    Getting Help With Crystal Reports 1-7
    Crystal Reports Certification 1-7
    What's New In SAP Crystal Reports 2011 1-8
    Start Page Tab 1-8
        Start A New Report 1-9
        My Recent Reports 1-9
        Start Page Tab Menu Options 1-9
    Checking For Software Updates 1-10
    Exercise 1.1: Create A Folder For Your Reports 1-11

TOOLBARS, MENUS AND CUSTOMIZATION OPTIONS 2-1
    Crystal Reports Toolbars 2-2
        Standard Toolbar 2-2
        Formatting Toolbar 2-3
        Insert Tools Toolbar 2-4
        Navigation Tools Toolbar 2-4
        Expert Tools Toolbar 2-5
        External Command Toolbar 2-6
    Crystal Reports Menus 2-7
        File Menu 2-7
        Edit Menu 2-8
        View Menu 2-10
        Insert Menu 2-11
        Format Menu 2-12
        Database Menu 2-13
        Report Menu 2-14
        Chart Menu 2-16
        Map Menu 2-16
        Window Menu 2-17
        Help Menu 2-17
    Customizing The Crystal Reports Design Environment 2-18

DATABASE TERMINOLOGY AND THE CRYSTAL REPORTS WORKSPACE   3-1
    Database Terminology 3-2
    Database Concepts 3-2
    Data Types 3-3
    Crystal Reports Terminology 3-4
    Report Design Process 3-4
        Step 1: Define The Purpose Of The Report 3-5
        Step 2: Determine The Layout Of The Report 3-6
        Step 3: Find The Data For The Report 3-6
        Step 4: Organize The Data 3-7
    Report Prototype 3-8
    Sections Of A Report 3-8
        Section 1: Report Header (RH) 3-8
        Section 2: Page Header (PH) 3-9

Section 3: Group Header (GH) 3-9
Section 4: Details (D) 3-9
Section 5: Group Footer (GF) 3-9
Section 6: Report Footer (RF) 3-10
Section 7: Page Footer (PF) 3-10
Report Creation Options 3-10
Wizards 3-10
Create A Report Based Off Of An Existing Report 3-11
Create A Report From Scratch 3-11
Wizard Types 3-11
Report 3-11
Cross-Tab 3-11
Mailing Label 3-11
OLAP Cube 3-11
Xtreme Database 3-11
Xtreme Database Tables 3-12
Crystal Reports Workspace 3-13
Preview Tab 3-13
The Status Bar 3-14
Preview Panel 3-15
The Group Tree 3-16
Design Tab 3-17
The Workbench 3-18
Exercise 3.1: Create A Folder In The Workbench 3-19
Adding Reports To The Workbench 3-19
Deleting Projects And Reports From The Workbench 3-20
Maintaining The Workbench 3-20
Explorers 3-21
Field Explorer 3-22
Field Explorer Shortcut Menu (For Fields) 3-23
Field Explorer Shortcut Menu (For Databases And Tables) 3-24
Sort Fields In The Field Explorer 3-25
Repository Explorer 3-25
Docking The Explorers 3-26
The Push Pin 3-27

CREATE YOUR FIRST REPORT 4-1
Exercise 4.1: Create Your First Report 4-2
Why Do I Have To Connect To A Data Source? 4-2
Step 1: Create A Connection To The Data Source 4-3
Step 2: Select The Tables 4-4
Step 3: Select The Fields 4-7
Step 4: Select The Grouping Options 4-8
Step 5: Select The Summary Options 4-9
Step 6: Select The Chart Type 4-10
Step 7: Select The Fields To Filter On 4-11
Step 8: Select A Template 4-12
Step 9: Save The Report 4-12
Step 10: Add The Current Report To The Workbench 4-16
Selecting A Data Source 4-16
Report Bursting Indexes 4-16
Exercise 4.2: Create A Product List Report 4-17
Exercise 4.3: Create An Employee Contact List Report 4-17

Linking Tables..4-17
    Index Legend 4-18
Crystal Reports Report Processing Model 4-21
Saving An Existing Report With A New File Name.......................4-21

CREATING REPORTS FROM SCRATCH **5-1**
The Database Expert..5-2
Data Source Options 5-2
    Tables...5-2
    Business Views 5-2
    Commands 5-3
    SQL 5-3
    Stored Procedures 5-3
    Other Data Source Options..5-4
Exercise 5.1: Create Your First Report From Scratch....................5-4
Exercise 5.2: Create A Report Using Multiple Tables 5-6
How To Add And Remove Databases And Tables 5-8
Relational Databases 5-9
    Primary Key Fields 5-9
    Types Of Relationships...5-10
    How Linking Works 5-11
    Join Types..5-12
    Recursive Join 5-14
    Smart Linking 5-14
    Manual Join Types 5-15
Exercise 5.3: Create A Customer Orders Report 5-16
Exercise 5.4: Create An Orders Report.......................................5-17
Using A Table Alias...5-17

ALIGNING OBJECTS ON A REPORT **6-1**
Shortcut Menus...6-2
Selecting Fields And Objects 6-3
Exercise 6.1: Moving Objects 6-4
Aligning Objects Vertically...6-4
Aligning Objects Horizontally...6-5
Guidelines..6-6
    How To Manually Add Guidelines 6-8
    Turning The Guidelines On 6-8
    Using Guidelines To Move Objects 6-8
Using The Grid..6-9
Resizing Objects...6-9
Size Options...6-10
Nudging Objects 6-12
Using Object Layering 6-12

EDITING AND FORMATTING REPORTS **7-1**
Exercise 7.1: How To Edit Text Objects 7-2
    How To Add A Text Object 7-3
    How To Format A Text Object 7-4
Combining Text Objects And Database Fields...............................7-5
Exercise 7.2: Adding Image Files To A Report 7-5
    How To Resize An Image 7-6

Exercise 7.3: Adding Graphics From Fonts 7-6
The Format Editor 7-7
Exercise 7.4: Format A Text Object 7-10
Exercise 7.5: Using The Can Grow Option 7-11
Exercise 7.6: Format A Numeric Field 7-14
Format A Date/Time Field 7-16
Resize The Image File 7-17
Exercise 7.7: Format A Boolean Field 7-18
Exercise 7.8: Using The Format Painter 7-19
Exercise 7.9: Centering Data Under A Heading 7-21
How To Add Horizontal Lines To A Report 7-21
Exercise 7.10: Add Vertical Lines To A Report 7-22

USING SUBSECTIONS, SPECIAL FIELDS AND THE REPORT EXPLORER 8-1
Subsections 8-2
Exercise 8.1: How To Create Subsections 8-2
Exercise 8.2: Add A Background Color To A Report Section 8-3
Exercise 8.3: Add A Border To A Field 8-3
Exercise 8.4: Adding Boxes To A Report 8-5
Use The Rounding Options 8-6
Add A Box Around A Text Object 8-6
Special Fields 8-7
Exercise 8.5: Add Special Fields To A Report 8-9
Report Explorer 8-12
Custom Colors 8-15
Exercise 8.6: Swapping Fields 8-16

SELECTING RECORDS 9-1
The Select Expert 9-2
Operators 9-3
Is In The Period Functions 9-4
Using The Select Expert 9-5
Exercise 9.1: Using The Is Equal To Operator 9-6
Exercise 9.2: Using The Is One Of Operator 9-8
Exercise 9.3: Using The Is Greater Than Or Equal To Operator 9-9
Exercise 9.4: Modify Selection Criteria 9-10
Exercise 9.5: Using The Is Between Operator 9-10
Exercise 9.6: Using Multiple Selection Criteria 9-11
Viewing Formulas 9-11
How To Delete Selection Criteria 9-13
Understanding How Date/Time Fields Work In Selection Criteria 9-13
Edit An Existing Formula 9-15
Record Selection Performance Considerations 9-16
Case Sensitive Considerations 9-17
Using Wildcard Characters As Selection Criteria 9-18
Document Properties 9-18
    Summary Tab Options 9-18
    Statistics Tab Options 9-19
    Add Summary Information To A Report 9-19

GROUPING, SORTING AND SUMMARIZING RECORDS 10-1
Grouping Records 10-2
Insert Group Dialog Box 10-3

Custom Grouping 10-5
    User Defined Sort Order 10-5
Sorting Records 10-6
Summary Information 10-7
Creating Groups 10-10
Exercise 10.1: Group Customer Information By Region 10-11
Exercise 10.2: Group Orders By Customer 10-18
Displaying The Record Selection Formula Field 10-23

CREATING CUSTOM GROUPS 11-1
Exercise 11.1: Change The Group Order 11-2
Custom Group Names 11-3
    Use A Different Field As The Group Name 11-3
Exercise 11.2: Group Customer Orders By Month 11-5
How To Create Percent Calculations 11-6
How To Check Or Edit Summary Fields 11-7
How To Create A Custom Group Name 11-9
Group Selection Criteria On Summary Fields 11-10
Using The Group Expert 11-11
User Defined Groups 11-12
Exercise 11.3: Create A User Defined Group Report 11-13
Exercise 11.4: Create A Custom Group Name Report 11-14

USING THE REPORT CREATION WIZARDS 12-1
Report Wizards 12-2
Common Report Wizard Screens 12-3
    Data Screen 12-4
    Fields Screen 12-4
    Grouping Screen 12-4
    Summaries Screen 12-5
    Group Sorting Screen 12-5
    Chart Screen 12-6
    Record Selection Screen 12-6
    Template Screen 12-7
Exercise 12.1: Create The Region = OH Or FL List Report 12-8
Exercise 12.2: Create The Order Date And Order Amount Report 12-9
Exercise 12.3: Create A Group Summary Report 12-9
Exercise 12.4: Create A Top N Report 12-10
Exercise 12.5: Fix The Top 5 Order Days Report 12-12
Exercise 12.6: Use The Mailing Label Wizard 12-13

PRINTING AND EXPORTING REPORTS 13-1
Printing Options 13-2
Page Setup Options 13-2
    Page Orientation 13-3
    Page Margins 13-3
    Paper Size 13-3
Using The Adjust Automatically Option 13-3
Printer Options 13-4
Exercise 13.1: Use The Set Print Date And Time Options 13-5
Exercise 13.2: Use The Preview Sample Option 13-6
Report Options Dialog Box 13-7

Report Export Overview 13-8
    Export Format Options... 13-8
    Export Destination Options..13-11
    Default Export Options 13-12
Exercise 13.3: Create A PDF Export File 13-13
Exercise 13.4: Create An Excel (97-2003) Export File 13-14
Exercise 13.5: Create An Excel Workbook Data Only Export File 13-16
Exercise 13.6: Create A Separated Values (CSV) Export File 13-19
Exercise 13.7: Create A Crystal Reports Read-Only Export File..........13-20
ODBC Export Format..13-20
Text Export Format..13-21
XML Export Format 13-21
Crystal Reports Viewer 13-21

FORMULAS AND FUNCTIONS **14-1**
What Is The Difference Between Formulas And Functions? 14-2
Formulas.. 14-2
Syntax Rules 14-3
Functions 14-4
Syntax Language And Editors 14-4
Formula Workshop... 14-6
    Workshop Tree 14-9
    Formula Editor 14-10
    SQL Expression Editor..14-12
    Formula Expert 14-12
Formula Evaluation Order...14-14
Formula Naming Conventions...14-14
Exercise 14.1: Create A Formula Field 14-15
Exercise 14.2: Create A Sales Tax Formula 14-18
Exercise 14.3: Create A Weekly Salary Formula 14-20
Exercise 14.4: Combine Two String Fields 14-22
Exercise 14.5: Use The Subscript Operator 14-23
Exercise 14.6: Combine A Text And Numeric Field 14-23
Exercise 14.7: Use The Picture Function 14-25
Formatting Strings With A Mask..14-26
Exercise 14.8: Create A Date Formula To Calculate The Order Processing Time....................14-28
Exercise 14.9: Calculate The Employee Age..14-28
Run-Time Errors 14-31

CONDITIONAL FORMATTING **15-1**
Conditional Formatting Tips.. 15-2
Highlighting Expert 15-3
    Item List Section Options.. 15-4
    Item Editor Section Options 15-4
Exercise 15.1: Use The Background Highlighting Option....................... 15-5
Exercise 15.2: Use One Field To Highlight Another Field And Set A Priority 15-5
If...Then...Else Statements 15-7
IsNull Function 15-9
Exercise 15.3: Use The If Then Else Statement And IsNull Function...........15-10
Exercise 15.4: Using Nested If Statements In Formulas 15-11
Exercise 15.5: Suppressing Fields 15-12
Comparison Conditional Formatting 15-14
Exercise 15.6: Compare Customer Averages.......................................15-14

Exercise 15.7: Font Color Conditional Formatting 15-15
Exercise 15.8: Suppress Currency Formatting 15-16
Select Case Statement 15-17
Exercise 15.9: Use The Select Case Statement 15-18
Boolean Formulas 15-18

USING THE SECTION EXPERT **16-1**
The Section Expert 16-2
    Common Tab 16-3
    Paging Tab 16-4
    Layout Tab 16-5
Exercise 16.1: Create Page Breaks 16-6
Exercise 16.2: Conditionally Format The Page Break 16-6
Exercise 16.3: Resetting Page Numbers 16-7
Exercise 16.4: Use The Change Group Options Dialog Box 16-8
Exercise 16.5: Use The InRepeatedGroupHeader Function 16-10
Exercise 16.6: Suppress A Section Of The Report 16-10
Exercise 16.7: Suppress A Group 16-11
Exercise 16.8: Use The Color Tab Section Expert Options 16-13
Exercise 16.9: Create Odd And Even Page Headers 16-16

CREATING CHARTS **17-1**
The Chart Expert 17-2
    Type Tab 17-3
    Data Tab 17-6
    Axes Tab 17-14
    Options Tab 17-17
    Color Highlight Tab 17-18
    Text Tab 17-18
Exercise 17.1: Create A Bar Chart 17-20
Exercise 17.2: Create A Line Chart 17-21
Exercise 17.3: Create An Area Chart 17-22
Exercise 17.4: Create A Pie Chart 17-23
Exercise 17.5: Detach A Slice Of A Pie Chart 17-24
Exercise 17.6: Create A Doughnut Chart 17-24
Exercise 17.7: Create A 3D Riser Chart 17-25
Exercise 17.8: Create An XY Scatter Chart 17-25
Exercise 17.9: Show The Bottom 20% Of Orders Chart 17-26
Exercise 17.10: Create A Radar Chart 17-27
Exercise 17.11: Create A Bubble Chart 17-28
Exercise 17.12: Create A Stock Chart 17-28
Exercise 17.13: Create A Numeric Axis Chart 17-30
Exercise 17.14: Create A Gauge Chart 17-31
Exercise 17.15: Create A Gantt Chart 17-31
Exercise 17.16: Create A Histogram Chart 17-32
Exercise 17.17: Create A Color Highlighting Chart 17-32

FORMATTING AND EDITING CHARTS **18-1**
Zooming In And Out 18-2
Resizing Charts 18-3
Exercise 18.1: Use The Chart Expert Preview Tab Shortcut Menu Options 18-3
Trendlines 18-6

Exercise 18.2: Use The Underlay Following Sections Option..18-7
Chart Options Dialog Box 18-9
Exercise 18.3: Move Labels On A Chart 18-12
Customizing 3D Charts..18-13
Customizing Individual Elements On A Chart 18-14
Exercise 18.4: Apply Color To Chart Elements...18-17
Chart Templates 18-20

PARAMETER FIELD BASICS 19-1
How Do Parameter Fields Work?.. 19-3
The Create New Parameter Dialog Box.. 19-3
Data Types.. 19-5
Using Parameter Fields With The Select Expert... 19-7
Enter Values Dialog Box 19-9
Exercise 19.1: Create An Is Equal To Parameter Field 19-9
Parameters Panel 19-10
Exercise 19.2: Create An Is Greater Than Or Equal To Parameter Field 19-11
Calendar Control...19-12
Exercise 19.3: Set A Default Date For A Parameter Field 19-13
List Of Values 19-14
Static And Dynamic List Of Values 19-14
Exercise 19.4: Create A Static List Of Values Manually 19-15
How To Sort The Entire List At One Time 19-18
Importing A Static List Of Values 19-18
Exercise 19.5: Create An Imported Static List Of Values 19-18

CREATING DYNAMIC AND CASCADING PARAMETER FIELDS........................... 20-1
Dynamic List Of Values 20-2
Exercise 20.1: Create A Dynamic List Of Values.. 20-2
Cascading Prompts And List Of Values 20-3
Exercise 20.2: Create Cascading Prompts For Countries And Regions..................... 20-3
Exercise 20.3: Create Cascading Prompts For Customers And Their Orders 20-4
Allow Range Values And Allow Multiple Values Options 20-5
Exercise 20.4: Use The Allow Range Values Option With Dates............................... 20-6
Using Range Values For Non Date Data 20-7
Long List Of Values.. 20-7
Exercise 20.5: Use The Allow Range Value Option With A Currency Field 20-8
Exercise 20.6: Use The Allow Multiple Values Option With A Static List Of Values 20-9
Exercise 20.7: Use The Allow Multiple Values Option With A Dynamic List Of Values 20-10
Exercise 20.8: Combine Range And Multiple Values For A Date Field.....................20-11
Cascading Parameter Groups And Multi Value Parameter Options 20-11
Exercise 20.9: Create Dynamic Cascading Prompts For Customers And Their Orders..............20-12
Exercise 20.10: Rearrange The Parameter Fields Order...20-14
Exercise 20.11: Allowing All Values In A Parameter Field.......................................20-15
Using Formula Fields In Parameter Fields 20-16
Exercise 20.12: Create A Parameter Field For A Top N Report 20-16
Using Parameter Fields To Highlight Data...20-18
Exercise 20.13: Create A Parameter Field To Highlight Rows Of Data 20-18
Using Parameter Fields To Select The Sorting And Grouping Options 20-21
Exercise 20.14: Create A Parameter Field To Sort The Records................................20-21
Exercise 20.15: Create A Parameter Field To Group Data 20-22
Boolean Parameter Fields..20-24
Exercise 20.16: Conditional Section Suppression Using A Parameter Field 20-24
. . . .

Managing Data Entry In Parameter Fields 20-25
Edit Masks 20-26
Adding Parameter Field Criteria To A Report 20-26
    Printing Parameter Range Fields 20-27
Exercise 20.17: Print Parameter Range Fields 20-27
Exercise 20.18: Print Multi Value Parameter Fields 20-28
Deleting Parameter Fields From A Report 20-28
Customizing The Enter Values Dialog Box 20-29

CROSS-TAB REPORTS 21-1
Going From Standard Reports To Cross-Tab Reports 21-2
Cross-Tab Wizard 21-4
Exercise 21.1: Create A Cross-Tab Product Report 21-5
Exercise 21.2: Create A Sales Per Year Per Sales Rep Cross-Tab Report 21-6
Exercise 21.3: Create Charts From Cross-Tab Data.. 21-8
Cross-Tab Expert 21-10
    Cross-Tab Tab 21-11
    Style Tab... 21-12
    Customize Style Tab 21-13
Cross-Tab Shortcut Menu 21-15
Formatting Formulas 21-16
Exercise 21.4: Use The Cross-Tab Expert.. 21-16
Creating And Using Embedded Summaries 21-18
Exercise 21.5: Add Percents To A Cross-Tab Report 21-19
Exercise 21.6: Top N Cross-Tab Reports 21-20
Exercise 21.7: Create Conditional Formatting In Cross-Tabs................................... 21-22

ADDITIONAL CRYSTAL REPORTS FUNCTIONALITY 22-1
Barcodes 22-2
Sort Controls.. 22-2
Exercise 22.1: Using Sort Controls.. 22-3
Running Total Fields.. 22-4
Exercise 22.2: Create Two Order Processing Time Running Total Fields.................... 22-7
Exercise 22.3: Use Running Total Fields With Parameter Fields 22-8
Hierarchical Group Reports 22-10
Exercise 22.4: Create A Hierarchical Group Report 22-11
Optional Hierarchical Report Options 22-12
The Group Sort Expert.. 22-12
Exercise 22.5: Sort On The Customer Group By Order Amount Field....................... 22-13
Exercise 22.6: Create A Group Selection Formula 22-14
Multi Column Reports 22-15
Exercise 22.7: Add A Watermark To A Report Using An Image............................... 22-16

GETTING STARTED WITH SAP CRYSTAL REPORTS 2011

 Overview

After reading this chapter and completing the exercises you will be able to:

- ☑ Have a better understanding of what Crystal Reports is and what you can use it for
- ☑ Understand the options on the Start Page tab
- ☑ Check for updates for Crystal Reports
- ☑ Download the practice files

CHAPTER 1

Welcome To SAP Crystal Reports 2011!

Crystal Reports is a software package that is used to create reports. It is the leading report writing software on the market. Almost all businesses today that maintain data, have a need for reports to help them get their job done and to make business decisions. Often, businesses have data in a variety of data sources and need a way to pull data from several data sources to create a variety of reports including business intelligence analysis and proprietary business requirements.

Reports allow one to be able to read and make sense of large amounts of data that is most often stored in a database. Most databases have limited reporting capabilities and only allow reports to be created in that "type" of database. Database types include Sybase, Microsoft SQL Server and Oracle, to name a few. These are often called SQL databases and are usually stored on a database server. If you need to create a report that has data (information) in both Oracle and Sybase databases for example, you would have to use Crystal Reports because neither database allows you to create reports that have data in other types of databases.

Crystal Reports provides the ability to use data from a variety of database types and display the data in one report. Crystal Reports can use databases of any size. In addition to the SQL databases mentioned above, you can also use mainframe databases and what I call desktop or PC databases like Microsoft Access and Visual FoxPro. This type of database usually contains a lot less data than SQL databases and do not have the capacity to support hundreds or thousands of end-users like SQL databases do. Crystal Reports also comes bundled with several leading software packages like PeopleSoft. In addition to creating paper reports, reports can be exported to Word, Excel and PDF formats from Crystal Reports. You can create almost any type of report that you can dream up.

Normally, Crystal Reports is a read-only program, meaning that when you create or modify reports, the data in the database is not changed. You can however, include SQL commands in the report, which will allow the report to edit, delete and add records to a database.

The primary goal of Crystal Reports is to allow a wide range of users to have the ability to work with the raw data in databases to be able to create reports that allow data to be interpreted and analyzed. Crystal Reports makes creating basic reports easier through the use of report wizards, which are similar to wizards that you may have used in other software packages. You can also create complex reports that include subreports, formulas, charts and much more.

A hands-on approach is usually the best way to learn most things in life. This book is a visual guide that shows you how to create or modify over 130 reports. There are over 675 illustrations that practically eliminate the guess work and let you know that you are doing the steps correctly.

Another goal of this book is to discuss report design issues and potential solutions on how to resolve them. The good thing is that you have taken a great first step towards learning Crystal Reports by purchasing this book. Now, all you have to do is use this book to learn how to overcome the hurdles. From time to time, I will point out functionality that may not work as expected. When I do this, I am not complaining, merely pointing out things that you should be aware of.

It is my sincere hope that whatever your current skill level is with Crystal Reports, that you will learn more about features that you are already familiar with as you go through this book and that you learn about features that you did not know existed. Learning new tips and shortcuts will let you work faster and smarter. The more you know about Crystal Reports, the easier your day to day report design experiences will be.

So sit back and lets get started!

How This Book Is Organized

Topics and exercises in one chapter build on ones covered in previous chapters. To get the most out of this book, it is not advised that you skip around. The first reason is because some of the reports used in later chapters are created in exercises earlier in the book. The other reason is that a topic or option may have been covered in more detail earlier in the book. If you decide to skip around and cannot complete an exercise because there is something that you do not understand, you will have to go back and find the section that covers the topic in question. Below is an overview of what is covered in each chapter.

Chapter 1, Getting Started With SAP Crystal Reports 2011 covers background information about Crystal Reports, what's new in Crystal Reports, the Start Page and how to check for software updates.

Chapter 2, Toolbars, Menus And Customization Options covers the toolbars and menus in Crystal Reports, as well as how the workspace can be customized.

Chapter 3, Database Terminology And The Crystal Reports Workspace covers data types, the report design process, sections of a report, save data options, the design and preview tabs, the Preview Panel, Workbench and group tree.

Chapter 4, Create Your First Report covers creating a connection to a data source, linking tables and creating a basic report with a wizard.

Chapter 5, Creating Reports From Scratch covers the Database Expert, relational databases and creating a report without using a wizard.

Chapter 6, Aligning Objects On A Report covers how to line up objects on a report, resize objects, use the grid and guidelines.

Chapter 7, Editing And Formatting Reports covers adding images to a report, using the Format Editor and Format Painter.

Chapter 8, Using Subsections, Special Fields And The Report Explorer covers using the Section Expert, Special Fields and the Report Explorer.

Chapter 9, Selecting Records covers using the Select Expert to determine which records will appear on the report, using operators and creating report summary information.

Chapter 10, Grouping, Sorting And Summarizing Records covers the grouping and sorting techniques that are used to select how records will appear on the report.

Chapter 11, Creating Custom Groups covers using the Group Expert, setting up a user defined sort order and user defined groups.

Chapter 12, Using The Report Creation Wizards covers using the report and mailing label wizards to create reports.

Chapter 13, Printing And Exporting Reports covers the options on the Page Setup and Report Options dialog boxes. Exporting report options are also covered.

Chapter 14, Formulas And Functions covers what formulas and functions are, selecting a syntax editor, using the Formula Workshop and creating formulas.

Chapter 15, Conditional Formatting covers using the Highlighting Expert and If Then Else statements to create conditional formatting. Suppressing fields and sections of the report are also covered.

Chapter 16, Using The Section Expert covers formatting entire sections of a report at one time and creating formulas for options on the Section Expert.

Chapter 17, Creating Charts covers creating the majority of chart types that Crystal Reports has.

Chapter 18, Formatting And Editing Charts covers basic chart formatting and editing techniques.

Chapter 19, Parameter Field Basics covers using the Create Parameter Field dialog box to create parameter fields to customize reports, using parameter fields with the Select Expert and creating a static list of values for a parameter field.

Chapter 20, Creating Dynamic And Cascading Parameter Fields covers creating a dynamic list of values for parameter fields, create cascading parameter fields, creating parameter fields for Top N reports and using parameter fields to suppress data.

Chapter 21, Cross-Tab Reports covers using the Cross-Tab wizard and Cross-Tab Expert to create reports. Creating charts from a cross-tab grid is also covered.

Chapter 22, Additional Crystal Reports Functionality covers barcode functionality, running total fields, creating hierarchical groups and adding a watermark to a report.

Objectives Of The Book

This book is written to accommodate self-paced, classroom and online training. While there are no required prerequisites to successfully complete the exercises in this book, having a general knowledge of any of the following would be helpful.

- ☑ Prior version of Crystal Reports
- ☑ Database structures
- ☑ Basic programming
- ☑ Report design

Step-by-step instructions are included throughout this book. This book takes a hands-on, performance based approach to teaching you how to use Crystal Reports and provides the skills required to create reports efficiently. After completing the exercises in this book, you will be able to perform the following tasks and more:

- ☑ Create a connection to a database and link tables
- ☑ Utilize report design and planning techniques
- ☑ Understand database concepts
- ☑ Use the report wizards and create reports from scratch
- ☑ Modify existing reports
- ☑ Edit and format reports
- ☑ Utilize the Workbench to organize reports that you work on
- ☑ Create report selection criteria
- ☑ Sort and group data

- ☑ Create charts
- ☑ Create reports that have subtotals, counts, running totals and summary information
- ☑ Export data
- ☑ Add Special Fields to reports
- ☑ Create mailing labels using a wizard
- ☑ Create Cross-Tab reports
- ☑ Use the Formula Editor and Formula Workshop to create formulas and use functions
- ☑ Use the Highlighting and Section Experts to format data conditionally
- ☑ Create If...Then...Else formulas
- ☑ Create parameter fields

Conventions Used In This Book

I designed the following conventions to make it easier for you to follow the instructions in this book.

- ☑ The Courier font is used to indicate what you should type.
- ☑ **Drag** means to press and hold down the left mouse button while moving the mouse.
- ☑ **Click** means to press the left mouse button once, then release it immediately.
- ☑ **Double-click** means to quickly press the left mouse button twice, then release the mouse button.
- ☑ **Right-click** means to press the right mouse button once, which will open a shortcut menu.
- ☑ Click **OK** means to click the OK button on the dialog box.
- ☑ Press **Enter** means to press the Enter key on your keyboard.
- ☑ Press **Tab** means to press the Tab key on your keyboard.
- ☑ Click **Save** means to click the Save button in the software.
- ☑ Click **Finish** means to click the Finish button on the dialog box.
- ☑ SMALL CAPS are used to indicate an option to click on or to bring something to your attention.
- ☑ This icon indicates a shortcut or another way to complete the task that is being discussed. It can also indicate a tip or additional information about the topic that is being discussed. Some of this information comes from my personal experience using Crystal Reports.
- ☑ This icon indicates a warning, like a feature that has been removed or information that you need to be aware of.
- ☑ NEW This icon represents a new or modified feature in Crystal Reports 2011.
- ☑ [See Chapter 3, Database Concepts] refers to a section in a chapter that you can use as a reference for the topic that is being discussed.
- ☑ [See Chapter 2, Figure 2-8] refers to an illustration (screen shot) that you can use as a reference for the topic that is being discussed.
- ☑ When you see "YOU SHOULD HAVE THE OPTIONS SHOWN IN FIGURE X-X", or something similar in the exercises, check to make sure that your screen does look like the figure. If it does, continue with the next set of instructions. If your screen does not look like the figure, redo the steps that you just completed so that your screen does match the figure. Not doing so may cause you problems when trying to complete exercises later in the book.
- ☑ The section heading EXERCISE X.Y: (where X equals the chapter number and Y equals the exercise number) represents exercises that have step-by-step instructions that you should complete. You will also see sections that have step-by-step instructions that are not an exercise. Completing them as you go through the book is optional, but recommended.

☑ "E2.1 Report Name" is the naming convention for reports that you will create. E2.1 stands for Chapter 2, Exercise 1. You may consider some of the report file names to be long. I did this on purpose, so that it is easier to know what topic the report covers. If you do not like to type or do not want to type the full report name, you can just type the first part as the report file name. That way when you have to find a report to complete another exercise, you will be able to find the correct report. For example, if the report name is E5.5 Orders shipped between 4-1-2010 and 6-30-2010, you can type E5.5 as the file name for the report.

☑ "Chapter 15 Report Name" refers to a report in the zip file for this book.

☑ "Save the My practice report as" means to open the My practice report and save it with the new file name specified in the instruction. The reason that I have you do this is if you want to view a report after completing this book, all of the reports will be intact.

☑ Many of the dialog boxes in Crystal Reports have OK, Cancel and Help buttons at the bottom of the dialog box. Viewing these buttons on all of the figures adds no value, so they are not shown.

☑ FILE ⇒ NEW ⇒ CROSS-TAB REPORT means to open the FILE menu, select the option NEW, then select the option CROSS-TAB REPORT, as shown in Figure 1-1.

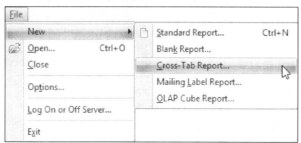

Figure 1-1 Menu navigation technique shown

Assumptions

Yes, I know one should never assume anything, but the following assumptions have been made. It is assumed that . . . .

☑ You have Crystal Reports 2011 installed on your computer. If you are not sure what version Crystal Reports you have, open Crystal Reports, then select Help ⇒ About SAP Crystal Reports. At the top of the dialog box shown in Figure 1-2, you will see the version that is installed.

☑ You are familiar with the Windows environment, including Windows Explorer and that you are comfortable using a mouse.

☑ You know that the operating system used to write this book is Windows 7. If you are using a different version of Windows, any or all of the following can apply:

① Some of the screen shots may have a slightly different look

② Some of the instructions for Windows tasks may be different.

③ The path to folders and files on your computer may be different then the paths listed in this book.

☑ You have Crystal Reports open at the beginning of each chapter.

☑ You have access to the Internet to download the practice files needed to complete the exercises in this book and to download any updates to Crystal Reports that are available.

☑ When you see <smile>, that signifies my attempt of adding humor to the learning process.

☑ Optional: That you have access to a printer, if you want to print any of the reports that you create.

☑ Optional: That you have Microsoft Excel installed if you want to view the reports that will be exported to this format.

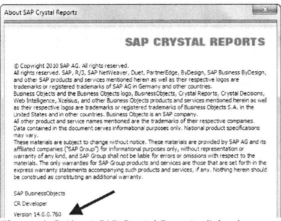

Figure 1-2 About SAP Crystal Reports dialog box

 Crystal Reports does not have a spell checker.

Getting Help With Crystal Reports

As explained below, there are four primary ways to get help if you have a question on how to use a feature or option in Crystal Reports.

① Read this book from cover to cover and complete the exercises. Many of the basic questions that you may have are probably covered in this book.

② The Online Help file. It is helpful for the basic definitions of features.

③ Crystal Reports forum. You can post questions and learn how other people are using the software. The forum is also a great way to keep current on the latest Crystal Reports trends and for getting ideas on how to enhance the reports that you create. It is an invaluable resource. The name of the forum is SAP Crystal Reports Design. The web site is https://forums.sdn.sap.com/category.jspa?categoryID=45. If you do not already have a free account, you will have to create one to be able to post and answer questions. On the Development tab in Crystal Reports, click on the Support Forums link in the Community section.

④ Hire a Crystal Reports consultant. Need I say that this is the most expensive option and you probably will not get an answer to your question as fast as you would like. Never mind the cost <smile>.

Crystal Reports Certification

At the time this book went to print, I could not find any information on certification for Crystal Reports 2011. When it becomes available, you should be able to find a link to the information from the web page listed below.

Certification information http://www.sap.com/services/education/certification/levels/index.epx

If you purchased this book as part of your arsenal for preparing for the certification exams, you may want to spend more time completing the exercises to make sure that you have an above average understanding of the concepts presented. Good luck on the exam!

What's New In SAP Crystal Reports 2011

What you will notice that's new, depends on the previous version of Crystal Reports that you used, if any. The older the version of Crystal Reports that you are upgrading from, the more new features you will notice. The two major new features are explained below.

Export Reports To Excel 2007 Format This feature allows reports to be exported to the .xlsx Excel 2007 file format. This means that up to one million rows of data from a report can be exported to Excel.

Read-Only Format This feature allows reports to be exported to an .rptr file. The read-only format does not allow the report to be modified, not even in Crystal Reports.

NEW Start Page Tab

The Start Page tab is the first page that you see when you open Crystal Reports. It has been modified. It provides a lot of options that you may find helpful. The options on this tab may save you some time because you do not have to remember which menu the option is on.

Open Crystal Reports

1. Open Crystal Reports. You will see the Register dialog box if you have not registered the software. If that is the case, click the **REGISTER LATER** button. You will see the window shown in Figure 1-3.

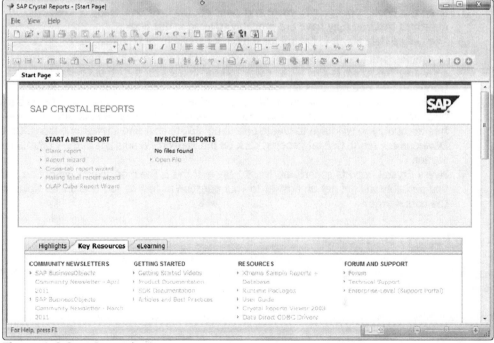

Figure 1-3 Start Page tab

There are three tabs on the Start Page tab. They provide information, help, updates and add-ons for Crystal Reports if your computer is connected to the Internet. Each tab is explained below.

① **HIGHLIGHTS** Provides links to sample reports, free product add-ons and blog posts.
② **KEY RESOURCES** Has links to newsletters, getting started information, forums and resources.
③ **ELEARNING** Has links to tutorials for Crystal Reports.

 If you close the Start Page tab either on purpose or by accident, you can still get to all of the options at the top of the tab through the menu, toolbar or shortcuts.

Start A New Report The options in this section of the Start Page tab are the report wizards. Having them here makes them easy to get to. The **STANDARD REPORT** option (File ⇒New) opens the same report wizard as the **REPORT WIZARD** link.

 The **BLANK REPORT** option is what you would select when you want to create a report from scratch (not use a wizard).

My Recent Reports This section displays the last five reports that you opened. The first report listed is the most recent one that you opened. I think that it would be great if there was an option to display the last nine reports, like the bottom of the File menu does.

The **OPEN FILE** link will display the last folder that you opened from inside of Crystal Reports. Clicking on this link allows you to look for the report that you want to open. You can navigate to another folder, if the folder that opens is not the one that you need.

Start Page Tab Menu Options

The Start Page tab menu contains some of the options available in Crystal Reports. This menu is a subset of the menu options that are available when a report is open in Crystal Reports. For example, Figure 1-4 shows the options on the File menu on the Start Page tab. Figure 1-5 shows the options on the File menu when a report is open. The section above the Exit option at the bottom of the File menu will display the last nine reports that were opened, compared to the last five reports that are displayed in the My Recent Reports section.

 File Menu Differences
One difference in the location of items on the File menu that I noticed is the **LOG ON OR OFF SERVER** option. It is on the File menu on the Start Page tab shown in Figure 1-4. When a report is open, this option is on the Database menu.

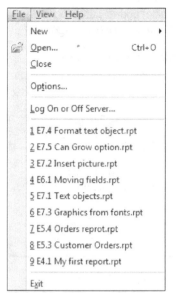

Figure 1-4 File menu options on the Start Page tab

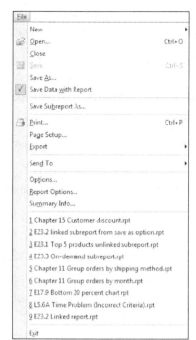

Figure 1-5 File menu options when a report is open

Checking For Software Updates

There are several ways that you can check for software updates, as explained below.

① **CHECK FOR UPDATES ON START UP** If this option is selected, every time that you open Crystal Reports you will be prompted to check for updates. I don't know about you, but this would get on my nerves <smile>.

② **CHECK FOR UPDATES** This option is used to control when the check for updates will occur. When you select this option, the software will check for updates.

③ Use the Technical Support option on the Key Resources tab on the Start Page tab to manually check for updates.

The Help menu displays the first two update options explained above, as illustrated in Figure 1-6.

Clear the **CHECK FOR UPDATES ON START UP** option, if you do not want to check for updates every time that you open Crystal Reports.

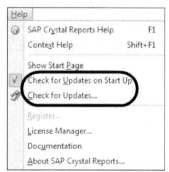

Figure 1-6 Update options illustrated

At the time this book went to print, the Check for updates menu options did not work.

Depending on the security that you have set in your firewall software, you may be prompted to grant Crystal Reports access to the Internet. It is probably a good idea to grant the access so that you can check for updates. Your firewall software may prompt you if you have the Check for Updates on Start Up option on the Help menu selected.

Exercise 1.1: Create A Folder For Your Reports

You will create and modify several reports in this book. It is a good idea to store all of them in the same folder on your computers hard drive so that you can find them easily. I will refer to this folder as "your folder" throughout the book. The instructions below show you how to create the folder at the root of the C drive. If you want to create the folder in another location or under an existing folder, navigate to that location prior to starting step 2.

1.   Open Windows Explorer, then click on the C drive.

2.   File ⇒ New ⇒ Folder.

3.   Type Crystal Reports Book as the folder name, then press Enter.

4.   The reports and files needed for this book are in a zip file named cr2011.zip. To have the link for the zip file sent to you, send an email to cr2011@tolanapublishing.com. If you do not receive an email in a few minutes with the subject line Crystal Reports 2011 Files, check the spam folder in your email software.

5.   Open Windows Explorer, then click on the folder that you just created. Right-click on the zip file and select **EXTRACT TO HERE**, as shown in Figure 1-7.

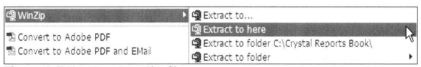

Figure 1-7 How to extract the files

Backing Up Your Work

I cannot stress how important it is to back up your work frequently. Doing so will save you frustration in the event a power failure occurs or if your computer has a hardware failure. The majority of times that you lose work, it can't be recovered or if it can, it may cost you a few hundred dollars or more to recover it. I use to tell my students this and it never failed that a student lost some, if not all of their work. Don't say that I didn't warn you <smile>.

If you aren't already, you should also be saving a copy of your work to an external source like an external hard drive or USB drive. My favorite file backup and imaging device at the moment is the ClickFree C6 external drive.

TOOLBARS, MENUS AND CUSTOMIZATION OPTIONS

 Overview   In this chapter you will learn about the options on the toolbars and menus in Crystal Reports. You will also learn about the report design customization options.

CHAPTER 2

Crystal Reports Toolbars

There are five toolbars in Crystal Reports: Standard, Formatting, Insert Tools, Navigation Tools and Expert Tools, as explained below. They are right below the menu that you will learn about later in this chapter. The buttons on the toolbars provide quick access to features that you will probably use the most. Like toolbars in other applications, you can rearrange the toolbars by clicking on the dots at the beginning of the toolbar with the left mouse button and dragging the toolbar to a new location in the workspace. You cannot add or delete buttons on the toolbars, but you can turn off (remove) toolbars that you do not need or use. If you have used other Windows based applications, you are already familiar with many of the menu options. You will probably find that you will use the toolbar buttons more frequently then the options on the menu.

 Keep in mind that the buttons on the toolbars are available based on what you are doing and the object that is selected. There are some differences between the toolbar buttons and their menu counterparts. These differences will be pointed out.

Standard Toolbar

The Standard toolbar shown in Figure 2-1 contains the most commonly used options from the File, Edit, Format, View, Report and Help menus. Table 2-1 explains the buttons on the toolbar.

Figure 2-1 Standard toolbar

Button	Description
1	Creates a new report.
2	Opens an existing report. If you click on the arrow at the end of the button, you will see the last nine reports that you opened.
3	Saves the active report.
4	Opens the Print dialog box.
5	Displays the active report on the Preview tab. This is the same as clicking on the Preview tab. You can click this button if the Preview tab is not visible.
6	Displays the active report as a web page in the HTML Preview window if the HTML Preview options are configured on the Options dialog box. [See Figure 2-36 later in this chapter]
7	Opens the Export dialog box, which is used to export the report to a different file format.
8	Removes the selected object from the report and places it on the clipboard.
9	Copies the selected object to the clipboard.
10	Pastes objects from the clipboard into the report.
11	Copies formatting properties from one object to one or more other objects. This is a shortcut to the Format Painter tool.
12	Undoes an action. (1)
13	Redoes the last action that was undone. (1)
14	Toggles the Preview Panel (on the left side of the workspace) on and off on the Preview tab.

Table 2-1 Standard toolbar buttons explained

Button	Description
15	Opens the Field Explorer so that fields and other objects can be added to the report. (2)
16	Opens the Report Explorer, which is used to view the objects in the report in a tree view format. (2)
17	Opens the Repository Explorer, which is used to view the contents of the repository. (2)
18	Opens the Dependency Checker so that you can check reports for errors.
19	Displays the Workbench.
20	Opens the Find dialog box, which is used to search for information in the report.

Table 2-1 Standard toolbar buttons explained (Continued)

(1)   You can select how many changes that you want to undo and redo from the drop-down list. This functionality is not available from the Edit menu.
(2)   Clicking this button a second time does not close the Explorer window.

Formatting Toolbar

The Formatting toolbar shown in Figure 2-2 contains options to modify object properties, like borders and fonts. Table 2-2 explains the buttons on the toolbar. This toolbar is only enabled after an object on the report is selected. Many of these options are on the Format menu.

Figure 2-2 Formatting toolbar

Button	Description
1	Select a font.
2	Change the size for the font that is currently selected.
3	Increases the font size of the selected object one point each time this button is clicked. (3)
4	Decreases the font size of the selected object one point each time this button is clicked. (3)
5	Makes the selected object bold.
6	Makes the selected object italic.
7	Underlines the selected object.
8	Aligns the selected object flush left.
9	Centers the data of the selected object in the frame.
10	Aligns the data in the selected object flush right.
11	Justifies the data in the selected object between the length of the frame that the object is in.
12	Applies the selected color to the object. This button is used to select or define colors in the Color dialog box. If you click on this button, the font color will change to the color that is on the line at the bottom of the button. Click on the arrow to change the color.
13	Applies the selected border to the object. You can select from several border style options. Click on the arrow to change the border style.

Table 2-2 Formatting toolbar buttons explained

Button	Description
14	Suppresses the selected object. This means that the object will not be displayed or printed on the report.
15	Locks or unlocks the formatting of an object so that it can't be changed accidentally.
16	Locks the size and position of an object in relation to the object to its right.
17	Adds or removes the currency symbol in the selected numeric field.
18	Adds or removes the comma in the selected numeric field.
19	Adds or removes the percent sign in the selected numeric field.
20	Moves the decimal point in the selected numeric field one place to the right each time this button is clicked. (4)
21	Moves the decimal point in the selected numeric field one place to the left each time this button is clicked. (4)

Table 2-2 Formatting toolbar buttons explained (Continued)

(3)   There is no menu option that has this functionality.
(4)   Rounding is set to the number of decimal places in the field.

 Font Size Tip
If the font size that you want is not in the drop-down list, highlight whatever size is showing in the font size drop-down list and type in the size that you want. You can also type in half sizes like 9.5.

Insert Tools Toolbar

The Insert Tools toolbar shown in Figure 2-3 contains options to add objects other then data fields to the report. Table 2-3 explains the object type that each button will add to a report. These options are also available on the Insert menu.

1   2   3   4   5   6   7   8   9 10 11 12
Figure 2-3 Insert Tools toolbar

Button	Is Used To Insert A . . .
1	text object
2	group section
3	summary field
4	Cross-Tab object
5	OLAP grid object
6	subreport
7	line
8	box
9	picture
10	chart
11	map
12	Flash object

Table 2-3 Insert Tools toolbar buttons explained

Navigation Tools Toolbar

The Navigation Tools toolbar shown in Figure 2-4 contains options to display different parts of a report and refresh the reports data. This toolbar is activated after you preview a report. Table 2-4 explains the buttons on the toolbar. The Refresh option is available on the Reports menu. The other options are only available on this toolbar.

Figure 2-4 Navigation Tools toolbar

Button	Description
1	Refreshes the report data.
2	Stops the processing of data and only displays the report with the data that has been processed prior to clicking this button.
3	Displays the first page of the report.
4	Displays the previous page of the report.
5	Displays the next page of the report.
6	Displays the last page of the report.
7	Displays the previous page of the report. (5)
8	Displays the next page of the report. (5)

Table 2-4 Navigation Tools toolbar buttons explained

(5)   This button is only available when you are using the HTML Preview option.

Expert Tools Toolbar

The Expert Tools toolbar shown in Figure 2-5 provides access to the experts, including the database, group and template experts. The buttons on this toolbar open dialog boxes that provide options to complete a task. Table 2-5 explains the buttons on the toolbar. These options are also available on the Database and Report menus.

Figure 2-5 Expert Tools toolbar

Button	Opens The . . .
1	Database Expert. It is used to add (or remove) data sources for the report.
2	Group Expert. It is used to create, modify and delete groups.
3	Group Sort Expert. It is used to find the Top or Bottom N records and sort the report on summary fields.
4	Record Sort Expert. It is used to select the order that the detail records will be sorted in.
5	Select Expert. It is used to create report selection criteria. (6)
6	Section Expert. It is used to format any section of the report or create a new section.
7	Formula Workshop. It is used to create and edit formulas.
8	OLAP Design Wizard. It is used to create a report that uses an OLAP cube or **.CAR** file as the data source.
9	Template Expert. It is used to apply a template to a report.
10	Appropriate Format Editor based on the object that is selected. It is used to modify the formatting properties of the selected object.
11	Hyperlink tab on the Format Editor. It is used to add a hyperlink to a report.

Table 2-5 Expert Tools toolbar buttons explained

Button	Description
12	Highlighting Expert. It is used to apply conditional formatting to an object.

Table 2-5 Expert Tools toolbar buttons explained (Continued)

(6) The Select Expert button has the options shown in Figure 2-6.

Table 2-6 explains the options.

Figure 2-6 Select Expert button options

Option	Description
Record	Creates selection criteria based on a field.
Group	Creates selection criteria based on a group name or summary field. Group processing is done after the record processing.
Saved Data	This option only filters data that has already been saved with the report instead of retrieving data from the database. This option reduces the number of times a database has to be refreshed. This is helpful for reports that have parameter fields.

Table 2-6 Select Expert button options explained

External Command Toolbar

By default, this toolbar is not displayed because it is empty. After you have added an application to the toolbar, the toolbar can be displayed. This toolbar provides access to third party applications that you add to it. The **ADD-INS** menu can also be used to store custom controls. The add-ins menu is not displayed by default.

How To Remove Toolbars

There are two ways to remove a toolbar, as explained below.

① View ⇒ Toolbars. Opens the dialog box shown in Figure 2-7. Clear the check mark next to the toolbar that you do not want to be visible in the workspace, then click OK.

② Right-click near the toolbars at the top of the workspace. You will see the **TOOLBAR SHORTCUT MENU** shown in Figure 2-8. Click on the check mark in front of the toolbar that you want to remove. Notice the **TOOLBARS** option at the bottom of the shortcut menu. Selecting this option will open the Toolbars dialog box shown in Figure 2-7.

Figure 2-7 Toolbars dialog box

Figure 2-8 Toolbar shortcut menu

Crystal Reports Menus

While the toolbars provide quick access to the most commonly used features in Crystal Reports, the menus provide access to almost all of the functionality in Crystal Reports. Tables 2-7 to 2-17 explain the Crystal Reports menu options. Many of the menu options will be familiar from the toolbars that you learned about earlier in this chapter.

File Menu

The options on the File menu are used to open, close, print and save reports. The options are explained in Table 2-7.

Menu Option	Description
New	Is used to select how the new report will be created and the type of report that will be created. [See Chapter 1, Figure 1-1]
Open	Is used to open an existing report. The default setting is to only display Crystal Reports files in the dialog box. You can change the Files of type option to open other types of files. The **UPDATE REPOSITORY OBJECTS** option on the Open dialog box causes objects in a report that are connected to the repository to be updated when the report is opened.
Close	Closes the active report. (7)
Save	Saves the active report. If the report is new, you will be prompted to give the report a file name.
Save As	Saves the active report with a new name.
Save Data With Report	[See Chapter 4, Options For Saving Data]
Save Subreport As	Saves an existing report as a subreport with a different file name, even if it has already been inserted into another report.
Print	[See Chapter 13, Printer Options]
Page Setup	[See Chapter 13, Page Setup Options]
Export	[See Chapter 13, Export Report Overview]
Send To	Sends the active report via email using the dialog box shown in Figure 2-9 or to an Exchange mail folder. The first time that you use the Mail Recipient option, you may be prompted to install the additional required components.
Options	Opens the Options dialog box, which is covered in detail later in this chapter.
Report Options	[See Chapter 13, Report Options Dialog Box]
Summary Info	[See Chapter 9, Document Properties]
Exit	Closes Crystal Reports. (7)

Table 2-7 File menu options explained

(7) If changes were made to the report before this option is selected, you will be prompted to save the report.

Figure 2-9 Send Mail dialog box

 The **ADDRESS** button on the **SEND MAIL** dialog box will open the default address book that is associated with the email software that you use. To send a report via email, you must use a MAPI compliant email software package. [See Chapter 13, Table 13-3]

Edit Menu

Many of the options on the Edit menu may be familiar, especially if you have used a word processing software package. The options are used to modify different parts of the report. Some of the options on the Edit menu require an object to be selected before it can be used. The options are explained in Table 2-8.

Menu Option	Description
Undo	Undoes the last action that you did. If this menu option is not enabled, the last action cannot be undone. (8)
Redo	Redoes the last action that you did. If this menu option is not enabled, the last action cannot be repeated. (8)
Cut	Deletes the selected object from the report and places it on the clipboard.
Copy	Copies the selected object and places it on the clipboard.
Paste	Pastes an object from the clipboard into the report.
Paste Special	This option is primarily used for OLE (Object Linking and Embedding) objects because it gives more control than the Paste option, in terms of how an object is pasted into the report.
Delete	Deletes the selected object from the report. Unlike the Cut option, the Delete option does not send the object to the clipboard.
Select All	Selects all of the objects in the report at one time. This will let you perform the same task to all of the objects on the report at the same time.
Find	Opens the dialog box shown in Figure 2-11. The options are used to search for text in the report. The **ADVANCED FIND** button opens the dialog box shown in Figure 2-12 in preview mode. These options search for data (values in a field in the report). It is similar to the Select Expert because you can search in more than one field at the same time.
Go To Page	The dialog box shown in Figure 2-13 will display any page in the report. Type in the page number that you want to view in the field across from the Page field, then click OK. This option is only available in preview mode.

Table 2-8 Edit menu options explained

Menu Option	Description
Edit Report Object	The name of this menu item will change depending on the type of object that is selected. This option is only available for fields that can be edited, like summary and formulas fields. Editing a field is different then formatting a field. It is similar to right-clicking on an object and selecting Edit <Object Type>.
Subreports Links	This option is only available in reports that have a subreport. The dialog box shown in Figure 2-14 is used to check and modify the link between the subreport and main report.
Object	Is used to edit an embedded or linked OLE object.
Links	Is used to modify the link properties of the OLE object that is selected.

Table 2-8 Edit menu options explained (Continued)

 (8) The Undo and Redo options will change depending on the action (what you did) right before you opened the Edit menu. Figure 2-10 shows the Undo and Redo options after an action was taken.

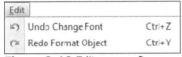

Figure 2-10 Edit menu after an action was taken

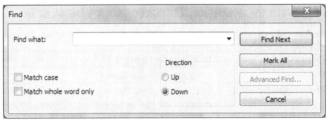

Figure 2-11 Find dialog box

 The difference between the Search Expert and the Select Expert is that the Search Expert searches through the data in the report. It does not search the records in the database like the Select Expert does.

Figure 2-12 Search Expert dialog box

Figure 2-13 Go To dialog box

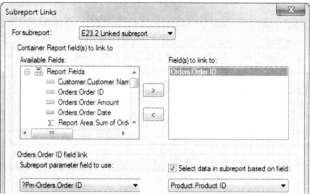

Figure 2-14 Subreport Links dialog box

View Menu

The options on the View menu contain many of the tools in Crystal Reports. There are also options to customize the workspace. The options are explained in Table 2-9.

Menu Option	Description
Design	Displays the design tab.
Preview	Displays the preview tab.
Print Preview	Is used to view the report as it will look when printed. This is the same as clicking on the preview tab. This option is only available on the design tab.
Preview Sample	Displays the report with limited data.
HTML Preview	Displays the report as it will look on the web. You may have to set some of the options on the Smart Tag & HTML Preview tab on the Options dialog box before you can use this option.
Close Current View	Closes the active tab. This option is only available in preview mode.
Field Explorer	Opens the Field Explorer so that you can add fields and other objects to the report.
Report Explorer	Displays all of the fields and objects on the report.
Repository Explorer	Opens the Repository Explorer so that an item from the repository can be added to the report.
Dependency Checker	Opens the Dependency Checker so that reports can be checked for errors.
Workbench	Displays the Workbench.
Toolbars	Is used to display and hide toolbars on the workspace.
Status Bar	Displays or hides the status bar at the bottom of the workspace. The status bar provides additional information about the object that you are holding the mouse pointer over, as well as, other information about the active report.
Preview Panel	The Group Tree, Parameters Panel and Find tab are stored in the Preview Panel.
Zoom	Sets the zoom level for viewing a report, as shown in Figure 2-15.
Rulers	Displays or hides the rulers. (9)
Guidelines	Displays or hides the guidelines. (9)

Table 2-9 View menu options explained

Menu Option	Description
Grid	Displays or hides the grid. (9)
Tool Tips	Displays or hides the tool tips. (9)
Product Locale	Is used to change the language that the menus and commands are displayed in.
Preferred Viewing Locale	Is used to select a different language then the one that was selected during the installation, to display on the menus and commands.

Table 2-9 View menu options explained (Continued)

(9) This option works on the design and preview tabs.

You can change the zoom percent by typing in the percent that you want on this dialog box.

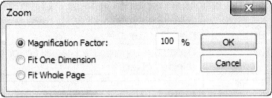

Figure 2-15 Zoom dialog box

Insert Menu

The options on the Insert menu are used to add objects to a report. The options are explained in Table 2-10. Many of these options are also available on the shortcut menu for the object.

Menu Option	Description
Text Object	Adds a text object to the report.
Summary	Adds a summary field to the report.
Field Heading	Creates a field heading for the selected field. If the **INSERT DETAIL FIELD HEADINGS** option is checked on the Layout tab of the Options dialog box, you will probably not have the need to use the field heading option because field headings will be created automatically for fields that are added to the details section.
Sort Control	Adds a control that will let the report be sorted in a different order or on a different field, by the person running the report.
Group	Adds a group to the report.
OLAP Grid	Opens the OLAP Expert, which is used to create an OLAP grid. (10)
Cross-Tab	Opens the Cross-Tab Expert, which is used to create a cross-tab object. (10)
Subreport	Opens the Insert Subreport dialog box, which is used to create a subreport or select an existing report to use as a subreport.
Line	Draws lines on the report. You can draw horizontal and vertical lines.
Box	Draws a box on the report. Boxes can also be drawn across sections of the report.
Picture	Is used to add image files to a report. The supported file types are bmp, jpeg, png, tiff and Windows metafile.
Chart	Is used to create a chart using the Chart Expert.
Map	Is used to create a map using the Map Expert.
Flash	Is used to add a Flash (SWF) file to the report.
OLE Object	Is used to add an OLE object to the report.

Table 2-10 Insert menu options explained

Menu Option	Description
Template Field Object	This object is used as a placeholder for a field in a template. Template field objects are not connected to fields in a database.

Table 2-10 Insert menu options explained (Continued)

(10) There can be more than one OLAP grid or cross-tab object in the same report.

Format Menu

The options on the Format menu are used to change the appearance and alignment of the objects on the report. The options are explained in Table 2-11.

Menu Option	Description
Format Field	Opens the appropriate Format Editor to modify the properties of the selected object.
Format Painter	Copies the formatting properties from one object to another.
Hyperlink	Create a hyperlink.
Use Expert	Opens an expert based on the object that is selected, so that the object can be edited. You may find it easier to right-click on an object and select the expert that you want to use, instead of selecting the object and then opening the Format menu.
Highlighting Expert	Opens the Highlighting Expert which is used to apply conditional formatting to a field.
Text Formatting	Is used to apply formatting to a text field.
Move	Is used to move a field from one layer to another on the report.
Align	Is used to line up objects.
Make Same Size	Is used to make two or more objects the same size by width, height or both.
Size and Position	[See Chapter 6, Object Size And Position Dialog Box]
Pivot OLAP Grid	Is used to switch the rows to columns and the columns to rows in the OLAP grid.
Pivot Cross-Tab	Is used to switch the rows to columns and the columns to rows in the cross-tab grid. Figure 2-16 shows the cross-tab before the pivot option is applied. Figure 2-17 shows the cross-tab after the pivot option is applied.

Table 2-11 Format menu options explained

	2010	2011	2012	Total
Davolio	$71,862.70	$450,865.83	$138,028.42	$660,756.95
Dodsworth	$29,049.94	$513,545.52	$140,253.75	$682,849.21
King	$21,093.75	$512,406.60	$215,255.59	$748,755.94
Leverling	$44,121.64	$447,235.19	$157,745.16	$649,101.99
Peacock	$38,458.39	$446,150.56	$147,190.82	$631,799.77
Suyama	$54,804.22	$496,881.48	$158,715.78	$710,401.48
Total	$259,390.64	$2,867,085.18	$957,189.52	$4,083,665.34

Figure 2-16 Cross-tab before option is applied

	Davolio	Dodsworth	King	Leverling	Peacock	Suyama	Total
2010	$71,862.70	$29,049.94	$21,093.75	$44,121.64	$38,458.39	$54,804.22	$259,390.64
2011	$450,865.83	$513,545.52	$512,406.60	$447,235.19	$446,150.56	$496,881.48	$2,867,085.18
2012	$138,028.42	$140,253.75	$215,255.59	$157,745.16	$147,190.82	$158,715.78	$957,189.52
Total	$660,756.95	$682,849.21	$748,755.94	$649,101.99	$631,799.77	$710,401.48	$4,083,665.34

Figure 2-17 Cross-tab after option is applied

Database Menu

The options on the Database menu are used to interact with the databases that you use to create reports. The options are explained in Table 2-12.

Menu Option	Description
Database Expert	Opens the Database Expert, which is used to add or delete data sources to or from the report.
Set Data Source Location	Is used to select a different database for the report or a different location for the database that the report is currently using. This option is useful when you are using a copy of the database to create and test the reports and are now ready to move the reports into production (go live).
Log On or Off Server	Is used to log on or off of an SQL or ODBC server, set database options and maintain the Favorites folder. Most of the tasks that you can complete on the Data Explorer window can be done another way.
Browse Data	Is used to view data in a field. This is the same as the Browse button that is on some dialog boxes.
Set OLAP Cube Location	Is used to select a different location for the OLAP cube in the report.
Verify Database	Is used to compare the structure of the data source that is used in the report to the structure of the actual database.
Show SQL Query	Is used to view SQL queries if the report is using any. Parameter fields are included if they are used in the selection formula. Figure 2-18 shows the dialog box.
Perform Grouping on Server	If checked and the report has a group and the details section of the report is hidden, the grouping process will be done on a server.
Select Distinct Records	If checked, duplicate records will not appear on the report. A duplicate record has the same data in every field in both records.
Query Panel	Opens the Business Objects Query Panel, which is used to create queries (by using objects in a Business Objects universe) that will be used in the report.

Table 2-12 Database menu options explained

The query on this dialog box is automatically created when you create selection criteria for a report.

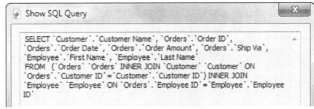

Figure 2-18 Show SQL Query dialog box

Report Menu

Many of the options on the Report menu will open an Expert. Some of the wizard screens look similar to some of the Experts that you will learn about throughout the book. The options are explained in Table 2-13.

Menu Option	Description
Select Expert	Opens the Select Expert, which is used to create selection criteria to filter records.
Selection Formulas	[See Chapter 9, Using The Select Expert]
Formula Workshop	Opens the Formula Workshop, which is used to create, edit and view formulas and functions.
Alerts	Is used to create and edit report alerts.
Report Bursting Indexes	This option is only available on reports that have saved data. It is used to create indexes on the saved data. This improves the record selection processing time.
Section Expert	Opens the Section Expert, which is used to format any section of the report.
Group Expert	Opens the Group Expert, which is used to create, modify and delete groups in a report.
Group Sort Expert	Sort the groups in the report by group summary fields.
Record Sort Expert	Opens the Record Sort Expert, which is used to select the order that the detail records will be sorted in.
Template Expert	Opens the Template Expert shown in Figure 2-19. It is used to apply a template to the report.
OLAP Design Wizard	Opens the OLAP Expert. This menu option is only available after an OLAP grid is selected in the report.
Hierarchical Grouping Options	Is used to create a hierarchical report.
Show Current Parameter Values	Opens the dialog box shown in Figure 2-20, if the report has parameter fields. It is used to view the parameter values that were selected the last time that the report was run.
Check Dependencies	Is used to view the results of running the Check Dependencies tool.
Refresh Report Data	Refreshes the data in the report. If the report has parameter fields, you can select the parameter options that you want to use.
Set Print Date and Time	Overrides the values that would print if the Print Date or Print Time special fields are on the report.
Performance Information	Displays information similar to what is shown in Figure 2-21. This may help you troubleshoot report performance problems. For example, the options in the **REPORT DEFINITION** section provide information on objects that could impact the performance of the report.

Table 2-13 Report menu options explained

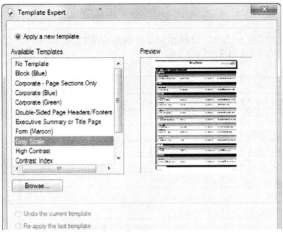

Figure 2-20 Current Parameter Values dialog box

Figure 2-19 Template Expert

From time to time throughout this book, I let you know about options and functionality that can cause a report to run slow or cause the server to run slow. The options on this dialog box may help you resolve the problem.

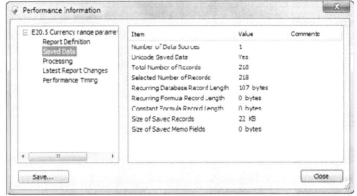

Figure 2-21 Performance Information dialog box

The **LATEST REPORT CHANGES** options are useful when a report that did not run slow in the past, now is.

It could be because of some of the recent changes made to the report.

Figure 2-22 Latest Report Changes options

The **PERFORMANCE TIMING** options are used to show the processing time for different stages of the report.

Figure 2-23 Performance Timing options

Chart Menu

The options on the Chart menu are used to customize a chart. This menu is only available when a chart is selected on a report. The options are explained in Table 2-14.

Menu Option	Description
Format Background	Change the color or font of the selected item.
Chart Options	[See Chapter 18, Chart Options Dialog Box]
Axis Options	Change the grid options.
Series Options	Change the options for the chart series that is selected.
3D Viewing Angle	Change the angle of a 3D chart.
Edit Axis Label	Change the axis label that is selected.
Trendlines	Modify the trendlines.
Auto-Arrange Chart	Arrange all of the objects on the chart.
Apply Changes To All Charts	Apply the same formatting to all of the same group level charts.
Discard Custom Changes	Delete all customizations that you made to the chart.
Load Template	Select a template to apply to the chart.
Save As Template	Saves the chart as a user defined template.
Select Mode	Prevents accidental zooming or panning on the chart.
Zoom In	Zoom in closer on the chart.
Zoom Out	Zoom out on the chart.
Pan	This option is only available when a chart has been zoomed in on. It is used to move through the data in the chart.

Table 2-14 Chart menu options explained

Map Menu

The options on the Map menu are used to customize a geographic map. This menu is only available when a map is selected on the preview tab. The options are explained in Table 2-15.

Menu Option	Description
Select Mode	This option is enabled as soon as you click on a map on the preview tab. Once enabled, the Map menu is visible.
Zoom In	Zoom in closer on the map.
Zoom Out	Zoom out on the map.
Pan	This option is only available when a map has been zoomed in on. It is used to move through the data on the map.
Center Map	Center a map in its frame. You may need to use this option after you have used the Pan option.
Title	Add or change a title on the map.
Type	Change the type of map.
Layers	Opens the Layer Control dialog box, which is used to change the order of the layers, so that the map can display more or less detail.
Resolve Mismatch	Opens the Resolve Map Mismatch dialog box, which is used to select the map that you want to have the data values associated with.
Map Navigator	Turns the Map Navigator on and off. You can use the Map Navigator to center, zoom and pan on the map.

Table 2-15 Map menu options explained

Window Menu

The options on the Window menu are used to change the default layout of the open windows in Crystal Reports. These options work the same way that they do in Windows. The options are explained in Table 2-16.

Menu Option	Description
Tile Vertically	Arranges all open windows side by side.
Tile Horizontally	Arranges all open windows in rows so that they do not overlap.
Cascade	Arranges all open windows so that the title bar of each window is visible.
Arrange Icons	Arranges the icons at the bottom of the window.
Close All	Closes all open windows. You will be prompted to save any reports that have not been saved.

Table 2-16 Window menu options explained

Open Reports

At the bottom of the Window menu, you will see a list of all of the reports that are currently open, as shown in Figure 2-24.

The report that is currently displayed has a check mark in front of it. If you want to switch to a different report that is open, you can select it from the bottom of the Window menu. I am not sure how much this option is used because it is easier and faster to click on the tab for the open report that you want to view.

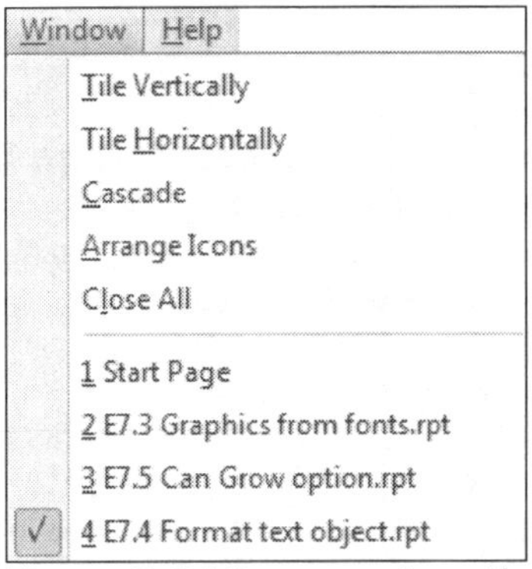

Figure 2-24 Open reports on the Window menu

Help Menu

The options on the Help menu provide several ways to get assistance. The other options are used to register and manage Crystal Reports. The options are explained in Table 2-17.

Menu Option	Description
SAP Crystal Reports Help	Opens the Online Help file.
Context Help	Displays help for windows, buttons and menus that you click on. After selecting this option, click on an item in the Crystal Reports workspace. A tool tip will appear that explains the item that you clicked on.
Show Start Page	Displays the Start Page tab if it is closed.
Check for Updates on Start Up	This option will automatically check for software updates each time that Crystal Reports is opened. (11)
Check for Updates	This option is used to immediately check for software updates. (11)
Register	Opens the registration wizard, which is used to register your copy of Crystal Reports or change your address. (11)

Table 2-17 Help menu options explained

Menu Option	Description
License Manager	Add and remove Crystal Reports and Integration kit key codes and license information.
Documentation	Opens the SAP Business Objects Knowledge Center web page. (11)
About SAP Crystal Reports	Opens the About dialog box. [See Chapter 1, Figure 1-2] It displays information about the version of Crystal Reports that is installed. Clicking the **MORE INFO** button on the dialog box displays the Loaded Modules shown in Figure 2-25.

Table 2-17 Help menu options explained (Continued)

(11) The computer needs to be connected to the Internet to use this option.

The information on this dialog box could be helpful if you have to troubleshoot some types of report problems.

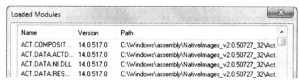

Figure 2-25 Loaded Modules dialog box

Customizing The Crystal Reports Design Environment

If you need to customize the report design environment, you can learn how, by reading the rest of this chapter. These options are used to set the default properties for the majority of features that you will use to create and modify reports. An example would be if you wanted all date fields placed on reports to use the same format.

Many companies have standards and requirements for how reports are formatted. If you are in this type of an environment, it would be a good idea to set up as many of these standards as possible. Doing so will keep you from having to always change certain options in every report that you create. Once you have used Crystal Reports for a while and find yourself always having to change an option, you should come back to this section and review the options on the Options dialog box and change the ones that you use to better meet your needs.

 While looking at the options, pay particular attention to the options on the layout, database and reporting tabs, as they have the options that you are likely to need to change first. They contain the options that most effect the functionality in the design tab.

 Options Dialog Box
The changes that you make on the Options dialog box effect all of the reports that you create or modify after the changes on this dialog box are saved. Any changes that are made are not applied to reports that were saved prior to the changes made on the Options dialog box. If you want to apply changes that you make on the Options dialog box to existing reports, delete the object from the report that the change will effect and then add the object back to the report. It would be nice if there was an easier way to apply the change to existing reports.

 If you click the Help button on the Options dialog box, you will see that the Online Help file automatically opens to the page for the options on the tab that you have open, as shown in Figure 2-27. In this example, the help button was clicked on the Layout tab shown in Figure 2-26.

Options Dialog Box

File ⇒ Options, opens the dialog box shown in Figure 2-26.

The options on the **LAYOUT TAB** are used to select what will appear on the design and preview tabs.

The options in the Design View section are used to select the look and functionality of the design tab.

The **SHORT SECTION NAMES** option provides more space on the design and preview tabs because it abbreviates the section names.

The options in the Preview section are used to select the look and functionality of the preview tab.

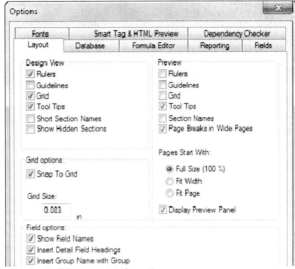

Figure 2-26 Layout tab options

The options in the Grid Options section are used to select how the grid will or will not be displayed on the design tab.

The options in the Field Options section are used to select how fields are displayed on the design tab. The **INSERT DETAIL FIELD HEADINGS** option is what causes field headings to be added to the report when you add a field to the details section. If the **SHOW FIELD NAMES** option is not checked, characters that indicate the field type will be displayed in fields on the design tab instead of the field name.

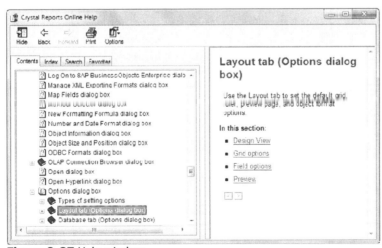

Figure 2-27 Help window

Figures 2-28 to 2-37 show some of the options that can be changed. When you are finished viewing the options, close the dialog box.

The **DATABASE TAB** options are used to select how data is displayed and how queries are processed.

The options in the Tables and Fields section are used to configure how tables and fields are displayed.

The options in the Data Explorer section are used to select how database objects are displayed in the Field Explorer and Database Expert.

The options in the Advanced Options section are used to help resolve performance issues like determining how queries will be run and when changes in the database structure will be checked. The first two options in this section are only available for SQL tables, not queries.

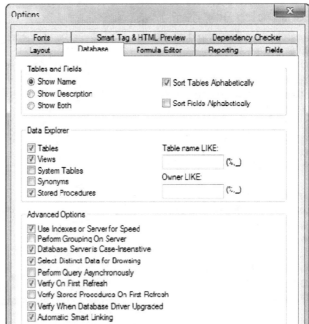

Figure 2-28 Database tab options

The **FORMULA EDITOR TAB** options are used to customize the fonts and colors used in the Formula Editor.

The **DEFAULT FORMULA LANGUAGE** option is used to select the default syntax language for the formulas that you create.

For the exercises in this book, this option should be set to Crystal Syntax.

Figure 2-29 Formula Editor tab options

The **REPORTING TAB** options are used to select how data is saved and retrieved for the report. These settings can be changed on a report by report basis, using the Report Options dialog box. [See Chapter 13, Report Options Dialog Box]

The options in the Enterprise Settings section are used to select report functionality in the SAP Business Objects Enterprise environment.

The options in the Reading Data section are used to select how null values and sorting will be handled.

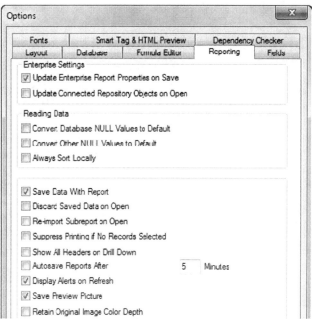

Figure 2-30 Reporting tab options

The **FIELDS TAB** options are used to select the default options for the field types that Crystal Reports supports.

For example, if you want all string fields to have the Can Grow option selected by default, click the **STRING** button. You will see the dialog box shown in Figure 2-32.

The Date and Time button displays the options shown in Figure 2-33.

Select the option that you want applied to all reports, then click OK.

Figure 2-31 Fields tab options

You may want to click on the buttons on the Fields tab now to become familiar with the default options. One option that you may want to change after completing the exercises in this book is the default date format if you think that you will use the same date format for the majority of reports that you will create. You do not have to change anything to complete the exercises in this book.

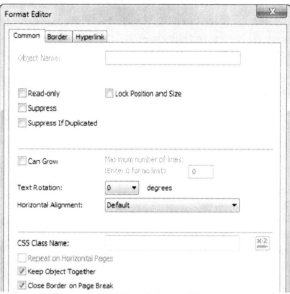

Figure 2-32 Format Editor string options

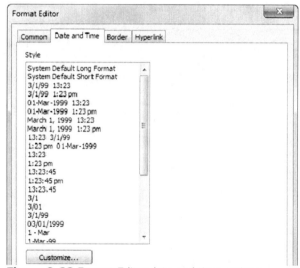

Figure 2-33 Format Editor date and time options

The **FONTS TAB** options are used to select the default font options for a variety of fields and objects that Crystal Reports supports.

The default font and size for fields is Arial, size 10.

As you will see, some of the defaults may not meet your reporting needs. Figure 2-35 shows the Group Name Fields font options.

All of the buttons on the Fonts tab display this dialog box. It is how you can select different font options for each field or object.

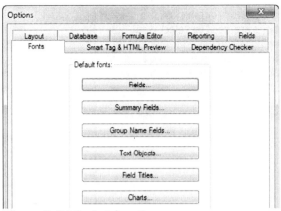

Figure 2-34 Fonts tab options

This dialog box is also used to select font options for other objects.

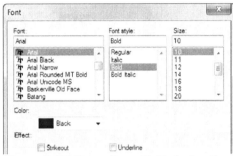

Figure 2-35 Group Name Fields font options

The **SMART TAG & HTML PREVIEW TAB** options are used to select how Crystal Reports Smart Tags will be used in Microsoft Office applications.

The HTML Preview options are used to select and configure how reports will be displayed as web pages.

If your reports are not stored in the SAP Business Objects Enterprise you may want to check the **ENABLE HTML PREVIEW** option so that you can preview reports as web pages.

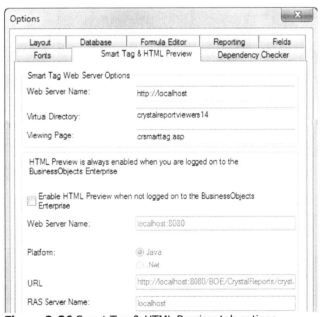

Figure 2-36 Smart Tag & HTML Preview tab options

The **DEPENDENCY CHECKER TAB** options are used to select what conditions you want to verify when you check reports for formula errors, broken links, database errors and more.

This tool can check one report or all reports in a project in the workbench.

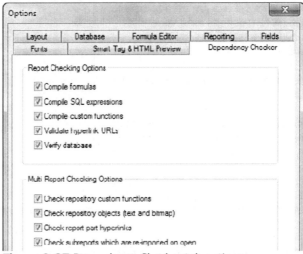

Figure 2-37 Dependency Checker tab options

DATABASE TERMINOLOGY AND THE CRYSTAL REPORTS WORKSPACE

After completing the exercises in this chapter you will be able to:

- ☑ Have a foundation of database terminology
- ☑ Understand data types
- ☑ Have a foundation of Crystal Reports terminology
- ☑ Understand the report design process
- ☑ Understand the sections of a report
- ☑ Understand the report creation options
- ☑ Use the design and preview tabs in the workspace
- ☑ Use the Group Tree
- ☑ Organize reports in the Workbench
- ☑ Use the Field Explorer
- ☑ Understand the purpose of the Repository Explorer

CHAPTER 3

Database Terminology

Below are key terms that would be helpful to understand about databases, in order to work with them effectively.

Field A field contains one piece of information and is stored in a record. Examples of fields include customer name and customer address.

Record A record has one or more fields. Each of the fields in a record are related. A record looks like a row of data in a spreadsheet.

Table A table is stored in a database and is a collection of records. Most databases have more than one table. Tables are linked on fields. Tables may remind you of a spreadsheet, because SQL databases have rows and columns, which Crystal Reports refers to as records and fields. Each table contains information about a specific topic. For example, a customer table would only contain information about customers. The customer table would not contain information about products.

Database A database is a collection of information that is stored in one or more tables.

Relational Database A relational database is a collection of RELATED information that is stored in one or more tables in the database. It is important to note that there are different types of physical database structures.

Database Concepts

There are several database concepts that you need to be aware of. Having an understanding of these concepts would be helpful when creating reports.

Data Source A data source is where the data is stored. Examples of data sources are databases, .cub files and spreadsheets.

Data Dictionary A data dictionary contains detailed information about a data source and includes the following types of information: Database and table names, field names, types, sizes, indexes and related files. A data dictionary can be handwritten or typed. It can also be generated by some database software packages.

Relationship A relationship is how two or more tables are joined (linked). Tables can be joined when they have at least one field that is the same in each table. For example, an invoice table can be joined to a products table because each invoice record will have at least one item from the products table. Crystal Reports has a SMART LINKING feature that will automatically join tables that have related information. Crystal Reports also has a built-in visual utility that will help you link tables.

Length Is used to select the maximum number of characters that the field can have. This means that if the length of a field is set to 20, the field cannot have more than 20 characters.

Null Any of the data types explained in Table 3-1 can be null (empty). Null means that the field does not have a value. Depending on the data source, an empty string may or may not be set to null. An empty numeric field is not equal to zero.

Index The purpose of indexes is to make the retrieval of records from tables faster. Knowing which fields in the table are indexed is important when you need to optimize a report. Crystal Reports can indicate which fields are indexed in some types of databases and in other types of databases it can't.

If Crystal Reports does not recognize the indexes in the tables that you are using, you can get the information from the data dictionary for the database.

> **PRIMARY KEY FIELDS** should always be indexed. **FOREIGN KEY FIELDS** are usually indexed. Other fields in a table that are used frequently to retrieve (select) records should be indexed. Fields that fall into this category are fields that are used to sort, group or link data.

> Databases that have too many indexes will retrieve records slower. Indexes are usually created by the DBA (Data Base Administrator). If you need to have an index created contact the DBA, unless you have the rights to create an index in the database.

Data Types

Each field must have a data type. The data type determines what type of information can be stored in the field. Table 3-1 explains the data types that Crystal Reports supports. The data types listed are available in most databases. If you use a database that has data types other then the ones listed in Table 3-1, they will automatically be mapped to a data type that Crystal Reports recognizes.

Data Type	Description
String	String fields are also known as **TEXT FIELDS** because they primarily contain text. They can also store numbers, spaces and other special characters. Numeric data that is stored in a string field is treated like text because there is no need to use the data in any type of calculation. An example of numeric data that is treated like text is zip codes. Numeric data stored in a string field cannot be formatted with any number data type formatting options.
Number	This data type can only contain numbers and decimal points. It can be used in a calculation like addition, multiplication and formulas.
Currency	This data type can only contain monetary data. You can use currency fields in calculations, just like number fields. Currency is a special number data type. By default, Crystal Reports will automatically display and print a dollar sign with this data type.
Date	Date fields are used to store dates, which can be stored in several formats. Date fields contain the month, day and year.
Time	This data type is used to store time, which can be stored in several formats. Time fields contain hours, minutes and seconds. Crystal Reports does not recognize fractional seconds even if the underlying data source has them.
Date and Time	Displays the date and time in one field in this format - MM/DD/YYYY HH:MM:SS. You can hide the time portion of this data type on reports.
Boolean	Boolean fields are used to set a logical value of true/false, yes/no or 1/0.
Memo	The memo data type is a free form text field, meaning that it can store almost any type of information. This data type may not be available in all databases. Memo fields can contain large amounts of data and embedded formatting. Crystal Reports can recognize **RICH TEXT (RTF)** and **HTML FORMATTING** in memo fields. A common use for memo fields is to store comments about the data in the other fields in the record.

Table 3-1 Data types explained

Data Type	Description
Picture	This data type stores an image file or a link to the location of the image file. (This is known as the DYNAMIC IMAGE LOCATION.) Crystal Reports recognizes the following image file types: JPEG (.jpg), bitmap (.bmp), Tagged Image (.tiff), Portable Network Graphics (.png) and Windows Metafile (.wmf). Some databases refer to this data type as a BLOB (Binary Large Object). This field type can only be displayed on a report. It cannot be used in a formula.

Table 3-1 Data types explained (Continued)

Crystal Reports Terminology

Below are some key terms that you need to understand about Crystal Reports in order to work with databases effectively. The four field types explained below are not stored in a table like the data types explained above in Table 3-1 are.

① **FORMULA FIELDS** can include any of the 300 built-in functions that Crystal Reports has, or you can create a formula from scratch. Formula fields are calculated each time the report is run.

② **SPECIAL FIELDS** contain information that is system generated. Examples of system generated fields include the date the report was printed and the page number. There are 26 special fields that you can use.

③ **SUMMARY FIELDS** are calculated fields and like formula fields, they are also calculated each time the report is run. You create summary fields.

④ **TEXT OBJECT FIELDS** are free form fields that are used to place information on the report that is not in any of the fields in the database. Text objects are often used to create a report title or a heading for fields that you create.

Report Design Process

I know that you are anxious to create your first report, but there are several items that need to be addressed and worked out before you create a report, whether this is your first report or your 100th report. This section is an overview of the report design process. Report design could be an entire chapter or two all by itself, but I am giving you the abridged version <smile>. The report design process is part of what is known as the "Business Requirements" phase of a project. As you gain experience, you will see that if you do not get the business requirements right, the project will be delayed, potentially be over budget and not produce the results that the business owner (requestor) or client is looking for. Many call this a "bad career move".

When you learn the concepts presented in this chapter, it will be easier for you to create reports. You should write down the answers to the questions that will be presented in the report design process. The more planning that you do before you create the report, the less you will have to modify a report after it is created. There are four main steps to the report design process. Each step can have multiple tasks.

You will see how these steps come together through the exercises in this book. When creating reports, especially ones that other people will use, it is imperative that you fully understand the requirements, which often includes you asking a lot of questions. This is not a task that you can be bashful about. Not asking questions or worse, asking the wrong questions will more than likely cause you grief down the road.

Step 1: Define The Purpose Of The Report

Yes, I know what you are saying: "How hard can it be to figure out the purpose of a report?".
The answer is it depends on how well the person or group of people are able to explain what they
want the report to provide and how well you understand what they tell you.

The majority of reports that you create will probably be used by someone other than yourself, which
means that you should meet with the person or group of people that will use the report. These
meetings are part of the report requirement gathering process. Keep in mind that you may have to
have more than one meeting to get a good idea of what the report needs to include, because the
users may not tell you or be able to clearly articulate their needs in one meeting. Reports are often
used as a decision making tool, which means that poor decisions will be made or the decision
making process will be ineffective due to missing or incorrect data that is presented on the report.
The data must be presented in a logical manner in order to be an effective decision making tool.

> Keep in mind that one report can be used by people at different levels in the company.
> This means that at each level people can have slightly different needs. If this is the case,
> you will have to plan and design the report accordingly, so that it meets the needs of all of
> the users.

Your role as the report designer is to gather the information needed, which will help the users of the
report to be able to read it easily, as well as, understand the data on the report. If the information
is not presented in a way that works for the users, trust me, they will let you know and you will be
spending a lot of time modifying the report.

In my opinion, the more that users have you modify a report, the quicker your credibility goes down
hill. That is not something that you want to happen. What I have discovered is that if you create a
prototype (which is explained later in this chapter) of the report for the users, they can discuss what
they like and do not like about the prototype report. Usually, you will gain valuable information that
is often hard to get users to discuss in a regular meeting. The worst thing that you can do in many
cases, is give the users the impression that you know more about their needs than they do. I am
not saying that in some cases that you won't know more about their data or needs, just don't give
them that impression, if you know what I mean. To define the expected outcome of the report,
write a descriptive sentence or two about the purpose of the report or what the report needs to
accomplish. Below are some example purpose statements.

① The purpose of the report is to compare last years sales data to this years sales data by
   region.
② The purpose of the report is to show products that are low on inventory and need to be
   reordered.
③ The purpose of the report is to show the top 10 best selling products by sales team.

In addition to defining the expected outcome of the report you have to take into consideration who
will be using the report. It is very possible that managers and their staff will request similar reports.
In some cases it is better to create separate reports, even if there is only one field that is different,
then to try and get multiple parties to try and come up with one report that works for both groups
of users. As you gain report design experience, understand business requirements and know the
requestors, you will be able to quickly determine which is the best solution.

Step 2: Determine The Layout Of The Report

Now that you have determined the purpose of the report, you need to determine where each piece of data should be placed on the report. If you are creative you will like this step. In addition to determining where the data should be placed, you need to determine some or all of the following:

① Create a list of fields that need to appear on the report. If you know what database and table each field is in, include that on the list. If the data does not currently exist, include that on the list also. You will use this list to complete tasks in future steps in the report design process.

② What should the report title be and where should it be placed on the report. Should it only be printed on the first page or on all pages of the report?

③ Does the report need page numbers or dates? If so, what format should they be in and where should they be placed on the report; in the page header or footer section or someplace else?

④ Are any Special Fields other then the page number or date needed on the report?

⑤ Which fields or sections of the report need totals, summary information, statistical information or some other type of calculated field? (**Hint**: Summary fields do not exist in a table.)

⑥ An important question to answer during this step is what format the report needs to be in. This is known as the **DELIVERY METHOD** (for example, paper, PDF or web based). The way that a report needs to be distributed can influence the layout of a report. You should also find out if the report needs to be distributed in more than one format.

Step 3: Find The Data For The Report

This step is very important because without the data there is no report. As the person creating the report, life will be much easier for you if you are familiar with the data needed for the report and how it is organized. If you are not familiar with the data or are not technical, you may have to rely on Information Technology specialists like database administrators to help you with the tasks in this step. There are three tasks that you have to work on to complete this step successfully.

Task 1 The first task that you have to complete is to find out which databases and tables contain the data for the report. Use the list of fields that you created in step 2 to find the databases and tables. You may also have to find out what servers the databases are on. There are several types of databases that the data can be stored in. The data may also be stored in a Crystal dictionary, an OLAP cube or something other than a database, like a spreadsheet. This task is known as finding the **DATA SOURCE**.

Task 2 This task involves selecting the actual fields in the tables that are needed for the report. Use the list that you created in step 2. Once the fields are selected, determine the formatting for each field and how the fields should be displayed on the report. You also have to determine if the field names in the table are the best choice for the field headings on the report. One example of when a field name needs to be changed on a report is for fields that have the word ID as part of the field name.

Task 3 Now that you have found some of the data in the tables, there are probably fields left on the list that you created in step 2 that you have not found. Some may be special fields that you read about earlier in this chapter. More than likely, many of the fields that are left on the list are calculated fields. This task involves writing out the formulas for the calculated fields. Some calculated fields may use a built-in function and others may require a field that is in a data source, but will not be placed on the report.

In order to be able to create calculated fields, you have to become familiar with the database field types and the Crystal Reports fields explained earlier in this chapter. Several Crystal Reports functions are designed to only work with specific types of data. Examples of calculated fields include:

① Sales price times quantity
② Number of days between the order date and the ship date
③ How long the person has been employed at the company

Step 4: Organize The Data

This step involves organizing all of the data. Many of the options that you decide on in task 1 below, will automatically dictate which section of the report certain fields will be placed in.

Task 1 To complete this task you have to organize all of the data, both from the tables and calculated fields, as well as, any other data source. Organizing the data means at a minimum, answering the following questions.

① Does the data need to be sorted? If so, which fields should the data be sorted on?
② Does the data need to be grouped? If so, which fields should the data be grouped on?
③ Does the report need summary data? Summary data is a calculated field, like grand totals, averages and counts.
④ Does the report need to have any data flagged? If so, how should the data be flagged? The primary reason data would be flagged is so that it can easily be identified on a report. Make a list of any data that needs to be flagged. Crystal Reports has several options including borders, symbols, changing the font size and other formatting techniques that you can use to indicate that the data is flagged.
⑤ Decide if the report needs any of the following: Charts, cross-tabs, maps or alerts, which notify the person running the report that a specific condition has been met.

Task 2 To complete this task you have to determine which section of the report each field should be placed in. Task 1 had you make decisions on how to organize the data at a high level. There are several sections of a report that the data and objects can be placed in. The sections of a report are explained later in this chapter.

Task 3 One way that you organize the data is by selecting which records will actually appear on the report. This is important because most reports do not require that all records in a table appear on the report. For example, if the report needs to display sales (orders) for a specific sales rep, you would create selection criteria that would only allow orders for the particular sales rep to appear on the report. Another example would be to display all customers that purchased a specific product or group of products.

In addition to record selection, it may be necessary to create parameter fields which will make the report more flexible in terms of record selection. Parameter fields allow the person running the report to select the criteria that will be used to retrieve the records that will appear on the report. Parameter fields allow one report to be run with a variety of selection criteria. An example of this would be an order report. If the report had parameter fields for the order date, order amount and sales rep fields, all of the following reports and more, could be generated from the same report.

① A report to show all orders for a specific date.
② A report to show all orders for a specific sales rep.
③ A report to show all orders over or under a specific total order amount.

④ A report to show all orders in a date range.

⑤ A report to show all orders in a certain date range for a specific sales rep.

Task 4 Depending on the company, it may be necessary to have the person or group of people sign a document that states that all of the tasks discussed above will produce the report that they need.

Report Prototype

Even though you will go through the entire report design process, it is very possible that the users are still somewhat unclear or cannot visualize what the finished report should look like. If that is the case, creating a report prototype will be a life saver. A report prototype can be hand drawn on paper or you can create a sample report that displays the data based on the information that you gather during the initial portion of the report design process. The reason prototypes are helpful is because the users will get a pretty good idea of what the finished report will look like, based on the information that they supplied.

The feedback that you receive from the users about the prototype is invaluable in my opinion, because users get to "see" what they asked for. I have found this process to be a very effective way for users to tell me what they like, don't like, need and don't need.

Sections Of A Report

There are seven sections of a report that you can place data and other objects in. Each section has its own properties that can be customized on a section by section basis. If you place the same calculated field (numbers, totals or amounts) in different sections of the report, it can produce different results. It is important that you understand how each section of the report functions because they function independently of each other. Keep the following in mind when deciding where to place fields and objects on the report.

① If a report does not need a section, it can be suppressed so that it does not display blank space on the report.

② If you create a report using a wizard, the majority of fields are automatically placed in an appropriate section of the report.

③ All of the report sections except the group header and footer, will automatically appear in the report, whether you use them or not. Grouping is optional.

④ The order of the report sections cannot be changed.

⑤ Sections can be resized vertically as needed.

⑥ Formulas, charts and cross-tabs will display different results, depending on which section of the report they are placed in. These differences are explained below in each report section.

 By default, the letters in parenthesis after each report section is what you will see to the left of the report when it is previewed. These are known as **SECTION SHORT NAMES**. On the design tab you will see the full section name by default. If you want to change either of these options, File ⇒ Options ⇒ Layout tab.

Section 1: Report Header (RH)

Data fields and other objects placed in this section will only print on the first page of the report. It is quite possible that many of the reports that you create will not have anything in this section. Something that you may want to include in this section of the report is the selection criteria and parameter fields that the report has. If the report needs a cover page, the report header section can be used for the cover page. If this is what you need to do, add a page break after this section so that the actual report starts on a new page.

FORMULAS are calculated for the entire report.
CHARTS and **CROSS-TABS** will contain data for the entire report.

 If the report header section requires more than one page, the information in the page header and footer sections of the report will not print until all of the information in the report header section has printed.

Section 2: Page Header (PH)

Data fields and other objects placed in this section will appear at the top of every page in the report except the report header page if it prints on a page by itself. This is where most people put the report title. Other objects that are commonly placed in this section include the date, page number and headings for the fields in the details section of the report. Report wizards will automatically place field headings and the system generated "print date" field in this section.

FORMULAS are calculated at the beginning of every page of the report.
CHARTS and **CROSS-TABS** cannot be placed in this section.

Section 3: Group Header (GH)

This section is only used if the data is grouped. Data fields and other objects placed in this section will print at the beginning of each group on the report. Each time the data in the field that the group is based on changes, another group header and footer section is dynamically created. This section is always right above the details section. If a report is grouped on two or more fields, a new group header and footer section will automatically be created for each field that the report is grouped on.

FORMULAS are calculated one time at the beginning of the group, based on the data in the group, not on all of the data in the report.
CHARTS and **CROSS-TABS** will only contain data from the group.

Section 4: Details (D)

Data fields and other objects placed in this section will print for each record that meets the selection criteria. The data fields and other objects in this section usually have field headings in the page header section. This section is automatically repeated once for each record that will be printed on the report.

FORMULAS are calculated for each record in this section, unless the record does not meet the condition of the formula.
CHARTS and **CROSS-TABS** cannot be placed in this section.

Section 5: Group Footer (GF)

This section is only used if the data is grouped. Data fields and other objects placed in this section will print at the end of each group section on the report. The group footer section often includes subtotals and other summary data for the group. This section is always right below the details section.

FORMULAS are calculated one time at the end of the group, based on the data in the group, not on all of the data in the report.

CHARTS and **CROSS-TABS** will only contain data from the group.

Section 6: Report Footer (RF)

Data fields and other objects placed in this section will print once at the end of the report. This is usually where grand totals and other types of report summary information is placed.

FORMULAS are calculated once at the end of the report.
CHARTS and **CROSS-TABS** will contain data for the entire report.

> If the report footer section requires more than one page to print the information, the page header and footer sections will print on the additional pages that the report footer needs. This is the opposite of what happens if the report header requires more than one page. If you think about it though, that makes sense because by the time the report footer section is printed, the "switch" if you will, for the page header and footer sections is turned on.

Section 7: Page Footer (PF)

Data fields and other objects placed in this section will print at the bottom of each page of the report. The page footer section is similar to the page header section. Page numbers are often placed in this section. Report wizards will automatically place the page number in this section.

FORMULAS are calculated at the end of every page of the report. This would be useful if the report needs to have totals by page.
CHARTS and **CROSS-TABS** cannot be placed in this section.

Report Creation Options

There are three ways (wizards, from an existing report and from scratch) that you can create a report. Each option has pros and cons. Once you understand all of the options, you can select the one that best meets the needs for each report that you create. You can also use one of the templates that come with Crystal Reports to format the report differently.

Wizards

This is the easiest way to create a new report. The wizards will walk you through the steps required to create a report. The wizards are helpful when learning the basics of Crystal Reports. Some report designers sometimes use the wizards to save time to create a basic report and then add advanced features manually. Keep in mind that the wizards do not provide all of the options that are needed to create the functionality that all reports need. The wizards are limited because they use default options which often do not meet the needs of the report that you are creating.

Based on your selections on the wizard screens, the fields are placed in the most appropriate section of the report. This does not mean that if you make a mistake when using the wizard, that the wizard will correct the mistake. It is possible to create a report that displays results that are very different then you intended when using a wizard. There are four report wizards that you can select from. What you will find, depending on the options that you select, is that additional fields are automatically added to the report, which you may not need. If this happens, you can delete the fields once you have the report open on the design tab.

Create A Report Based Off Of An Existing Report

If a report exists that is similar to the report that you now need to create, select this report creation option. Save the existing report with a new file name and make the necessary changes to the new report. You will use this option in several exercises in this book.

An example of when to create a report based off of an existing report would be when two groups of people need to see the majority of the same fields and one group needs additional information that the other group does not need, or when one group needs the same fields in a different layout.

Create A Report From Scratch

This option provides the most flexibility to create a report. You start with a blank canvas so to speak and add the fields, formulas and other objects without any assistance. For many, this can be intimidating especially in the beginning, but being the fearless person that you are, I'm sure that when you get to the exercises that have you create a report from scratch, you will do just fine.

Wizard Types

As mentioned earlier, there are four report wizards that you can select from to create reports. They are explained below.

① **REPORT** This is probably the most used wizard because it provides the majority of options needed to create a wide variety of reports. The name displayed on the dialog box for this wizard is Standard Report Creation. The report wizards discussed below create specific types of reports.

② **CROSS-TAB** This wizard will create a report that presents data in a grid. Cross-Tab reports resemble spreadsheets because they have rows and columns. The grid often contains totals at the end of each row and column. An example of when a cross-tab should be used would be if you needed to know how many of specific products were sold by each sales rep. You should only use this wizard if the cross-tab will be the only object on the report.

③ **MAILING LABEL** This wizard will walk you through the process of creating labels. While you can format a report created with the Report wizard to print labels, the advantage of using the mailing label wizard is that it has an option to select the label size that you need. This means that you will not have to manually format the report to match the dimensions of the label size that you need.

④ **OLAP CUBE** This wizard is used to create a report that is similar to a cross-tab report. The difference is that this wizard connects to an OLAP data source. You can filter the data and create a chart.

Xtreme Database

This is the database that is often used to test and learn Crystal Reports. You will use a modified version of it (which I named crystalxtreme.mdb) as the basis for the reports that you will create in this book. As you saw in Chapter 1, there are links on the Start Page tab for sample reports that you can view. Downloading the sample reports is not a requirement to complete the exercises in this book.

The Xtreme database is a Microsoft Access database. This database contains the data for a fictitious company called Xtreme Mountain Bikes. As the company name suggests, they sell mountain bikes and accessories. The database has tables that store the following types of information: Customers, Employees, Orders, Suppliers, Products and more.

Figure 3-1 shows the data model for some of the tables in the Xtreme database. The fields in bold are the Primary Key fields. Table 3-2 contains information for tables in the database that are shown in Figure 3-1.

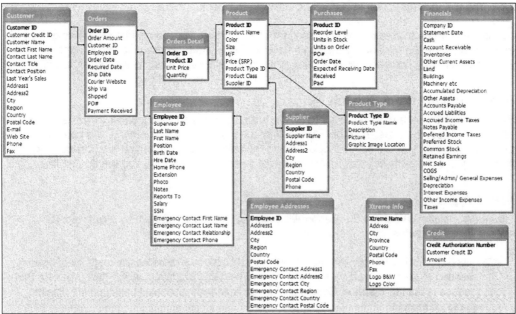

Figure 3-1 Xtreme database data model

Table	Primary Key Field	Indexed Fields	Records
Credit	Credit Authorization Number	Credit Authorization Number, Customer Credit ID	322
Customer	Customer ID	Customer ID, Postal Code	269
Employee	Employee ID	Employee ID, Supervisor ID, Reports To	15
Employee Addresses	Employee ID	Employee ID, Postal Code, Emergency Contact Postal Code	15
Financials	Company ID	Company ID	4
Orders	Order ID	Order ID, Customer ID, Employee ID	2,192
Orders Detail	Order ID, Product ID	Order ID, Product ID	3,684
Product	Product ID	Product ID, Product Type ID, Supplier ID	115
Product Type	Product Type ID	Product Type ID	8
Purchases	Product ID	Product ID	44
Supplier	Supplier ID	Supplier ID, Postal Code	7
Xtreme Info	Xtreme Name	Xtreme Name, Postal Code	1

Table 3-2 Xtreme database table information

Xtreme Database Tables

In order to help you become more familiar with the data contained in each table, this section provides a description of the data in the tables that you will use in this book. The table name is in bold.

Customer Contact and address information for all of the companies customers.

Employee Detail information for each employee.

 The Supervisor ID field in the Employee table contains the Employee ID of a different person in the Employee table. The Supervisor ID field contains who the employee reports to. This is known as a **RECURSIVE JOIN,** which you will learn about Chapter 5.

Employee Addresses Home address and emergency contact information for each employee.

Orders Information about each customer order. Fields that apply to the entire order, like the order date and order amount are in this table. This table is often referred to as the **ORDER HEADER** table. This table does not contain information about the items on the order.

Orders Detail Information about each item in each order.

Product Information for each item that the company sells. Each product only has one product type and supplier. This does not mean that there cannot be two suppliers that have the same product. For example, Supplier A has blue hats. Supplier B has blue hats and brown hats. There would be a record in the Product table for each of these three hats.

Product Type General categories for the products like gloves, locks and helmets.

Supplier Information about the companies that Xtreme purchases the products from that they sell. Contact and address information for each supplier is stored in this table.

Crystal Reports Workspace
The workspace is also known as the Report Designer. It is where you will create, edit and preview reports. Therefore, it is important to know what tools are available in the workspace. As you will see, the workspace has a lot of options. The toolbars, menus and customization options were covered in detail in Chapter 2. The workspace has two tabs: The design tab and the preview tab.

Design And Preview Tabs
When a report is opened, two tabs will appear below the Start Page tab: the preview and design tabs. (The display area of these tabs are often referred to as the preview and design windows.) The majority of functionality available on the design tab is also available on the preview tab including the menus, toolbars and formatting options.

Preview Tab
The preview tab is used to view the report as it will look when it is printed. Reports can look different on this tab depending on the printer that is selected. Also notice the following:

① That some of the toolbars at the top of the workspace are now available.
② The report opened on its own tab. The tab name is either the report file name or the report title.
③ The blue area to the left of the report contains the "sections" of the report. Having the sections visible, lets you know which section of the report each piece of data or object is in. You learned about the seven report sections earlier in this chapter.
④ The options down the far left side of the report are the groups that the report has. This section is called the **GROUP TREE**.

⑤ You can modify reports on the preview tab. Unless stated otherwise, the instructions in this book are written to be completed in the design tab.

 The preview tab will not automatically appear for a report that was created from the **BLANK REPORT** option or for a report that is open, but the data has not been refreshed. If you need the preview tab and it is not visible, you can use one of the five options listed below.

How To Display The Preview Tab

① Click the **PRINT PREVIEW** button on the Standard toolbar.
② Click the **REFRESH** button on the Navigation Tools toolbar.
③ Press the **F5** key.
④ View ⇒ Print Preview.
⑤ View ⇒ Preview Sample.

Design And Preview Tab Differences

As much as these tabs have in common, there are some differences between the tabs that you should be aware of, as explained below.

① The section names display differently. On the design tab you can display the section names as long or short names. On the preview tab, the section names can be hidden or displayed as short section names, but not long section names.
② The design tab displays the fields from the tables and objects. The preview tab displays the data from the fields and the objects.
③ Only the preview tab has the Parameters Panel, which has the group tree. Page controls and refreshed data information are also only available on the preview tab.
④ If you select a field on the preview tab, every occurrence of the field in the report is selected.
⑤ If you modify a field on the preview tab, the report will take longer to be redisplayed then it will if you make the same change in the design tab. This is because the data is displayed on the preview tab.
⑥ The design tab does not display the page margins. On the preview tab, the margins are indicated by a black border around the page.

The Status Bar

The status bar shown in Figure 3-2 is located at the bottom of the workspace. It displays helpful information when you are designing and previewing reports. The information on the status bar will change, depending on what you are doing. It also displays tool tips when the mouse is hovered over an option on a menu or over a button on a toolbar. Like the toolbars, the status bar can also be turned off (View ⇒ Status Bar), but it can't be moved.

On the preview tab you will see the number of records in the report on the status bar. If you do not see the number of records, resize the window. The date and time shown, 3/11/2008 4:46 PM in Figure 3-2 is the last time that the data in the report was refreshed.

If the data was refreshed or retrieved today, only the time will be displayed. If you clicked the **REFRESH** button, the date and time information will change. The percent shown in the far right is the zoom level percent of the report. If an object is selected on the report, its name will be displayed in the left corner of the status bar instead of the date and time, as shown in Figure 3-3. The object size and position are displayed on the right. You can also see the number of records in the status bar on the design tab, as shown in Figure 3-3.

3/11/2008 4:46PM   Records: 83

Figure 3-2 Status bar with report information

Field: Product.Product Name   3/11/2008 4:46PM   Records: 83   2.8 , 2.8 : 1.3 x 0.1

Figure 3-3 Status bar with field information

Zoom Options

On the right side of the status bar are the **ZOOM** options shown in Figure 3-4.
The first button displays the entire report in the workspace.
The second button displays the report so that it takes up the entire size of the available workspace.
The slider is used to change how large or small the report will be displayed.

100%

Figure 3-4 Zoom options

Navigation Tools Toolbar

The **PAGE INDICATOR** section shown in
Figure 3-5 displays what page of the report
is currently displayed. This section also
displays how many pages are in the report.

2 of 2+

Figure 3-5 Navigation Tools toolbar

 If you see **1 OF 1+** or something similar and want to know how many pages the report has, click the **SHOW LAST PAGE** button on the Navigation Tools toolbar. The plus sign shown above in Figure 3-5 means that Crystal Reports has not formatted all of the pages for the report. This means that the total number of pages in the report is currently unknown.

Preview Panel

The Preview Panel is a section on the preview tab. It contains the Group Tree, Parameters Panel and the Find Panel, as shown in Figure 3-6. This panel adds more interactive options. The Preview Panel can be displayed or hidden by clicking the **TOGGLE PREVIEW PANEL** button on the Standard toolbar.

If the report has a parameter field you will see options similar to those shown in Figure 3-7 on the Preview Panel.

Figure 3-6 Preview Panel

The **FIND PANEL** shown in Figure 3-8 is used to search the report for words or phrases. Type in the word or phrase that you are looking for, then click the magnifying glass button or press Enter to start the search. You will see results similar to what is shown in Figure 3-9. Double-clicking on a search result option will display that part of the report.

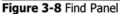

Figure 3-8 Find Panel

Figure 3-9 Search results

Figure 3-7 Parameters Panel

The Group Tree

If the report has groups, a group section is automatically added to the Preview Panel. If you click on the groups button you will see the groups that the report has. Clicking on a group will display that section of the report.

This feature is helpful when you need to navigate through a report that has a lot of groups. The group tree is located on the far left side on the preview tab in the Preview Panel. It displays all of the groups and subgroups in the report. Clicking on an option in the group tree will display the corresponding section in the report. You can customize the group name.

If a group has a subgroup, you will see a plus sign (+) in front of the group name, as shown in Figure 3-10. Clicking on the plus sign will expand the group and display the subgroup, as shown in the figure. The plus sign is also known as the **EXPAND BUTTON**. The minus sign is also known as the **COLLAPSE BUTTON**.

If you click on the plus sign in front of the number 4, then click on the name under the group, as shown in Figure 3-10, the section of the report for this group would be displayed.

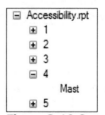

Figure 3-10 Group tree options

Group Tree Shortcut Menu

If you right-click in the group tree section on the preview tab you will see the shortcut menu shown in Figure 3-11.

The options are explained below.

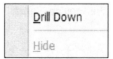

Figure 3-11 Group tree shortcut menu

① **DRILL DOWN** This option will open another tab, as illustrated in Figure 3-12. The new tab contains the detail information for the branch in the group tree that you right-clicked on. The name on the tab represents the heading in the group tree that was right-clicked on.

② **HIDE** This option will hide the branch that was selected before it was right-clicked on.

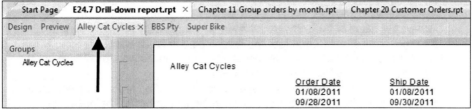

Figure 3-12 Drill Down result with several other reports open

 The Drill Down and Hide options are not available from a menu or toolbar.

 If you can't see the groups on the left side of the window, place the mouse pointer on the bar illustrated above in Figure 3-12, then drag the bar over to the right, as much as needed.

Viewing Reports

Notice that each report opens on its own tab to the right of the Start Page tab, as shown above in Figure 3-12. You can have several reports open at the same time.

 The tab with the X indicates the active report. To close a report click on the X. If changes were made to the report you will be prompted to save them.

 You can make some changes to the report like formatting and moving objects on the preview tab, but you will probably find it easier to use the design tab.

Design Tab

When you click on the **DESIGN** tab, you will see the window shown in Figure 3-13. The design tab is where you will create and modify reports, as well as, see the structure of the report. When fields are added to a report, the data is not retrieved. The data is not retrieved until the report is previewed. This means that when fields and objects are added to the report, formulas are created or fields are formatted, no processing is taking place. Figure 3-13 illustrates parts of the design tab. Table 3-3 explains the illustrated parts of the design tab.

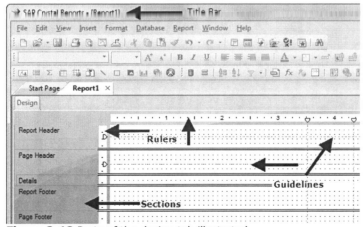

Figure 3-13 Parts of the design tab illustrated

Option	Description
Title Bar	Displays the name of the software followed by the file name of the report.
Sections	Like other parts of the design tab, the section portion has a shortcut menu, which you access by right-clicking in the section that you want to work on. These are the same report sections that you read about earlier.
Rulers	The rulers help you place fields in a specific location on the report. The default unit of measurement for the rulers is set by the regional settings of the operating system installed on your computer.
Guidelines	The guidelines are used to line up fields and other objects in the design area.
Design area	The design area is all of the white space below and to the right of the rulers. This is where you will add, change and format fields and other objects on the report. You can place objects as close to the edge of this area as necessary because this area is inside of the report page margins.

Table 3-3 Parts of the design tab explained

 Everything on a report is an object. Each object has its own set of properties. Almost all of these properties can be modified. The properties can also be modified based on a condition that you set. You will learn about conditional formatting in Chapter 15.

Report Sections

As shown above in Figure 3-13, the design tab is divided into sections. The sections are divided by boundary lines, which are also called **SECTION BARS** and is how I will reference them. The sections can be resized by moving the section bars up or down. Figure 3-14 shows a smaller page header section and a larger details section, then shown above in Figure 3-13.

To resize a section of the report, place the mouse pointer over the section bar that you need to move, as illustrated in Figure 3-14. The mouse pointer will change to a double arrow, as shown in the figure. Drag the section bar up or down. If you do not need to display data in a section of the report, you can **SUPPRESS** (hide) the section and it will not appear on the preview tab or on the printed report.

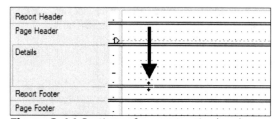

Figure 3-14 Sections of a report resized and mouse pointer in position to move the section bar

 You cannot make a section smaller than the objects that are in the section.

The Workbench

This tool is used to organize the reports that you create or are responsible for maintaining. By default, the Workbench is on the right side of the workspace. The way that you organize the reports in the Workbench is by placing them in folders which Crystal Reports calls **PROJECTS**. You can also add **REPORT PACKAGES** to the Workbench if you are using the Crystal Reports Server or the SAP Business Objects Enterprise.

Project folders can only contain reports. Unlike other file management tools, you cannot create a folder under an existing folder in the Workbench. A benefit of using the Workbench is that you will be able to access reports without having to know where they are located on your computers hard drive or which server they are on. The downside is that you have to add the reports one by one to the Workbench.

Once you have added reports to the Workbench, you can move them from one folder to another by dragging the report. You can also rearrange the order of the project folders by dragging them to where you want them to be. You can create a folder in the Workbench for this book. That way, when you need to go back to a report you will be able to find it easily. Placing the report files in the Workbench to complete the exercises in this book is optional.

 If you rename, delete or move a report, when you double-click on the link for it in the Workbench you will get an error message when you try to open the report. If this happens, you have to add the report to the Workbench again.

Exercise 3.1: Create A Folder In The Workbench

The Workbench has been discussed as a way for you to organize the reports that you create. In preparation for the first report that you will create, you will create a folder in the Workbench by following the steps below.

 View ⇒ Workbench, will display the Workbench if you do not see it on the design tab or on the Start Page tab. It is probably a good idea to leave the Workbench open all the time if you add reports to it, because you can use it to quickly open reports that you have already created.

1. Add ⇒ Add New Project, as shown in Figure 3-15.

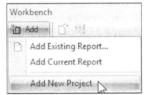

Figure 3-15 Menu option to create a new project folder

2. Type Crystal Reports Book, as shown in Figure 3-16, then press Enter.

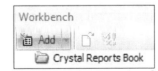

Figure 3-16 New project folder name

Adding Reports To The Workbench

There are four ways to add reports to the Workbench, as explained below.

① Add ⇒ Add Existing Report.
② Add ⇒ Add Current Report.
③ Right-click in the Workbench and select Add ⇒ Add Existing Report.
④ Drag a report from Windows Explorer to the Workbench.

If you need to add a report to the workbench, it is easier to do it while the report is open in the workspace.

 The Workbench does not sort the reports in a folder. This means that they appear in the folder in the order that they are added, opposed to be sorted alphabetically. You can rearrange the order of the reports in the Workbench.

 You can publish an entire project to the SAP Business Objects Enterprise.

The Workbench Toolbar

Table 3-4 explains the purpose of each button on the Workbench toolbar.

Button	Description
1	The **Add Report** button is used to add the three types of objects explained below to the Workbench. ① **ADD EXISTING REPORT** Is used to add an existing report to the Workbench. ② **ADD CURRENT REPORT** Is used to add the active report to the Workbench. If the workbench does not have a project folder a project folder is automatically created and then the active report is automatically added to it. ③ **ADD NEW PROJECT** Is used to create a project folder.
2	The **Open** button is used to open a report or report package that is in the Workbench. I find it easier to double-click on the report in the Workbench, then to click this button.
3	The **Check Dependencies** button will start the Dependency Checker as long as there is one report in a project folder in the Workbench. This tool is used to check one report or all reports in a folder in the Workbench for errors.

Table 3-4 Workbench toolbar buttons explained

Deleting Projects And Reports From The Workbench

Deleting projects and reports from the Workbench works similar to how you delete folders and files in other applications. Reports deleted from the Workbench are not deleted from the hard drive or server that they are stored on. You are only deleting the reference (link) to the report in the Workbench. There are two ways to delete items in the Workbench, as explained below.

① Click on the project folder or report that you want to delete, then press the DEL key on your keyboard.
② Right-click on the project folder or report that you want to delete, then select REMOVE on the shortcut menu.

Maintaining The Workbench

The information for the Workbench is saved in the file **PROJECTEXPLORER.XML**. This file is automatically saved in the folder listed below.
C:\Users\Your account name\App Data\Local\Crystal Reports

If you have to reinstall Crystal Reports and want to retain your Workbench project folder and report links, you should copy this file to another location before reinstalling Crystal Reports and then copy the file back. If you get a new computer, in addition to copying any reports from the old computer to the new one, you can copy this file to the new computer and you will have the same project folders displayed in the Workbench on the new computer if you keep the same folder structure on the new computer that you have on the old computer.

Explorers

As illustrated in Figure 3-17, Crystal Reports comes with three explorers that you can use to help create and manage reports. These design tools provide quick access to objects and their properties.

The explorer that you will probably use the most is the Field Explorer.

The Report Explorer is covered in detail in Chapter 8.

The other two explorers are explained below.

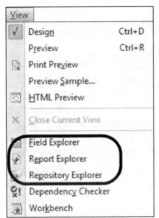

Figure 3-17 Explorer options illustrated on the View menu

 The View menu shown above in Figure 3-17 has the options for the explorers. Buttons for the explorers are also on the Standard toolbar.

1. If the Field and Report Explorers are not visible in the workspace, add them now.

   Figure 3-18 is how I have the explorer windows docked, but you can configure them however you want.

   Pay attention to the symbols (icons) that are next to each of the options in the Field Explorer. You will see them again when you learn how to create formulas

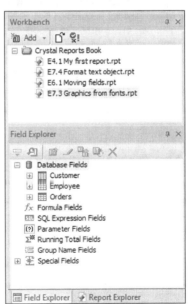

Figure 3-18 Field and Report Explorers docked

Field Explorer

The Field Explorer is used to add the seven types of fields shown above in Figure 3-18 to a report. Table 3-5 explains each of the field types.

Field Type	Description
Database	The fields in this folder come from tables and are usually placed in the details section of the report. This is the only field type in the Field Explorer that is stored in a database.
Formula	These are calculated fields that you create using the Formula Workshop. They are recalculated every time the report is run or previewed. (1)
SQL Expression	This field type queries (searches) the data to select records that meet the criteria in the query. They are usually stored on and run from a server. This type of field is written in a language called SQL. (1)
Parameter	Parameter fields prompt the person running the report to provide information. The information gathered from parameter fields is used to query the tables to select the records that will appear on the report. (1)
Running Total	This is a formula field that sums (adds) the values in a numeric field (or column of data). Running Total fields can be placed in the details section of the report and will provide a total up to the current record. Running Total fields can be reset to zero. They can be used to create totals by group or for the entire report. Summary fields can only be placed in a group or report section of the report. (1)
Group Name	This field type is automatically created for each group that the report has. When a group is created, by default the group name field is added to the group header section of the report and will display the value in the field. You can customize the group name to display something other than the value in the field. (1)
Special Fields	These are system generated fields. Some of the more popular special fields include the page number and Page N of M. Special Fields can be formatted like the other field types explained in this table. [See Chapter 8, Special Fields] (1)

Table 3-5 Field types explained

(1)   This field type is not stored in a database.

Field Explorer Toolbar

Figure 3-19 shows the Field Explorer toolbar. Table 3-6 explains the buttons on the toolbar.

Figure 3-19 Field Explorer toolbar

Button	Description
1	The **INSERT TO REPORT** button is used to add a field to the report.
2	The **BROWSE** button is used to view the data in the field that is selected.
3	The **NEW** button is used to create formula, parameter, SQL Expression or running total fields. (2)

Table 3-6 Field Explorer toolbar buttons explained

Button	Description
4	The **EDIT** button is used to modify formula, parameter, SQL Expression or running total fields. (2)
5	The **DUPLICATE** button is used to create a copy of a formula, SQL Expression or running total field. This option does not duplicate parameter fields. (3)
6	The **RENAME** button is used to rename formula, parameter, SQL Expression or running total fields. (2)
7	The **DELETE** button is used to delete formula, parameter, SQL Expression or running total fields. (2)

Table 3-6 Field Explorer toolbar buttons explained (Continued)

(2)   Before clicking on this button, click on the category (below the toolbar) of the field type that you want to use.

(3)

> **Duplicating A Formula Field**
> If you need to create a formula that is similar to one that is already in the report, you can duplicate the formula, instead of creating the second formula from scratch.
>
> To duplicate a formula field, right-click on it in the Field Explorer and select Duplicate. You can accept the default formula name or you can right-click on the duplicated formula field, then select **RENAME** to change the name.

> **Copying A Formula Field From One Report To Another**
> You can also copy a formula from one report to another. Open the report that has the formula that you want to copy and the report that you want to copy the formula to. Click on the formula field that you want to copy in the report layout, then Edit ⇒ Copy. Click on the tab of the report that you want to copy the formula to, then Edit ⇒ Paste. Click in the section of the report where you want the formula field placed.

Field Explorer Shortcut Menu (For Fields)

The shortcut menu shown in Figure 3-20 is available when you right-click on a database field in the Field Explorer.

Table 3-7 explains the options on the shortcut menu that are not in the Field Explorer toolbar.

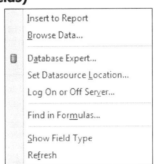

Figure 3-20 Field Explorer shortcut menu for fields

Option	Description
Database Expert	[See Chapter 5, The Database Expert]
Set Data Source Location	Is used to select a different location for the current database or to select a different database for the report.
Log On or Off Server	Is used to logon or logoff of the Business Objects Enterprise Server.
Find In Formulas	Use this option if you need to find out if a field is used in a formula. Right-click on the field either in the report or in the Field Explorer and select Find in formulas. If the field is being used in a formula, the Formula Workshop will open and display all of the formulas that use the field. [See Chapter 14, Figure 14-9]
Show Field Type	The field type and field length if applicable, will be displayed at the end of the field, as illustrated in Figure 3-21.
Refresh	This option works the same as the Refresh button on the Navigation Tools toolbar.

Table 3-7 Field Explorer shortcut menu options (for fields) explained

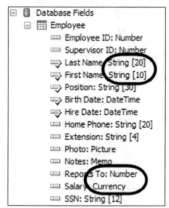

Figure 3-21 Field types and lengths illustrated in the Field Explorer

Field Explorer Shortcut Menu (For Databases And Tables)

The shortcut menu shown in Figure 3-22 is available when you right-click on a database or table in the Field Explorer.

The **SORT TABLES ALPHABETICALLY** option displays the tables in alphabetical order instead of the order that they are in, in the database.

The other options were explained above in Table 3-7.

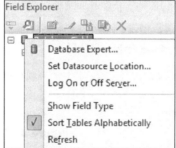

Figure 3-22 Field Explorer shortcut menu for databases and tables

Field Type Symbols And Naming Conventions

In Table 3-5 you read about the field types that can be added to a report. Four of these field types; Formula, SQL Expression, Parameter and Running Total are fields that you create. Each of these field types must have a unique name. Crystal Reports will add a symbol to the beginning of the field name as explained below. This is done to help you know what type of field it is when you are viewing fields on the design tab.

① **@ symbol** is a formula field.
② **% sign** is an SQL Expression field.
③ **? question mark** is a parameter field.
④ **# sign** is a running total field.

 Do not use the field type symbols listed above as part of a field name that you create. Formula, SQL Expression, Parameter and Running Total fields must have a unique name within each field type. Therefore, it is possible to use the same field name for a parameter, formula and running total field in the same report. This is why understanding what the field type symbols represent is important.

Sort Fields In The Field Explorer

By default, the fields are displayed in the Field Explorer in the order that they are in the table that they come from. If you do not like the default order that the fields are displayed in the Field Explorer, you can sort the fields alphabetically by right-clicking on the table name and selecting **SORT FIELDS ALPHABETICALLY**. Figure 3-23 shows the fields in the Employee table after they have been sorted alphabetically. Compare this to Figure 3-21 shown earlier.

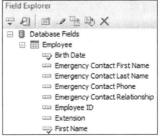

Figure 3-23 Fields in table after sorting

Repository Explorer

The Repository Explorer is used to share and save objects like images, queries and functions that you want to use in more than one report.

When you use this explorer, you will be prompted to log on to the SAP Business Objects Enterprise, as shown in Figure 3-24.

Figure 3-24 Business Objects Enterprise Log On dialog box

The Repository Explorer can only be accessed through the Repository, which is stored in the SAP Business Objects Enterprise or the Crystal Reports Sever. Prior versions of Crystal Reports came with all of the components required to use the Repository Explorer and did not require access to another system.

Repository Explorer Toolbar

Figure 3-25 shows the Repository Explorer toolbar. Table 3-8 explains the buttons on the toolbar.

Figure 3-25 Repository Explorer toolbar

Button	Description
1	The **CHANGE VIEW SETTINGS** button is used to select options that will change how the Repository Explorer window looks. It is used to limit the items that are displayed in the Repository Explorer.
2	The **ADVANCED FILTERING** button is used to only display items in the repository based on the author or by specific words.
3	The **DELETE THE ITEM/FOLDER** button is used to permanently delete a file or folder from the repository. If you delete a folder, all of the files in the folder are also deleted.
4	The **INSERT A NEW FOLDER** button is used to create a folder in the repository.
5	The **LOGON/LOGOFF SERVER** button is used to logon or logoff of the Business Objects Enterprise Server.

Table 3-8 Repository Explorer toolbar buttons explained

 Formulas cannot be stored in the Repository.

Docking The Explorers

Docking explorers is not a requirement to complete the exercises in this book, but doing so will make the explorer windows easier to use. I find it easier to dock the explorers as shown earlier in Figure 3-18. I also dock the Workbench with the explorers. To accomplish this, you can follow the steps below.

1. Open two of the explorer windows, as shown in Figure 3-26.

Figure 3-26 Two explorer windows opened in the workspace

2. With the left mouse button, drag the explorer window that you want to dock over to the explorer window that you want to dock it to, then release the mouse button when the window has a tab for the explorer window that you moved, as illustrated at the bottom of Figure 3-27.

   The docked window will now contain the explorer window that you added, as shown in the figure. As you saw earlier in Figure 3-18, I have the explorers docked below the Workbench. To do that, make the Workbench window smaller, then drag the explorer windows below it.

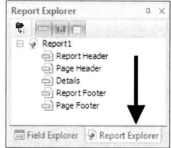

Figure 3-27 New window docked

Docking Tips

Below are several tips that you may find useful when using the explorers. It could be me, but when I mistakenly move an explorer window, I have difficulty getting it back to where it was. This truly drives me nuts. The reason that I am telling you this is so that if you have trouble getting the explorers exactly where you want them, you know that you aren't the only one that it happens to.

① To select the explorer that you want to use, click on the tab for it at the bottom of the explorer windows.
② If you double-click on an explorer's title bar, it will toggle between being in docked and free floating modes.
③ If you double-click on the title bar of a free floating explorer window, it will go back to where it was the last time that you used Crystal Reports.
④ In free-floating mode, the explorer window can be moved to a new location in the workspace.
⑤ I prefer to keep the Workbench separate from the explorers because I use the Workbench frequently and like to always keep it displayed. If it was docked with the explorers, I would have to keep clicking on the tab to get to it.

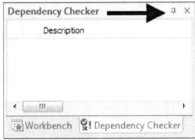

The Workbench and Dependency Checker windows can also be docked together, as shown in Figure 3-28.

Figure 3-28 Workbench and Dependency Checker windows docked together

The Push Pin

If you click on the push pin illustrated in the upper right corner of Figure 3-28 above, the toolbar shown in Figure 3-29 will be displayed. This toolbar will give you more space to work on reports.

To access one of the explorers from this toolbar, hold the mouse pointer over the icon and the corresponding explorer window will open.

To close the toolbar and return to the docked explorer windows, open an explorer window from the toolbar and click on the push pin.

Figure 3-29 Explorer toolbar

Explorer Shortcut Menu

If you right-click on the title bar of an explorer window you will see the shortcut menu shown in Figure 3-30.

The **UNDOCK** option removes the explorer window from the other windows that is it docked with.

The **AUTOHIDE** option will display the toolbar shown above in Figure 3-29.

The **CLOSE** option closes the explorer window.

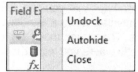

Figure 3-30 Explorer window shortcut menu

CREATE YOUR FIRST REPORT

Overview

In addition to creating your first report, after completing the exercises in this chapter you will be able to:

- ☑ Create a connection to a database
- ☑ Understand the save data report options
- ☑ Link tables
- ☑ Have an understanding of the basics of the report processing model

CHAPTER 4

Learning To Create Reports

For some, learning to create reports can be intimidating. **LEARNING TO CREATE REPORTS REQUIRES TIME, PATIENCE, DEDICATION AND ATTENTION TO DETAIL.** Crystal Reports is a very robust package and has a lot of features and options. As you go through the exercises in this book, take your time and try to understand how the concepts that you are learning can be applied to reports that you will create on your own. It is possible to go through this entire book in a few days if you already have above average report design experience with another report design software package or if you have used a previous version of Crystal Reports and have a solid foundation of relational databases.

The reality is that you will make some mistakes along the way. If you have a fear of making mistakes, this is the time to let go of the fear because the fear will prevent you from learning. It is also normal to initially get confused on what to do next. Even though you may not understand why you are being instructed to do something, the steps in each exercise will allow you to achieve the expected result. This is how you will begin to build a foundation for creating reports and learning Crystal Reports.

The first time that a concept or technique is presented, a lot of information is provided. Each subsequent time that you have to perform the same task, less and less information (aka hand holding) will occur. As you will see, there are a lot of repetitious tasks involved in creating reports. These are the tasks that less and less information will be provided for as you go through the book. The purpose behind this learning technique is to allow you to rely more on your knowledge instead of flipping through this book months from now to find the answer, which in turn allows you to complete an exercise in less time.

Exercise 4.1: Create Your First Report

I suspect that this is the moment that you have been waiting for; to create your first report. You will use the report wizard to create the reports in this chapter. The first report that you will create is a report that only uses data from one table. The report layout is basic, but you will use almost every screen on the wizard dialog box so that you can become familiar with all of the options.

Why Do I Have To Connect To A Data Source?

First, I should explain what a data source is. A data source contains the underlying data for the report that you will create or modify. The most common data source is a database. In addition to there being several types of data sources that you can connect to, there are multiple ways to connect to the same data source including the Xtreme database. You can connect to this database via the Access/Excel (DAO) connection type (which uses a direct access driver) or the ODBC connection type (which uses an indirect access driver). There are two reasons that you would need to connect to a data source, as explained below.

① If you viewed any of the reports that come with the Xtreme database you would see data. The reason that you are able to view data in the sample reports is because the data was saved with the report. If the data is not saved with the report, you would have to create a connection to the database that the report gets the data from to view data with the report.

② If you want to create a new report or modify an existing report that does not have the data saved with it.

> **Direct vs Indirect Access Drivers**
> These are the types of drivers that you can use to connect to a data source. Direct drivers, when available, are the best option because they are designed to work with a specific type of database, like Access or Sybase. They usually provide better performance. Indirect drivers are not designed for a specific database. They are generic in a way because one driver can be used to connect to more than one type of database. The two most popular indirect drivers are **ODBC** and **OLE DB**.

Step 1: Create A Connection To The Data Source

There are several types of data sources that you can use.

Figure 4-1 shows the categories of connection options that are available.

You may see different data source options then those shown, depending on the data components that were selected when you installed Crystal Reports. You will also see data source options that you have added.

Table 4-1 explains some of the connection options.

Figure 4-1 List of available connection options

NEW The four data source options shown above in Figure 4-1 that start with SAP are new in Crystal Reports 2011.

> **Data Source Options**
> Crystal Reports supports over 100 data source types. The order that data sources appear in the list were rearranged in Crystal Reports 2008. The more frequently used data sources have their own folder. Data sources that the Crystal Reports project team thought are used less, have been moved to the **MORE DATA SOURCES** folder. Some of the connection types have been renamed. For example, XML has been renamed to XML and Web Services. ACT! was moved from the More Data Sources folder to its own folder in Crystal Reports 2008 and in Crystal Reports 2011, it was moved back under the More Data Sources folder.

Connection Option	Is Used To Connect To . . .
Access/Excel (DAO)	Access databases and Excel spreadsheets. The spreadsheets can be converted to tables in an Access database.
Database Files	Standard PC databases including FoxPro, Paradox, Clipper and dBASE.
ODBC (RDO)	Any ODBC complaint database including Oracle, Sybase, Access and Visual FoxPro. This is probably the most common data driver.
OLAP	OLAP cubes and **.CAR** files. OLAP stands for Online Analytical Processing. CAR stands for Crystal Analysis Reports file.

Table 4-1 Connection options explained

Connection Option	Is Used To Connect To . . .
OLE DB (ADO)	Data link files that contain connection information (for a data source) that is saved in a file.
Universes	Business Objects query and analysis tools like Web Intelligence.
More Data Sources	Data sources that are available, but the driver was not installed during the Crystal Reports installation. These drivers will be installed on demand when you select the data source.

Table 4-1 Connection options explained (Continued)

How To Create An Access/Excel (DAO) Connection

Follow the steps below to create an Access/Excel (DAO) connection for the crystalxtreme database.

1. Click on the **REPORT WIZARD** link on the Start Page tab.

2. Click on the plus sign in front of the **CREATE NEW CONNECTION** folder, then click on the plus sign in front of the Access/Excel (DAO) option.

3. Click on the button at the end of the **DATABASE NAME** field. Navigate to your folder.

4. Double-click on the **CRYSTALXTREME.MDB** database file.

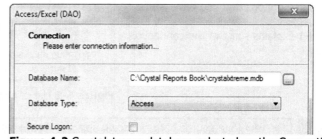

    The database should have been added to the Database Name field on the dialog box, as shown in Figure 4-2.

    Click the **FINISH** button.

Figure 4-2 Crystalxtreme database selected on the Connection dialog box

You have completed creating your first connection to a database in Crystal Reports. That wasn't so bad, was it?

Logging Onto A Database
If the database required logon information, you would check the **SECURE LOGON** option shown above in Figure 4-2. The remaining fields on the dialog box would become available for you to enter the logon information.

Step 2: Select The Tables

1. Click on the plus sign in front of the **CREATE NEW CONNECTION** folder, then click on the plus sign in front of the Access/Excel (DAO) folder.

2. Select the crystalxtreme database, then click on the plus sign in front of the Tables folder.

   You should see the tables shown in Figure 4-3. These are the tables that are in the crystalxtreme database.

   They are also the tables that are used for the sample reports that you can download from the Highlights tab on the Start Page tab.

Figure 4-3 Tables in the crystalxtreme database

Available Data Sources List Shortcut Menu

If you right-click on an item (a view or table name for example) in this list you will see the shortcut menu shown in Figure 4-4. The options are explained in Table 4-2.

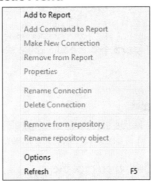

Figure 4-4 Available Data Sources list shortcut menu

Option	This Option . . .
Add To Report	Adds a table, view or stored procedure to the report.
Add Command To Report	Adds a table that was created from an SQL command. A query can also be created to select the records for the report from this option.
Make New Connection	Creates a connection to a data source.
Remove From Report	Removes a table or stored procedure from the report.
Properties	Displays the information shown in Figure 4-5 about the selected table or data source.
Rename Connection	Is used to give the connection a more friendly user name.
Delete Connection	Removes the connection from the list.
Remove From Repository	Is used to delete an SQL command from the SAP Business Objects Enterprise Repository.
Rename Repository Object	Is used to rename an SQL command in the SAP Business Objects Enterprise Repository.
Options	Displays the Database tab on the Options dialog box. [See Chapter 2, Figure 2-28]
Refresh	Redisplays the list of available data sources.

Table 4-2 Available Data Sources list shortcut menu options explained

Figure 4-5 Properties dialog box

3. Click on the **PRODUCT** table, then click the **>** button. The Product table should now be in the **SELECTED TABLES** list, as shown on the right side of Figure 4-6.

Figure 4-6 Product table selected

Click Next.

Viewing The Data In A Field

The **BROWSE DATA** button on the Fields screen is used to view data. This is helpful if you are not familiar with the data. This button is on several dialog boxes in Crystal Reports.

1. Click on the **PRODUCT NAME** field, then click the **BROWSE DATA** button. You will see the dialog box shown in Figure 4-7. What you see is the data in the Product Name field.

   Notice that the field **TYPE** and **LENGTH** are displayed at the top of the dialog box. This information is helpful because it tells you the type of field and the length of the field.

Figure 4-7 Data in the Product Name field

2. Click the Close button when you are finished viewing the data.

> **Selecting The Number Of Records To View**
> You can also view the data on the design tab. By default, the first 500 distinct values in a field are displayed. The actual values that you see can be changed by clearing the **SELECT DISTINCT DATA FOR BROWSING** option on the Database tab on the Options dialog box or on the Report Options dialog box, if you only want the change applied the current report. OK, that's the way that it is suppose to work, but it doesn't.

Selecting The Number Of Records To View (Continued)
If this actually worked, it probably is not a good idea to turn this option off because you could see duplicate data in the Browse Data dialog box shown above in Figure 4-7. But since it doesn't work, turning it off has no effect. If you want to view a different number of records, you have to modify the following registry key. HKEY_CURRENT_USER\Software\SAP Business Objects\ Suite XI 4.0\Crystal Reports\DatabaseServer.
Change the **MAXNBROWSEVALUES** key to the maximum number of records that you want to see. (Select the Decimal Base option)

How To Find A Field

The **FIND FIELD** button on the Fields screen on the Standard report wizard is used to search for a field in the table. You will see this button on a few dialog boxes in Crystal Reports. I'm not sure that I understand the purpose of this button because all of the fields in a table are displayed on this dialog box. It could be helpful if you don't know which table a field is in.

The Find Field button will only find the first field that matches the text that you enter in the dialog box shown in Figure 4-8. The first matching field that it finds depends on what field is currently selected in the Available Fields list. The search starts from the field that is selected and goes down the list. You can also enter a partial field name. Even if the same field name is in more than one table, the search does not continue.

Figure 4-8 Enter Search Name dialog box

If you were creating a report on your own, in the report design process you would have already written down a list of fields and where they are located because you learned how to do this in Chapter 3 <smile>.

Step 3: Select The Fields

1. Click on the Product Name field if it is not already selected, then click the **>** button. You should see the field in the **FIELDS TO DISPLAY** list.

2. Add the following fields to the Fields to Display list: Size, Price (SRP) and Product Class. Figure 4-9 shows the fields that should have been added. Click Next.

All of the items in the **AVAILABLE FIELDS** list are the fields that are in the Product table.

To add all of the fields in a table at one time, click the **>>** button. You do not have to select any fields before clicking this button.

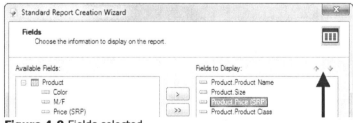

Figure 4-9 Fields selected

To remove a field that you do not need on the report, click on the field in the Fields to Display list, then click the **<** button. To remove all of the fields from the Fields to Display list, click the **<<** button.

How To Add Several Fields At The Same Time
You can add several fields at the same time by clicking on the first field that you want to add, then press and hold down the **CTRL** key and click on the other fields that you want to add, one by one. When you have all of the fields selected that you want to add, click the **>** button.

The order that you add the fields to the Fields to Display list is the order that they will appear on the report in the details section, from left to right. If you discover that the fields are not in the order that you want them to appear on the report, click on the field in the Fields to Display list, then click the **UP** or **DOWN** arrow buttons, illustrated above in Figure 4-9, to move the field to where it should be.

The Wizard Can Change The Field Order
When using a wizard to create a report, the order that the fields are placed in on the report will change automatically if at least one field is selected to group on. Fields that are grouped on are moved to the beginning of the details section. You can rearrange the fields after the wizard has created the report. This does not happen when you create a report from scratch that has groups.

Notice in Figure 4-9 above that fields in the Fields to Display list have the table name in front of the field name. This is done to let you know which table the field is in. This is helpful when you are using more than one table to create the report. Primary key fields in tables often have the same field name when the tables have related information. Without adding the table name, you would not know which table a field is in.

Primary key fields are fields that are used to link one table to another table.

Step 4: Select The Grouping Options

Grouping is used to organize and sort the data. Grouping data forces all records that have the same value in the field that is being grouped on, to be displayed together. Grouping data makes reports that have a lot of data easier to read. Grouping the data in a report is optional. You can group on more than one field. You can group on fields that have already been added to the report, or you can select fields to group on that will not appear on the report.

1. Add the Product Class field to the Group By list. The default grouping option **IN ASCENDING ORDER** is correct. Figure 4-10 shows the grouping options that you should have selected. Click Next.

There are two options that you can select from to group the records by, as explained below. This is how you sort the values in the field that is being grouped on.

IN ASCENDING ORDER This is the default grouping option. The values in the field being grouped on will be sorted in A to Z order if the field is a string field. If the field is numeric, the values will be sorted in 0 to 9 order.

IN DESCENDING ORDER The values in the field being grouped on will be sorted in Z to A order if the field is a string field. If the field is numeric, the values will be sorted in 9 to 0 order.

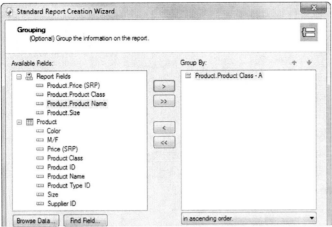

Figure 4-10 Field added to the Group By list

 Using The Cancel Button On The Wizard
The only reason that I can think of to click the CANCEL button on a screen in the wizard is if you decide that you no longer want to create the report. You will lose all of the options that you have selected if you click the Cancel button. It is better to use the BACK button to go back and make changes because you cannot reopen the wizard to make changes or pick up where you left off.

Step 5: Select The Summary Options

Creating summary fields is optional. Summary options involve calculated fields. By default, the wizard will create a summary field for all numeric fields that were selected to print on the report. You can remove the ones that are not needed.

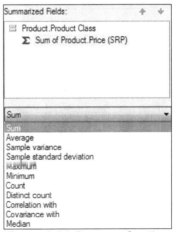

There are built-in summary functions that you can use. Some of them are shown at the bottom of Figure 4-11.

The number of summary functions that are in the list depends on the data type of the field that you are summarizing on. Not all data types can use all of the summary functions. Many of the summary functions are only for numeric fields.

Figure 4-11 Summary function options

1. Add the Product Class field to the SUMMARIZED FIELDS list.

2. Open the drop-down list shown above in Figure 4-11 and select **COUNT**.

    Notice that the Product Class field has different options in the drop-down list, then those shown above for the Product Price (SRP) field.

    Figure 4-12 shows the summary options that should be selected.

Figure 4-12 Summary options

    Click Next.

3. Select the **TOP 5 GROUPS** option.

    Figure 4-13 shows the group sorting options that should be selected.

    Click Next.

Figure 4-13 Group Sorting options

 The Top 5 Groups option will only display data for the five groups that have the highest value in the field selected in the **SUMMARY VALUES** field. Selecting **NONE**, which is the default, will display all groups. It is possible that you will not get the five groups that you think should appear on the report. This is because of the way that Crystal Reports processes data. In Chapter 12 you will create a Top 5 group report that illustrates unexpected results because a wizard was used to create the report.

Step 6: Select The Chart Type

Adding a chart to a report is optional. Once you select a chart type, the wizard will fill in information for the other fields on the Chart screen. If you are not sure what options to select, accept the defaults, preview the report and then decide which chart options need to be modified.

1. Select the **PIE CHART** option.

   Figure 4-14 shows the chart options that should be selected.

   Click Next.

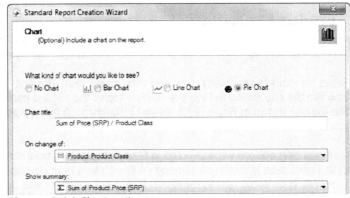

Figure 4-14 Chart options

Step 7: Select The Fields To Filter On

Creating filters is optional. Filters are another way that you can narrow down the number of records that will appear on the report. You can create more than one filter. In this step you will create a filter for the Product Size field to only display records that have a size that is in a specific range.

1. Add the Size field to the **FILTER FIELDS** list. Open the drop-down list and select **IS BETWEEN**.

2. Open the next drop-down list and select 16. Open the last drop-down list and select **XLRG**. Figure 4-15 shows the filter options that should be selected. Click Next.

The filter that you just created will only display products that have a size that is between 16 and XLRG.

The data in the last two drop-down lists is the actual data in the field that you are creating the filter for. If the values that you want are not in the last two drop-down lists, you can type them in.

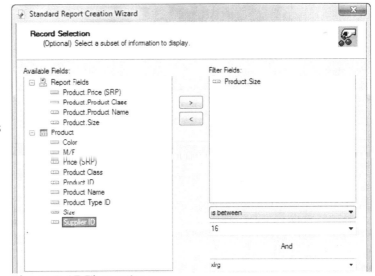

Figure 4-15 Filter options

Step 8: Select A Template

Selecting a template is optional. If you do not want to use a template, select the **NO TEMPLATE** option. You can preview what the other template options look like by clicking on them.

1. Select the **CORPORATE (BLUE)** template, then click Finish. The first page of the report should look like the one shown in Figure 4-16. The top of the second page of the report should look like the one shown in Figure 4-17. As you scroll through the report, you may see things that you would like to change.

Because grouping options were selected in Step 4, the **GROUP TREE** shown down the left side of the report in Figure 4-16 is displayed. Clicking on the options in the group tree will display that section of the report. If for some reason the group tree is not visible or you do not want to see it, you can click the **TOGGLE PREVIEW PANEL** button on the Standard toolbar to display or hide it.

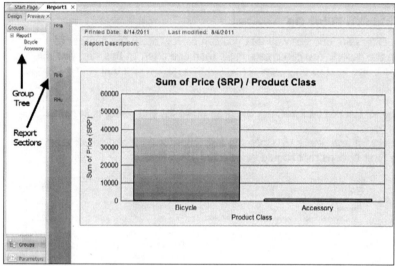

Figure 4-16 First page of the report

Product Class	Product Name	Size	Price (SRP)
Bicycle	Descent	22	$2,939.85
Bicycle	Descent	17	$2,939.85
Bicycle	Descent	17	$2,939.85
Bicycle	Descent	18.5	$2,939.85
Bicycle	Descent	18.5	$2,939.85
Bicycle	Descent	20	$2,939.85

Printed Date: 8/4/2011   Last modified: 6/4/2011

Bicycle

Figure 4-17 Second page of the report

Step 9: Save The Report

As shown earlier in Figure 4-16, the report was given a default name of **REPORT x** (X is a number) which you can use. You should save the report with a name that is more meaningful. In addition to giving the report a meaningful name, you have to decide whether or not you want to save the data with the report, which is explained below.

Options For Saving Data

Unless you changed the default options after Crystal Reports was installed, the data is saved with the report by default.

Figure 4-18 illustrates the **SAVE DATA WITH REPORT** option on the File menu. There are pros and cons to saving data with a report, as explained below.

Figure 4-18 Save data option on the File menu illustrated

Save The Report With Data

As stated earlier, this is the default option. You can preview and print reports faster with this option selected because the data does not have to be retrieved from the database. This option is also useful if you need to send the report to someone that does not have access to the data. One downside to saving the data with the report is that the report requires more hard drive space. A second downside is that anyone that runs the report with saved data will probably not be using the most current data. A third downside occurs if the database has security. Unless the report has been published to a Crystal Reports Server, the security is bypassed and anyone that opens the report will have access to the data, whether they should or not.

 If you do not want the **SAVE DATA WITH REPORT** option set as the default, File ⇒ Options. Click on the **REPORTING** tab. Clear the option, **SAVE DATA WITH REPORT**, then click OK.

Fields in tables are indexed to reduce the time it takes to retrieve the records needed to create the report. Fields that are used in the record selection criteria are often used as an index.

 Indexes are not usually helpful in reports that use saved data. The exception to this is reports that have parameter fields that can be used to change the record selection formula. The **REPORT BURSTING INDEXES** command is used to create indexes in reports that are saved with data.

Report Menu

Save The Report Without Data

Selecting this option requires less hard drive space. With this option, the report uses live data each time it is run. The downside is when you need to preview or print the report, it will take a little longer to process because the data has to be retrieved. Most of the time, you will not notice the delay.

 From a report designers perspective if you have the hard drive space, it will save a considerable amount of time if there are thousands of records for the report, if you save the data with the report while you are creating and modifying it. The mistake that some designers make <not us of course> is that they forget to change the save data option before putting the report into production. Another danger is not testing the report with live data. Remember that most data is volatile, meaning that it changes frequently, because data is deleted, modified and added to on a regular basis. Not testing with live data before putting the report into production could be a bad career move, if you know what I mean. Testing with live data before putting the report into production also means that it won't go into production with the saved data.

> **When To Save A Report**
> As a rule, I save a report before I preview it. Over the years, I have noticed that from
> time to time when I did not save a report, especially one that used a lot of tables and
> tried to preview it, the report would freeze (aka crash). When this happened, the entire
> report was lost. Take from this what you will.

Refreshing Report Data

F5

As you just learned, you have to decide whether to save the data with the report or not. If you
decide to normally save data with a report to save processing time while designing the report that's
fine. Anytime that you want to work with the current data, click the REFRESH button on the
Navigation Tools toolbar.

If the changes that you make to a report fall in the formatting category, like changing fonts, moving
fields around on the report or adding titles to summary fields that were already saved with the
report, you do not have to refresh the data.

Automatic Data Refreshing

If any of the options listed below occur after a report have been saved, the data will automatically
be refreshed, regardless of the save data option that is selected for the report.

1. A field is added to the report.
2. The Refresh command is used.
3. A formula field is added to the report that uses a field that is not already being used on
   the report.
4. An existing formula is modified that uses a field that is not already being used on the
   report.
5. The linking parameter field on a subreport changes.
6. If any report criteria or parameter fields are added or changed that include a field that is
   not already being used on the report.
7. If the grouping is not done on a server, the detail record data will be refreshed.
8. The logon to the database has changed.

> If you drill-down on hidden data, the data is not a full refresh. If the grouping is taking
> place on a server, drilling down in the details section will only retrieve the new data
> required by the drill-down for the details section.

Yes, I can sense that you are shaking your head about the save data with report options. Keep in
mind that only the fields on the report and fields needed for formulas or functions that the report
uses are saved with the report. Other fields in the table are not saved with the report. This is why
you are prompted frequently to refresh data when the save data option is enabled. As you become
more familiar with modifying reports, you will know which save data option is best suited for each
report that you are modifying or creating.

Real World Data

Many companies have what is known as a "development server" that has a copy of "live data" and
applications (live data is also known as production data). This is done so that anyone that is
creating new applications, modifying existing applications or testing software, can do so without
putting the companies data in danger. If this is the type of environment that you working in, keep

in mind while going through this book, the differences between "live" and "refreshed" data, when these terms are referenced.

When creating reports on a development server and you click the **REFRESH** button in Crystal Reports, you are not getting a copy of the data from a production server. You are getting another copy of the data from the development server. The same is true if you have placed a copy of the production data on your computers hard drive. Usually, data on a development server is refreshed from a production server at pre-defined intervals (daily, weekly, monthly). If you want to know when the data on a development server is refreshed, ask the DBA or the person that manages the databases that you are using.

Save The Report

Report File Extension
The default file extension for reports is **.RPT** in Crystal Reports. Report file names can have up to 255 characters and can include spaces and special characters. Reports can be stored in almost any folder on a computers hard drive or server. You should not store reports in operating system folders.

1. File ⇒ Save As. Open the **SAVE IN** drop-down list on the Save As dialog box and navigate to the Crystal Reports Book folder that you created.

You can also click the **SAVE** button on the Standard toolbar when saving a report for the first time.

2. Type E4.1 My first report as the file name, as shown at the bottom of Figure 4-19.

    Press Enter or click the Save button.

Figure 4-19 Save As dialog box

Report file names like the one shown at the bottom of Figure 4-19 above are different then report titles. Report file names are what you save the report as. Report titles come from the **DOCUMENT PROPERTIES** dialog box. By default, the name displayed on the design and preview tabs is the report file name. If the report has a report title, it will be displayed on the tab instead.

Step 10: Add The Current Report To The Workbench

When you save a report it is not automatically added to the Workbench. You have to manually add it, as explained below.

1. In the Workbench, Add ⇒ Add Current Report. The report should now be under the Crystal Reports Book folder in the Workbench, as shown in Figure 4-20.

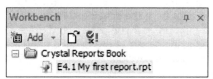

Figure 4-20 Report added to the Workbench

Selecting A Data Source

In the previous exercise you used the options in the **CREATE NEW CONNECTION** folder to create a connection to the crystalxtreme database. That connection stays live until you close Crystal Reports.

When you reopen Crystal Reports any connections that are in the Create New Connection folder are automatically moved to the **MY CONNECTIONS** folder shown in Figure 4-21.

If you right-click on the connection in this folder, you will see the shortcut menu shown earlier in Figure 4-4.

Figure 4-21 My Connections data source folder

Report Bursting Indexes

The Report Bursting Indexes command (Report ⇒ Report Bursting Indexes) is used to create indexes in reports that have saved data.

Figure 4-22 shows the **SAVED DATA INDEXES** dialog box, which is used to select the fields to create indexes for the next time the report data is refreshed.

After the fields are selected, the report should be refreshed so that the indexes can be created.

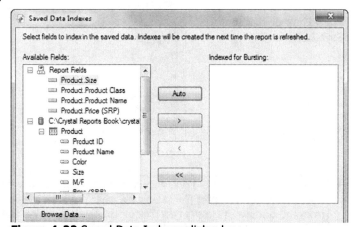

Figure 4-22 Saved Data Indexes dialog box

 Clicking the **AUTO** button will automatically add all of the fields that are used in the report record selection criteria to the Indexed for Bursting list.

Exercise 4.2: Create A Product List Report

In this exercise you will create a product list report that will print the Product ID, Product Name and Price fields.

1. Click on the Report Wizard link on the Start Page tab.

2. Select the crystalxtreme database connection, then add the Product table to the Selected Tables list and click Next.

3. Add the Product ID, Product Name and Price (SRP) fields to the Fields to Display list.

Click Finish because the report does not require any options on the other wizard screens.

The report should look like the one shown in Figure 4-23. As you can see, the Product Name field needs to be made larger so that more of the data in the field can be displayed.

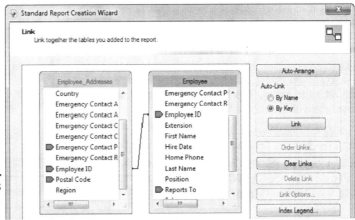

Product ID	Product Name	Price (SRP)
1,101	Active Outdoors Crochet Glo	$14.50
1,102	Active Outdoors Crochet Glo	$14.50
1,103	Active Outdoors Crochet Glo	$14.50
1,104	Active Outdoors Crochet Glo	$14.50
1,105	Active Outdoors Crochet Glo	$14.50
1,106	Active Outdoors Lycra Glove	$16.50
1,107	Active Outdoors Lycra Glove	$16.50
1,108	Active Outdoors Lycra Glove	$16.50

8/4/2011

Figure 4-23 Product list report

4. Save the report as E4.2 Product list.

Exercise 4.3: Create An Employee Contact List Report

The fields that are needed to create this report are stored in two tables. This report will be grouped by the Supervisor ID field so that each supervisor can have a list of their employees.

1. Open the Report Wizard, then select the crystalxtreme database.

2. Add the Employee and Employee Addresses tables to the Selected Tables list, then click Next.

Linking Tables

You will see the screen shown in Figure 4-24.

This screen displays the relationships between tables that are connected to the report.

The options on this screen are used to select the appropriate links for the tables that you have selected. Each window on the screen is a different table. The fields in the table are also displayed.

Figure 4-24 Link screen

Most of the time, the link (a line between two tables) that is automatically created between tables is correct. Fields are automatically linked if they have the same name and compatible data type. In this exercise, the tables should be linked by the Employee ID field.

Link Screen Tips

① You may need to make the dialog box wider to see both tables. To make the dialog box wider, place the mouse pointer on the right side of the dialog box and drag the border of the dialog box to the right. You can also make the tables longer if you want to see all of the fields in the table.

② If you right-click on a field and select **BROWSE FIELD**, as shown in Figure 4-25, you will be able to see the first 500 unique values for the field. If you see more than one occurrence of the same value, it means that the Select Distinct Data For Browsing option on the Database tab on the Options dialog box or on the Report Options dialog box is not enabled.

③ By default, Crystal Reports only uses a link if the record selection query requires it. If you want to enforce a link, right-click on the link that you want to enforce and select **LINK OPTIONS**, as shown in Figure 4-26.

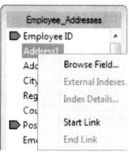

Figure 4-25 Link screen field shortcut menu

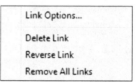

Figure 4-26 Link shortcut menu

Index Legend

As you saw earlier in Figure 4-24, there are colored arrows next to some fields. If you click the **INDEX LEGEND** button, you will see the index that each colored arrow represents, as shown in Figure 4-27.

As much as possible, you should use indexed fields as the fields to link tables with because they allow records to be retrieved faster. This improves and increases the performance of the database.

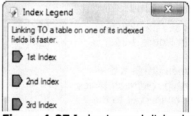

Figure 4-27 Index Legend dialog box

Add The Fields To The Report

1. Click Next on the dialog box shown earlier in Figure 4-24, then add the fields in Table 4-3 to the Fields to Display list.

   Figure 4-28 shows the order that the fields should be in. Click Next.

Employee	Employee Addresses
Supervisor ID	Region
First Name	
Last Name	
Home Phone	

Table 4-3 Fields to add to the report

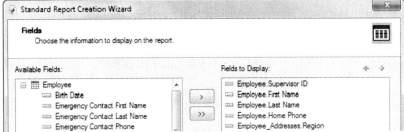

Figure 4-28 Fields selected for the report

Select The Grouping Options

This report would look better if it was grouped on the Supervisor ID field and within each Supervisor ID group, the employee names were sorted by last and first name. It would also be helpful if there was a count of employees per supervisor.

1. Add the Supervisor ID field to the **GROUP BY** list, then click Next.

2. Add the Employee ID field to the **SUMMARIZED FIELDS** list.

3. Open the drop-down list and select **COUNT**. Figure 4-29 shows the summary options that should be selected.

   This option will count the number of employee ID's under each supervisor ID. When you want a count of records, you should select a field that has unique values. Each employee is assigned a unique ID. Think of ID fields as being the equivalent of social security numbers, where each persons social security number is unique.

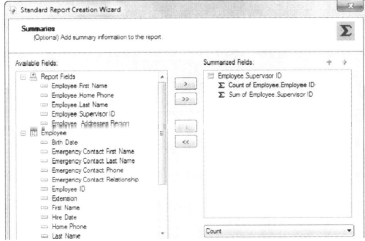

Figure 4-29 Summary options

4. Click Next. Click Next again on the Group Sorting screen because you do not need to change any of the options.

Select The Chart Options

1. Select the **BAR CHART** option.

2. Type `Count of employees per supervisor` in the **CHART TITLE** field.

Figure 4-30 shows the chart options that should be selected.

Click Next.

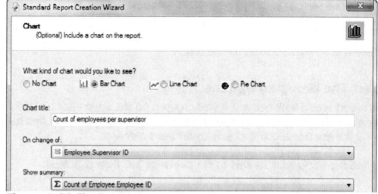

Figure 4-30 Chart options

Finish The Report

1. Click Next on the Record Selection screen because you do not need to select any fields to filter on.

2. Select the **NO TEMPLATE** option, then click Finish.

The report should look like the one shown in Figure 4-31.

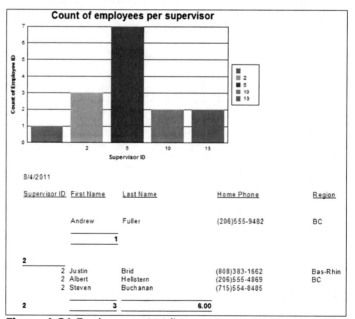

Figure 4-31 Employee contact list report

3. Save the report as `E4.3 Employee contact list`.

Crystal Reports Report Processing Model

Reports are processed in three main passes. The first pass reads all of the records, calculates the formulas and summary fields, suppresses fields and creates a temporary data file. This temporary file only contains the records needed for the report, opposed to all of the records in the database. The second pass sorts records, calculates totals for groups, calculates running totals, generates charts, maps, cross-tabs, OLAP grids and subreports as needed. The second pass also formats the pages. The third pass calculates the total page count and Page N of M special fields if necessary.

Formulas can be placed in all sections of a report. Formulas are not processed in report section order. The processing model uses the following criteria to help determine the order to process formulas in.

① Formulas that use database fields are processed while the records are being read in the first pass.
② There is no order to how formulas are processed in the same section of the report.
③ Formulas that only use variables are processed before records are read.
④ Formulas that use summary and group fields are processed after the records are read.
⑤ Cross-Tab summary fields are calculated in the first pass.

The link below provides more information on the processing model that Crystal Reports uses. http://msdn2.microsoft.com/en-us/library/ms225477.aspx

If this report processing model seems complicated, remember the following:

① The first pass reads the records in the database, retrieves the records that match any selection criteria and calculates formulas where all of the fields in the calculation are fields in a table.
② The second pass selects data for groups and evaluating summary functions, calculating running total fields, in-place subreports and charts based on cross-tabs or OLAP data are generated.
③ The third pass is mainly used to calculate the total page count (Page N of M) if needed.

Saving An Existing Report With A New File Name

This is a task that you will do a lot in this book. The steps below show you how.

1. Open the report that you want to save with a new file name.

2. File ⇒ Save As.

    For the exercises in this book, save the reports in the folder that you created. On your own, you can save the reports in any folder that you want.

CREATING REPORTS FROM SCRATCH

After completing the exercises in this chapter you will be able to:

☑ Use the Database Expert
☑ Create basic reports from scratch
☑ Add and remove tables in the Field Explorer
☑ Understand relational databases
☑ Understand the different types of relationships
☑ Understand Linking, Join Types and Smart Linking techniques

CHAPTER 5

Overview

While you may be frowning at the title of this chapter because you know that there are wizards that will help you create reports, you should keep in mind that the wizards may not be able to create a report that you need. If you only use the wizards to create reports, you will not learn how to use the majority of features that Crystal Reports has. If you create a report and do not get the output that you need, you could have a hard time trying to figure out how to modify it to get what you need, if you only know the options on the wizards. You will experience not getting the correct output when using a wizard in Chapter 12, Exercise 12.4. Therefore, learning to create reports from scratch is essential for being able to create new reports and modify existing ones.

The Database Expert

The Database Expert shown in Figure 5-1 is used to select the data sources for the report.

Database ⇒ Database Expert, will open this dialog box.

Figure 5-1 Database Expert dialog box

As you can see, this dialog box is very similar to the Data screen in the report wizard. Like the Data screen, the Database Expert has a Links screen.

Data Source Options

Each of the four data source options (tables, views, commands and stored procedures) provide a different way to access data for the reports that you create. These are the most popular data source options. The other data source options are System Tables and Synonyms. For the most part, as the report designer, you will not be required to create or maintain the data sources. You do however, need a good understanding of them so that you can select the best option, based on the requirements for the report. They are explained below.

Tables are probably the most used of the four data sources because accessing the tables does not require any code or programming skills, like the other three data source options require.

Business Views are a set of components, (data connections, dynamic data connections, data foundations and business elements) that report designers and end-users can use to access the data that is needed to create the report. Business Views are usually created by a database administrator or someone that has administrator rights to the databases. Business Views can be used to gather data from a variety of types of databases and combine the data into a "view". This makes it easier to access the data.

Many databases have the ability to present different views of the data. A Business View is a **RECORDSET** (the result) of a query. Business Views usually display a subset of the data from the data sources. Business Views are stored in the database and are like tables, but they do not have the physical characteristics of a table. For example, records cannot be added or deleted from a Business View, fields cannot be added to a view or the length of a field cannot be changed in a Business View.

If you know that you will create several reports that use the same sorting, grouping or data selection options, you could create and save a Business View, if you have the appropriate administrator rights to do so. Doing this means that you would not have to select the same options over and over again for each report. Instead of selecting all of the tables, fields and options, select the view that already has all of this information.

Business Views are one way to optimize reports that use tables that have a lot of data. For example, a customer table will hold all customers world wide. If there is a need to create several reports that are specific to a certain country for marketing or sales analysis purposes, create a Business View (a query) that retrieves all of the customer records for the country. When the reports are created for that country, select the "country view" if you will, as the data source, instead of the customer table. The report will run faster because it does not have to read the entire customer table to find the records for the specific country. Instead, the "view" is read. This makes it easier to access the data. The Xtreme database comes with several Business Views that you can use. The first one is explained below.

① **TOP CUSTOMERS** This view contains customers that have purchased $50,000 or more worth of products. The fields in this view are from the Customer table.

Commands are queries (code that retrieves data from tables) that are created with a **STRUCTURED QUERY LANGUAGE (SQL)** and have been brought into Crystal Reports. These queries are often complex. They are usually created (by a DBA or programmer) in another software package.

Using a command as a data source allows the report to process faster, because the selection of records for the report is already done before the report that you create is run. Commands are very useful when you need data from several databases to create one report.

SQL is the language that is most used to interact with databases. It is used to create and populate tables with data, modify data and retrieve data from a database. The **SQL SELECT** command is what is used to retrieve data. This is also known as a **QUERY**. Before you start to frown, the answer is no, you do not have to write a lot of SQL code to retrieve the data that you need for the reports that you will create in this book. Crystal Reports has tools, like the Select Expert and Group Expert, that you can use to retrieve the data from the tables. At some point you may have requests for functionality that these tools can't provide, which means that you will have to write code.

When that is the case, select the **ADD COMMAND** option shown above in Figure 5-1, then click the Add button. You will see the dialog box shown in Figure 5-2. This dialog box is used to create the SQL query. (1)

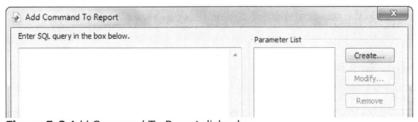

Figure 5-2 Add Command To Report dialog box

Stored Procedures, like commands and views, do not contain data. A stored procedure is a compiled SQL program and contains at least one SQL statement. The majority of the time, stored procedures are created by a database administrator or programmer. Stored procedures can be used over and over and can be used in more than one report. The Xtreme database comes with two stored procedures that you can use. Figure 5-1 shown earlier, shows the stored procedures in the database. (1)

> **(1) Command And Stored Procedure Advantage**
> The advantage that commands and stored procedures have over views is that they can use parameter fields. This means that the stored procedure can return a different recordset each time that it is run, based on the values in the parameter fields.

Other Data Source Options

As mentioned earlier, there are two other types of data sources. To enable these data sources, open the Options dialog box and click on the Database tab, then select the options that you want to enable.

System Tables These tables require administrator rights. The data stored in these tables work behind the scenes by keeping track of things like groups, queries and relationships, as shown in Figure 5-3.

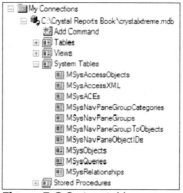

Figure 5-3 System tables

Synonyms These are virtual tables that some databases support.

Exercise 5.1: Create Your First Report From Scratch

1. Click on the **BLANK REPORT** link on the Start Page tab. You will see the Database Expert dialog box. It looks similar to the Data screen on the Standard report wizard. All of the wizards have this screen except for the OLAP Cube report wizard.

2. Select the crystalxtreme database.

3. Add the Customer table to the **SELECTED TABLES** list, then click OK. You will see an empty design tab.

How To Add The Fields To A Report

There are several ways to add fields in the Field Explorer to a report, as explained below. If you are not familiar with the techniques, take some time to try each of them to see which one you like the best. These options are for adding one field at a time to the report. Later in this chapter you will learn how to add more than one field to the report at the same time.

① Drag the field to the report.

② Select the field. Click the **INSERT TO REPORT** button on the Field Explorer toolbar, then click in the report where you want to place the field.

③ Right-click on the field that you want to add to the report and select Insert To Report on the shortcut menu, then click in the report where you want to place the field.

Dragging A Field To The Report
When you drag a field to the report you will see a frame, as shown in Figure 5-4. The frame is the approximate size of the data in the field.

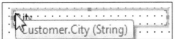

Figure 5-4 Frame for a field being added to the report

If you add a field to the report from the preview tab, the value in the field will be displayed instead of the field name.

Add The Fields To The Report

1. On the Field Explorer window, click on the plus sign in front of the **DATABASE FIELDS** option. then click on the plus sign in front of the Customer table. You will see all of the fields in the table.

2. Drag the Customer Name field to the **DETAILS** section. Notice that a field heading is automatically added to the page header section.

If you add a field to a section other then the details section, a field heading will not automatically be added to the page header section.

3. Add the following fields to the **DETAILS** section: Address1, Region, Country and Postal Code. When you are finished, the report layout should look like the one shown in Figure 5-5.

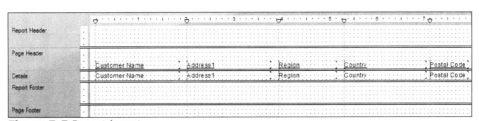

Figure 5-5 Report layout

The green check marks illustrated in the Field Explorer in Figure 5-6 indicate that the field has been added to the report or is being used in a formula field that has been added to the report.

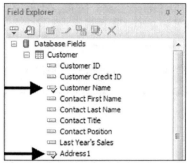

Figure 5-6 Checked fields illustrated

 Find In Field Explorer Option
This option will highlight the field in the Field Explorer window. I am not sure of the benefit of this feature because if you have the tool tips option turned on, you can see which table the field is in by holding the mouse pointer over the field on the design tab. This option is on the shortcut menu when you right-click on a field.

4. Save the report in your folder. Type E5.1 Customer information as the file name. If prompted to generate the data, click Yes.

5. Preview the report. It should look like the one shown in Figure 5-7. Not bad for your first time creating a report from scratch. Close the report. If prompted to save the changes, click Yes.

Customer Name	Address1	Region	Country	Postal Code
City Cyclists	7464 South Kingsway	MI	USA	48358
Pathfinders	410 Eighth Avenue	IL	USA	60148
Bike-A-Holics Anonymous	7429 Arbutus Boulevard	OH	USA	43005
Psycho-Cycle	8287 Scott Road	AL	USA	35818
Sporting Wheels Inc.	480 Grant Way	CA	USA	92150

Figure 5-7 Customer information report

 Adding More Than One Field To The Report At The Same Time
There are three options that you can select from to add more than one field to the report at the same time.

① Select all of the fields that you want to add, then drag them onto the report. This is probably the easiest option.
② Click on a field in the Field Explorer, then press and hold down the **CTRL** key and click on the other fields that you want to add. This option can be used to select fields that are next to each other in the Field Explorer or not next to each other.
③ Clicking on a field, then holding down the **SHIFT** key will let you select fields that are next to each other. If you click on the Customer Name field in the Customer table shown earlier in Figure 5-6, then hold down the Shift key and click on the Last Year's Sales field, all of the fields between these two fields will be selected. This option can only be used to select fields that are next to each other.

Exercise 5.2: Create A Report Using Multiple Tables

In the previous exercise the report that you created was based on one table. Many of the reports that you will need to create will use two or more tables. The report that you will create in this exercise uses more than one table.

Select The Tables And Add The Fields To The Report

1. Open a blank report and add the Employee, Employee Addresses and Orders tables to the report.

 Adding More Than One Table To The Report At The Same Time
You can add more than one table at the same time by clicking on the first table that you want to add. Press and hold down the Shift key and select the other tables, then click the Add button.

You can also double-click on the table in the **AVAILABLE DATA SOURCES** section to add it to the Selected Tables list.

2. Click on the **LINKS** tab and make the dialog box larger. This will make it easier to see how the tables are linked. Notice that all of the tables have an Employee ID field.

 The Database Expert calls the screen that you link tables on, the **LINKS** screen. The wizards call the same screen the **LINK** screen. They both do the exact same thing, so I don't know why they have slightly different names.

The **ORDER LINKS** button opens the dialog box shown in Figure 5-8. It is used to verify the order of how the tables are linked. Most of the time, the order that is automatically selected is correct.

When you are using several tables it is a good idea to check the link order to make sure that the links are correct, because an incorrect linking order will produce an outcome different then what you expect.

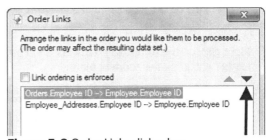

Figure 5-8 Order Links dialog box

If you need to rearrange the order of the links, click on the link that you need to move, then click the **UP** or **DOWN** arrow to move the link, as illustrated above in Figure 5-8.

If you are using a command or query as the basis of the report you do not have to create links because the links are created and stored in the command or query. Linking data in tables is an important concept to understand and will be covered in detail after you finish creating this report.

3. Close the Order Links dialog box, then click OK to close the Database Expert dialog box.

4. Add the following fields in the Employee table to the details section: Photo, First Name and Last Name.

5. Add the following
    fields in the Employee
    Addresses table to the
    details section:
    Address1 and Region.

    Figure 5-9 shows
    the report layout.

Figure 5-9 Fields added to the report

6. Save the report. Type E5.2 Employee list as the file name. Leave the report open to
    complete the next part of the exercise.

How To Add And Remove Databases And Tables

It is possible that during the report design process you may need to add or delete a database or
table. You just realized that you do not need any fields from the Orders table and want to remove
the table from the report. You can make changes like this on the design tab by following the steps
below.

1. Right-click on the **DATABASE FIELDS** option in the Field Explorer, then select the **DATABASE
    EXPERT** option on the shortcut menu.

> **Other Ways To Open The Database Expert**
> ① Right-click on a table in the Field Explorer and select Database Expert.
> ② Right-click on a field in the Field Explorer and select Database Expert.
> ③ Click the Database Expert button on the Expert Tools toolbar.

2. Click on the Orders table in the **SELECTED TABLES** list, then click the **<** button and click OK.

> If you need to add a table, select it from the **AVAILABLE DATA SOURCES** list and add it to the
> Selected Tables list on the Database Expert dialog box.

3. Click OK to close the Database Expert
    dialog box, then preview the report.

    Click OK if prompted to refresh the
    report data.

    The report should look like the one
    shown in Figure 5-10.

    Save the changes.

Figure 5-10 Employee list report

Relational Databases

Earlier in this chapter you read a little about linking tables. The reason tables can be linked is because there is a relationship between them, thus the term "Relational Databases". Yes, this is a complicated topic and there are a lot of books on the concepts associated with relational databases and how to create them, so I won't bore you with the details, but please hear me out and don't skip this section.

If the databases that you will use out in the real world are created properly, you will not have to learn a lot about linking or relational databases, because Crystal Reports will automatically create the links that you need. However, this doesn't mean that you do not have to learn anything about these topics.

While databases are not the primary focus of this book, it is important that you understand a little more than the fundamentals and basic database terminology that were covered in Chapter 3. The reason that you need to understand databases is because they are the foundation for the reports that you will create and modify. If you have never created a database, or have very little experience creating them, the next few sections in this chapter will be your crash course in databases, relationships and linking. You will learn how all of the components fit together. Figures 5-11 and 5-12 show the layout of two tables.

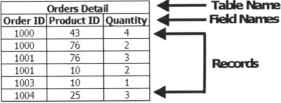

Figure 5-11 Orders table layout

Figure 5-12 Orders Detail table layout

Primary Key Fields

In Chapter 3, Table 3-2 you saw the primary keys for some of the tables in the Xtreme database. The fields in the Primary Key column are the ID fields. You will see these two terms (Primary key and ID fields) used interchangeably. I prefer to use the term ID field because primary key fields usually have "ID" as part of the field name.

 ID is short for identification. It is jargon that the programming community uses to reference a field that can be used to link the data in one table to the data in another table.

All of the tables that you will use in the Xtreme database have at least one ID field. Hopefully, you will find that this is also true out in the real world. The reason ID fields are used is because by design they provide a way for each record in the table to have a unique way to be identified.

I have taught several database classes and almost without fail, this topic causes a lot of confusion. For some reason, people want to create links on string (text fields). Please don't do that. It can cause you problems.

If you needed to create a report that showed all of the orders and what items were on each order, you would need a way to link the Orders and Orders Detail tables. Think of "linking" as having the ability to combine two or more tables "virtually" and being able to display the result of this "virtual linking" on a computer screen or on a printed report.

In Figures 5-11 and 5-12 above, the common ID field is the Order ID field. If you look at the data in the Orders Detail table, you will see that some records have the same Order ID number. That's okay. This means that some customers placed orders with more than one item. Each record in the Orders Detail table represents one item that a customer ordered. If you were to "virtually" join the data in the tables shown in Figures 5-11 and 5-12 above, it would look like the table shown in Figure 5-13.

Orders				Orders Detail		
Order ID	Order Date	Order Amount	Cust ID	Order ID	Product ID	Quantity
1000	1/2/2005	$263.99	48	1000	43	4
1000	1/2/2005	$263.99	48	1000	76	2
1001	1/2/2005	$322.45	57	1001	76	3
1001	1/2/2005	$322.45	57	1001	10	2
1002	1/3/2005	$196.00	3			
1003	1/4/2005	$124.99	48	1003	10	1
				1004	25	3

Figure 5-13 Virtually joined tables

This "virtual" join is what happens when tables are **LINKED**. If all of this data was stored in one table instead of two, at the very minimum, the Order Date and Order Amount fields would be repeated for every record that is in the Orders Detail table. Repetition of data is why this information is stored in two tables instead of one. It is considered poor table design to have the same information (other than fields that are used to join tables) stored in more than one table.

> Usually if you see a record in the Orders Detail table, like Order ID 1004 shown above in Figure 5-13, or any child table that is in a parent-child relationship, there is a problem with the data in at least one of the tables because all of the records in the child table should have at least one matching record in the parent table. Parent tables are used to get data from a child table.

Types Of Relationships

The Employee List report that you just created required two tables. These tables are linked by a common field, the Employee ID field. This field is what connects (joins) data from both tables and allows you to use data from both tables in the same report.

The Employee ID field in the Employee table is how you find the matching record (known as a **ONE-TO-ONE RELATIONSHIP**) or records (known as a **ONE-TO-MANY RELATIONSHIP**, which is the most popular type of relationship) in the Employee Addresses table. These are two of the most common types of relationships. The **MANY-TO-MANY RELATIONSHIP** is a third type of relationship. It is not used as much as the other two.

How Linking Works

More than likely, most reports that you create will require data from more than one table. Reports like the Product List report that you created in Chapter 4 only used one table, so there is no linking involved. For reports that require two or more tables, the tables need to be linked. The tables are usually linked in the database. The links that you see on the Link screen the first time that the screen is displayed, are the same as the links in the database. When you create a report and need to view or modify the links, you can do so by opening the Database Expert and clicking on the Link tab. Even though most of the time the links that you need are created for you, it is important to understand what is going on behind the scenes, as they say.

The best way to understand the basic concept of linking tables is to look at the records or a portion of the records in the tables that need to be linked. When you create a report that is based on data that you are not familiar with, you should take the time to look at the data in the tables.

Figures 5-14 and 5-15 show the records in the Employee and Employee Addresses tables. The field that these tables have in common is the Employee ID field.

Employee ID	Supervisor ID	Last Name	First Name	Position	Birth Date	Hire Date
1	5	Davolio	Nancy	Sales Representative	12/8/1972	3/29/1991
2		Fuller	Andrew	Vice President, Sales	2/19/1969	7/12/1991
3	5	Leverling	Janet	Sales Representative	8/30/1971	2/27/1991
4	5	Peacock	Margaret	Sales Representative	9/19/1973	3/30/1992
5	2	Buchanan	Steven	Sales Manager	3/4/1975	9/13/1992
6	5	Suyama	Michael	Sales Representative	7/2/1963	9/13/1992
7	5	King	Robert	Sales Representative	5/29/1972	11/29/1992
8	5	Callahan	Laura	Inside Sales Coordin	1/9/1974	1/30/1993
9	5	Dodsworth	Anne	Sales Representative	1/27/1976	10/12/1993
10	2	Hellstern	Albert	Business Manager	3/13/1968	3/1/1993
11	10	Smith	Tim	Mail Clerk	6/6/1973	1/15/1993
12	10	Patterson	Caroline	Receptionist	9/11/1979	5/15/1993
13	2	Brid	Justin	Marketing Director	10/8/1977	1/1/1994
14	13	Martin	Xavier	Marketing Associate	11/30/1975	1/15/1994
15	13	Pereira	Laurent	Advertising Specialis	12/9/1970	2/1/1994
0	0					

Figure 5-14 Employee table data

Employee ID	Address1	Address2	City	Region	Country	Postal Code
1	507 - 20th Ave. E.		Port Moody	BC	Canada	V3D 4F6
2	908 W. Capital Way	Suite 100	Coquitlam	BC	Canada	V3H4J7
3	722 Moss Bay Blvd.		Vancouver	BC	Canada	V6M 8S9
4	4110 Old Redmond Rd.		Richmond	BC	Canada	V5S 6H7
5						
6	Coventry House		London		UK	EC2 7JR
7	Edgeham Hollow	Apt #243	London		UK	RG1 9SP
8	4726 - 11th Ave. N.E.		New Westminster	BC	Canada	V7J 5G5
9	7 Houndstooth Rd.		Nottingham		UK	WG2 7LT
10	13920 S.E. 40th Street		Burnaby	BC	Canada	V2C 8H3
11	30301 - 166th Ave. N.E.	Apt #3D	North Vancouver	BC	Canada	V3K 2G9
12	16 Maple Lane		West Vancouver	BC	Canada	V3L 5S3
13	2 impasse du Soleil		Haguenau	Bas-Rhin	France	67500
14	9 place de la Liberté		Schiltigheim	Bas-Rhin	France	67300
15	7 rue Nationale		Strasbourg	Bas-Rhin	France	67000
0						

Figure 5-15 Employee Addresses table data

Depending on the table structure, tables can have more than one field that they can be linked by. An example of this would be the Orders Detail table. This table has an ID field that can be used to link it to the Orders table. There is a Product ID field in the Orders Detail table that is used to retrieve the Product Name from another table (the Product table) to print on the report, instead of printing the Product ID number. Displaying the product name on the report is more meaningful then displaying the Product ID field, which usually contains a sequential number. If you are asking why the Product Name is not stored in the Orders Detail table, there are two reasons.

① The ID field takes up less space, thereby keeping the size of the Orders Detail table smaller.

② If a Product Name has to be changed for any reason, it only has to be changed once in the Product table. Every place that the Product Name field is used on any report would automatically be updated with the revised product name. If the product name was stored in the Orders Detail table, every record in the Orders Detail table that had that product name would have to be changed, as well as, any other table that stored the product name in a field. That would be a lot of extra work.

Join Types

Hopefully, you are still with me. Don't worry, the relational database "lecturette" is almost over. There are several types of links that can be created. These different types of links are called **JOIN TYPES**. Crystal Reports has several join types that you can select from. Each join type will display different results from the same tables, which you will see in Figures 5-16 to 5-19. **INNER** joins are the most common.

If you use any of the three **OUTER** join types explained below, the order that the tables are added to the report is important. The four join types that are explained in Table 5-1 are the join types that are automatically created and are the most common. The other join types have to be created manually. They are covered later in this chapter.

 The "matching" explained in Table 5-1 is usually done on ID fields.

Join Type	How Records Are Selected . . .
Inner	Selects records that have matching records in both tables, as shown in Figure 5-16. This is the default join type.
Left Outer	Selects all records from one table (usually the left most table on the Links tab) and only matching records in the table on the right, as shown in Figure 5-17.
Right Outer	Selects all records from the right table and only matching records from the table on the left, as shown in Figure 5-18. This join type works the opposite of the Left Outer join type.
Full Outer	Selects all records from both tables whether or not there are matching records in the other table, as shown in Figure 5-19. Full Outer joins are also known as a **UNION** join type.

Table 5-1 Join types explained

In the Orders and Orders Detail tables, the Orders table is known as the **LEFT** table and should be added to the list of tables for the report first. The Orders Detail table is known as the **RIGHT** table and should be added to the list of tables after the Orders table. The reason the tables need to be added in this order is because for each record in the Orders table, there can be multiple records in the Orders Detail table that have the same ID. If the tables were added in the wrong order you can use the options on the Order Links dialog box to change the order.

Join Type Examples

When walking through these examples compare the data in the example to the data shown earlier in Figure 5-13. The examples in this section illustrate how the same data would be retrieved differently depending on the join type that is selected. This is why it is important to understand linking and join types. The arrows between the tables represent the flow of the data.

In Figure 5-16, the record for Order ID 1002 in the Orders table would not be retrieved in an Inner join because there is no related record in the Orders Detail table.

Orders					Orders Detail		
Order ID	Order Date	Order Amount	Cust ID		Order ID	Product ID	Quantity
1000	1/2/2005	$263.99	48		1000	43	4
1001	1/2/2005	$322.45	57		1000	76	2
1003	1/4/2005	$124.99	48		1001	76	3
					1001	10	2
					1003	10	1

Figure 5-16 Inner join recordset

In Figure 5-17, the record for Order ID 1004 would not be retrieved from the Orders Detail table in a Left Outer join because there is no related record in the Orders table.

Orders					Orders Detail		
Order ID	Order Date	Order Amount	Cust ID		Order ID	Product ID	Quantity
1000	1/2/2005	$263.99	48		1000	43	4
1001	1/2/2005	$322.45	57		1000	76	2
1002	1/3/2005	$196.00	3		1001	76	3
1003	1/4/2005	$124.99	48		1001	10	2
					1003	10	1

Figure 5-17 Left Outer join recordset

In Figure 5-18, the record for Order ID 1002 in the Orders table would not be retrieved in a Right Outer join because there is no related record in the Orders Detail table.

Orders					Orders Detail		
Order ID	Order Date	Order Amount	Cust ID		Order ID	Product ID	Quantity
1000	1/2/2005	$263.99	48		1000	43	4
1001	1/2/2005	$322.45	57		1000	76	2
1003	1/4/2005	$124.99	48		1001	76	3
					1001	10	2
					1002	10	1
					1004	25	3

Figure 5-18 Right Outer join recordset

In Figure 5-19, all records would be retrieved in a Full Outer join whether there is a related record in the other table or not.

Orders					Orders Detail		
Order ID	Order Date	Order Amount	Cust ID		Order ID	Product ID	Quantity
1000	1/2/2005	$263.99	48		1000	43	4
1001	1/2/2005	$322.45	57		1000	76	2
1002	1/3/2005	$196.00	3		1001	76	3
1003	1/4/2005	$124.99	48		1001	10	2
					1003	10	1
					1004	25	3

Figure 5-19 Full Outer join recordset

Tables Without A Link

If you added the Orders and Orders Detail tables to a report but did not link them, Crystal Reports would not know which record in the Orders table went with which record in the Orders Detail table. The result would be that each order record would be displayed (matched) with each of the records in the Orders Detail table, as shown in Figure 5-20. In total, 24 records would print on the report. When a report uses more than one table, this is usually not what you want.

Orders					Orders Detail		
Order ID	Order Date	Order Amount	Cust ID		Order ID	Product ID	Quantity
1000	1/2/2005	$263.99	48		1000	43	4
1000	1/2/2005	$263.99	48		1000	76	2
1000	1/2/2005	$263.99	48		1001	76	3
1000	1/2/2005	$263.99	48		1001	10	2
1000	1/2/2005	$263.99	48		1003	10	1
1000	1/2/2005	$263.99	48		1004	25	3
1001	1/2/2005	$322.45	57		1000	43	4
1001	1/2/2005	$322.45	57		1000	76	2
1001	1/2/2005	$322.45	57		1001	76	3
1001	1/2/2005	$322.45	57		1001	10	2
1001	1/2/2005	$322.45	57		1003	10	1
1001	1/2/2005	$322.45	57		1004	25	3
1003	1/4/2005	$124.99	48		1004	25	3

Figure 5-20 Tables not joined recordset

Recursive Join

In addition to the join types explained above, there is another join type called RECURSIVE JOIN. This type of join is not always obvious when looking at the table structures. A recursive join occurs when the same data is stored in two different ID fields in the same table. This is not the same as a parent/child (also known as a master/detail) relationship because this type of relationship does not require two tables like the Orders and Orders Detail tables that you read about earlier.

An example of a recursive join is in the Employee table. The Supervisor ID field in the Employee table contains the Employee ID of another record in the Employee table. This is because supervisors are also employees. Refer back to Figure 5-14. Seven employees have the number 5 in the Supervisor ID field (the second field from the left). This is because they all have the same supervisor, Steven Buchanan, whose Employee ID is number 5. Recursive joins are often used to create hierarchical reports.

Smart Linking

The AUTOMATIC SMART LINKING option is enabled by default. Crystal Reports uses this feature to create links based on an index or common fields in tables. You can change the default smart linking option on the Database tab of the Options dialog box. [See Chapter 2, Figure 2-28] Some people turn this option off and always create the links manually to make sure that the correct join type is selected.

Another reason people turn this feature off is because it causes Crystal Reports to create a link for every field that tables have in common, usually fields that have the same name and data type, which may not be what you want. This often causes fewer records to be retrieved then what you are expecting.

View The Current Links

1. Open a blank report, then add the Customer, Orders and Orders Detail tables.

2. Click on the Links tab, then click the **CLEAR LINKS** button. Click Yes, when prompted if you want to remove all of the links.

How To Manually Create Links

When you have the need to manually create links, follow the steps below.

1. Select a field in one table and drag it to a field in the other table. In this example, you can use the report that you used in the View The Current Links section above. Select the Quantity field in the Orders Detail table and drag it to the Customer Name field in the Customer table, then release the mouse button.

> Fields that are used to link tables must have the same data type. You could not create a link between a date field and a string field. If there is something wrong with the link that you are trying to create, you will see a warning message similar to the one shown in Figure 5-21. This message informs you that the link that you are trying to create is not valid.

2. Click OK to close the Visual Linking Editor message window, then close the Database Expert.

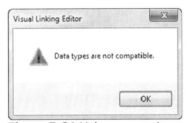

Figure 5-21 Link error warning message

Manual Join Types

As explained earlier, there are other join and link types that can be used to link tables. Table 5-2 explains the enforce join type options. Table 5-3 explains the link types.

Enforce Join Type	Selecting This Option . . .
Not Enforced	Doesn't mean that the link will be included in the SQL statement. At least one field must be used to join tables in order for the linking criteria to be included in the SQL statement. This is the default option.
Enforced From	Forces the link to the right table. When a field from the right table is used, but not one from the left table, the SQL statement requires that both tables be referenced.
Enforced To	Forces the link from the left table, whether or not a field is used from the right table. This means that the SQL statement will include both tables.
Enforced Both	Forces the link between the tables, regardless of where the fields that are used in the report are stored.

Table 5-2 Enforce Join types explained

Link Type	Creates A Recordset Where The Linked Field . . .
Equal =	Has related records in the left and right tables.
Greater Than >	From the left table is greater than the linked field in the right table.
Greater Than or Equal To >=	From the left table is greater than or equal to the linked field in the right table.
Less Than <	From the left table is less than the linked field in the right table.
Less Than or Equal To <=	From the left table is less than or equal to the linked field in the right table.
Not Equal !=	From the left table does not match the linked field in the right table.

Table 5-3 Link Types explained

Exercise 5.3: Create A Customer Orders Report

In this exercise you will create a report that displays customers and their orders.

1. Open a blank report and add the Customer and Orders tables, then click OK twice to close the Database Expert dialog box.

2. Add the Customer Name field in the Customer table to the details section.

3. Add the Order Date and Ship Date fields in the Orders table to the details section.

Add Another Table To The Report

You have decided that the report would look better if it also had fields from the Orders Detail table. To add a table to the report, follow the steps below.

1. Right-click on the **DATABASE FIELDS** option in the Field Explorer and select Database Expert.

2. Add the Orders Detail table, then click OK. When you see the **LINKS** tab, Click OK. You will then see the Orders Detail table in the Field Explorer window.

Add More Fields To The Report

1. Add the Order ID, Unit Price and Quantity fields in the Orders Detail table to the details section. The report layout should look like the one shown in Figure 5-22.

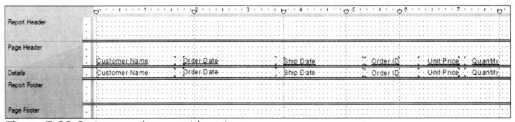

Figure 5-22 Customer orders report layout

2. Save the report. Type E5.3 Customer orders as the file name.

3. Preview the report. It should look like the one shown in Figure 5-23.

Customer Name	Order Date	Ship Date	Order ID	Unit Price	Quantity
City Cyclists	12/2/2010 12:00:00AM	12/10/2010 5:32:23PM	1	$41.90	1
Deals on Wheels	12/2/2010 12:00:00AM	12/2/2010 6:45:32AM	1,002	$33.90	3
Deals on Wheels	12/2/2010 12:00:00AM	12/2/2010 6:45:32AM	1,002	$1,652.86	3
Warsaw Sports, Inc.	12/2/2010 12:00:00AM	12/5/2010 12:10:12AM	1,003	$48.51	3
Warsaw Sports, Inc.	12/2/2010 12:00:00AM	12/5/2010 12:10:12AM	1,003	$13.78	3

Figure 5-23 Customer orders report

The reason that the information in the Customer Name, Order Date, Ship Date and Order ID fields is repeated, is because on some orders the customer ordered more than one item. (See Order ID 1002 and 1003). As you can see, all of the reports that you have created so far in this book need to be edited and formatted so that they are more presentable. You will learn how to edit reports in the next two chapters.

Exercise 5.4: Create An Orders Report

Create a Customer Orders report from scratch that uses the Customer, Employee and Orders tables. Add the fields in Table 5-4 in the order they are shown in the report in Figure 5-24.

The Last Name field may not fit on the report. It's okay to let it hang off of the right edge of the report for now. Later you will learn how to resize fields and change the page orientation so that the fields will fit on the report.

Save the report as E5.4 Orders report.

Customer	Employee	Orders
Customer Name	First Name	Order ID
	Last Name	Order Date
		Order Amount
		Ship Via

Table 5-4 Fields to add to the Orders report

Customer Name	Order ID	Order Date	Order Amount	Ship Via	First Name	Last Name
City Cyclists	1	12/2/2010 12:00:00A	$41.90	UPS	Nancy	Davolio
Deals on Wheels	1,002	12/2/2010 12:00:00A	$5,060.28	Pickup	Janet	Leverling
Warsaw Sports, Inc.	1,003	12/2/2010 12:00:00A	$186.87	UPS	Margaret	Peacock
Bikes and Trikes	1,004	12/2/2010 12:00:00A	$823.05	Pickup	Margaret	Peacock
SAB Mountain	1,005	12/3/2010 12:00:00A	$29.00	Loomis	Janet	Leverling

Figure 5-24 Orders report

Using A Table Alias

There may be times when a table needs to be added to a report twice to be able to retrieve different data. The second time that a table is added to a report, you will see the message shown in Figure 5-25.

Figure 5-25 Adding the same table twice message

. . . .

The second occurrence of the table is automatically renamed to include an underscore and incremental number, as illustrated in Figure 5-26. The second occurrence table is known as the alias table. You can rename the alias table.

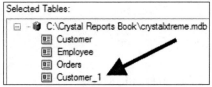

Figure 5-26 Alias table added to the report

ALIGNING OBJECTS ON A REPORT

Overview

As the title of this chapter indicates, you will learn alignment techniques that you can use to make the reports that you create look better. After completing the exercises in this chapter you will be able to:

- ☑ Understand the formatting options on shortcut menus
- ☑ Select objects
- ☑ Align objects
- ☑ Use guidelines
- ☑ Understand the purpose of the grid
- ☑ Resize objects
- ☑ Nudge objects

CHAPTER 6

Shortcut Menus

Crystal Reports has several shortcut menus that you can use instead of selecting menu options or clicking on toolbar buttons. As you will see, you will spend a lot of time formatting and editing reports. A great time saver in my opinion to completing these tasks is using the options on the shortcut menus.

The options will change on the shortcut menu depending on the object that is right-clicked on.

In addition to the object shortcut menu, there is a general shortcut menu available when you right-click on an empty space on the design or preview tab, as shown in Figure 6-1. Several of the options on this shortcut menu are explained in detail later in this chapter. The options that aren't, are explained below.

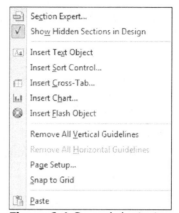

Figure 6-1 General shortcut menu

 You can also open this shortcut menu by right-clicking on the design or preview tab.

① **SHOW HIDDEN SECTIONS IN DESIGN** By default, this option is enabled. It is used to view hidden sections of the report on the design tab. If this option is turned off (not checked), hidden sections have a small space between them, as illustrated in Figure 6-2. Suppressed sections have slanted lines, as illustrated in Figure 6-3.

② **INSERT SORT CONTROL** [See Exercise 22.1, Using Sort Controls]

③ **INSERT CROSS-TAB** Is used to add a cross-tab object to the report.

④ **INSERT CHART** Is used to add a chart to the report.

⑤ **INSERT FLASH OBJECT** Is used to add a Flash (SWF) file to the report.

⑥ **REMOVE ALL VERTICAL GUIDELINES** This option will hide (not delete) vertical guidelines. (1)

⑦ **REMOVE ALL HORIZONTAL GUIDELINES** This option will hide (not delete) horizontal guidelines. (1)

⑧ **PAGE SETUP** [See Chapter 13, Page Setup Options]

(1) These options are not the same as clearing the **GUIDELINES** option on the Layout tab on the Options dialog box.

Figure 6-2 Page header section with the Show Hidden Sections in Design option turned off

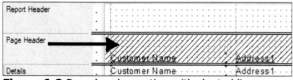

Figure 6-3 Page header section with slanted lines

Selecting Fields And Objects

A lot of the report editing that you will do requires fields and other objects to be selected. Often, you will have the need to apply the same changes to several fields or objects.

To select a single field or object, click on it with the left mouse button.

When an object is selected you will see a blue frame around it, as illustrated in Figure 6-4. You will also see squares.

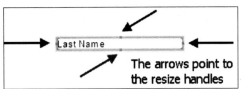

The arrows point to the resize handles

Figure 6-4 Resize handles illustrated

These squares are called **RESIZE HANDLES**. They are used to change the size of the object to make it wider, longer, shorter or smaller. You will learn how to resize objects later in this chapter.

 When I use the word "field", I am referring to a field in the details section of the report, or a field from a table or a calculated field that you create. "Objects" refer to items like the field heading, a text field or an image.

Selecting Multiple Fields And Objects

There are three ways to select the fields that you need, as explained below.

① Click on one field or object. Press and hold down the **CTRL** or **SHIFT** key and click on the other fields or objects that you need to select.

② Draw what is called a **MARQUEE** or **LASSO** around the fields or objects with the mouse. To do this successfully, the objects need to be near each other, either side by side or up and down from each other. To use this technique, no objects can already be selected. Click outside of the first field or object that you want to select. Hold the left mouse button down and draw around the objects that you need to select. You will see a frame being drawn. When you are finished selecting the objects and release the mouse button, you will see that several objects have been selected.

③ If you need to select all of the objects in one section of the report, right-click in the section (page header, details, etc.) on the far left side of the design window and select the option **SELECT ALL SECTION OBJECTS**, shown at the bottom of Figure 6-5.

The top of the shortcut menu displays which section of the report you are about to select all of the objects in. As shown in Figure 6-5, the objects that will be selected are in the page header section.

Figure 6-5 Report section shortcut menu

Exercise 6.1: Moving Objects

One of the tasks that you will do from time to time is rearrange fields and other objects on a report. This exercise shows you how to move fields and objects on a report.

1. Save the E4.2 report as `E6.1 Moving fields`. Make sure that you save the report in your folder.

2. Click on the design tab. Drag the **PRICE** field in the details section to the right.

 Interestingly enough, when you have multiple objects selected, the last one that you select is the **MAIN OBJECT**. The main object is the one that the other selected objects emulate (follow). If you have multiple objects selected and you move the main object to a place in the report where it does not fit, none of the objects that are selected will be moved. If you move multiple objects to a location where some objects will fit, including the main object, the objects that will fit in the new location will be moved and those that will not fit, will not be moved.

3. Move the Print Date field up and over to the far left of the page header section.

Aligning Objects Vertically

In addition to moving objects, you will have the need to have multiple objects line up. The **ALIGN** option is used to line up several objects at the same time. Follow the steps below to learn how to align objects. Because everything on the report is currently aligned, you need to move an object to get it out of alignment to see how the align option works.

1. In the E6.1 report, drag the Price field heading to the right, as shown in Figure 6-6.

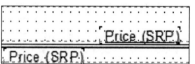

Figure 6-6 Field heading moved to the right

2. Select the Price field and heading, then right-click on the Price field.

 In the step 2, you have to right-click on the object that has the alignment that you want duplicate. In this example you want to align the field heading with the field in the details section. If you right-clicked on the field heading in the step above and selected Align ⇒ Rights, the field in the details section would have been aligned on the right side with the field heading.

You can right-click on any object and select the **ALIGN** option. Just remember which object that you right-click on before selecting an align option, because you may get results different then what you expected. The alignment of the object that you right-click on will be applied to the other objects that are selected.

3. Align ⇒ Lefts, as shown in Figure 6-7. The field and heading should be where it was before you started this exercise.

   Table 6-1 explains the align options.

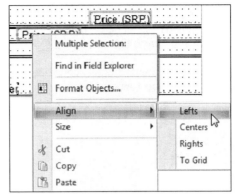

Figure 6-7 Align options

 At the top of the shortcut menu if you see the words **MULTIPLE SELECTION**, as shown above in Figure 6-7, it means that multiple objects have been selected. When selecting multiple fields or objects, whatever change you make will be applied to all of the selected fields and objects as long as the change can be applied to the data type. Not all data types can have the same changes applied.

Align Option	How It Aligns . . .
Lefts	On the left side of the object.
Centers	On the center of the object.
Rights	On the right side of the object.
To Grid	To the closest grid point of the object that you right-click on. The **GRID** option needs to be enabled to see how this works.

Table 6-1 Vertical align options explained

4. Save the changes and leave the report open.

Aligning Objects Horizontally

This type of alignment is very similar to the vertical align options that you just read about. The horizontal align option is useful when you manually add fields or objects to a report. The difference is that these alignment options are only available when all of the selected objects are in the same section of the report. If you rush and add fields to a report like I do, meaning that you just drop them on the report without paying attention to whether or not they are lined up properly, you will really appreciate this feature. In order to demonstrate how this feature works, you need to rearrange objects on the report first.

1. In the E6.1 report, drag the Product ID and Product Name field headings up in the page header section, as shown in Figure 6-8.

![Report layout showing Print Date, Product ID, Product Name, and Price (SRP) fields in page header and detail sections]

Figure 6-8 Field headings moved

2. Select the Product ID, Product Name and Price field headings, then right-click on the Price heading.

3. Align ⇒ Bottoms, as shown in Figure 6-9.
   The field headings should be back where they
   were before you moved them.

   Table 6-2 explains the horizontal alignment
   options on the shortcut menu.

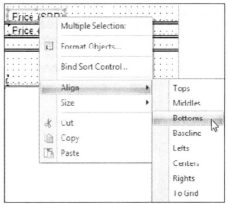

Figure 6-9 Horizontal align options

Align Option	How It Aligns . . .
Tops	On the top of the object.
Middles	On the middle of the object.
Bottoms	On the bottom of the object.
Baseline	On the bottom of the text, not the bottom of the frame like all of the other alignment options explained in this table. The baseline alignment option is useful when you are aligning objects that have a different font, font size or frame size.
Lefts	On the left side of the object.
Centers	On the center of the object.
Rights	On the right side of the object.
To Grid	To the closest grid point of the object that you right-click on. The **GRID** option needs to be enabled to see how this works.

Table 6-2 Horizontal align options explained

4. Save the changes and leave the report open.

Guidelines

As you add fields to the report you will see triangles called **GUIDELINES**, automatically being added
to the beginning or end of the field. Text and date fields will have the guideline marker at the
beginning of the field. Numeric fields will have the guideline marker at the end of the field.
In Figure 6-10, the Customer Name (a text field) and Order Date (a date field) fields have the
guideline markers at the beginning of the field. The Order ID (a numeric field) and Unit Price
(a numeric field) fields have the guideline marker at the end of the field. These markers let you
know visually where a field starts or ends on the report. Each field also has brackets around it to
let you know how long the field is.

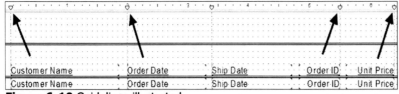

Figure 6-10 Guidelines illustrated

As a general rule, the brackets for one field should not be inside of the brackets for another field, unless you are combining objects and fields.

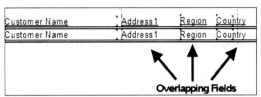

Figure 6-11 Fields overlapped in the design window illustrated

Overlapping fields, as illustrated in Figure 6-11, will cause the fields to print on top of each other as shown in Figure 6-12.

Customer Name	Address1	Region	Country
City Cyclists	7464 South Kingsway	USA	
Pathfinders	410 Eighth Avenue	USA	
Bike-A-Holics Anonymous	7429 Arbutus Boulevard	USA	
Psycho-Cycle	8287 Scott RoadIL	USA	
Sporting Wheels Inc.	480 Grant WayCA	USA	

Figure 6-12 Overlapping fields shown on the report

It may not always be easy to move or align objects. Guidelines are used to move all objects that are anchored to the guideline at the same time. This means that you can move the field in the details section, the field heading in the page header section and all calculated or summary fields in other sections that are anchored to the same guideline at the same time, without selecting them.

Guidelines are the **TRIANGLE BUTTONS** on the ruler at the top of the report, illustrated in Figure 6-13. The dotted lines that you see coming down from the guidelines in the page header and group header sections are **MARKERS** on the ruler. The reason that you do not see the markers in the report header section in the figure is because the section has a chart. The dotted lines for the markers are behind the chart. The dotted lines do not print on the report.

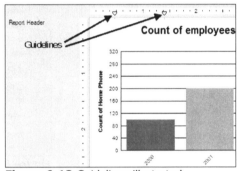

Figure 6-13 Guidelines illustrated

If you moved the guideline that is anchored to the Last Name field, all of the following objects would move at the same time: The field heading, the Sum of Employee.Supervisor ID field in the first group footer section and the Count of Employee.Home Phone field in the report footer section.

You will see red marks on the side of objects that the guideline is on, if the object is anchored to a guideline. If you do not see the red marks, drag the object towards the guideline or drag the guideline towards the object.

Guidelines are automatically added to a report if any of the follow actions occur:

① A field is added to the details section.
② You right-click in a **REPORT SECTION** on the design tab, as shown earlier in Figure 6-5, then select **ARRANGE LINES**.
③ A summary field is added to the report.

How To Manually Add Guidelines

If the need arises to manually add guidelines, you can select one of the options below.

1. Click on the horizontal ruler where you want to add a guideline.
2. Click on the vertical ruler where you want to add a guideline.

Turning The Guidelines On

If you do not see the guidelines,
View ⇒ Guidelines ⇒ Design,
will turn the guidelines on (on the design
tab), as shown in Figure 6-14.

The **PREVIEW** option will display the
guidelines on the preview tab.

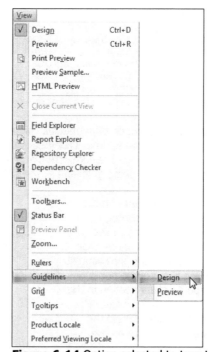

Figure 6-14 Option selected to turn the guidelines on

Guidelines Tips
① By default, the **VERTICAL GUIDELINE** option is enabled. To verify this, File ⇒ Options ⇒
Layout tab. The **INSERT DETAIL FIELD HEADINGS** option should be checked.
② To remove a guideline, drag the triangle marker off of the ruler. Removing guidelines
does not delete the objects attached to it.
③ By default, reports created with a wizard other then the **BLANK WIZARD** will have
horizontal guidelines inserted automatically. You can manually add horizontal guidelines to
reports created with the Blank wizard. The horizontal guidelines for all fields are at the top
or bottom of the field or the baseline of the text in the field.

Using Guidelines To Move Objects

You can move all of the objects that are attached to the same guideline at the same time,
by following the steps below.

1. Click on the guideline marker for the Product ID field on the E6.1 report and drag the marker to the left, to the 1 inch mark on the ruler, as illustrated in Figure 6-15.

    The field and field heading should have moved. If there were other objects anchored to this marker, they would have moved also.

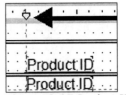

Figure 6-15 Product ID field guideline marker moved

Guideline Issues

Depending on how much you use guidelines, you may notice that a few strange things happen with the guidelines. The ones that I have noticed are explained in Table 6-3.

Issue	Solution
You delete objects from the report, but the guidelines stay.	Delete the guidelines that are no longer needed.
You moved an object, but the guideline did not move with it.	Move the object towards the guideline until the object snaps to the guideline.
You resized or moved an object and the object now appears to be attached to two guidelines.	Move the object away from the guideline that you do not want it attached to, then resize the object and attach it to the guideline that you want.

Table 6-3 Solutions to guideline issues

Using The Grid

When you need to have greater precision over lining up objects on a report then the guidelines provide, you can turn on the **GRID** option. This option is not enabled by default. In addition to the grid option, turning on the **SNAP TO GRID** option provides additional precision. The Snap to Grid option affects the guidelines.

View ⇒ Grid ⇒ Design, will display the grid on the design tab, as shown above in Figure 6-15. The grid is the dot pattern in the background. When new fields or objects are added to the report manually, they are automatically placed on the closest grid position to where you release the mouse button. If you need to change any of the grid settings, they are located on the Layout tab on the Options dialog box.

Resizing Objects

When fields are added to a report, the size is the larger of the field or the field heading. It appears that Crystal Reports estimates the horizontal space needed for string fields. Sometimes this works and sometimes the data in a string field in the details section gets cut off using this method. I suspect this happens because there is not enough space in the row to display all of the fields, so text fields are often truncated. This is what happened with the Product Name field on the report illustrated in Figure 6-16.

Product ID	Product Name		Product Type Name
1,101	Active Outdoors Crochet Glo		Gloves
1,102	Active Outdoors Crochet Glo		Gloves
1,103	Active Outdoors Crochet Glo	**Truncated Data**	Gloves
1,104	Active Outdoors Crochet Glo		Gloves
1,105	Active Outdoors Crochet Glo		Gloves
1,106	Active Outdoors Lycra Glove		Gloves

Figure 6-16 Truncated data illustrated

To fix this you need to resize the field. Depending on how close you placed the fields on the report, you may have to move the Product Type Name field to the right. To resize a field, follow the steps below.

1. Click on the field that you need to resize.

2. Place the mouse pointer on the right side of the field. The mouse pointer will change to a double headed arrow, as illustrated at the bottom of Figure 6-17. Drag the **RESIZE HANDLE** that you saw earlier in Figure 6-4 to the right. You will see the color on the ruler change above the field, as illustrated at the top of Figure 6-17. This may make it easier to see the size that you are adjusting the field to. Notice that the field heading was also resized.

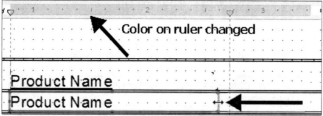

Figure 6-17 Mouse pointer in position to resize the field and color on ruler illustrated

3. Preview the report to see if you can now see all of the data in the field, as shown in Figure 6-18. Save the changes.

Product ID	Product Name	Product Type Name
1,101	Active Outdoors Crochet Glove	Gloves
1,102	Active Outdoors Crochet Glove	Gloves
1,103	Active Outdoors Crochet Glove	Gloves
1,104	Active Outdoors Crochet Glove	Gloves
1,105	Active Outdoors Crochet Glove	Gloves
1,106	Active Outdoors Lycra Glove	Gloves

Figure 6-18 Product Name field resized

Size Options

In the previous section you learned how to manually resize fields and objects. If you need to make one or more fields the same width, height or size, select the fields or objects.

On the shortcut menu, select the size option shown in Figure 6-19. The options are explained in Table 6-4.

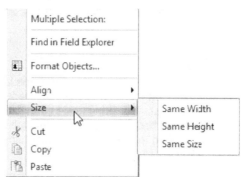

Figure 6-19 Shortcut menu sizing options

Option	Makes The Selected Fields The Same . . .
Same Width	Width.
Same Height	Height.
Same Size	Width and height.

Table 6-4 Size options explained

Object Size And Position Dialog Box

The options on this dialog box provide greater control over the size and position of an object, then sizing the object manually. You can use these options by following the steps below.

1. Right-click on the field that you want to resize and select **SIZE AND POSITION**, as illustrated in Figure 6-20. In this exercise, right-click on the Product Type Name field.

   Notice that the options on the shortcut menu are different then the ones shown earlier in Figure 6-7.

   The options on the menu change, depending on how many objects are selected or the type of object that is selected.

Figure 6-20 Object shortcut menu

2. Change the **WIDTH** to 1.0, as shown in Figure 6-21, then click OK. Save the changes and leave the report open.

This change will make the field shorter. If you enter a larger number in the Width field, the field will be longer. If you do not have a need for this much field size precision, you will probably not have a need to use the options on this dialog box. I have been using Crystal Reports for years and other then writing this book, I have never used this dialog box.

Figure 6-21 Object Size and Position dialog box

 The options that you change on the Object Size and Position dialog box will **NOT** automatically be applied to the fields title.

Unit Of Measurement
This option is on the Object Size and Position dialog box shown above in Figure 6-21, is set in Windows. As shown, the unit of measurement is inches. You may have a different unit of measurement.

Nudging Objects

So far in this chapter you have learned how to move and resize objects using the mouse. You can also move and resize objects using the keyboard. This is helpful if you use a laptop and do not use a mouse. Using the keyboard to move or resize objects is known as **NUDGING** an object.

 If the **SNAP TO GRID** option is enabled, the arrow key will move the object one grid point each time an arrow key is pressed.

How To Move An Object By Nudging It

1. Without using the mouse, select the object that you want to move.

2. Use one of the four arrow keys on the keyboard to move the object in the direction that you need to reposition it.

How To Resize An Object Using The Nudge Feature

1. Without using the mouse, select the object that you need to resize, then press and hold down the **SHIFT** key.

2. Use the arrow key that points in the direction that you want to resize the object. If you used the nudging feature on the E6.1 report, close the report but do not save the changes.

Using Object Layering

In Exercise 6.1 you learned how to move objects around on the report. In Figure 6-22, you can see the Move option on the shortcut menu. The options on the right of the figure are used to place objects on top of each other. This is known as **TRANSPARENT OBJECT LAYERING**. The options are explained in Table 6-5.

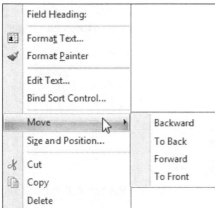

Figure 6-22 Move options

Option	Moves The Selected Object . . .
Backward	Back one layer.
To Back	To the last layer.
Forward	Up one layer.
To Front	To the top layer.

Table 6-5 Move options explained

EDITING AND FORMATTING REPORTS

As the title of this chapter indicates, you will learn editing and formatting techniques that you can use to make the reports that you create look better. Chapters 14, 15 and 16 will teach you other ways to format reports. After completing the exercises in this chapter you will be able to:

- ☑ Add images to a report
- ☑ Use the Format Editor
- ☑ Format Boolean fields
- ☑ Use the Format Painter

Overview

It can take an hour or more to create a report. You may struggle to write the formulas, make sure that the sorting and grouping options meet the report requirements and come up with an appropriate title for the report. You are pleased that you were able to accomplish all of these tasks and give a copy of the report to the person that requested it. You see them frown, but can't figure out why, especially because you checked the formulas by hand and know that the data is correct. You ask why they are frowning and they say, "Some of the fields are not lined up and there are too many fonts". As they say, "Perception is everything". Take from this what you will.

Crystal Reports provides a variety of options that you can use to make the reports that you design look better. Reports that are not visually appealing, are formatted ineffectively or are not user friendly, can be difficult to understand. You can draw boxes, apply templates, add color (probably best suited for reports that will be viewed on a web page or printed on a color printer) and more. You can also apply formatting conditionally to fields or sections of the report depending on whether the value in a field meets specific criteria. This type of formatting can be applied to any field that is on the report including summary and group name fields.

Earlier in this book you learned that everything on a report is an object, including charts, data fields, headings and formula fields. I realize that this may take some getting use to. The good news is that each type of object has its own set of properties that you can modify. The options on the Standard, Formatting and Insert Tools toolbars contain many of the options that are covered in the exercises in this chapter.

Adding And Editing Text Objects

Text objects are used to add additional information to a report. Text objects include field headings, report titles or any text that you want to add to a report that is not automatically created based on a field in a table.

Exercise 7.1: How To Edit Text Objects

In this exercise you will learn how to edit text objects.

1. Save the E5.4 report as `E7.1 Text objects`.

The majority of the field headings on the report are clear and easy to understand. The one field heading that would be easier to understand is the one for the Order ID field. Most end-users (people that will use the report) would not understand the term "ID", so it would be better to change this field heading.

2. Right-click on the Order ID field heading in the page header section and select **EDIT TEXT**.

 You can also double-click on the Order ID field heading to change the text.

3. Select (highlight) the text shown in Figure 7-1.

    Type `Order #`, then click on a blank space on the report.

Figure 7-1 Text selected to change

You can also select a portion of the text in a field and change that. For example, you could select "ID" in Figure 7-1 above and just change that instead of retyping text that is already there.

 Pressing the **ENTER** key does not end the editing session like it does in other software packages. Pressing Enter in Crystal Reports starts a new line in the text object. When you finish adding or editing text, click outside of the text object to end the editing session.

Make The Page Header Section Longer

The report that you have open does not have a report title. As you can see, there is not a lot of space in the page header section above the field headings to add a report title. The page header section needs to be longer to add a report title. Follow the steps below to learn how to make a section of the report longer.

1. Click on the section bar below the page header section. The mouse pointer is in the right position when you see the double arrow illustrated in Figure 7-2. Drag the section bar down below the details section.

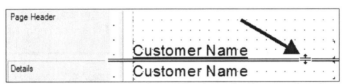
Figure 7-2 Mouse pointer in position to make the page header section longer

2. Move all of the field headings in the page header section down, then click on a blank space on the report.

 The easiest way to move all of the field headings at one time is to select all of them first and then move them.

 If you need to make a section in the report shorter, drag the section bar up.

How To Add A Text Object

1. Click the **INSERT TEXT OBJECT** button on the Insert Tools toolbar. The mouse pointer will change to a plus sign when placed over the report.

2. Click in the page header section and type Customer Orders Report in the text object. Click on a blank space on the report.

 You can right-click on a blank space in the report and select **INSERT TEXT OBJECT**.

 When selecting fonts to use on a report, it is best to use the default fonts that come with Windows, otherwise the report could look different on computers that do not have the font that you selected. If you have to use a font that does not come with Windows, you should export the report to Adobe PDF format. Doing that will allow the report to be viewed and printed with the font that you selected.

How To Format A Text Object

Follow the steps below to learn how to format a text object.

1. Click on the object that you want to apply formatting to. In this exercise, click on the report title that you just created.

2. Click the **BOLD** button and change the font size to 14, then resize the object so that you can see all of the text.

3. Move the report title so that it is centered (left to right) across the page header section. The top of the report should look like the one shown in Figure 7-3. Save the changes.

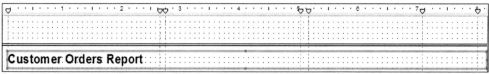

Customer Orders Report						
Customer Name	Order #	Order Date	Order Amount	Ship Via	First Name	Last Name
City Cyclists	1	12/2/2010 12:00:00/	$41.90	UPS	Nancy	Davolio
Deals on Wheels	1,002	12/2/2010 12:00:00/	$5,060.28	Pickup	Janet	Leverling

Figure 7-3 Modified page header section

Centering Text Across A Page
I use to find it difficult to center text like a report title across a page. I finally came up with the steps below to center a report title across the page.

① Make the report title object the width of the report, as shown in Figure 7-4.

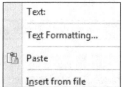

Customer Orders Report

Figure 7-4 Text object resized to the width of the report

② Click the **ALIGN CENTER** button.

How To Import A Text File Into A Text Object

Crystal Reports does not have spell check functionality. If you are creating a mail merge report, you can create and format the document in word processing software, then import it into a text object. If there is text in a file that you want to add to a report, you can, by following the steps below.

1. Add a text object to the report, then double-click in the text object to start the edit mode.

2. Right-click in the text object and select **INSERT FROM FILE**, as shown in Figure 7-5.

Text:
Text Formatting...
Paste
Insert from file

Figure 7-5 Text object shortcut menu

3. Find the text file on your computers hard drive or in another location, that has the content that you want to add to the report, then double-click on it. The content of the text file will be added to the text object. Save the changes.

Combining Text Objects And Database Fields

Text objects are more powerful then they may appear. If you have spent any time trying to get a text object and a field to line up side by side with spacing that looks right, but have had trouble doing so, you are in luck. Text objects can have data fields embedded in them. Text objects will automatically resize to accommodate the embedded field so that there is no extra space. The steps below explain how to embed a database field in a text object.

1. Add a text object to the report, then add text to the object.

2. Drag a database field either from the report or from the Field Explorer into the text object, as shown in Figure 7-6, then release the mouse button. You will see a flashing cursor in the text object before you release the mouse button. This is where the database field will be added.

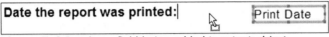

Figure 7-6 Database field being added to a text object

Combining Text Objects Tips
① You can edit the combined field or add more text or another database field to the text object.
② You can format part of a text object. If this is what you need to do, only select (highlight) the part that you want to format.
③ If you discover that you have added the wrong field to the text object, click on the database field in the text object, then press the DEL key.
④ I find it easier to drag the fields that I want to add to the report and format them there and then drag them into the text object instead of trying to format the fields inside of the text object.

Exercise 7.2: Adding Image Files To A Report

This exercise will show you how to add a logo or any image file to a report. There are two ways to open the Open dialog box, as explained below.

① Click the **INSERT PICTURE** button on the Insert Tools toolbar.
② Insert ⇒ Picture.

1. Save the E6.1 report as E7.2 Insert picture.

2. Make the page header section longer by dragging the section bar (below the section) down almost to the end of the report footer section. Delete the Print Date field. Move the field headings down in the page header section.

Tip For Adding An Image
In the step above you made the page header section longer to add the image. If you add an image file to a section that is not long enough, the section will automatically be expanded.

3. Open the Insert Picture dialog box, then navigate to the folder or location where the image file is that you want to use. For this exercise, navigate to your folder. You may have to change the Files of type field at the bottom of the Open dialog box to **ALL FILES** to be able to see the logo file.

4. Double-click on the file image6.jpg.

    The mouse pointer should have changed to a shadow box that is the actual size of the image, as shown in Figure 7-7.

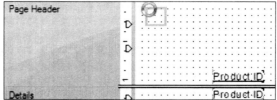

Figure 7-7 Mouse pointer in the Insert Picture mode

5. Click in the upper left corner of the page header section. You should see the image. Save the changes and leave the report open to complete the next part of the exercise.

How To Resize An Image

The image would look better if it were larger. Follow the steps below to resize the image.

1. Select the image if it is not already selected. Drag the mouse pointer down and to the right to make the image larger.

2. The report should look like the one shown in Figure 7-8. Save the changes.

    If you look at other pages in the report you will see the image at the top of the page because it was placed in the page header section, which prints on every page.

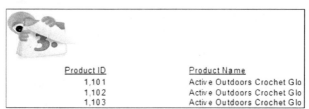

Figure 7-8 Insert picture report with an image added

Exercise 7.3: Adding Graphics From Fonts

In addition to being able to add images to a report, you can also add graphics that are stored in fonts like the Wingdings font. Fonts that have graphics can be accessed from the Character Map application in Windows. These graphics have to be placed in a text object. In this exercise you will add a graphic from a font to a report.

1. Save the E7.1 report as E7.3 Graphics from fonts.

2. Delete the first and last name fields on the report.

3. Click the Windows Start button ⇒ All Programs (or Programs) ⇒ Accessories ⇒ System Tools ⇒ Character Map.

4. Open the Font drop-down list on the Character Map dialog box and select **WINGDINGS**, if it is not already selected.

   You should see the dialog box shown in Figure 7-9.

   Double-click on the document picture (the third picture from the right in the first row), then click the Copy button and close the dialog box.

Figure 7-9 Character Map dialog box

5. Add a text object to the details section after the Ship Via field, then press the CTRL+V keys to paste the picture in the text object.

6. Click on a blank space on the report. Save the changes. The report should look like the one shown in Figure 7-10.

Customer Orders Report

Customer Name	Order #	Order Date	Order Amount	Ship Via	
City Cyclists	1	12/2/2010 12:00:00	$41.90	UPS	🗎
Deals on Wheels	1,002	12/2/2010 12:00:00	$5,060.28	Pickup	🗎

Figure 7-10 Graphics from fonts report

One reason to add an image next to each detail record is to create a hyperlink to another section of the report or to open a document or another report that has information that relates to the specific detail record.

The Format Editor

So far, all of the formatting that you have read about is considered basic formatting. For many reports that is all of the formatting that is required. When you need to create additional formatting, you can use the Format Editor. If the standard options on the Format Editor do not handle your needs, you can write conditional formulas. As you will see, the Format Editor provides a lot of options for changing how objects look on a report.

There are three ways to open the Format Editor **AFTER** selecting at least one object in the report, as explained below.

① Click the **FORMAT** button on the Expert Tools toolbar.

② Right-click and select **FORMAT <OBJECT TYPE>**. Depending on the object that is selected, a different format option type would be displayed. If the selected object is a graphic, **FORMAT GRAPHIC** would be displayed. The option for the Format Editor is always the first "Format" option on the shortcut menu. Notice that the icons to the left of the menu options shown in Figure 7-11 are the same icons that are on the buttons on the Expert Tools toolbar.

③ Format ⇒ Format <object type>.

Field: Orders.Order Date

Find in Field Explorer

Find in Formulas

 Format Field... ◀

Format Painter

Figure 7-11 Format Editor menu option illustrated

The options that are on the Format Editor dialog box vary depending on the type of object that is selected. When you open the Format Editor, you will only see tabs that can be used for the field type that was selected before the dialog box was opened. Table 7-1 explains all of the tabs on the Format Editor. In the next few exercises you will learn how to use the Format Editor.

> If you need to make the same change to several objects, select all of the objects that need the same change, prior to opening the Format Editor.

Tab	Data Type	Description
Common	All	The options shown in Figure 7-12 can be used by most objects on a report. Table 7-2 explains the options on the Common tab.
Border	All	Add lines and drop shadows to fields.
Font	All except OLE & graphic objects	Select font, font size, font color, underlining, strike out and character spacing. Most of the options on this tab are also on the Formatting toolbar.
Hyperlink	All	Uses the selected object as a link to a web site, file, email address or a field on a web page.
Paragraph	String & Memo fields	Format paragraphs that are stored in string or memo fields.
Number	Number & Currency	Apply formatting options that are only for number fields. (1)
Date & Time	Date & Time fields	Apply formatting options that are only for date and date/time fields. (1)
Picture	Graphic	Crop, scale, reset and resize image files.
Boolean	Boolean	Select how Boolean values will be displayed.

Table 7-1 Format Editor tab options explained

(1)   Options on this tab support custom formatting.

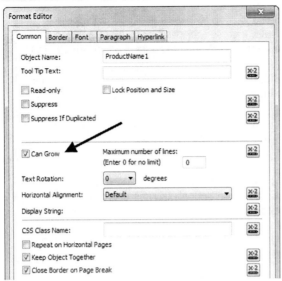

Figure 7-12 Common tab options

Option	Description
Object Name	This field is filled in by default. You can accept the default name unless you have a need to use the field in a formula and want to use a shorter or more descriptive name. It is not mandatory to change the object name.
Tool Tip Text	Enter text in this field that you want displayed when the mouse pointer hovers over the field on the report on the preview tab. You can type the text in the field or you can create a formula that will display the Tool Tip. The Tool Tip option on the Layout tab on the Options dialog box must be enabled to use this feature.
Read-only	Prevents the objects properties from being changed.
Lock Position and Size	Prevents the object from being moved or resized on the report.
Suppress	Keeps the object from being viewed or printed.
Suppress If Duplicated	Keeps the data in the field from being displayed on the report or printed, if it has the same value as the one in the previous record.
Suppress Embedded Field Blank Lines	Suppresses the field if it does not have data. This prevents blanks lines from appearing on the report. This option is only for text objects which is why it is not visible in Figure 7-12 above.
Can Grow	Allows the field to expand vertically to accommodate more data. When selected, the **MAXIMUM NUMBER OF LINES** option is enabled, which lets you select the number of lines the field will display on the report.
Text Rotation	Is used to rotate the object 90° or 270°.
Horizontal Alignment	Is used to select the horizontal alignment type for the selected object.
Display String	Is used to create conditional formatting to control how the data is formatted.
CSS Class Name	If the report will be displayed on the web and the field will be formatted with a style sheet, enter the CSS Class Name that should be applied to the field.

Table 7-2 Common tab options explained

Option	Description
Repeat on Horizontal Pages	This option is mostly used with a cross-tab, chart or OLAP grid that will print horizontally across more than one page because it allows an object to be repeated.
Keep Object Together	Keeps the object that will fit on one page from printing on more than one page. The object will be printed on the next page if it does not fit on the current page.
Close Border on Page Break	This option is used for fields that will print on more than one page and have a border. This option will print the bottom of the border of the object on the first page and print another border around the remaining data that prints on the next page.
![X+2 icon]	The Formula button (opens the Formula Workshop) is used to create a conditional formatting formula for the option. You can also attach an existing formula to the option. You would use a formula when you need to control when the option is turned on or off, based on a condition. For example, if you wanted to highlight the order amount field of records that were in a certain dollar amount range.

Table 7-2 Common tab options explained (Continued)

Exercise 7.4: Format A Text Object

1. Save the E7.1 report as E7.4 Format text object.

2. Right-click on the report title, then select **FORMAT TEXT**.

3. On the **BORDER** tab you will see the options shown in Figure 7-13.

   Table 7-3 explains the options on this tab.

Figure 7-13 Border tab options on the Format Editor dialog box

Option	Description
Line Style	These four options are used to select the line style for each side of the object. Notice that these options can be set conditionally. You can use the Bottom option to apply a double line below a field. This is often used in financial reports.
Tight Horizontal	Removes space from around the border. This option can resize fields because the border is around the length of the value in the field, not the physical size of the field.
Drop Shadow	Adds the shadow effect to the lower right corner of the object.
Border Color	Select a color for the border and drop shadow.
Background Color	Select the color for the background of the object.

Table 7-3 Border tab options explained

4. Change the **LINE STYLE** to single for the Left, Right and Top options. Look at the bottom of the dialog box in the **SAMPLE** section. You can see how the options that you selected will be applied to the object.

5. Check the **DROP SHADOW** and **BACKGROUND** options, then open the drop-down list across from the Background option and select **YELLOW**, as shown in Figure 7-14.

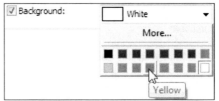

Figure 7-14 Background color options

 The **MORE** option shown above in Figure 7-14 will open the Color dialog box, which is used to select from additional colors or create a custom color.

6. Click OK to close the Format Editor. The report should look like the one shown in Figure 7-15. Save the changes.

Customer Orders Report						
Customer Name	Order #	Order Date	Order Amount	Ship Via	First Name	Last Name
City Cyclists	1	12/2/2010 12:00:00	$41.90	UPS	Nancy	Davolio
Deals on Wheels	1,002	12/2/2010 12:00:00	$5,060.28	Pickup	Janet	Leverling
Warsaw Sports, Inc	1,003	12/2/2010 12:00:00	$186.87	UPS	Margaret	Peacock

Figure 7-15 Format text object report with formatting applied to the report title

Exercise 7.5: Using The Can Grow Option

Earlier I mentioned that one reason data gets truncated is because there may not be enough room in the section of the report to accommodate all of the data. If you have tried everything possible to get all of the data to fit but it won't, the **CAN GROW** option can be used to fix the problem. This option will cause the data in the field to wrap to a new line, only when needed. Fields that have this option enabled, will only grow longer, not wider. Follow the steps below to learn how to use this option.

 The Can Grow option can only be used with string fields, text objects and memo fields.

1. Save the E7.2 report as E7.5 Can Grow option.

2. Move the Product ID field to the far left of the report. Move the Product Name field to the left to the 1 inch mark. Move the Price field to the 3 inch mark.

3. Right-click on the objects that you want to apply the Can Grow option to and select **FORMAT FIELD**. You will see the Format Editor dialog box. For this exercise, use the Product Name field.

4. On the **COMMON** tab check the **CAN GROW** option, then click OK.

If you want to limit the maximum number of lines that a field can display on the report, enter it in the **MAXIMUM NUMBER OF LINES** field. For example, if you are applying the Can Grow option to a memo field that could have 500 characters or more of text, you may not want to have all of the text in the field printed on the report. If this is the case, you would enter a number in the Maximum number of lines field so that only the first two or three lines of information in the field will actually print on the report. The Can Grow option, even when enabled will only be activated when needed. It does not force every record to expand to the number of lines entered in the field.

If you use the Can Grow option on a field and there is another field below it in the same section of the report, it is possible that the field below will be overwritten. To prevent this, the following options are available.

① Put the field with the Can Grow option at the bottom of the report section.

② Not as effective as the first option, but you can check the spacing by previewing the report to make sure that the field with the Can Grow option is not close to other fields.

5. Resize the Product Name field so that it ends at the 2 inch mark.

    The report should look similar to the one shown in Figure 7-16.

    Save the changes.

Product ID	Product Name	Price (SRP)
1,101	Active Outdoors Crochet Glove	$14.50
1,102	Active Outdoors Crochet Glove	$14.50
1,103	Active Outdoors Crochet Glove	$14.50
1,104	Active Outdoors Crochet Glove	$14.50

Figure 7-16 Can Grow option applied to the Product Name field

Text Rotation

There may be times when some of the text on a report will look better if it is rotated.

Figure 7-17 illustrates the degrees that text can be rotated. Select the text that you want to rotate, then select the degree rotation and click OK.

Figure 7-18 shows the Product ID heading on the E7.5 report rotated 90 degrees.

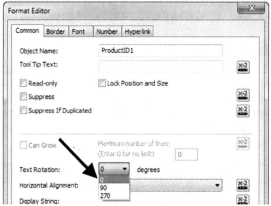

Figure 7-17 Text Rotation options illustrated

Product ID	Product Name	Price (SRP)
1,101	Active Outdoors Crochet Glove	$14.50
1,102	Active Outdoors Crochet Glove	$14.50

Figure 7-18 Product ID heading rotated 90 degrees

Font Tab

The options shown in Figure 7-19 are used to format the font of the selected field.

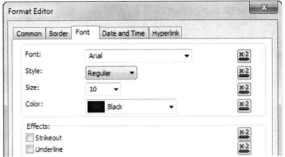

Figure 7-19 Font tab options

Paragraph Tab

When you are applying formatting to a string or memo field, you will see the Paragraph tab shown in Figure 7-20.

The options on this tab are used to select how text fields that have multiple lines of data or text will be indented or formatted.

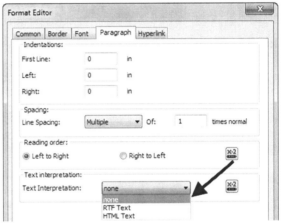

Figure 7-20 Paragraph tab options

 The **TEXT INTERPRETATION** option illustrated above in Figure 7-20 is not available for text objects. This option is helpful if the field has HTML (Hypertext Markup Language) formatting, which is used to create web pages or RTF (Rich Text Format) formatting for text that may have special formatting that was created in word processing or publishing software.

Hyperlink Tab

The options shown in Figure 7-21 are used to create a hyperlink to a website, email address, file, current website field value or current email field value.

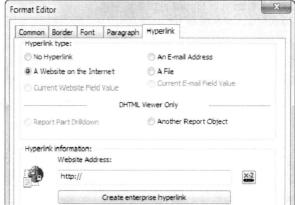

Figure 7-21 Hyperlink tab options

Exercise 7.6: Format A Numeric Field

Usually, order numbers do not have any formatting. As you saw earlier in Figure 7-15, the Order Number field has a comma. This field would look better if it did not have any formatting. Follow the steps below to change the formatting of the Order Number field.

1. Save the E7.4 report as
   `E7.6 Format a numeric field`.

   Right-click on the Order ID field in the details section, then select **FORMAT FIELD**.

   You will see the dialog box shown in Figure 7-22.

   The options are explained in Table 7-4.

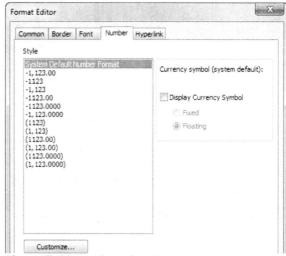

Figure 7-22 Number tab options

 The **CUSTOM STYLE** option was removed from the Style list on the Number tab in Crystal Reports 2008.

Option	Description
Style List	The options in this list are used to select how the number will be formatted.
Display Currency Symbol	Select this option to display the $ symbol. This option enables the Fixed and Floating options.
Fixed	This option displays the $ sign to the far left of the field. All of the $ signs in the column will line up.
Floating	This option displays the $ sign before the left most number in the field.

Table 7-4 Number tab options explained

2. Click on the third option **-1123**, from the top. The minus sign will only print if the number is negative. Click OK and preview the report. The Order ID field should not have a comma in it. Save the changes and leave the report open to complete the next part of the exercise.

If none of the options shown above in Figure 7-22 meet your needs to format currency or number fields, click the **CUSTOMIZE** button.

You will see the options shown in Figure 7-23 if the field is a currency field.

You will see the options shown in Figure 7-24 if the field is a number field.

Figure 7-23 Currency symbol custom style options

 Usually, the **DECIMALS** and **ROUNDING** options shown in Figure 7-24 are set to the same number of decimal places.

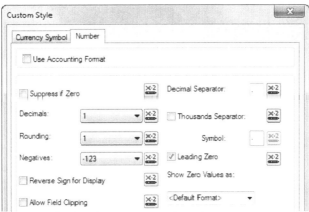

Figure 7-24 Number custom style options

If you find it difficult or confusing figuring out if a field on a report is a string or a numeric field based on the field name, you can clear the SHOW FIELD NAMES option on the Layout tab of the Options dialog box. Clearing this option will display X's in string fields and 5's in numeric fields, as shown in Figure 7-25. The number of X's displayed in the object is the maximum number of characters defined for the field in the database. By default, the width of the field on the report is the maximum number of characters, but you can resize the field as needed.

Customer Name	Order #	Order Date	Order Amount	Ship Via
XXXXXXXXXXXXXXX	-5555555	11/14/2007 11:23:45	($55,555.56)	XXXXXXXXXX

Figure 7-25 Fields displayed without field names

Format A Date/Time Field

Displaying the time as part of a date field is usually not needed on reports. To keep the time portion of a Date/Time field from printing on the report, the Date/Time field needs to be formatted, if they have not been globally modified on the Options dialog box. Follow the steps below to change the formatting of a Date/Time field.

1. Right-click on the Order Date field in the E7.6 report and select Format Field. You will see the dialog box shown in Figure 7-26.

   If you click the CUSTOMIZE button you will see the dialog box shown in Figure 7-27. The options on this tab are used to change the formatting for a date field or the date portion of a date/time field.

   The options shown in Figure 7-28 are used to change the formatting for the time portion of a date/time field.

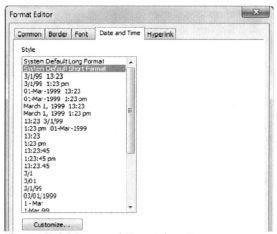

Figure 7-26 Date and Time tab options

Figure 7-27 Date custom style options

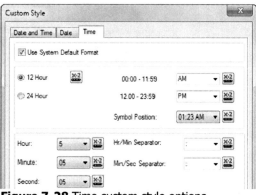

Figure 7-28 Time custom style options

2. Click on the option **3/1/99** on the Date and Time tab shown earlier in Figure 7-26, then click OK. The report should look like the one shown in Figure 7-29. You should not see the time on the Order Date field like you did earlier in Figure 7-15. Save the changes.

Customer Orders Report						
Customer Name	Order #	Order Date	Order Amount	Ship Via	First Name	Last Name
City Cyclists	1	12/2/10	$41.90	UPS	Nancy	Davolio
Deals on Wheels	1002	12/2/10	$5,060.28	Pickup	Janet	Leverling
Warsaw Sports, Inc.	1003	12/2/10	$186.87	UPS	Margaret	Peacock

Figure 7-29 E7.6 report with the Order Number and Order Date fields modified

Picture Tab

Earlier in this chapter you added an image to the E7.2 Insert picture report. The image would look better if it had a border and was scaled down. The options on the Picture tab are used to scale an image, as well as, crop and resize the image. The Picture object supports the following image formats: JPG, which is usually used for photos, TIFF, PNG and BMP, which is not used much these days.

Resize The Image File

1. Open the E7.2 report, then right-click on the image and select Format Graphic.

   Click on the **PICTURE** tab.

   You will see the dialog box shown in Figure 7-30.

   Table 7-5 explains the options on the Picture tab.

Figure 7-30 Picture tab options

Option	Description
Crop From	Removes the part of the image that is on the outside of the crop lines that are created when you enter the dimensions in any or all of the four crop options (left, right, top or bottom). Positive numbers cut into the image. Negative numbers add a white space between the edge of the image and the frame around the image. Cropping starts at the edge of the image.
Scaling	Enlarge or reduce the image by a percent.
Size	Change the width and height of the image.
Reset	Removes all of the formatting that was applied to the image on the Picture tab. When you crop, scale or size an image, the original image file is not changed. It is only displayed differently on the report, based on the options that are selected.

Table 7-5 Picture tab options explained

2. Change the scaling **WIDTH** option to 200, then change the scaling **HEIGHT** option to 200 and click OK. Preview the report. Figure 7-31 shows the image before it was scaled. Figure 7-32 shows the image after scaling. Save the changes and leave the report open.

Product ID
1,101

Figure 7-31 Image before scaling

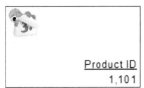

Product ID
1,101

Figure 7-32 Image after scaling

Add A Border To The Image

1. Click on the image, then open the Format Editor and click on the Border tab.

2. Change all four **LINE STYLE** options to Dotted, then click OK. The image should look like the one shown in Figure 7-33.

   Save the changes.

Product ID
1,101

Figure 7-33 Image border modified

Exercise 7.7: Format A Boolean Field

In this exercise you will change how the data in a Boolean field is displayed on a report.

1. Create a new report and add the following fields from the Orders table: Order ID, Order Date, Shipped and Payment Received.

2. Save the report as E7.7 Boolean formatting. The report should look like the one shown in Figure 7-34.

The Shipped and Payment Received fields are Boolean fields. As you can see, they both are displaying true or false.

Order ID	Order Date	Shipped	Payment Received
2,798	3/8/2012 12:00:00AM	True	True
2,799	3/8/2012 12:00:00AM	True	True
2,800	3/8/2012 12:00:00AM	True	False
2,801	3/8/2012 12:00:00AM	True	False
2,802	3/8/2012 12:00:00AM	True	False

Figure 7-34 Boolean formatting report

You will format these fields so that they display Yes and No instead of true and false. Doing this does not change the data in the table.

3. Select both Boolean fields, then right-click and select Format Objects.

4. On the Boolean tab open the **BOOLEAN TEXT** drop-down list shown in Figure 7-35, then select Yes or No.

   Click OK.

   Preview the report. The value in the Shipped and Payment Received fields is now displayed as Yes or No, instead of True and False.

Figure 7-35 Boolean tab options

5. If you go to page 37, you will see that not all of the data in these fields is Yes, as shown in Figure 7-36.

   Save the changes.

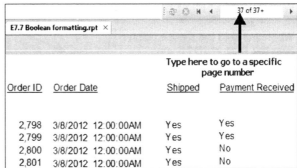

Figure 7-36 Boolean fields displayed differently on the Boolean formatting report

 Instead of clicking on the right arrow 36 times, you can type 37 in the Navigation Tools toolbar, as illustrated above in Figure 7-36, then press Enter.

Exercise 7.8: Using The Format Painter

This is a pretty cool feature. It is used to copy the formatting from one object to several other objects with a mouse click. Formatting properties like the font, font size, font color and borders can be taken from a text object and applied to a numeric object. This is because this type of formatting is not specific to a data type. Usually, number specific formatting cannot be applied to other data types. There are three ways to start the Format Painter as explained below, **AFTER** you have clicked on the object that has the formatting that you want to apply (copy) to other objects.

① Right-click on the object and select Format Painter.
② Click the **FORMAT PAINTER** button on the Standard toolbar.
③ Format ⇒ Format Painter.

There are some things that the Format Painter cannot do, as explained below.

① The Format Painter cannot copy a format that is created with the Highlighting Expert.
② Formatting cannot be copied from text objects or templates to fields in a table.
③ Formatted objects in the repository can be copied to reports. Formatting from reports cannot be copied to objects in the repository.
④ The Format Painter does not copy hyperlink properties.

⑤ The Format Painter will copy all formatting to other objects of the same data type. If formatting is copied from one data type to a different data type, only the formatting options that the objects have in common will be copied.

Change The Formatting Of An Object

In order to use this feature you need to change the formatting of an object.

1. Save the E7.2 report as E7.8 Format Painter.

2. Change the font of the Product Name heading to Times New Roman, size 10 and bold.

Apply The Formatting To Other Objects

1. With the Product Name heading selected, turn on the Format Painter.

2. When you hold the mouse pointer over the Product ID heading, it will change to a **PAINT BRUSH**, as illustrated in Figure 7-37.

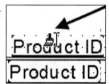

Figure 7-37 Mouse pointer in position to apply formatting

3. Click on the Product ID heading. The formatting from the Product Name heading should have been applied to the Product ID heading.

4. Move the Price field to the right, then add the Color field to the report after the Product Name field.

Using The Format Painter On Multiple Objects

If you need to apply the same formatting to more than one object, follow the steps below.

1. Select the object that has the formatting that you want to apply to other objects. For this exercise, click on the Product ID heading.

2. Turn on the Format Painter, then press and hold down the **ALT** key.

3. Click on the first object that you want to change. In this exercise, click on the Color heading, then click on the Price heading. The headings should all have the same formatting. Save the changes.

If you tried to apply this formatting to the logo, the mouse pointer would change to the symbol illustrated in Figure 7-38.

Figure 7-38 Symbol indicating that the formatting cannot be applied to the object

This symbol is used to let you know that the formatting cannot be applied to the object that you are holding the mouse pointer over.

Exercise 7.9: Centering Data Under A Heading

The customer information report that you created in Exercise 5.1 would look better if the following changes were made.

    ① Center the region field under the heading.

    ② Put a line under each detail record to make the report easier to read.

1. Save the E5.1 report as E7.9 Modified customer information.

2. Select the Region field and heading, then click the **ALIGN CENTER** button on the Standard toolbar.

3. Make the Region field and heading smaller. The data should now be centered under the heading.

How To Add Horizontal Lines To A Report

One way to make the data in the details section of a report easier to read is to place a line under the fields. Like other objects, you can format lines that you add to a report. There are two ways to open the **LINE** tool, as explained below.

    ① Click the **INSERT LINE** button on the Insert toolbar.

    ② Insert ⇒ Line.

Follow the steps below to add a line to the details section.

1. Move the details section bar down a little. Move it to the first row of dots in the grid in the report footer section.

2. Open the **LINE** tool. The mouse pointer will change to a pencil. Draw a line under the fields in the details section.

 It is easier to draw a long line like this if you can see the entire width of the report. To do this, I often change the **ZOOM CONTROL** option to 75%.

Format The Line

Follow the steps below to learn how to format a line.

1. Right-click on the line in the details section and select **FORMAT LINE**.

   You will see the dialog box shown in Figure 7-39.

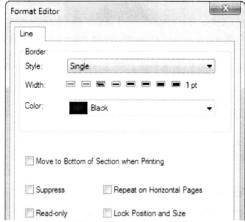

Figure 7-39 Format Editor line options

 The **MOVE TO BOTTOM OF SECTION WHEN PRINTING** option is often used for lines in a section of the report that has a field with the Can Grow option enabled, like a Notes field. Checking this option will force the line to print at the bottom of the section, which is what you usually want. You can test how this option works by checking this option and making the section of the report longer that has the line and preview the report.

2. Open the **STYLE** drop-down list and select Single, if it is not already selected.

3. Click on the first button in the **WIDTH** section. You should see the word **HAIRLINE** at the end of the Width options.

4. Click OK. The report should look like the one shown in Figure 7-40. Notice that the Region field data is centered under the heading. Save the changes.

Customer Name	Address1	Region	Country	Postal Code
City Cyclists	7464 South Kingsway	MI	USA	48358
Pathfinders	410 Eighth Avenue	IL	USA	60148
Bike-A-Holics Anonymous	7429 Arbutus Boulevard	OH	USA	43005
Psycho-Cycle	8287 Scott Road	AL	USA	35818

Figure 7-40 Modified customer information report with a modified details section

Exercise 7.10: Add Vertical Lines To A Report

In the previous exercise you learned how to add horizontal lines to a report. In this exercise you will learn how to add vertical lines to a report.

1. Save the E5.1 report as E7.10 Vertical lines.

2. Make the Region, Country and Postal Code fields smaller, then move the Country and Postal Code fields over to the left.

3. Insert ⇒ Line. Draw a vertical line in the details section after the Customer Name field. Make sure that the line touches the section bar above and below the details section.

4. Right-click on the vertical line that you just created and select Copy, then right-click anyplace in the report and select Paste. The mouse pointer will have a picture of the line next to it.

5. Click at the end of the next field (the Address field) on the report.

6. Repeat steps 4 and 5 to place a vertical line after every field in the details section, then save the changes. The report should look like the one shown in Figure 7-41.

Customer Name	Address1	Region	Country	Postal Code
City Cyclists	7464 South Kingsway	MI	USA	48358
Pathfinders	410 Eighth Avenue	IL	USA	60148
Bike-A-Holics Anonymous	7429 Arbutus Boulevard	OH	USA	43005
Psycho-Cycle	8287 Scott Road	AL	USA	35818

Figure 7-41 Vertical lines report

 You can also draw vertical lines through sections of the report. In the report that you just added vertical lines to, if you made the vertical lines longer by clicking on the line and dragging the top blue square on the line up, so that it is above the field heading in the page header section, the report would look like the one shown in Figure 7-42.

Customer Name	Address1	Region	Country	Postal Code
City Cyclists	7464 South Kingsway	MI	USA	48358
Pathfinders	410 Eighth Avenue	IL	USA	60148
Bike-A-Holics Anonymous	7429 Arbutus Boulevard	OH	USA	43005
Psycho-Cycle	8287 Scott Road	AL	USA	35818

Figure 7-42 Vertical lines report with lines extended into the page header section

USING SUBSECTIONS, SPECIAL FIELDS AND THE REPORT EXPLORER

After completing the exercises in this chapter you will be able to:

- ☑ Use the Section Expert
- ☑ Add subsections to a report
- ☑ Add Special Fields to a report
- ☑ Understand how the Report Explorer works

CHAPTER 8

Subsections

In some reports that you will create, all of the fields in the details section will not fit. Crystal Reports allows you to split any section of the report into **SUBSECTIONS**. One reason that you would create subsections is to be able to spread the fields out so that they are easier to read. This allows fields to be in multiple rows.

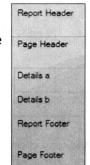

Yes, you can make the section longer, but depending on the requirements of the report, creating subsections may be a better solution. One reason that comes to mind that subsections is a better solution is because you may need to apply conditional formatting to some fields in a section. When a section of the report is split, the subsections are labeled, a, b, c, etc, as shown in Figure 8-1.

Figure 8-1 Details subsections

Ways To Add A Subsection

① Use the Section shortcut menu. Right-click on the section on the left that you want to split and select **INSERT SECTION BELOW**.
② Click the Section Expert button on the Expert Tools toolbar.
③ Report ⇒ Section Expert.

The benefit of using the Section Expert to add a section to the report is that you can apply other options to the new section at the same time. These options are on the right side of Figure 8-2.

You will learn about the options on the Section Expert in Chapter 16.

Figure 8-2 Section Expert

Exercise 8.1: How To Create Subsections

1. Save the E5.3 report as E8.1 Subsections.

2. Open the Section Expert. Click on the report section that you want to add a section to. Select the details section in this exercise, then click the **INSERT** button. You will see the section that you added, as illustrated in Figure 8-3.

3. Add a page header section, then click OK to close the Section Expert. The report layout should look like the one shown in Figure 8-4.

Section Expert
Sections:
Insert
Delete
Merge
Report Header
Page Header
Details
Details a
Details b
Page Footer
Report Footer

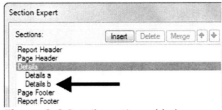

Figure 8-3 Details section added

Page Header a
Customer Name
Page Header b
Details a
Customer Name
Details b

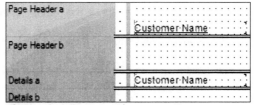

Figure 8-4 Report with new sections

4. Rearrange the fields in the details section as shown in Figure 8-5, then save the changes.

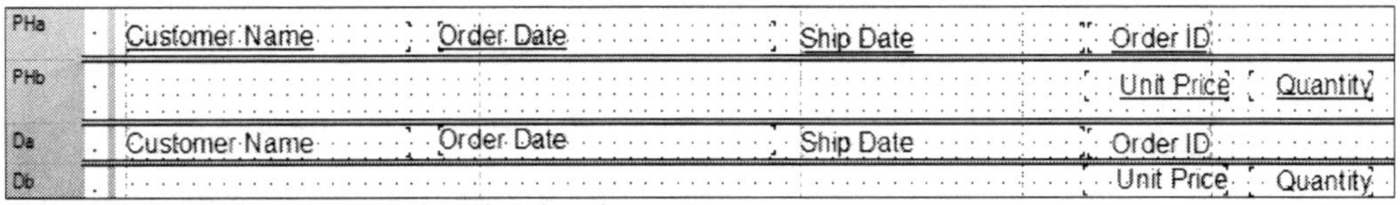

PHa
Customer Name
Order Date
Ship Date
Order ID
PHb
Unit Price
Quantity
Da
Customer Name
Order Date
Ship Date
Order ID
Db
Unit Price
Quantity

Figure 8-5 Fields rearranged in the details section

Exercise 8.2: Add A Background Color To A Report Section

If you applied a background color to the page header section, all of the objects in the section would have the background. Fortunately, there is a solution for this. If you only want the background color applied to the field headings and not the other objects in the page header section, you have to move the field headings to a new section.

1. Save the E6.1 report as `E8.2 Section background color.`

2. Insert a new page header section using the Section Expert, then click on the Color tab for the page header b section on the Section Expert.

3. Check the Background Color option, then open the drop-down list and select the color Gray. Click OK.

4. Select all of the field headings and change the font color to white. (**Hint**: Use the Font tab on the Format Editor.) Remove the underline and make the headings bold.

5. Move the fields to the page header b section. Save the changes. The report should look like the one shown in Figure 8-6.

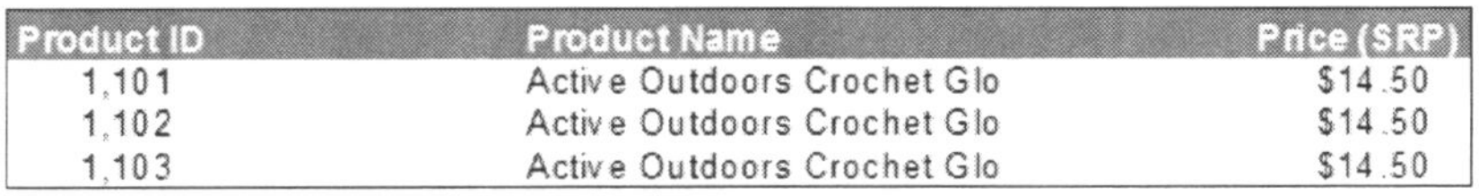

Product ID
Product Name
Price (SRP)
1,101
Active Outdoors Crochet Glo
$14.50
1,102
Active Outdoors Crochet Glo
$14.50
1,103
Active Outdoors Crochet Glo
$14.50

Figure 8-6 Section background color report

Exercise 8.3: Add A Border To A Field

You have learned several formatting techniques that you can use to make reports look better. Another technique that you can use is to put borders around a field. Borders are often used to make a field stand out on the report. In this exercise you will add a border to the Notes field. In the previous chapter you learned about the Can Grow option. A notes field is a good field to use this option on.

1. Save the E5.2 report as `E8.3 Border around field.`

2   Delete the Photo field, then move the remaining fields to the left.

3. Make the details section smaller, then add another details section.

4. Add the Notes field in the Employee table to the details b section under the First Name field. Make the Notes field longer and wider.

5. Right-click on the Notes field and select Format Field. Check the **CAN GROW** option on the Common tab if it is not already checked.

6. On the Border tab check the **DROP SHADOW** option.

7. Change the Line Style to **DOTTED** for the Left and Right options, then change the Top and Bottom Line Style options to **SINGLE**.

    You should have the options selected that are shown in Figure 8-7.

    Click OK, then save the changes.

    The report should look like the one shown in Figure 8-8.

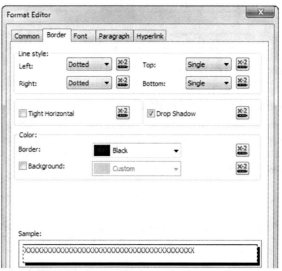

Figure 8-7 Border options

Figure 8-8 Border around field report

 It may be a good idea to check the **CLOSE BORDER ON PAGE BREAK** option on the Common tab on the Format Editor for fields that have a border because it is possible that the field could print on more than one page, especially a field that has the Can Grow option enabled.

Exercise 8.4: Adding Boxes To A Report

If you need to make something on a report stand out or you want to put a more decorative border around a field or heading then the border options that you learned about in Exercise 8.3, you can use the options on the Box tab on the Format Editor. In this exercise you will add a box to a field and a box to a report title. There are two ways to open the Box tool, as explained below.

① Click the **INSERT BOX** button on the Insert toolbar.

② Insert ⇒ Box.

Add A Box Around A Field

1. Save the E8.3 report as E8.4 Box around objects.

2. Delete the Notes field, then add it back to the details b section under the Customer Name field. Make the Notes field longer and wider. Leave space in the section above and below the Notes field.

3. Apply the **CAN GROW** option to the Notes field, then click OK.

4. Open the Box tool and draw a box around the Notes field.

5. Right-click on the box and select Format Box.

 If you have trouble selecting the box, open the Report Explorer and select it from there.

6. Select the **DOTTED** Border Style, then check the **FILL COLOR** option and select Silver as the color.

   Check the **EXTEND TO BOTTOM OF SECTION WHEN PRINTING** option. You should have the options selected that are shown in Figure 8-9.

   As you can see, the Box tab has many of the same options that the Line tab has. Table 8-1 explains the options that are different on the Box tab.

   Leave the Format Editor open to complete the next part of the exercise.

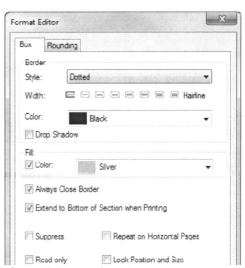

Figure 8-9 Box tab options

Box Option	Description
Fill Color	This option is used to apply a background color to the box.
Always Close Border	This option will close a box by adding additional lines if a box also prints on the next page of the report. The box at the bottom of the page will have a bottom line added to the border. The box at the top of the next page will have a line added to the border.
Extend to Bottom of Section when Printing	Checking this option allows the box to extend to the bottom of the section as the field that it is being used for extends (grows).

Table 8-1 Box tab options explained

Use The Rounding Options

The options on the Rounding tab are used to make the corners of the box round.

1. On the Rounding tab change the **ROUNDING PERCENT** option to 50.

    Figure 8-10 shows the options that should be selected.

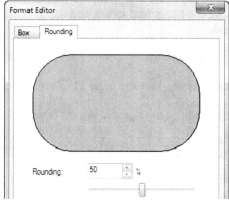

Figure 8-10 Rounding tab options

2. Click OK, then save the changes. Leave the report open to complete the next part of the exercise.

 If you move the slider all the way to the right, the box will change to a circle.

Add A Box Around A Text Object

Just like you can place a box around a data field, you can place a box around a text object.

1. Add a text object to the report header section. Type Employees Contact Info in the text object.

2. Make the border of the text object smaller, so that it is close to the words in it.

3. Draw a box around the text object, then open the Format Editor for the box.

4. Accept the default options on the Box tab.

   Change the rounding percent to 100 on the Rounding tab.

   Click OK and save the changes.

   If prompted to generate the data to save, click No.

   The report should look like the one shown in Figure 8-11.

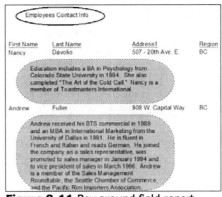

Figure 8-11 Box around field report

Special Fields

Crystal Reports has 26 built-in fields that you can add to reports. You can drop and drag these fields from the Field Explorer to the report, just like you drop and drag fields from tables in the Field Explorer.

Figure 8-12 shows the Special Fields that are available. Because these are system fields, the data in the field can change each time the report is run.

Table 8-2 explains the data that each of the Special Fields contains.

Special Fields, like the fields that are added to the details section, have headings automatically created in the page header section.

Figure 8-12 Special Fields

Special Field	The Field Will Print The . . .
Content Locale	Information in the **LOCATION** field, which comes from the Regional and Language Options dialog box (which is part of Windows) shown in Figure 8-13. (1)
Current CE User ID	ID number of the SAP Business Objects user. (1)
Current CE User Name	Username of the SAP Business Objects user. (1)
Current CE User Time Zone	Time zone that the SAP Business Objects user is in. (1)
Data Date	Date that the data was last refreshed in the report. (1)
Data Time	Time that the data was last refreshed in the report. (1)
Data Time Zone	Time Zone that the data was last refreshed in the report. (1)
File Author	Information in the **AUTHOR** field. (2)
File Creation Date	Date that the report was first created.
File Path And Name	File path and name of the report. (The location of the report file on the hard drive or server). For example: C:\Crystal Reports Book\E3.2 Employee list.rpt.
Group Number	Number of each group in the group header or footer section. If the report does not have any groups, this field will print a "1". This number is created each time the report is run.
Group Selection Formula	Group selection formula if applicable. It is created when the Select Expert is used.
Horizontal Page Number	Page number on pages that have a horizontal alignment. When this option is selected, the **REPEAT ON HORIZONTAL PAGES** option on the Common tab on the Format Editor dialog box is automatically enabled.
Modification Date	Date that the report was last modified. This would be helpful during the report creation and modification process.
Modification Time	Time that the report was last saved.
Page N of M	Page number and total number of pages in this format: Page 3 of 24. (3)
Page Number	Current page number.
Print Date	Date that the report was printed. (1) (4)
Print Time	Time that the report was printed. (1) (4)
Print Time Zone	Time zone that the report was printed in. This data comes from the Date & Time Properties dialog box (which is part of Windows) shown in Figure 8-15. (1)
Record Number	System generated number that is a counter for each detail record. It is based on the sort order in the report.
Record Selection Formula	Record selection criteria.
Report Comments	Information in the **COMMENTS** field. (2)
Report Title	Information in the **TITLE** field. (2)
Selection Locale	Locale setting (the country). (1)
Total Page Count	Total number of pages in the report. (3)

Table 8-2 Special Fields explained

(1) This data comes from the computer that the report is run from.
(2) This data comes from the Summary tab on the Document Properties dialog box shown in Figure 8-14. These fields can be added to a report just like the other special fields in Table 8-2 can, even though they come from a dialog box that is part of Windows.

(3) The Page N of M and Total Page Count fields add to the processing time when the report is generated. If the report has hundreds of pages, you may notice a delay while the data is being processed, but it is bearable. If the report will contain hundreds or thousands of pages, it is best to leave the Page N of M field off of the report while you are designing it because Crystal Reports has to generate the entire report prior to displaying or printing these fields, which will take some time. Right before you put the report into production, add these fields to the report as needed.

(4) Or this field will print the date on the Set Print Date and Time dialog box.

To view the dialog box shown in Figure 8-13, open the Control Panel in Windows. Double-click on the **REGION AND LANGUAGE OPTIONS** icon then click on the Location tab. In Crystal Reports, File ⇒ Summary Info, opens the dialog box shown in Figure 8-14.

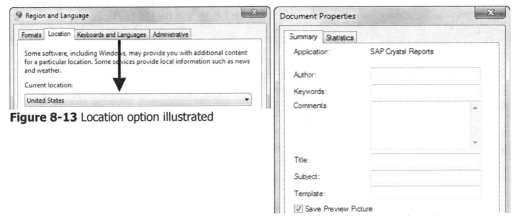

Figure 8-13 Location option illustrated

Figure 8-14 Summary tab options

To view the dialog box shown in Figure 8-15, open the Control Panel in Windows.

Double-click on the **DATE AND TIME** option, then click the Change time zone button.

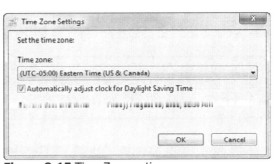

Figure 8-15 Time Zone options

Exercise 8.5: Add Special Fields To A Report

As you learned in Table 8-2 above, there are several Date and Time fields. To better understand what each of these fields will print, you will add all of them to one report in this exercise.

1. Save the E6.1 report as E8.5 Date special fields.

2. Make the report header section longer by dragging the section bar down to the seventh row of dots in the grid in the page header section. Delete the Print Date field in the page header section.

3. Open the Special Fields section of the Field Explorer, then drag the **DATA DATE** field to the upper right corner of the report header section.

4. Add the **DATA TIME** field to the upper right corner of the report header section and place it below the Data Date field.

Adding Text Objects

As you noticed, the headings were not created for the special fields that you added to the report header section. You have two options for using a text object with special fields, as explained below. I tend to use the second option because I find it easier to move the objects when they are combined, but you can use either option.

① Create a text object. Enter a title for the field and place the text object next to the special field.
② Complete ① above, then press the **SPACE BAR** and drag the special field into the text object.

1. Create two text objects in the report header section.
    Type Date the data was last refreshed: in one of the text objects.
    Type Time the data was last refreshed: in the other text object.
    Make both text objects bold.

2. Rearrange the fields and text objects so that they look like the ones shown in Figure 8-16. Save the changes and leave the report open to complete the next part of the exercise.

	Date the data was last refreshed: 8/4/2011
	Time the data was last refreshed: 1.01:16AM

Product ID	Product Name	Price (SRP)
1,101	Active Outdoors Crochet Glo	$14.50
1,102	Active Outdoors Crochet Glo	$14.50

Figure 8-16 Fields and text objects arranged on the report

 You may need to use the **ALIGN** options to line up the objects that you just added to the report. This would be a good use of the Align ⇒ Baseline option, so that you can line up the text object and the corresponding field because the text object is bold and the field is not.

Add More Date And Time Special Fields To The Report

1. In the report header section, add the Special Fields and Text Objects listed in Table 8-3.

    Arrange the objects so that they look like the ones shown in Figure 8-17.

Special Field	Text For The Text Object
File Creation Date	Date the report was designed:
Modification Date	Date the report was last saved:
Modification Time	Time the report was last saved:
Print Date	Date the report was printed:

Table 8-3 Fields and text objects to add to the report

 You can select all of the special fields and then drag them to the report header at the same time.

Date the report was last saved:	Modification	Date the data was last refreshed:	Data Date
Time the report was last saved:	Modification	Time the data was last refreshed:	Data Time
Date the report was printed:	Print Date	Date the report was designed:	File Creatic

| Product ID | Product Name | | Price (SRP) |

Figure 8-17 Special Fields and text objects arranged on the report

2. Save the changes. If prompted to refresh the data, click **NO**. Make any changes that are needed. The report should look similar to the one shown in Figure 8-18. Write down the dates and times that are displayed in the report. You can write them next to the headings in Figure 8-18.

Date the report was last saved:	8/5/2011	Date the data was last refreshed:	8/4/2011
Time the report was last saved:	1:15:42AM	Time the data was last refreshed:	1:01:16AM
Date the report was printed:	8/5/2011	Date the report was designed:	8/4/2011

Product ID	Product Name	Price (SRP)
1,101	Active Outdoors Crochet Glove	$14.50
1,102	Active Outdoors Crochet Glove	$14.50

Figure 8-18 Date special fields report run on day one

3. Tomorrow, run this report twice as follows:

① Run the report without refreshing the data. Compare the dates and times to those that you wrote down in step 2 above. My report looks like the one shown in Figure 8-19. Notice that the data in some fields changed and others did not.

② Move the Print Date field and title to the upper left corner of the report and save the changes. Refresh the data and run the report. Compare the data to what you wrote down in step 2 above. My report looks like the one shown in Figure 8-20. The only field that should still have the same data is the **DATE THE REPORT WAS DESIGNED**, as shown in Figure 8-18 above.

Date the report was last saved:	8/5/2011	Date the data was last refreshed:	8/4/2011
Time the report was last saved:	1:15:42AM	Time the data was last refreshed:	1:01:16AM
Date the report was printed:	8/6/2011	Date the report was designed:	8/4/2011

Figure 8-19 Date special fields report run on day two without modifications

Date the report was printed:	Date the report was last saved: 8/5/2011	Date the data was last refreshed: 8/4/2011
8/6/2011	Time the report was last saved: 1:15:42AM	Time the data was last refreshed: 1:01:16AM
		Date the report was designed: 8/4/2011

Figure 8-20 Date special fields report run on day two with modifications

4. Save the changes.

Report Explorer

By default, the Report Explorer displays the following report sections, whether or not they are actually being used in the report: Report header, page header, details, report footer and page footer.

This explorer is available from the design and preview windows.

Figure 8-21 shows the Report Explorer window. At the top of the tree structure is the report name. Each of the branches in the tree represents one section of the report.

If you click on an object in the Report Explorer, the object will be displayed and highlighted on the design tab.

You may find it easier to locate the object that you need to edit or format in this window, then in the Field Explorer once it has been added to the report. Like the Field Explorer, the Report Explorer is used to view all of the fields on the report. The Report Explorer also displays all of the other objects that are on the report, like charts and images.

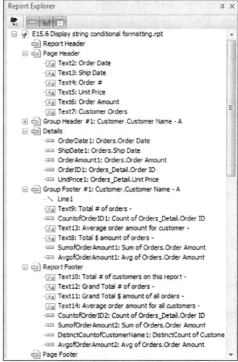

Figure 8-21 Report Explorer window

The icon next to a report section in the Report Explorer will change if the section has been suppressed (hidden) on the report. I find it hard to tell one icon from the next for the report sections. The field shortcut menus are the same as the ones in the Field Explorer.

 The group header and footer sections are only displayed in the Report Explorer if they are being used in the report.

Report Explorer Toolbar

Figure 8-22 shows the Report Explorer toolbar. Table 8-4 explains the buttons on the Report Explorer toolbar. The last three buttons on the toolbar are used to filter the object types that are displayed on the Report Explorer, which means that you do not have to display all of the objects in the Report Explorer. This is helpful if you need to only see certain object types in the Report Explorer.

Figure 8-22 Report Explorer toolbar

Button	Description
1	The **EXPAND** button opens all of the sections in the Report Explorer that have a plus sign.
2	The **SHOW/HIDE DATA FIELDS** button displays or hides the data objects, like text objects and formula fields.

Table 8-4 Report Explorer toolbar buttons explained

Button	Description
3	The **SHOW/HIDE GRAPHICAL OBJECTS** button displays or hides the lines, boxes, charts, maps and images (like photos or logos).
4	The **SHOW/HIDE GRIDS AND SUBREPORTS** button displays or hides the cross-tabs, OLAP grids and subreports.

Table 8-4 Report Explorer toolbar buttons explained (Continued)

 You can delete objects in the Report Explorer, but you cannot add new objects to the report from the Report Explorer.

Report Explorer Shortcut Menu

If you right-click on an object in the Report Explorer, you will see the shortcut menu editing options shown in Figure 8-23. You can modify fields and formulas by selecting the appropriate option on the shortcut menu. The shortcut menu options vary depending on the object that is selected. Figure 8-24 shows the shortcut menu if you right-click in the Report Explorer and an object is not selected.

 If you need to make the same change to more than one field or object, select all of the fields and objects that require the change, then open the shortcut menu. The fields that you select should be the same data type, to make the best use of editing multiple fields. If you select multiple fields that have different data types, the shortcut menu options that you can use will be limited to those that work for all of the data types of the fields that you have selected.

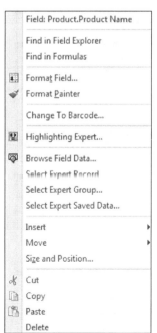

Figure 8-24 Report Explorer shortcut menu options when no object is selected on the report

Figure 8-23 Report Explorer shortcut menu editing options for a data field

Report Explorer Section Shortcut Menu

This shortcut menu has options that you can use to manage the sections of the report.

Many of the options on the Report Explorer section shortcut menu shown in Figure 8-25 are the same as the options on the report section shortcut menu.

Depending on the section that you right-click on in the Report Explorer, you will see different options on the shortcut menu.

Table 8-5 explains all of the options on the Report Explorer section shortcut menu, regardless of which section you right-click on.

Page Header a

Suppress (No Drill-Down)

Section Expert...

Show Long Section Names

Insert Line

Delete Last Line

Arrange Lines

Fit Section

Insert Section Below

Merge Section Below

Delete Section

Select All Section Objects

Figure 8-25 Report Explorer section shortcut menu

Option	Description
Hide/Show (Drill-Down OK)	Hides the section when the report is printed. The section can be viewed on the preview tab.
Suppress (No Drill-Down)	The section that this option is applied to will not be printed and cannot be viewed on the preview tab.
Section Expert	Opens the Section Expert.
Show Short/Long Section Names	Toggles between displaying long and short section names.
Insert Line	Adds a guideline to the section that is selected.
Delete Last Line	Deletes the last guideline that was added to the section.
Arrange Lines	Spaces the guidelines in a section evenly.
Fit Section	Moves the bottom section bar up to the lowest object in the section.
Insert Section Below	Creates a new section below the selected section.
Merge Section Below	Combines the fields in the selected subsection with the subsection below it.
Delete Section	Deletes a subsection of the report. (5)
Hide Area	Hides a subsection of the report. (5)
Suppress Area	Suppress a subsection of the report. (5)
Don't Suppress Area	When selected, the subsection cannot be suppressed. (5)
Select All Section Objects	Selects all of the objects in the section. This is useful when you need to apply the same formatting or change to all of the objects in a section.

Table 8-5 Report Explorer section shortcut menu options explained

(5)   This option is only available when you right-click on a report section (in the Report Explorer) that has at least one subsection, as shown in Figure 8-26.

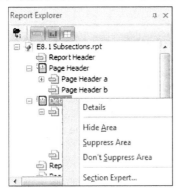

Figure 8-26 Report Explorer section shortcut menu

Custom Colors

If you create a custom color, it can be saved. To create a custom color, follow the steps below.

1. Open the Format Editor, then click on the Font tab or any tab that has a **COLOR** drop-down list field.

2. Open the Color drop-down list and select **MORE**, as illustrated in Figure 8-27.

   You will see the Color dialog box.

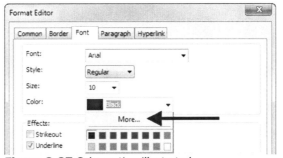

Figure 8-27 Color option illustrated

3. Use the options to create the custom color that you want.

   When you are finished, click the **ADD TO CUSTOM COLORS** button shown in Figure 8-28.

   The color that you created should be in one of the custom color boxes, as illustrated.

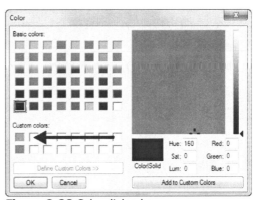

Figure 8-28 Color dialog box

4. Click OK twice to close both dialog boxes. Save the report. When you re-open the Color dialog box shown above in Figure 8-28, you will see the custom color that you created.

Exercise 8.6: Swapping Fields

You may have the need to swap a field on the report with a field in the database or a formula field. I find being able to swap fields helpful when I want the new field to have the same formatting as the original field on the report. Using this option saves some time because the formatting does not have to be applied to the field that is added to the report. The steps below show you how to swap a field.

1. Save the Chapter 8 Formula Field report as `E8.6 Swapping Fields`. Notice the formatting of the Order Amount field.

2. Display the Formula fields in the Field Explorer.

3. Press and hold down the Shift key, then drag the Line Item Total formula field in the Field Explorer on top of the Order Amount field in the detail section. You should see the two arrows shown in Figure 8-29. They indicate that the fields are being swapped.

Figure 8-29 Swap field arrows

4. You should see the Line Item Total field on the report with the formatting of the original field. Save the changes.

SELECTING RECORDS

Overview

After completing the exercises in this chapter you will be able to use the following techniques to control which records will appear on a report:

☑ The Select Expert
☑ Filter and query records
☑ Create report summary information

Overview

So far you have learned to create a variety of basic reports. All of the reports that you created without a wizard retrieved almost all of the records in the tables. As you saw, many of the reports contained 500 or more detail records. Most of the time reports provide specific information, which means that all of the records in the tables selected should not be on every report that is created. For reports that use tables similar to the size of the ones in the Xtreme database, this may not be a problem, but if the report is using tables or other data sources with thousands or millions of records (think credit card statements), the report will take a long time to run. Not only will you notice this on your computer, which may run out of memory, the network will also take a performance hit.

The Select Expert

One way that Crystal Reports can narrow down the records that will appear on the report is through a record selection process. Limiting data is one of the best ways to reduce the amount of time it takes to process a report. One selection process uses the **SELECT EXPERT**. This tool is used to select which records will appear on the report by entering **CRITERIA** that a record must meet. Records that do not meet the criteria will not appear on the report. This process is also known as **FILTERING RECORDS** or **QUERYING THE DATABASE**. Other ways to select records include writing formulas and using functions.

In Chapter 4 when you used a wizard to create a report, you created a filter on the Record Selection screen. The Record Selection screen has similar functionality to the Select Expert.

Examples of the types of information that can be retrieved when selecting records, filtering records or querying the database, include the following:

① Orders that were placed during a specific date range, like the month of June.
② All customers that purchased a specific product.
③ Orders that are over a certain dollar amount.
④ Products that need to be reordered.

Selecting, filtering or querying the database is used to ask a question about the data and then retrieve the records that meet the criteria. The records that are retrieved are known as a **RECORDSET**. The examples above are only asking one question. You can ask more than one question in the same query. You can ask the following types of multi-part questions.

① Orders that were placed during a specific date range and were more than $500.
② Customers that purchased a specific product and live in a specific state.
③ Orders that are over a certain dollar amount that were taken by a certain salesperson.
④ Customers that have a credit limit of $1,000 or more and have placed at least one order over $2,500, that shipped during a specific date range.
⑤ Orders that were placed or shipped during a specific date range.

Like SQL, the selection process produces the same results. Think of the Select Expert as an SQL code generator, without actually having to write code. The Select Expert creates the SQL code for you, which makes the Select Expert easy to use. The SQL code is what Crystal Reports uses to select records for the report.

In addition to selecting individual records, the Select Expert can also select groups. A group selection example would be to only display records in states that have an order total amount between $100,000 and $400,000.

The Select Expert provides two ways to select records, as explained below:

① Use the built-in **OPERATORS**. Table 9-1 explains the operators that are available. Not all of the operators listed in the table are available for all field types.

② **FORMULAS** are used to write the SQL code. This is not a contradiction to what I said earlier about not having to write code to use the Select Expert, because writing code in the Select Expert is not mandatory.

Operators

Operator	This Operator Selects Records That . . .
Is Equal To	Are equal to the value that you specify.
Is Not Equal To	Are not equal to the value that you specify. (1)
Is One Of	Match at least one of the values that you specify. If the criteria is NY, NJ or PA for the state field, any record that has one of these values in the State field would appear on the report.
Is Not One Of	Are not one of the values that you specify. (1)
Is Less Than	Are less than the value that you specify. If you want to see products that have a reorder level of less than 10 items in stock, enter 10 in the criteria field and the report will display products with a reorder level of nine or less. (2)
Is Less Than Or Equal To	Are less than or equal to the value that you specify. It works similar to the Is Less Than operator. The difference is that this operator will also select records that have the value that you specify. In the less than example above, the report would not display records with a reorder level of 10 items. The less than or equal to operator will. (2)
Is Greater Than	Have a value greater than the value that you specify. If you want to see all orders with an order amount over $500, enter $500 in the criteria field and the report will display records with an order amount of $500.01 or more.
Is Greater Than Or Equal To	Are greater than or equal to the value that you specify. It works similar to the Is Greater Than operator. The difference is that this operator will also select records that have the value that you specify. In the greater than example above, the report would not display records with an order amount of exactly $500. The greater than or equal to operator will.
Is Between	Fall between two values. If you want to see order amounts between $1,000 and $5,000 or orders between 6/1/10 and 6/15/10, this is the operator that you would use. This operator also selects records equal to the two values that you enter for the range.
Is Not Between	Are not in the range of values that you enter. It will retrieve records outside of the range that you select. (1)
Starts With	Begin with a specific character or set of characters. If you want to retrieve records of employees whose last name starts with the letter "M", use this operator. (3)
Does Not Start With	Do not start with the character or set of characters that you specify. (1) (3)
Is Like	Meet the wildcard criteria that you specify. The wildcard characters that you can use are a ? (question mark) and an * (asterisk). (3)
Is Not Like	Do not meet the criteria that you specify with the wildcards. (1) (3)

Table 9-1 Operators explained

Operator	This Operator Selects Records That . . .
Is In The Period	Meet the criteria of one of the functions explained in Table 9-2. These functions will save you a lot of time because you do not have to figure out what the formula should be. (4)
Is Not In The Period	Are not in the period that you select. (1) (4)
Is True	Have a value of true in the Boolean field. (5)
Is False	Have a value of false in the Boolean field. (5)

Table 9-1 Operators explained (Continued)

(1) This operator works the opposite of the operator above it in the table.
(2) This operator can also be used with a string field.
(3) This operator can only be used with a string field.
(4) This operator can only be used with date and date/time fields.
(5) This operator can only be used with a Boolean field.

> In addition to the operators listed above in Table 9-1, there is another operator,
> **IS ANY VALUE**, which is the default operator that you see when the Select Expert is first
> opened. This operator does not apply any condition to the field that it is associated to.
> In reports that do not select any criteria, this is the operator that is used by default when
> the report is run.

Is In The Period Functions

The functions in Table 9-2 provide a date range. You can create the same criteria using the
"Is Between" operator, but using these built-in functions is easier and does not require date values
to be hard coded in the formula.

Function	When The Period Starts And Ends . . .
Week To Date From Sun	From last Sunday to today
Month To Date	From the beginning of the current month to today
Year To Date	From the first day of the current year to today
Last 7 Days	From 7 days ago to today
Last 4 Weeks To Sun	From 4 weeks prior to last Sunday to last Sunday
Last Full Week	From Sunday of last week to Saturday of last week
Last Full Month	From the first day of last month to the last day of last month
All Dates To Today	From the earliest date in the table up to and including today
All Dates To Yesterday	From the earliest date in the table up to and including yesterday
All Dates From Today	From today forward
All Dates From Tomorrow	From yesterday forward
Aged 0 To 30 Days	From 30 days ago to today
Aged 31 To 60 Days	From 31 days ago from today to 60 days ago
Aged 61 To 90 Days	From 61 days ago from today to 90 days ago
Over 90 Days	More than 90 days ago
Next 30 days	From today to 30 days in the future
Next 31 To 60 Days	From 31 days from today to 60 days in the future
Next 61 To 90 Days	From 61 days from today to 90 days in the future
Next 91 To 365 Days	From 91 days from today to 365 days in the future

Table 9-2 Is in the period functions explained

Function	When The Period Starts And Ends . . .
Calendar 1st Qtr	From January 1 of the current year to March 31 of the current year
Calendar 2nd Qtr	From April 1 of the current year to June 30 of the current year
Calendar 3rd Qtr	From July 1 of the current year to September 30 of the current year
Calendar 4th Qtr	From October 1 of the current year to December 31 of the current year
Calendar 1st Half	From January 1 of the current year to June 30 of the current year
Calendar 2nd Half	From July 1 of the current year to December 31 of the current year
Last Year MTD	From the first day of the current month last year to the same month and day last year
Last Year YTD	From January 1 of last year to today's month and day last year

Table 9-2 Is in the period functions explained (Continued)

Using The Select Expert

As shown in Figure 9-1, the Select Expert is used to create criteria by record, group or saved data.

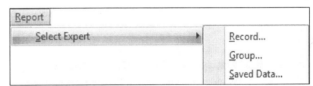

Figure 9-1 Select Expert submenu options

The **RECORD** option is used to create criteria for a field. This option filters records from being retrieved from tables.

Select the **GROUP** option when you want the criteria based on a group name or summary field. This option displays the groups based on the group selection criteria after the record selection has retrieved records. Group selection hides groups that do not meet the criteria.

Select the **SAVED DATA** option when you want to filter data that has been saved with the report. This option does not cause data to be refreshed like the record and group options do. Chapter 4 covered indexes and how they cause records to be retrieved faster because tables that are indexed are optimized. These indexes can be used with saved data. You can set indexes on saved data on the Saved Data Indexes dialog box. [See Chapter 4, Report Bursting Indexes]

For the most part, using the Select Expert is point and click. The only time that you have to type is if the value that you want to use is not in the drop-down list. This sometimes happens because the drop-down list only displays the first 500 unique values in a field. Any field that has multiple values that are identical will only display the value once in the drop-down list. An example of this would be a date field because it is possible that multiple records have the same date in the same field.

If you want to create a customer order report and only want to display records for the Wheels Company, this company name may not appear in the drop-down list because there could be more than 500 companies in the table and this company name is near the end of the alphabet. This is an example of when you would have to type something in the Select Expert.

The other time that you would need to type something in the Select Expert is if you are using a value that you know is not one of the values for the field. For example, if you want to select records that have an order amount greater than $600. You may have to type 600 in the field if the Order Amount field does not have that value in any of the first 500 values that are in the drop-down list.

Unless stated otherwise, when opening the Select Expert to complete exercises in this book, select the Record option or just click the Select Expert button. There are three ways to open the Select Expert, as explained below:

① Right-click on the field that you want to create criteria for and select the Select Expert option that you need.

② Click the **SELECT EXPERT** button on the Expert Tools toolbar.

③ Report ⇒ Select Expert.

If you click on the field that you want to create the criteria for before you select option two or three above, the Select Expert will open with the field selected and you can start to create the selection criteria.

 You can also use the Select Expert on the preview tab.

The exercises in this chapter will teach you how to create a variety of queries using the operators that you read about earlier in Table 9-1. Hopefully, this will make you feel comfortable using the Select Expert.

Exercise 9.1: Using The Is Equal To Operator

In this exercise you will use the Select Expert to find customers that are in the CA region. The region field contains the same data as a state field.

1. Save the E7.9 report as `E9.1 Region = CA`. Notice that there are 269 records in the report. The number of records is displayed in the Status bar.

2. Use one of the last two options explained earlier to open the Select Expert to create criteria per record. You will learn how to use the first option in the next exercise. You will see the dialog box shown in Figure 9-2.

The reason that you see the Choose Field dialog box is because a field was not selected prior to opening the Select Expert.

The **REPORT FIELDS** section at the top of the dialog box lists the fields that are currently on the report. Below that you will see all of the data sources that are connected to the report.

You can use any field in the Choose Field dialog box as a field for the selection criteria, whether or not it is being displayed on the report.

Figure 9-2 Choose Field dialog box

3. Click on the **CUSTOMER.REGION** field in the Report Fields section, then click OK. You will see the dialog box shown in Figure 9-3.

Notice that the field that you selected is the name on the first tab. Multiple tabs means that there is more than one set of selection criteria for the report. The type of criteria that you are creating is in the Title Bar on the dialog box.

Figure 9-3 Select Expert dialog box

The **NEW** button opens the Choose Field dialog box shown earlier in Figure 9-2.
The **DELETE** button deletes the tab that is selected.
The **BROWSE** button is used to view data in the field that is selected.
The **SHOW FORMULA** button displays the formula (in SQL) that was created by the selection criteria that you created.

4. Open the drop-down list and select **IS EQUAL TO**. You will see another drop-down list.
    The second drop-down list is connected to the field that is selected. The values in the second drop-down list are from the Region field in the table, as shown in Figure 9-4. As you learned earlier, drop-down lists that are connected to a field by default, only display the first 500 unique values in the field.

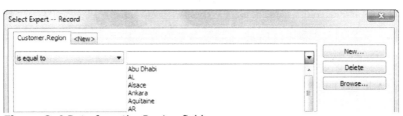

Figure 9-4 Data from the Region field

5. Select **CA** from the drop-down list shown above in Figure 9-4. Figure 9-5 shows the criteria that should be selected. When the report is run, this criteria will be used to find records that have CA (the state) in the Region field. Click OK, then preview the report. You may see the message shown in Figure 9-6.

Figure 9-5 Record selection criteria

Figure 9-6 Change In Record Selection Formula message

The message shown above in Figure 9-6 is asking if you want to use the data that is currently saved with the report or if you want to refresh the data. It also tells you the date and time the data that was saved with the report was last refreshed. If you know that the data in the report is current or you want to use the data that is saved with the report, click the **USE SAVED DATA** button. If you are not sure, click the **REFRESH DATA** button. When in doubt, refresh the data.

If you were creating this report and using live data, you would probably select the Refresh Data option the first time that you run the report after creating the selection criteria. Keep in mind that refreshing data can take a little longer than using saved data if there are tens of thousands of records in the table. Under certain conditions you may have to refresh the data, regardless of how long it takes. Don't worry, even with thousands of records, it only takes a few seconds. If the record selection criteria changes, Crystal Reports does not know if the database has to be re-queried. When this is the case, you will see the message shown above in Figure 9-6.

If you changed the selection criteria to include more records than the original selection criteria, you should refresh the data, so that the additional records that meet the criteria can be retrieved from the database. If you do not refresh the data when the modified selection criteria includes more records, the report will not display all of the records that should be on the report. It is also possible that no records will be displayed on the report depending on the revised selection criteria, if the data is not refreshed.

6.   Click the **REFRESH DATA** button. The report should look like the one shown in Figure 9-7. Notice that six records are displayed on the report. This means that there are only six records in the Customers table in the CA region. Save the changes.

Customer Name	Address1	Region	Country	Postal Code
Sporting Wheels Inc.	480 Grant Way	CA	USA	92150
Rowdy Rims Company	4861 Second Road	CA	USA	91341
Changing Gears	1600 Hyde Crescent	CA	USA	92750
Off the Mountain Biking	192 St. Luke Boulevard	CA	USA	92725
Tyred Out	3687 Kerrisdale Street	CA	USA	92721
Bike Shop from Mars	7071 Dundas Crescent	CA	USA	91338

Figure 9-7 Region = CA report

Exercise 9.2: Using The Is One Of Operator

In the previous exercise you used the "Is Equal To" operator to find customers in one region. In this exercise you will use the "Is One Of" operator to find customers that are in the OH or FL region.

1.   Save the E7.9 report as E9.2 Region = OH or FL.

2.   Right-click on the **REGION** field in the report and select, **SELECT EXPERT RECORD**.

3.   Open the drop-down list and select **IS ONE OF**, then open the next drop-down list and select OH.

 If the drop-down list is open and you type in the first letter of the value that you are looking for in the drop-down list, the first value that starts with the letter that you typed in will be displayed. You can also type in the exact value that you want.

4. Open the same drop-down list that you just used and select FL.

   Figure 9-8 shows the criteria that should be selected.

   Click OK.

Figure 9-8 Record selection criteria

5. Make the Country field smaller, then move the Postal Code field over to the left.

6. Preview the report. Click the **USE SAVED DATA** button. The report should look like the one shown in Figure 9-9. Save the changes.

Customer Name	Address1	Region	Country	Postal Code
Bike-A-Holics Anonymous	7429 Arbutus Boulevard	OH	USA	43005
Wheels and Stuff	2530 Bute Avenue	FL	USA	34666
Uni-Cycle	1008 Kerr Street	OH	USA	43042
Extreme Cycling	1925 Glenaire Avenue	FL	USA	34638
Karma Bikes	1516 Ohio Avenue	OH	USA	43092

Figure 9-9 Region = OH or FL report

Exercise 9.3: Using The Is Greater Than Or Equal To Operator

In this exercise you will use the "Is Greater Than Or Equal To" operator to find all orders that were placed on or after 6/24/2010.

1. Save the E5.3 report as E9.3 Order date GTE 6-24-2010. The report should have 3,683 records. (GTE is an abbreviation for greater than or equal to that I made up.)

2. Open the Select Expert to use with the Order Date field.

3. Select the "Is greater than or equal to" operator, then type 6/24/2010 in the next field.

   Figure 9-10 shows the criteria that should be selected.

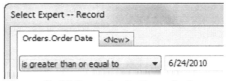

Figure 9-10 Record selection criteria

4. Click OK. The report should look like the one shown in Figure 9-11. The report should have 3,602 records. Notice that there are fewer records then before the selection criteria was applied. Save the changes and leave the report open to complete the next exercise.

Customer Name	Order Date	Ship Date	Order ID	Unit Price	Quantity
City Cyclists	12/2/2010 12:00:00AM	12/10/2010 5:32:23PM	1	$41.90	1
Deals on Wheels	12/2/2010 12:00:00AM	12/2/2010 6:45:32AM	1,002	$33.90	3
Deals on Wheels	12/2/2010 12:00:00AM	12/2/2010 6:45:32AM	1,002	$1,652.86	3
Warsaw Sports, Inc.	12/2/2010 12:00:00AM	12/5/2010 12:10:12AM	1,003	$48.51	3
Warsaw Sports, Inc.	12/2/2010 12:00:00AM	12/5/2010 12:10:12AM	1,003	$13.78	3
Bikes and Trikes	12/2/2010 12:00:00AM	12/2/2010 3:24:54PM	1,004	$274.35	3

Figure 9-11 Order date GTE 6-24-2010 report

Exercise 9.4: Modify Selection Criteria

In the previous exercise you created criteria to find orders that have an order date greater than or equal to a specific date. In this exercise you will add to this criteria to select orders that have an order amount that is at least $2,500.00.

Adding additional criteria via the Select Expert will reduce or increase the number of records that will appear on the report. As you have probably noticed, the report that you just added selection criteria to does not display the Order Amount field. If you need to have additional fields on the report you can add them at anytime. If you need to create criteria for a field, but do not need to see the field on the report, you can create the criteria without adding the field to the report.

> Creating the criteria IS GREATER THAN 2499.99 will produce the same results as creating the criteria, IS GREATER THAN OR EQUAL TO 2500.00.

1. Save the E9.3 report as
   E9.4 Order date GTE 6-24-10 and Order Amt GT 2499.99.

2. Delete the Quantity field, then add the Order Amount field from the Orders table and place it after the Ship Date field, as shown in Figure 9-12.

Page Header						
	Customer Name	Order Date	Ship Date	Order Amount	Order ID	Unit Price
Details	Customer Name	Order Date	Ship Date	Order Amount	Order ID	Unit Price

Figure 9-12 Order Amount field added to the report

3. Open the Select Expert to use with the Order Amount field. Notice that you see criteria on the Select Expert dialog box. This is the criteria that you created in the previous exercise.

Open the drop-down list and select IS GREATER THAN, then type 2499.99 in the next drop-down list.

Figure 9-13 shows the criteria that should be selected.

Figure 9-13 Record selection criteria

4. Click OK. Because you changed the selection criteria, you should refresh the data. The report should look like the one shown in Figure 9-14. The report should have 1,142 records. Save the changes.

Customer Name	Order Date	Ship Date	Order Amount	Order ID	Unit Price
Deals on Wheels	12/2/2010 12:00:00AM	12/2/2010 6:45:32AM	$5,060.28	1,002	$33.90
Deals on Wheels	12/2/2010 12:00:00AM	12/2/2010 6:45:32AM	$5,060.28	1,002	$1,652.86
Cyclopath	12/3/2010 12:00:00AM	12/3/2010 11:11:11PM	$14,872.30	1,010	$2,939.85
Cyclopath	12/3/2010 12:00:00AM	12/3/2010 11:11:11PM	$14,872.30	1,010	$2,645.87
Cyclopath	12/3/2010 12:00:00AM	12/3/2010 11:11:11PM	$14,872.30	1,010	$253.67

Figure 9-14 Order date GTE 6-24-2010 and Order Amt GT 2499.99 report

Exercise 9.5: Using The Is Between Operator

In this exercise you will use the "Is Between" operator to find all of the orders that were shipped between 4/1/2011 and 6/30/2011.

1. Save the E5.3 report as
   E9.5 Orders shipped between 4-1-2011 and 6-30-2011.
   There should be 3,683 records in the report.

2. Open the Select Expert to use with the Ship Date field. Select the "Is between" operator, then open the top drop-down list on the right and select 4/1/2011. If the date is not in the drop-down list, you can type it in.

3. Open the bottom drop-down list and select 6/30/2011. Click OK. Preview the report, then refresh the data. The report should have 780 records. Save the changes.

Exercise 9.6: Using Multiple Selection Criteria

In this exercise you will create a report that selects records that meet the following criteria: Country = USA, the order date is between 4/1/2012 and 4/30/2012 and the order was not shipped.

 Once you open the Select Expert and create the first set of criteria, you do not have to close it to add additional criteria. Click on the **NEW** tab to add more criteria.

☑ Table 9-3 contains the tables and fields for the report. The table names are in bold.
☑ Figure 9-15 shows the report layout.
☑ Figure 9-16 shows the report, which should have 44 records. Save the report as
   E9.6 US orders not shipped in April 2012.

Customer	Orders
Customer Name	Order Date (Change the format of this field to MM/DD/YYYY.)
Country	Order Amount
	Shipped

Table 9-3 Tables and fields to add to the report

Page Header					
	Customer Name	Country	Order Date	Order Amount	Shipped
Details	Customer Name	Country	Order Date	Order Amount	Shipped

Figure 9-15 Report layout

Customer Name	Country	Order Date	Order Amount	Shipped
City Cyclists	USA	04/29/2012	$63.90	False
Pathfinders	USA	04/26/2012	$3,185.42	False
Rockshocks for Jocks	USA	04/25/2012	$8,933.25	False
Rockshocks for Jocks	USA	04/30/2012	$31.00	False
Poser Cycles	USA	04/14/2012	$83.80	False
Trail Blazer's Place	USA	04/18/2012	$107.80	False

Figure 9-16 US orders not shipped in April 2012 report

Viewing Formulas

In Exercise 9.6 you created criteria that selected an order date greater than or equal to 6/24/2010. In another exercise you modified that criteria to only retrieve records that had an order amount greater than $2,499.99. To view the formula, click the **SHOW FORMULA** button on the Select Expert. The formulas for the selection criteria are similar.

Depending on the tab that is selected prior to clicking the Show Formula button, the formula will be in a different order then what is shown in Figure 9-17. The Country tab was selected for this figure.

```
{Customer.Country} = "USA" and
{Orders.Order Date} in DateTime (2012, 04, 01, 00, 00, 00) to DateTime (2012, 04, 30, 00, 00, 00) and
not {Orders.Shipped}
```

Figure 9-17 Selection criteria formula

 The zeros at the end of the date/time fields in the formula shown above in Figure 9-17 represent the time in HH MM SS format (hours, minutes, seconds).

 In Exercise 9.6 if the syntax in your formula looks different then what is shown above in Figure 9-17 and your report looks exactly like the one shown earlier in Figure 9-16, you are probably using the **BASIC SYNTAX** formula language instead of **CRYSTAL SYNTAX**.
[See Chapter 14, Syntax Language And Editors]

The bottom of Figure 9-18 shows the formula that was created for the selection criteria shown earlier in Figure 9-10. The bottom of Figure 9-19 shows the formula that was created for the E9.4 report shown earlier in Figure 9-14. It also shows all of the criteria that must be met. At the end of the first line of the formula, you see the word **AND**. If you changed the "and" to **OR**, the report would look like the one shown in Figure 9-20. If you made this change and ran the report, you would see that there are 3,622 records in this report, compared to the 1,142 records in the E9.4 report shown earlier in Figure 9-14.

 The **RECORD** and **GROUP SELECTION** options were removed from the Select Expert dialog box in Crystal Reports 2008.

{Orders.Order Date} >= DateTime (2010, 06, 24, 00, 00, 00)

Figure 9-18 Formula for the selection criteria shown earlier in Figure 9-10

{Orders.Order Amount} > $2499.99 and
{Orders.Order Date} >= DateTime (2010, 06, 24, 00, 00, 00)

Figure 9-19 Formula for the selection criteria for the E9.4 report shown earlier in Figure 9-14

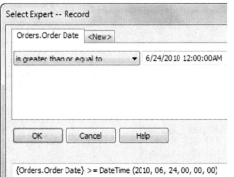

Customer Name	Order Date	Ship Date	Order Amount	Order ID	Unit Price
City Cyclists	12/2/2010 12:00:00AM	12/10/2010 5:32:23PM	$41.90	1	$41.90
Deals on Wheels	12/2/2010 12:00:00AM	12/2/2010 6:45:32AM	$5,060.28	1,002	$33.90
Deals on Wheels	12/2/2010 12:00:00AM	12/2/2010 6:45:32AM	$5,060.28	1,002	$1,652.86
Warsaw Sports, Inc.	12/2/2010 12:00:00AM	12/5/2010 12:10:12AM	$186.87	1,003	$48.51
Warsaw Sports, Inc.	12/2/2010 12:00:00AM	12/5/2010 12:10:12AM	$186.87	1,003	$13.78

Figure 9-20 Order date GTE 6-24-2010 OR Order Amt GT 2499.99 report

Reports can have more than one selection criteria. When this is the case, in order for records to appear on the report, they have to meet all of the selection criteria. That is because by default, Crystal Reports uses the logical **AND** operator on the Select Expert. If you need to create selection criteria where only one of the selection criteria options must be true in order for a record to appear on the report, you have to use the logical **OR** operator. To change the operator, you have to manually edit the selection formula that is created by the Select Expert.

How To Delete Selection Criteria

After you have created selection criteria you may decide that one or more of the criteria that you created is not needed. You do not have to delete everything and start over. The steps below show you how to delete specific criteria on the Select Expert dialog box.

1. Open the report that has the selection criteria that you want to delete.

2. Open the Select Expert. Click on the tab that has the selection criteria that you want to delete, then click the **DELETE** button shown earlier in Figure 9-4.

3. Click OK to close the Select Expert and save the changes.

Understanding How Date/Time Fields Work In Selection Criteria

In Exercise 9.4, a date/time field was used as part of the selection criteria. You entered a date and the records that have an order date greater than or equal to 6/24/2010 were retrieved, even though you did not enter a time for the date that you selected. That is because Crystal Reports will use midnight as the time when a date is entered without a time. This is fine for selection criteria that only uses a date/time field once. If the selection criteria uses the **IS BETWEEN** operator for example (or any operator that requires that two dates be entered for the selection criteria), the records that are retrieved may not be exactly what you are expecting.

The first date in the selection criteria will be compared to midnight as the time, meaning that all records that have a time of midnight or later will be included. So far, so good. The problem is with the second date in the selection criteria. If a time is not entered for the second date, only records that have midnight as the time will be retrieved. This means that a record that has the same date as the second date field in the selection criteria, but the time is something other then midnight will not appear on the report. To include all records on the date in the second date field, you should enter 23:59:59 (or 11:59:59 PM) as the time. If you enter 17.00.00 (or 05.00.00 PM) as the time, for the second date, records that have a time that is greater than 5 PM will not be included on the report.

If you were going to modify the E9.6 report to show all of the orders that were shipped between 1/1/2011 and 1/15/2011, Figure 9-21 shows what many people would enter as the selection criteria.

When the report is run with this selection criteria, 49 records will be retrieved.

This is incorrect because it does not account for records that have a time other than midnight on the Ship Date field.

Figure 9-21 Incorrect selection criteria

If the selection criteria shown in Figure 9-22 was entered, the report would retrieve 58 records.

As you can see in Figure 9-23, the times on the Ship Date field are different. Notice that there are nine records that have a ship date of 1/15/2011.

Figure 9-22 Correct selection criteria

If the second Ship Date field has the time entered as 03:00:00 PM as shown in Figure 9-24, the last three records on the 15th, shown in Figure 9-23 would not be displayed on the report because the time for these three records is after 3 PM.

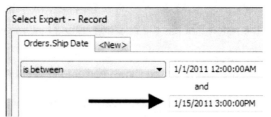

Figure 9-24 Criteria to show orders that were shipped between 1/1/2011 and 1/15/2011 by 3 PM

Figure 9-23 Ship Date field data

If you want to try this yourself, save the E9.6 report as E9.6A Time Problem (Incorrect Criteria) and delete all of the current selection criteria, then create the criteria shown earlier in Figure 9-21. Add the Ship Date field to the report and sort this field in ascending order. Refresh the data and run the report. If you scroll to the end of the report you will see that the last record on the report has a ship date of 1/14/2011. There are no records with a ship date of 1/15/2011 on the report.

Save the E9.6A report as E9.6B Time Problem (Correct Criteria). Use the criteria shown earlier in Figure 9-22. If you scroll to the end of the report you will see that there are nine records with the date 1/15/2011. These are the records that you were expecting to appear on the report when you created the criteria.

Save the E9.6A report as E9.6C Time criteria with a specific time. Use the criteria shown above in Figure 9-24. You will see that there are 55 records. This is what you were expecting because the time on the Ship Date criteria was 3 PM.

I don't know about you, but when I first figured this out it was somewhat scary. You do have options. You can always type in the time that you need on the second date field or you can type in the day after the last day that you want to include records for on the report. Instead of typing 1/15/2011 for the second date, you could type 1/16/2011 and let the time default to 00:00:00 AM. Doing this will produce the same result. Keep this in mind when you are creating reports on your own. In an effort to save time, when you create reports in this book that have similar selection criteria, you do not have to enter a time on the Select Expert dialog box.

Being able to enter a time is helpful for reports that are time sensitive. If you needed to create a report that displayed a list of medications that were given to patients between 8 AM and 2 PM, you would enter the times as part of the selection criteria.

Date/Time Field Update
As if all of the above time issues are not complicated enough, Crystal Reports now uses the current time as the default time instead of using 00:00:00, regardless of the data that you are using. The best advice that I can give you if you do not want to use a formula to fix this is to always type in the time that you need on all date/time fields.

If you do not mind modifying the selection criteria formula, you can add the Date function to the Date/Time field in the selection criteria. Doing this will force Crystal Reports to ignore the time portion of the field. Figure 9-25 shows the selection formula created for Figure 9-21 shown earlier. Figure 9-26 shows the same formula modified that uses the Date function. Another option is to change the default Date/Time option. [See Chapter 2, Figure 2-33]

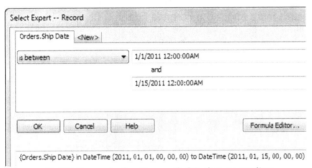

Figure 9-25 Formula for Figure 9-21 shown earlier

Figure 9-26 Modified formula for Figure 9-21 shown earlier

By now I think that you have figured out how important it is to understand how to create selection criteria to meet the requirements of the report. If the wrong criteria is created for the report, the output will not be what the user is expecting. This means that they could make decisions based on incorrect data and not know that the data is incorrect. If you aren't familiar with the data, it is a good idea to open the tables and look at the raw data.

Edit An Existing Formula

In Exercise 9.2, the criteria for the Region field is that it has to contain one of two values. If you needed to add another value you could use the Select Expert to add the value from the drop-down list or you could edit the formula that is at the bottom of the Select Expert dialog box.

If you type in the **FORMULA** field, Crystal Reports will disable the top portion of the Select Expert dialog box, as shown in Figure 9-27. Compare this to the Select Expert dialog box shown earlier in Figure 9-19, which displays criteria at the top and bottom of the dialog box.

In Figure 9-27 you do not see anything in the top portion of the dialog box.

That is because I typed "PA" in the formula field at the bottom of the dialog box.

Figure 9-27 Top half of the Select Expert dialog box disabled

The reason Crystal Reports disables the top half of the Select Expert when you create or edit a formula at the bottom of the dialog box is because the formula can't be duplicated by the options that the Select Expert has in the top section of the dialog box.

Opening The Formula Editor From The Select Expert

If you can create or edit the formula at the bottom of the Select Expert shown above in Figure 9-27, you do not have to use the Formula Editor. If you cannot remember the function or need help creating the formula, there are two ways that you can open the Formula Editor from the Select Expert, as explained below. You will learn more about the Formula Editor in Chapter 14.

① Click the **FORMULA EDITOR** button shown above in Figure 9-27.

② Open the operator drop-down list, then scroll to the bottom of the list and select the **FORMULA** option illustrated in Figure 9-28. The Select Expert will change, as illustrated in Figure 9-29 to let you create a formula.

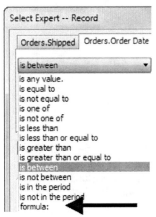

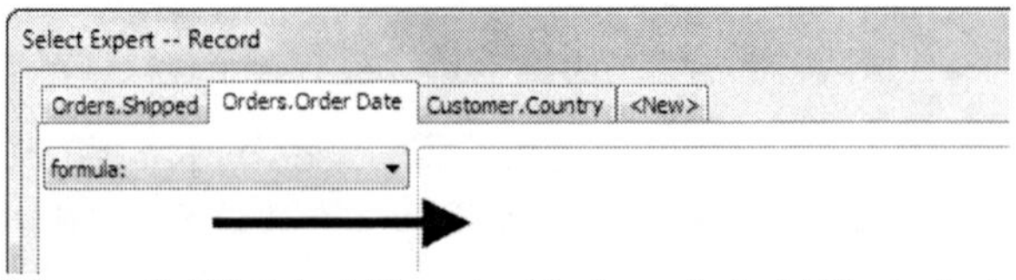

Figure 9-29 Select Expert with formula field illustrated

Figure 9-28 Formula option illustrated

Record Selection Performance Considerations

The type of database that the report is using determines the record selection process that Crystal Reports uses. Databases that are stored on a database server or desktop databases that use an ODBC connection have more performance issues than desktop databases that are local or are on a network drive, as explained below.

① If the database is on a server, Crystal Reports creates a **WHERE CLAUSE** and adds the clause to the query and sends the query to the database server. The query is run on the server and returns the records to Crystal Reports to use, to generate the report. If the database is on a server, performance improves if this record selection process is used.

② If the database is local or is a desktop database that is stored on a network drive (which is different then a database server), Crystal Reports runs the query that is created from the record selection criteria itself. Depending on the number of records, the report selection process can take some time.

Making changes to a formula created with the Select Expert via the **SHOW FORMULA** button can really slow down the record selection process if the database is on a database server, especially if the underlying tables have a lot of records.

The **USE INDEXES OR SERVER FOR SPEED** option will improve performance. If you want to use this option for the current report, it is on the Report Options dialog box. If you want this option to be the default for all reports that you will create going forward, select the option on the Database tab on the Options dialog box.

Using indexed fields will improve performance during the record selection process, especially when using tables that have a lot of records. When possible, you should use indexed fields for the record selection process because the fields index stores all of the values that are in the field, in sorted order, which makes retrieving records faster.

Case Sensitive Considerations

When Crystal Reports is installed, case insensitivity is set as the default. This means that entering "new orleans" or "New Orleans" will retrieve the same records. When creating selection criteria on text fields in Crystal Reports, keep the following in mind.

① PC and SQL databases that are connected to via an ODBC connection usually ignore case sensitivity.

② Some databases and ODBC drivers may not support case insensitivity, even though the **DATABASE SERVER IS CASE-INSENSITIVE** option is turned on.

③ If the server that the database is stored on is set to be case sensitive, you cannot override it by turning on the Database server is case-insensitive option on the Options dialog box. If you select the same option on the Report Options dialog box, you can turn the option on, only for the report that you are currently working with. If this is the case, you would have to convert the text field that you need to create the selection criteria for to all upper case and enter the criteria to support all upper case.

④ If the database is not stored on a server that is set to case sensitive and the database is set for case insensitivity, you can use the Database server is case-insensitive option to control what the selection criteria returns.

If you want the **DATABASE SERVER IS CASE-INSENSITIVE** option applied to reports that have already been created, you have to open each of the reports and select the option on the Report Options dialog box.

Using Wildcard Characters As Selection Criteria

Earlier in the chapter you learned that you could use the ? and the * as selection criteria using the "Is Like" and "Is Not Like" operators. Wildcard characters provide another way to retrieve records. Wildcards are characters that you can use to substitute all or part of the data in a field. You can also use wildcards to search for data that has a pattern. You can use these wildcard characters at the beginning or end of the search criteria.

① The question mark is used to replace one character in the data. If you entered t?n in the criteria field, the selection criteria would return records that have ten, tan, tune and ton, but not toon in the field.

② The asterisk is used to replace more than one character in the data. If you entered s*r in the criteria field, the selection criteria would return records that have star, start and sour, or any records that had the letter "s" come before the letter "r" in the field that the selection criteria is for. This wildcard character selection criteria is more flexible, but often returns a lot of results that may not be what you expect.

Document Properties

In Chapter 8 you learned about SPECIAL FIELDS and that they can be added to a report. You also learned that some of the special fields come from the Summary tab on the Document Properties dialog box.

Summary Tab Options

The information that is entered on this tab is used for identification purposes. The options on this tab are Windows file properties and are not specific to Crystal Reports. Other software packages have similar dialog boxes. For example, Microsoft Word has the Properties dialog box.

Earlier you learned that you could add a title to a report by using a text object. The content that is entered into the Title field shown in Figure 9-30, can be used as the report title.

The TEMPLATE field currently does not provide any functionality in Crystal Reports. It does not let you apply a template to the report or save the active report as a template.

If the report is based off of a template, you could enter the template name in this field so that you will know which template the report is using.

The SAVE PREVIEW PICTURE option will let you view a thumbnail size picture of the first page of the report in the Open dialog box in Crystal Reports or in Windows Explorer.

Figure 9-30 Summary tab options

Statistics Tab Options

The options shown in Figure 9-31 are **READ-ONLY**, which means that you cannot modify them.

The **REVISION NUMBER** is incremented each time the report is saved. If you are modifying a report that you did not create, the information on this tab may be helpful.

The **TOTAL EDITING TIME** field displays how long the report has been open.

Figure 9-31 Statistics tab options

Adding Summary Information To A Report

The special fields on the Document Properties dialog box can be added to a report. The report shown in Figure 9-32 has the **FILE AUTHOR** and **REPORT TITLE** special fields in the report header section.

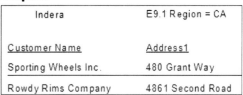

Figure 9-32 Report with summary information added

GROUPING, SORTING AND SUMMARIZING RECORDS

After completing the exercises in this chapter you will be able to use the techniques listed below to control which records appear on a report and how the records are organized.

- ☑ Group records
- ☑ Set up a user defined sort order
- ☑ Sort records
- ☑ Create summary subtotals and group totals

CHAPTER 10

Overview

Sorting rearranges the order that records will appear on the report. Grouping takes sorting one step further by displaying records that have the same value in a field or a value that is in a range of values together. After all of the records in a group print, there are often totals or some type of summary information about the records in the group. You can sort records whether or not the report has groups. In Exercise 4.1 you used a wizard to create a report that grouped the data.

Grouping Records

Grouping displays records together that meet specific criteria. Consider the following two examples:

① In the E9.2 Region = OH or FL report, at a glance it is hard to tell how many records are in OH and how many records are in FL. If the report was modified to print all of the records in the same region together, it would be easier to see how many records are in each region. This is known as grouping records.

② In the E9.6 US orders not shipped in April 2012 report, you cannot tell how many orders were not shipped on any particular day. If the records were grouped by ship date, you would be able to create a count summary field to show how many orders were not shipped by day. You could also have a total dollar amount by day, based on the Order Amount field, of orders that were not shipped.

There are three main tasks that need to be completed when records in a report need to be grouped. The three tasks are listed below and are explained in detail in this chapter.

① Select the fields to group on. [See Chapter 3, Report Design Process Step 4]

② Decide if the detail records in each group need to be sorted. [See Chapter 3, Report Design Process Step 4]

③ Decide if any fields in the details section of the report need summary information. [See Chapter 3, Report Design Process Step 2]

You learned about the group header and footer sections in Chapter 3. The name of the group is usually placed in the group header section. The summary information, which is not a requirement, is usually placed in the group footer section.

Being able to add this type of functionality to reports will make them much more useful in many cases, then the reports that were created in Chapter 9. Reports that have groups can also use the drill-down feature. In addition to creating the groups, Crystal Reports also has summary functions including statistical, averaging and totals that you can add to a report.

Records are placed together because they have the same value in a field (or fields). This is how the group header and footer sections are automatically recreated each time the value in a field the report is grouped on changes. You will not see this on the design tab. The process of creating another group each time the value changes is dynamic processing that happens behind the scenes, as they say. This is how you can create totals for a group. If you are shaking your head, after you complete the first exercise in this chapter, this should make more sense.

> **Selecting The Field To Group On**
> As you will see, you can create a group on just about any field in a table. It is best to select a field that has unique values like an ID field. Using a text field like a customer name or city field would work, but would probably produce unexpected results because there could be two or more customers that have the same name.

Selecting The Field To Group On (Continued)
In this scenario, the unexpected result would be that all customers with the same name would be grouped together. This means that the totals for the group would be incorrect because they included amounts for more than one customer. Grouping on the Customer ID field instead, would prevent this from happening.

Grouping Tips
Below are some tips that I follow to help determine if a report needs a group and if so, which fields to group on.

① Reports that retrieve hundreds or thousands of records, probably would be easier to read if there were one or two groups.
② If you need to provide a count or subtotal for a field.
③ If the report needs statistical information.

Insert Group Dialog Box

The options on the **COMMON** tab on this dialog box are used to create the groups. At a minimum, the field to group on (the first drop-down list shown in Figure 10-1) and the sort order of the group (the second drop-down list shown in Figure 10-1) have to be selected. Date and Boolean fields have an additional option that can be set. The **OPTIONS** tab is covered in detail in Chapter 16. There are two ways to open the Insert Group dialog box, as explained below.

① Click the **INSERT GROUP** button on the Insert Tools toolbar.
② Insert ⇒ Group.

In addition to using the Insert Group dialog box to create and edit groups, you can also use the Group Expert to create and edit groups.

Common Tab Options

The **GROUP BY** field is the first drop-down list. It contains all of the fields that the report can be grouped on.

This list contains the fields that are on the report and the fields in tables that are connected to with the report. You can also use formula fields as the field to group on.

Figure 10-1 Insert Group dialog box

Once a field is selected to be grouped on, it will appear under the text, **THE SECTION WILL BE PRINTED ON ANY CHANGE OF** at the bottom of the Insert Group dialog box.

Memo fields will not appear in the group by drop-down list because they cannot be used as a field to group on.

The **GROUP SORT ORDER** field is the second drop-down list. The sort order determines the order that the groups will appear in on the report. Table 10-1 explains the group sorting options. The first four options in the table are in the second drop-down list on the Insert Group dialog box.

Sorting Option	Description
In Ascending Order	Text fields are sorted in A to Z order. Numeric fields are sorted in low to high (1 to 9) order. Date fields are sorted in oldest to most recent date order. Boolean fields are sorted in False to True order.
In Descending Order	Text fields are sorted in Z to A order. Numeric fields are sorted in high to low (9 to 1) order. Date fields are sorted in most recent to oldest date order. Boolean fields are sorted in True to False order.
In Specified Order	This option is used to select the order of the groups. This is known as **CUSTOM GROUPING**. An example of a custom group would be to group customers by the amount of sales they placed last year. The option causes two tabs (Specified Order and Other) to appear on the Insert Group dialog box, as shown later in Figure 10-6.
In Original Order	Leaves the data in the order that it is retrieved from in the database. It may be me, but I don't find this option very useful.
Use A Formula As Group Sort Order	Check this option if you want to allow the person running the report to be able to sort the groups in ascending or descending order.

Table 10-1 Group sorting options explained

The **DATE/TIME** option is only available when a date, time or date/time field is selected in the Group By drop-down list. Figure 10-2 shows the options for date/time fields. The options in the drop-down list at the bottom of the dialog box are used to select the interval of time to group the records by.

The **BOOLEAN** option is only available when a Boolean field (for example a true/false or yes/no field) is selected in the group by drop-down list. The Boolean sort process does not work like the other sort options. Boolean fields sort false before true, when the ascending sort order is selected. The groups are created when the value in the Boolean field changes from yes to no, or from true to false. The exception to this is the **ON ANY CHANGE** option. Figure 10-3 shows the Boolean fields options. Table 10-2 explains the Boolean field options.

Figure 10-2 Date/Time field options

Figure 10-3 Boolean field options

Option	Description
On any change	This is the default option and will sort the values and place them next to each other.
On change to yes	Creates a new group each time a True value comes after a False value. (1)
On change to no	Creates a new group each time a False value comes after a True value. (1)
On every yes	Creates a group that always ends with a True value and includes any records in the middle that have a False value, back to the previous True value. (1)
On every no	Creates a group that always ends with a False value and includes any records in the middle that have a True value, back to the previous False value. (1)
On next is yes	Creates groups that always start with a True value and includes all records in the middle that have a False value until the next record with a True value is found. (1)
On next is no	Creates groups that always start with a False value and includes all records in the middle that have a True value until the next record with a False value is found. (1)

Table 10-2 Boolean field options explained

(1) The records are not sorted if this option is selected.

Custom Grouping

If the ascending and descending sort options are not sufficient, you can create custom groups by selecting the **IN SPECIFIED ORDER** option in the second drop-down list shown earlier in Figure 10-1. There are two custom group options available on the Insert Group dialog box: User defined sort order and user defined groups.

User Defined Sort Order

When you select the User defined sort order option, the **SPECIFIED ORDER** tab will appear on the Insert Group dialog box, as shown in Figure 10-4. The options on this tab are used to create the list of how the values in the groups will be sorted.

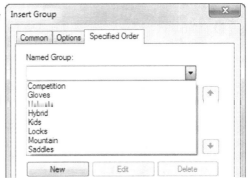

The **NAMED GROUP** drop-down list contains all of the values for the group field. Select the values in the order that you want the groups to appear in on the report, as shown at the bottom of Figure 10-5.

You can change the order of the values by clicking on the value that you want to move, then click the Up or Down arrow to the right of the list.

Figure 10-4 Specified Order tab

Once you add a value to the Named Group list, the **OTHERS** tab shown in Figure 10-6 will be available. The options on this tab are used to select what you want to happen to the group values that are not added to the Named Group list on the Specified Order tab. Table 10-3 explains the options on the Others tab.

 You do not have to order all of the group values. You can select just the ones that you need.

Figure 10-5 Values placed in a specific order

Figure 10-6 Others tab options

Option	Description
Discard all others	Causes the group values (and their detail records) that are not selected on the Specified Order tab to not be displayed on the report.
Put all others together, with the name	Is used to put all of the group values that are not selected on the Specified Order tab together under one group name that you type in the field.
Leave in their own groups	Prints all of the group values that you selected on the Specified Order tab first on the report. The remaining group values will be printed after, in ascending order.

Table 10-3 Others tab options explained

Sorting Records

Sorting records is the second task that has to be completed. Like grouping, sorting is used to rearrange the order that records appear on the report. Data can be sorted by a database field, formula or SQL Expression. Data cannot be sorted by a memo field. The data can be sorted on more than one field, including fields that are not on the report. There are two types of sorting, as explained below.

① You can sort the report as it is. The E9.1 report could be sorted by customer name. Another way to sort this report would be by postal code.

② You can sort the records within a group. After the groups for the report have been determined, you may decide that the report would be more meaningful if the detail records in the group were sorted. If you do not specify a sort order, the records in each group will print in the order that they are retrieved from the database.

The **RECORD SORT EXPERT** dialog box (shown later in Figure 10-16) is used to select the options to sort the records in the details section of the report. The Sort Fields list shows how the detail records will be sorted within the group. This expert does not sort groups. You can sort in ascending or descending order on each field.

 In addition to clicking on a field in the Available Fields list and clicking the arrow button to add it to the Sort Fields list, you can also drag fields to the Sort Fields list.

There are two ways to open the Record Sort Expert dialog box, as explained below.

① Click the **RECORD SORT EXPERT** button on the Expert Tools toolbar.

② Report ⇒ Record Sort Expert.

What I found interesting is that if you click on a group field on the Sort Fields list, all of the buttons become disabled on the dialog box. I suspect that this is because Crystal Reports is trying to protect you from changing the group order. Group field sorting is done before detail record sorting. Don't worry. If you need to change the order of the groups, you can change them on the design tab by dragging them or you can use the Group Expert.

 If you discover that the fields are in the wrong order in the Sort Fields list, click on the field that is not in the correct place, then click the Up or Down arrow button to move the field to the correct location.

Summary Information

This is the third major task that has to be completed when groups are created. One reason that groups are created is to make the report easier to read. Another reason groups are created is to provide summary information for fields in the details section of the report.

These summary calculated fields are usually placed in the group footer section of the report. Summary fields can also be placed in the group header section. Students have asked me how is it possible that summary fields that are in the group header section contain accurate totals. The answer is somewhat beyond the scope of this book, but I will answer the question because it may help you understand and allow you to use summary fields in the group header section with confidence, when needed. Crystal Reports actually builds (processes) the entire report before it is displayed or printed. This means that values for summary fields, regardless of where they are placed on the report, are calculated before the report prints. [See Chapter 4, Crystal Reports Report Processing Model]

The two types of calculations that you can perform on text (string) data is counting records in a group and determining the frequency of records in the group. These summary calculations are often also placed in the report footer section to create what is known as a grand total or report total. Summary fields have similarities of **RUNNING TOTAL** fields, which you will learn about later in this book. Summary fields that are in the report header or footer section are not dependant on groups.

You can create summary calculation fields in the report header and footer if the report does not have any groups. Summary fields in the report header and footer contain totals for all records on the report. Often you will find that group summary data is more useful then grand total summary data. Instead of having to manually count the number of orders on a report that each customer placed, a calculated field can be added to the report that would count the number of orders. Each summary field has to be created separately.

 To create a group summary field, the report must have at least one group. If you select the option to create a summary field and the report does not have a group, you will be prompted to create a group. If you place the same summary field in different sections of the report, it will produce different total amounts, which is what should happen.

There are three ways to open the Insert Summary dialog box shown in Figure 10-7 **AFTER** you have selected the field that you need to create a summary calculation field for, as explained below.

If the field that you need to create a summary calculation for is not on the report, you have to select option two or three below.

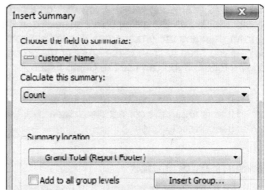

Figure 10-7 Insert Summary dialog box

① Right-click and select Insert Summary.
② Click the **INSERT SUMMARY** button on the Insert Tools toolbar.
③ Insert ⇒ Summary.

There are two types of summary calculations that you can create, as explained below.

① The **STRING** field summary calculation options are explained in Table 10-4. String fields can only create the calculations in Table 10-4.
② The **NUMERIC** field summary calculation options are explained in Table 10-5. They can also be used with currency fields. Numeric fields can also create the calculations in Table 10-4.

String Summary Calculation Options	
Calculation	**Description**
Count	Counts the detail records. By default, if the field that is being used to count on is **NULL**, it will not be included in the count. Select the **CONVERT DATABASE TO NULL VALUES TO DEFAULT** option on the Report Options dialog box if you need null values counted. Duplicate values in the field will also be counted. This may not be what you want.
Distinct Count	Counts all of the unique values in the field.
Maximum	Finds the highest value in the field.
Minimum	Finds the lowest value in the field.
Mode	Finds the most frequently used value in the field.
N^{th} Largest, N is:	Is used to select a number and calculate the Nth largest value in the selected field in the group. An example would be if you wanted to find out what the third largest (N^{th} largest) order amount (N) is in the group. (2)
N^{th} Most Frequent, N is:	Is used to select a number and calculate the Nth most frequently occurring value in the selected field. An example would be if you wanted to find out which product was ordered the most in the group, you would enter a 1 in this field. This is similar to the Mode function, but it is not limited to the frequent occurrences. (2)
N^{th} Smallest, N is:	Is used to select a number and calculate the Nth smallest occurring value. An example would be if you wanted to find out what the fifth (N^{th} smallest) smallest order amount (N) is in the group. You would enter a 5 in this field. (2)

Table 10-4 String summary calculation options explained

(2) When this option is selected, the **N IS** field illustrated in Figure 10-8 is displayed. N is the value that you type in.

Numeric Summary Calculation Options	
Calculation	**Description**
Average	Finds the average value of all of the values in the field.
Correlation With	Finds the relationship between the selected field and another field in the database or on the report. (3)
Covariance With	Finds the difference (often called the variance) between the selected field and another field in the database or on the report. (3)
Median	Finds the middle value of all the values in the field.
Mode	Finds the most frequently used value in the field.
P^{th} percentile, P is:	Is used to select a percent (the P is a value) between 0 and 100 and calculates that percentile of the values in the field.
Population Standard Deviation	Calculates how far from the mean (the average) each value in the selected field deviates.
Population Variance	Divides the sum of the number of items in the population. The result is the population variance.
Sample Standard Deviation	Calculates the mean (the average) value for the data in the sample.
Sample Variance	Calculates the square root of the standard deviation of the sample.
Sum	Adds the values in the selected field to get a total.
Weighted Average With	Calculates the average by the number of times the value is in the selected field. You can also adjust the average by selecting another field. (3)

Table 10-5 Numeric summary calculation options explained

(3) This summary type requires two fields. One that is used as the basis of the summary (this is the field that you select at the top of the Insert Summary dialog box). The other field is used for comparison. When this summary type is selected, the drop-down list illustrated in Figure 10-9 is displayed. This is where you select the second field that is discussed above.

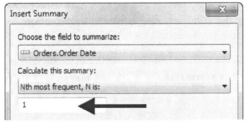

Figure 10-8 N is field illustrated

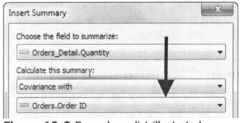

Figure 10-9 Drop-down list illustrated

 Date and Boolean fields can only use the following types of calculations: Count, distinct count, maximum, minimum, mode, N^{th} largest, N^{th} most frequent and N^{th} smallest.

In addition to the summary options that you read about in Tables 10-4 and 10-5, the summary options in Table 10-6 are also available. They are located at the bottom of the Insert Summary dialog box.

Option	Description
Summary Location	This option is used to select the section of the report where you want to place the summary field. The good thing is that you are not limited to the options in the drop-down list. You can manually copy or move the summary field to another section of the report.
Add to all group levels	This option will add the summary field to all existing groups on the report. This means that you do not have to create the same summary field manually for every group section that needs the same summary field.
Show as a percentage of	Calculates a comparison of the percent of one group that is part of a larger group. This option is used to select the group or total that you want the comparison to be based on. For example, this option can calculate the percent of sales for June compared to the sales for the entire year. The result would display what percent (out of 100%) the sales in June accounted for, compared to the sales for the entire year. This option is not available for all types of calculations. (4)
Summarize across hierarchy	On reports that have hierarchical groups (parent/child relationships), an identical summary field will be added to all subgroups under the primary hierarchical group. An example of a hierarchical group report would be one that displays a list of department managers (the parent group) and the employees (the child group) that are in each department.

Table 10-6 Summary options explained

(4) | Percentage summaries cannot be placed in the report footer section. |

If all of the summary calculation options seem a little confusing right now don't worry, you will only see options in the drop-down list that are available for the field type that you select to create the calculation for.

 Headings are not automatically created for group summary fields like they are for fields in the details section. By default, summary fields are usually placed in a section below the field that it is summarizing. The exception would be if the summary field is placed in the group header section.

 Creating Titles
Some exercises in this chapter will have you create a title for the report or a title for a field. When you see the phrase "Create a title", that means to add a text object to the report and type in the specified text. Report titles should be placed in the page header section unless stated otherwise. They should also be centered across the report.

Creating Groups

The reports that you modify in this chapter show you how to apply a variety of group and sorting options effectively. The name of each exercise describes how the data will be grouped. You will also learn more formatting techniques. As you will see, the more data that you add to a report, the more the report needs to be formatted.

Exercise 10.1: Group Customer Information By Region

In this exercise you will modify a report to include the following group and sorting options. These options are also used to create totals for the group.

- ① Group the data by the region field and sort the group in ascending order.
- ② Sort the detail records in each group in ascending order by the Postal Code field.
- ③ Create a count of detail records in each group.

1. Save the E7.9 report as E10.1 Customer info by region.

2. Change the line under the fields in the details section to the dotted style.

3. Open the Insert Group dialog box. Open the first drop-down list and select the **REGION** field from the Customer table, then click OK.

Notice that a **GROUP HEADER** and **GROUP FOOTER** section was added to the report, as illustrated in Figure 10-10.

If you also wanted to group this report on a second field you would see a second set of group header and footer sections, as illustrated in Figure 10-11.

Figure 10-10 Group header and footer sections added to the report

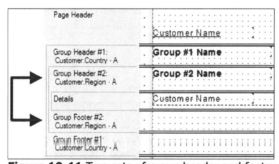

Figure 10-11 Two sets of group header and footer sections

 If you cannot see the entire group name on the left side of the design tab, as shown above in Figure 10-11, you can drag the section bar below the group section down until you can see the full name. Keep in mind that doing this will cause additional space to be added to that section of the report when you preview or print it. A better solution would be to turn on the **SHORT SECTION NAMES** option, by following the steps below.

How To Turn The Short Section Names Option On

1. Right-click in the **REPORT HEADER SECTION** on the design tab. You will see the shortcut menu shown in Figure 10-12. Select the option **SHOW SHORT SECTION NAMES**. The report section should look like the one shown in Figure 10-13.

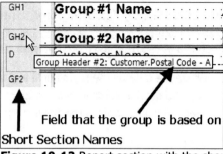

Figure 10-13 Report section with the short section names option turned on

Figure 10-12 Report section shortcut menu

 The **FIT SECTION** option shown above in Figure 10-12 is used to remove blank space in a section of the report. Selecting this option on the group header 1 section shown above in Figure 10-13 will cause the blank space below the group 1 name text object to be removed, so that the section looks like the group 2 section.

 If you hold the mouse pointer over the **GROUP SECTION NAME**, as illustrated above on the right, in Figure 10-13, you will be able to see which field the group is based on and the order that the group is sorted in.

2. Save the changes. The report should look like the one shown in Figure 10-14.

Customer Name	Address1	Region	Country	Postal Code
Abu Dhabi				
UAE Cycle	Post Box: 278	Abu Dhabi	United Arab Emirates	3453
AL				
Psycho-Cycle	8287 Scott Road	AL	USA	35818
The Great Bike Shop	1922 Beach Crescent	AL	USA	35857
Benny - The Spokes Person	1020 Oak Way	AL	USA	35861

Figure 10-14 Customer information grouped by region

Notice that the group name is bold on the report. This makes it easier to know where each group starts. If you look in the group tree section on the left of Figure 10-14 above, you will see all of the groups that the report has. If you scroll down the list of groups and click on the **PA** group, that section of the report will be displayed, as illustrated in Figure 10-15.

OR				
Whistler Rentals	4501 Third Street	OR	USA	97051
Rad Bikes	8217 Prince Edward Place	OR	USA	97068
PA				
Clean Air Transportation Co.	1867 Thurlow Lane	PA	USA	19453
Insane Cycle	5198 Argus Place	PA	USA	19442
Backpedal Cycle Shop	743 Three Rivers Way	PA	USA	19178

Figure 10-15 Customers in the PA region illustrated

By default, group name fields are added to the group header section of the report. If at some point you decide that you do not want the group name to automatically be added to the group header section, you can turn the **INSERT GROUP NAME WITH GROUP** option off on the Layout tab on the Options dialog box. If you turn this option off and then need to add a group name to a specific report, you can, without turning this option back on.

Sort The Detail Records

As you can see in Figure 10-14 shown earlier, the detail records in each group are not sorted on any field. Unless you specify a sort order, the detail records will appear in the report based on the order that they are retrieved from the database. In this part of the exercise you will sort the detail records by the Postal Code field (the Zip Code).

1. Open the Record Sort Expert dialog box. Click on the Postal Code field in the **AVAILABLE FIELDS** list, then click the **>** button. Select the **ASCENDING** sort order if it is not already selected. Figure 10-16 shows the sort options that you should have selected. Click OK.

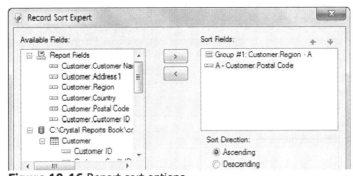

Figure 10-16 Report sort options

Notice that the group information for the report is the first entry in the **SORT FIELDS** list of the Record Sort Expert dialog box shown above in Figure 10-16. This is done to outline the sort order for the entire report. The first way that the report will be sorted is by group. Remember that the group is sorted in ascending order, which is denoted by the **A** at the end of the group field. If the field was sorted in descending order, you would see a **D** at the end of the field.

 If you need to sort a report by a persons name and the name is in two fields, you should sort on the last name field first and then sort on the first name field.

The detail records in each group will be sorted in ascending order by the Postal Code field. If you wanted to sort on other fields you can do that also, as shown in Figure 10-17.

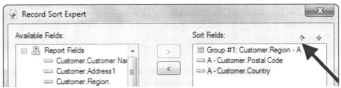

Figure 10-17 Second field in group to sort on

In this example, adding the Country field means that within each group, the detail records would be sorted by Postal Code first and then within each Postal Code in the group, the records would be sorted by Country. In reality, these sort options would produce strange results. It is shown here for illustration purposes only. A better way to sort on these two fields would be to sort on the Country field first because there are several Postal Codes within each Country.

Grouping, Sorting And Summarizing Records

If you wanted to sort on the Country field first you would click on the Country field and then click the **UP** arrow, as illustrated above in Figure 10-17. This would move the Country field up, as shown in Figure 10-18.

Figure 10-18 Sort order of the detail records changed

 More Sorting Options
In addition to being able to sort the detail records on fields in a table, detail records can be sorted on formula fields.

2. Save the changes. If prompted, click **YES** to generate (refresh) the data for the report. Preview the report. Go to the PA group. You should see the records shown in Figure 10-19. Notice the different order of the detail records in this version of the report compared to the order of the detail records in the report shown earlier in Figure 10-15. Leave the report open to complete the next part of the exercise.

PA					
Tek Bikes	8018 Meacon Crescent	PA	USA		19144
Backpedal Cycle Shop	743 Three Rivers Way	PA	USA		19178
Rocky Roadsters	1430 Hastings Boulevard	PA	USA		19440
Insane Cycle	5198 Argus Place	PA	USA		19442
Clean Air Transportation Co.	1867 Thurlow Lane	PA	USA		19453

Figure 10-19 Report with detail record sort order added

Count Summary Field Overview

Creating summary fields is the third step in the grouping and sorting process. In this part of the exercise you will create a summary field that will count the number of detail records in each group.

Create The Count Summary Field

1. On the Insert Summary dialog box open the first drop-down list and select the Customer ID field.

2. Open the second drop-down list and select **COUNT**. You should see all of the options that were explained earlier in Tables 10-4 and 10-5 for the Customer ID field because it is a numeric field.

 Notice that you can create a group from this dialog box. If you click the **INSERT GROUP** button, you will see the Insert Group dialog box that you saw earlier in Figure 10-1.

3. Open the **SUMMARY LOCATION** drop-down list and select the Group 1 option.
Figure 10-20 shows the summary options that should be selected.
Click OK. The summary field should be in the group footer section.
Save the changes. The report should look like the one shown in Figure 10-21. The number in bold below the dotted lines is the count field that you just created.

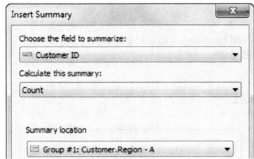

Figure 10-20 Summary options

Customer Name	Address1	Region	Country	Postal Code
Abu Dhabi				
UAE Cycle	Post Box: 278	Abu Dhabi	United Arab Emirates	3453
1				
AL				
Psycho-Cycle	8287 Scott Road	AL	USA	35818
The Great Bike Shop	1922 Beach Crescent	AL	USA	35857
Benny - The Spokes Person	1020 Oak Way	AL	USA	35861
3				

Figure 10-21 Report with the summary field added

 When used with detail level fields, summary functions like Average and Count will not include records when the detail level field is null because null fields do not contain anything, which is different then an empty string or a zero.

For example, if you were creating a summary field that counts on the city field and some records did not have any data in the city field and the database was set to use **NULL VALUES**, records that fall into this category would print on the report, but would not be included in the count summary calculation.

Often, this may not be what you want to happen. If this is the case, checking the **CONVERT DATABASE NULL VALUES TO DEFAULT** option on the Report Options dialog box will convert the null values in the database (if the database supports null values) to an empty string for string fields or zero for numeric fields. Selecting this option will include records in the count or average summary calculation. If you want this to be the default option for all reports, check the same option on the Reporting tab on the Options dialog box.

Modify The Report

The report would look better if the following changes were made.

① Add a report title and page number.
② Change the Postal Code heading to Zip Code.
③ Change the Address1 heading to Address.
④ Delete the Region field from the details section of the report. The field is not needed in this section because it is the field that the report is grouped on.
⑤ Create a title for the summary field that you created.
⑥ Create a grand total for the number of customers that are displayed on the report. Place this field in the report footer section.
⑦ Rearrange the fields in the details section so that the report is easier to read.

Add A Report Title And Page Number

1. Make the page header section longer, so that you will have room to add the report titles. Move all of the headings in the page header section down.

2. Create a report title and type `Customer Information Grouped By Region` in the object. Make the font size 16 and make the title bold.

3. Create a second report title and type `Sorted By Zip Code` in the object. Change the font size to 14 and make the title bold.

4. Center both of these titles across the page.

5. Add the Page N of M special field above and to the right of the Postal Code field. Right align the Page Number field.

Change The Field Headings And Delete Fields

1. Change the Address1 heading to `Address`, then change the Postal Code heading to `Zip Code`.

2. Delete the Region field.

3. Move the Address field over to the right, then make the Customer Name field wider.

Create A Title For The Summary Field

1. Create a title for the summary field in the group footer section and type `Total # of customers in region -` in the object. Right align the title.

2. Move the summary field over and place the field title that you just created before it, then remove the bold from the summary field and left align the field.

3. Make the group footer section a little longer so that there will be more blank space on the report before the next group prints.

Create A Grand Total Summary Field

Grand totals are also known as **RUNNING TOTALS** because they keep a total for all of the detail records that are on the report. Earlier in this chapter you learned how to create group summary totals, which are also known as **SUBTOTALS**. The difference between a group summary total and a running total is that a running total field cannot be summarized.

Another difference between group summary total fields and running total fields is that group summary total fields are automatically reset to zero each time a new group is started, as shown above in Figure 10-21. Running Total fields have the option of being reset to zero.

Grand or running total fields that are placed in the report footer section include all of the records in the report, regardless of which group the detail records are in. Earlier in this chapter, I stated that depending on the section of the report that the summary field is placed in, you will get different results. The summary field that you will copy to the report footer section in this part of the exercise will demonstrate this.

1. Right-click on the summary field in the group footer section and select **COPY**.

2. Right-click in the report and select **PASTE**, then click in the report footer section where you want to place the field.

3. Create a title in the report footer section and type
   `Grand Total # of customers on this report` – in the object.
   Place this title at the two inch mark, then move the grand total field to the right of the title.

> You could create another summary field by using the Insert Summary dialog box, just like the one you created for the group footer section and place it in the report footer section. I find it easier to copy the field and place the second field in the section that I need it in. You can also create a summary field by right-clicking on the field in the details section and selecting Insert ⇒ Summary or Insert ⇒ Running Total.

Rearrange The Fields

1. Move the fields in the details section to the right so that the Customer Name field starts at the half inch mark.

2. The report layout should look like the one shown in Figure 10-22. Save the changes.
   The first page of the report should look like the one shown in Figure 10-23.
   The last page of the report should look like the one shown in Figure 10-24.

The total number of pages in the report depends on the spacing that you have in each section of the report. Adjust the spacing if necessary, so that it is readable.

Customer Information Grouped By Region
Sorted By Zip Code

Page N of M

Customer Name	Address	Country	Zip Code
Group #1 Name			
Customer Name	Address1	Country	Postal Code
Total # of customers in region -	Count of (		
Grand Total # of customers on this report - Count of (			

Figure 10-22 Report layout

Customer Information Grouped By Region
Sorted By Zip Code

Page 1 of 17

Customer Name	Address	Country	Zip Code
Abu Dhabi			
UAE Cycle	Post Box: 278	United Arab Emirates	3453
Total # of customers in region - 1			
AL			
Psycho-Cycle	8287 Scott Road	USA	35818
The Great Bike Shop	1922 Beach Crescent	USA	35857
Benny - The Spokes Person	1020 Oak Way	USA	35861
Total # of customers in region - 3			

Figure 10-23 First page of the Customer info by region report

		Page 17 of 17

Customer Name	Address	Country	Zip Code
Blazing Saddles	4755 Seventieth Street	USA	53226
Rough Terrain	1502 Nelson Way	USA	53730
Pedals Inc.	8922 Field Street	USA	53795
Trail Blazer's Place	6938 Beach Street	USA	53795
Total # of customers in region - 4			
WV			
Two Wheelin'	5007 White Street	USA	25309
Total # of customers in region - 1			
	Grand Total # of customers on this report - 269		

Figure 10-24 Last page of the Customer info by region report

3. If you open the Field Explorer and click on the plus sign in front of the **GROUP NAME FIELDS** option, you will see the Region group that you created, as illustrated in Figure 10-25.

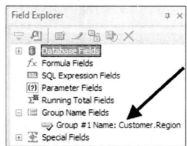

Figure 10-25 Group Name Fields section of the Field Explorer illustrated

You can drag the group name object from the **GROUP NAME FIELDS** section of the Field Explorer on to the report. If you prefer to keep the data in the group header or footer section visible, but not display it on the report, you can suppress the section.

 A group name field cannot be created in the Field Explorer like formula, parameter and running total fields can.

Exercise 10.2: Group Orders By Customer

In this exercise you will modify a report to include the following group and sorting options.

① Group on the Customer Name field and sort the group in ascending order.
② Sort the detail records in each group in ascending order by Order Date.
③ Create a count of detail records for each customer in each group.
④ Create a total amount per customer based on the order amount field. This will let the person reading the report know the total amount of the orders placed by each customer.

These options will create counts and totals for the group. The changes that you will make to the report will place all of the orders for each customer together. This will make the report more effective because you will be able to see all of a customers orders in one place.

In Exercise 10.1 you created a group based on a field that was not being printed on the report. Groups are often created on fields that are printed on the report, but it is not a requirement.

1. Save the E9.4 report as `E10.2 Orders grouped by customer`.

2. Change the Order Date selection criteria to 6/24/2011.

3. On the Insert Group dialog box, open the first drop-down list and select the **CUSTOMER NAME** field, if it is not already selected. Click OK. The report should look like the one shown in Figure 10-26.

Customer Name	Order Date	Ship Date	Order Amount	Order ID	Unit Price
Alley Cat Cycles					
Alley Cat Cycles	9/28/2011 12:00:00AM	9/30/2011 12:00:00AM	$2,559.63	2,157	$539.85
Alley Cat Cycles	9/28/2011 12:00:00AM	9/30/2011 12:00:00AM	$2,559.63	2,157	$313.36
Alley Cat Cycles	10/27/2011 12:00:00AM	11/6/2011 12:00:00AM	$2,699.55	2,272	$899.85
Alley Cat Cycles	1/31/2012 12:00:00AM	2/3/2012 12:00:00AM	$9,290.30	2,664	$2,792.86
Alley Cat Cycles	1/31/2012 12:00:00AM	2/3/2012 12:00:00AM	$9,290.30	2,664	$455.86
Alley Cat Cycles	2/19/2012 12:00:00AM	2/22/2012 12:00:00AM	$8,819.55	2,735	$2,939.85
Alley Cat Cycles	2/19/2012 12:00:00AM	2/22/2012 12:00:00AM	$8,819.55	2,735	$2,939.85
Backpedal Cycle Shop					
Backpedal Cycle Shop	7/2/2011 12:00:00AM	7/4/2011 12:00:00AM	$3,479.70	1,802	$1,739.85

Figure 10-26 Orders grouped by customer

Sort The Detail Records

As you can see in Figure 10-26 above, the report is now grouped by customer. The detail records in each group are not sorted. Because orders are entered into the database in the order that they are received, they are often already in date order. There are exceptions to this, including orders that may get changed some how during the ordering process.

Other exceptions that have to be accounted for include how the tables are linked and how the database sends the records to Crystal Reports. To be on the safe side, it is best to control the sort order. In this exercise that means that you should sort the records by the Order Date field to ensure that they are in date order, if that is a requirement for the report.

1. On the Record Sort Expert dialog box add the Order Date field to the Sort Fields list.

2. Select the Ascending sort order option, if it is not already selected. Figure 10-27 shows the sort options that should be selected. Click OK, then save the changes.

Figure 10-27 Sort options

Total Summary Fields Overview

In this part of the exercise you will create a summary field that will create a total dollar amount of orders for each customer. You will also create a count to show the number of orders for each customer.

 The default summary type is **SUM** for numeric fields.
The default summary type is **MAXIMUM** for Boolean, date and string fields.

Create The Total Summary Field

This summary field will create a total dollar amount of orders for each customer.

1. On the Insert Summary dialog box, open the first drop-down list and select the Order Amount field, then open the second drop-down list and select **SUM**.

2. Open the Summary Location drop-down list and select the Group 1 option. Click OK. The order amount summary field should be in the group footer section.

Create The Count Summary Field

This summary field will create a count of the number of orders for each customer.

1. On the Insert Summary dialog box, open the first drop-down list and select the Order ID field, then open the second drop-down list and select **COUNT**.

2. Open the Summary Location drop-down list and select the Group 1 option. Click OK. The count summary field should be in the group footer section.

Create The Distinct Count Summary Field

The distinct count summary will only count the information in a field once. If there are 20 orders for one customer, the distinct count calculation will only count that customer once. This will let you create a count for the total number of customers that are on the report.

1. On the Insert Summary dialog box, open the first drop-down list and select the Customer Name field if it is not already selected, then open the second drop-down list and select **DISTINCT COUNT**. Notice that the only options that are available for this text field are the ones explained earlier in Table 10-4.

2. Open the Summary Location drop-down list and select the **GRAND TOTAL (REPORT FOOTER)** option if it is not already selected. The distinct count only needs to appear once, at the end of the report.

   Figure 10-28 shows the summary options that should be selected.

   Click OK.

   The distinct count summary field should be in the report footer section.

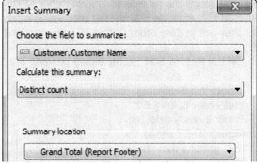

Figure 10-28 Distinct count summary options

3. Save the changes and refresh the data. The report should look like the one shown in Figure 10-29. As you can see, the report needs a little work.

Customer Name	Order Date	Ship Date	Order Amount	Order ID	Unit Price
Alley Cat Cycles					
Alley Cat Cycles	9/28/2011 12:00:00AM	9/30/2011 12:00:00AM	$2,559.63	2,157	$539.85
Alley Cat Cycles	9/28/2011 12:00:00AM	9/30/2011 12:00:00AM	$2,559.63	2,157	$313.36
Alley Cat Cycles	10/27/2011 12:00:00AM	11/6/2011 12:00:00AM	$2,699.55	2,272	$899.85
Alley Cat Cycles	1/31/2012 12:00:00AM	2/3/2012 12:00:00AM	$9,290.30	2,664	$2,792.86
Alley Cat Cycles	1/31/2012 12:00:00AM	2/3/2012 12:00:00AM	$9,290.30	2,664	$455.86
Alley Cat Cycles	2/19/2012 12:00:00AM	2/22/2012 12:00:00AM	$8,819.55	2,735	$2,939.85
Alley Cat Cycles	2/19/2012 12:00:00AM	2/22/2012 12:00:00AM	$8,819.55	2,735	$2,939.85
			$44,038.51	7	
Backpedal Cycle Shop					
Backpedal Cycle Shop	7/2/2011 12:00:00AM	7/4/2011 12:00:00AM	$3,479.70	1,802	$1,739.85

Figure 10-29 Orders grouped by customer report

If you view the last page of the report, you will see the number 102. This is the distinct count summary field that you just created, which displays how many customers are on the report. In the next part of this exercise you will create a title for this field.

Modify The Report

The report would look better if the following changes were made.

    ① Add a report title to the page header section.
    ② Create titles for the summary fields.
    ③ Create a grand total field for the order amount and a grand total count of order summary fields.
    ④ Remove the time from the Order Date and Ship Date fields.
    ⑤ Add a line above all of the summary fields.
    ⑥ Rearrange the fields in the details section so that the report is easier to read.

1.   Create a report title and type `Customer Orders` in the object. Change the font size to 16 and make the title bold. Center the title across the page.

 If a report has selection criteria, it is a good idea to incorporate the selection criteria in the report. Doing this lets the reader know what criteria the report is using. This report will print records for orders that were placed after a specific date and have a specific minimum order amount. How, or if you incorporate this information is up to you and the requestors of the report. Keep in mind that business decisions are based off of the data in reports, so providing as much helpful and useful information on the report as possible, is a good thing.

2.   Copy both of the summary fields in the group footer section and paste them in the report footer section.

 If you select all of the fields that you want to copy before you select the **COPY** command, you can copy all of the fields at the same time.

3.   Create the field titles in Table 10-7 for the summary fields. Make the titles bold. The middle column in the table is the section in the report where the title should be placed.

Summary Field	Section	Title
Order Amount	Group Footer	Total $ amount of orders -
Order ID	Group Footer	Total # of orders -
Customer Name	Report Footer	Total # of customers on this report -
Order Amount	Report Footer	Grand Total $ amount of all orders -
Order ID	Report Footer	Grand Total # of orders -

Table 10-7 Field titles for Exercise 10.2

 If I know that the report needs several field titles with the same formatting, I create one title field then copy it and just change the text. For me, this is quicker then using the Format Painter. Over time, you will find a process that works best for you.

I usually right align titles for calculated fields, when the title is placed to the left of the calculated field. Doing this reduces the amount of white space between the title and the calculated field. When I do this, I also left align the calculated field to further reduce the space between the field and the title. The other option is to drag the calculated field into the text object.

4. Remove the time from the Order Date and Ship Date fields. Delete the Customer Name field in the details section, then remove the bold from the Group Name field.

 Group Name objects can be formatted like any other object in the report.

5. Change the Order ID heading to `Order #`, then format the Order ID and Order ID count summary fields to display as a whole number without a comma.

6. Add a line at the bottom of the group footer section. Change the size of the line to 0.5 pt. Save the changes and leave the report open to complete the next part of the exercise.

Add A Line Above The Summary Fields

1. If necessary, move the summary fields in the group footer section down so that you have room to add the line above the fields.

2. Right-click on the Order Amount summary field in the group footer section and select **FORMAT FIELD**. On the Border tab, open the **TOP** drop-down list, select **SINGLE**, then click OK.

 The advantage of using the line option on the Border tab for a field is that if you move or resize the field, the line is automatically re-adjusted. You can also use the **LINE** tool to draw a line. If you use the Line tool and you move or resize the field, you will also have to move or resize the line.

3. Rearrange the fields so that they look like the layout shown in Figure 10-30.

Page Header						
			Customer Orders			
	Order Date	Ship Date	Order Amount	Order #	Unit Price	
Group Header #1	Group #1 Name					
Details	Order Date	Ship Date	Order Amount	Order ID	Unit Price	
Group Footer #1. Customer.Customer Name -	Total # of orders - Count of (		Total $ amount of orders - Sum of Order			
Report Footer	Total # of customers on this report - DistinctCount of Custo					
	Grand Total # of orders - Count of (					
	Grand Total $ amount of all orders - Sum of Orders.Order Am					

Figure 10-30 Report layout

4. Save the changes. The first page of the report should look like the one shown in Figure 10-31. The report footer section on the last page should look like the one shown in Figure 10-32.

 If you see **###'s** in a field on the report, make the field wider.

Notice that there are multiple line items for some order numbers. That is because there is more than one item on the order. Also notice that the order amount for these orders is repeated. This means that the totals for the Alley Cat customer for example, is incorrect because the number of orders and total amount of orders fields are being incremented when they should not be.
In Chapter 22, you will learn how to fix this by using a Running Total field.

Customer Orders

	Order Date	Ship Date	Order Amount	Order #	Unit Price
Alley Cat Cycles					
	09/28/2011	09/30/2011	$2,559.63	2157	$313.36
	09/28/2011	09/30/2011	$2,559.63	2157	$539.85
	10/27/2011	11/06/2011	$2,699.55	2272	$899.85
	01/31/2012	02/03/2012	$9,290.30	2664	$455.86
	01/31/2012	02/03/2012	$9,290.30	2664	$2,792.86
	02/19/2012	02/22/2012	$8,819.55	2735	$2,939.85
	02/19/2012	02/22/2012	$8,819.55	2735	$2,939.85
Total # of orders - 7		Total $ amount of orders -	$ 44,038.51		

Figure 10-31 First page of the Orders grouped by customer report

Total # of customers on this report - 78

Grand Total # of orders - 724

Grand Total $ amount of all orders - $ 4,015,868.71

Figure 10-32 Last page of the Orders grouped by customer report

5.   Make any changes that are needed.

Displaying The Record Selection Formula Field

In Chapter 8 you read that this special field can be added to a report to display the selection criteria for the report. Figure 10-33 shows the E9.6 report with the Record Selection Formula special field added to the report header section. Notice that this report displays multiple selection criteria.

Record Selection Formula	{Customer.Country} = "USA" and not {Orders.Shipped} and {Orders.Order Date} in DateTime (2012, 04, 01, 00, 00, 00) to DateTime (2012, 04, 30, 00, 00, 00)			
Customer Name	Country	Order Date	Order Amount	Shipped
City Cyclists	USA	04/29/2012	$63.90	False
Pathfinders	USA	04/26/2012	$3,185.42	False

Figure 10-33 E9.6 report with the Record Selection Formula special field displaying multiple criteria

CREATING CUSTOM GROUPS

Overview

After completing the exercises in this chapter you will be able to perform the following tasks:

- ☑ Create percent calculations
- ☑ Create a custom group name
- ☑ Set up user defined groups
- ☑ Use the Group Expert

CHAPTER 11

Overview

In the previous chapter you learned how to create basic groups. While the group functionality that you learned about will handle a large percent of your grouping needs, there will be times when you need to modify something about the group.

When you find that you cannot quite figure out how to use the group options that you learned about in the previous chapter to create the groups that you need, you can create what I call custom groups. That is the focus of this chapter.

Exercise 11.1: Change The Group Order

The Chapter 11 Group orders by shipping method report shown in Figure 11-1 is grouped on two fields: Ship Via and Customer Name. You will use this report to demonstrate how changing the order of groups changes how the same data is displayed. If after viewing the report you decide that the groups should be in the opposite order, meaning that the first group should be the Customer Name, follow the steps below.

Orders By Shipping Method

	Order #	Order Date	Order Amount		Salesperson
FedEx					
Alley Cat Cycles					
	2207	10/11/2011	$72.00	Janet	Leverling
	2301	10/31/2011	$1,664.70	Michael	Suyama
	2361	11/17/2011	$389.65	Robert	King
	Total # orders for customer - 3		Total order amount for customer - $ 2,126.35		
Backpedal Cycle Shop					
	1311	02/19/2011	$6,233.05	Robert	King
	1802	07/02/2011	$3,479.70	Anne	Dodsworth
	2198	10/08/2011	$93.50	Janet	Leverling
	Total # orders for customer - 3		Total order amount for customer - $ 9,806.25		

Figure 11-1 Chapter 11 Group orders by shipping method report

1. Save the Chapter 11 Group orders by shipping method report as `E11.1 Change group order`.

2. Open the Group Expert. Click on the Ship Via group on the right, then click the down arrow button. Click OK.

Notice that Group Header 1 is now grouped on the Customer Name field. This is now the first field that the report will be grouped on, as shown in Figure 11-2. If you look at the last page of the Chapter 11 Group orders by shipping method report, you will see that the report grand totals are the same as the ones on the E11.1 report, but in the E11.1 report, the totals for the shipping method are per customer.

Figure 11-2 First page of the Change group order report

If you open the Alley Cat Cycles group in the group tree, you will see options for different types of shipping methods, as shown in Figure 11-3. This means that this company has deliveries from each of these shipping methods. You will see totals for each shipping company if you click on it in the group tree.

Figure 11-3 Shipping method options for a group

Figure 11-4 shows the grand total of UPS shipments for the Alley Cat Cycles company.

Figure 11-4 Totals for the UPS shipping method for one company

3. Save the changes.

Custom Group Names

So far, the group names used in the reports have come from a field that the report is grouped on. In Crystal Reports there are options that are used to customize the group name, as explained below.

① Use a different field as the group name.
② Create a custom group name.
③ Create a user defined group name.
④ Create a formula to display the group name.

Use A Different Field As The Group Name

The custom group name option allows you to use one field to create the group and a different field to display as the group name. In Exercise 10.2, the report is grouped on the customer name.
[See Chapter 10, Figure 10-31]

If that report was grouped on the Customer ID field instead, the group name would be displayed, as shown in Figure 11-5.

If you selected the options shown in Figure 11-6 on the Options tab for the Customer ID group field, the report would look like the one shown in Figure 11-7.

	Order Date	Ship Date	Order Amount	Order #	Unit Price
1					
	09/01/2011	09/02/2011	$4,078.95	2054	$329.85
	09/01/2011	09/02/2011	$4,078.95	2054	$539.85
	09/01/2011	09/02/2011	$4,078.95	2054	$899.85
	01/26/2012	01/26/2012	$2,939.85	2640	$2,939.85
	04/09/2012	04/16/2012	$5,549.40	2900	$329.85
	04/09/2012	04/16/2012	$5,549.40	2900	$1,739.85
2					
	07/21/2011	07/27/2011	$3,526.70	1883	$1,739.85
	07/21/2011	07/27/2011	$3,526.70	1883	$23.50
	08/06/2011	08/14/2011	$5,879.70	1941	$2,939.85
	10/19/2011	10/19/2011	$8,819.55	2242	$2,939.85
	04/26/2012	05/01/2012	$3,185.42	2969	$726.61
	04/26/2012	05/01/2012	$3,185.42	2969	$899.85
	04/26/2012	05/01/2012	$3,185.42	2969	$832.35
3					
	09/16/2011	09/24/2011	$5,545.42	2112	$14.50
	09/16/2011	09/24/2011	$5,545.42	2112	$296.87
	09/16/2011	09/24/2011	$5,545.42	2112	$1,739.85

Figure 11-5 Report grouped by the Customer ID field

Figure 11-6 Options to use a different field as the group name

	Order Date	Ship Date	Order Amount	Order #	Unit Price
City Cyclists					
	09/01/2011	09/02/2011	$4,078.95	2054	$329.85
	09/01/2011	09/02/2011	$4,078.95	2054	$539.85
	09/01/2011	09/02/2011	$4,078.95	2054	$899.85
	01/26/2012	01/26/2012	$2,939.85	2640	$2,939.85
	04/09/2012	04/16/2012	$5,549.40	2900	$329.85
	04/09/2012	04/16/2012	$5,549.40	2900	$1,739.85
Pathfinders					
	07/21/2011	07/27/2011	$3,526.70	1883	$1,739.85
	07/21/2011	07/27/2011	$3,526.70	1883	$23.50
	08/06/2011	08/14/2011	$5,879.70	1941	$2,939.85
	10/19/2011	10/19/2011	$8,819.55	2242	$2,939.85
	04/26/2012	05/01/2012	$3,185.42	2969	$726.61
	04/26/2012	05/01/2012	$3,185.42	2969	$899.85
	04/26/2012	05/01/2012	$3,185.42	2969	$832.35
Bike-A-Holics Anonymous					
	09/16/2011	09/24/2011	$5,545.42	2112	$14.50

Figure 11-7 Report using a different field as the group name

Exercise 11.2: Group Customer Orders By Month

In this exercise you will modify a report to include the following group and sorting options. These options also allow you to create totals and counts so that the records will be grouped by the month the orders were placed.

① Group on the Order Date field.
② Sort the detail records in ascending order on the Order Date field.
③ Provide a count of orders per month.

The goal of this exercise is to create a report that displays all of the orders from 2011 and have a subtotal for each month. In order to create a subtotal of orders for each month, the report needs to be grouped on the Order Date field.

As you will see, when you group on a date or date/time field, the Insert Group dialog box will display the option, THE SECTION WILL BE PRINTED. This option is used to create the group by month, day, quarter, year and more.

Create The Order Date Group

1. Save the Chapter 11 Group orders by month report as E11.2 Group customer orders by month.

2. On the Insert Group dialog box, open the first drop-down list and select the ORDER DATE field.

    Open the last drop-down list and select FOR EACH MONTH. Figure 11-8 shows the group options that should be selected.

    Click OK.

Figure 11-8 Group options

Sort The Detail Records And Create Selection Criteria

1. On the Record Sort Expert add the Order Date field to the Sort Fields list.

2. Select the Ascending sort order if it is not already selected. Click OK, then save the changes.

3. Click on the Order Date field in the details section, then create criteria to select all of the orders in 2011.

Create The Summary Fields

The count summary field will create a total for the number of orders per month. You will copy it to the report footer section to create a grand total number of orders for the entire report. The order amount summary field will create a total dollar amount per month. You will also copy the summary field to the report footer section to create a grand total order amount.

1. On the Insert Summary dialog box, open the first drop-down list and select the Order ID field. Open the second drop-down list and select **DISTINCT COUNT**. Open the Summary Location drop-down list and select the Group 1 option, then click OK.

2. On the Insert Summary dialog box, open the first drop-down list and select the Order Amount field. Open the second drop-down list and select **SUM**. Open the Summary Location drop-down list and select the Group 1 option, then click OK.

How To Create Percent Calculations

Percent calculations are very useful when you have the need to show what percent each group on the report represents in comparison to the grand total value on the report. For example, on a report that shows the sales for an entire year, there could be a percent calculation by month on the order amount field. This would tell the person that reads the report the percent of sales each month represents for the year. Another example on a yearly sales report would be the percent of sales each salesperson had per month, per year or both.

 You can only create percent calculations on summary fields that have a numeric value. This means that if you are creating a count summary of customers based on the Customer Name field which is a text field, you can create a percent calculation, because the count summary field is a numeric value.

Each percent calculation on a report requires its own percent summary calculation field. The process of creating a percent summary calculation starts off the same as the calculations that you have already created in this book. The options to create percent calculations are at the bottom of the Insert Summary dialog box. To create a percent calculation check the **SHOW AS A PERCENTAGE OF** option, then select the group or total that you want the percent comparison based on.

 If you need a total field and a percent calculation field that are based off of the same field, you have to create two summary calculation fields: One for the total amount and one for the percent.

In the previous part of the exercise you created the Order Amount summary field. Now you will create the Order Amount percent calculation field.

1. On the Insert Summary dialog box, open the first drop-down list and select the Order Amount field, then open the second drop-down list and select **SUM**.

   Open the Summary Location drop-down list and select the Group 1 option, then check the **SHOW AS A PERCENTAGE OF** option.

   Figure 11-9 shows the summary options that should be selected.

   Click OK.

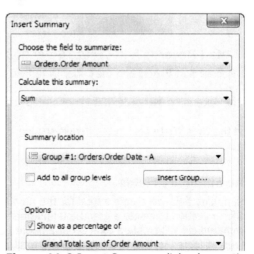

Figure 11-9 Insert Summary dialog box options

2. In the group footer section, move the percent summary field over to the right. On my report, it is currently on top of the Order Amount summary field that you just created. Save the changes and refresh the data. The third page of the report should look like the one shown in Figure 11-10. Notice that the percent summary field is already formatted with a percent sign. Leave the report open to complete the next part of the exercise.

E11.2 Group customer						
1/2011	Michael	Suyama	01/30/2011	1245	$3,419.25	
2/2011	Margaret	Peacock	01/30/2011	1246	$3,884.25	
3/2011	Margaret	Peacock	01/31/2011	1247	$36.00	
4/2011				127	$211,265.10	7.37%
5/2011	**2/2011**					
6/2011	Margaret	Peacock	02/01/2011	1248	$5,938.40	
7/2011	Michael	Suyama	02/02/2011	1249	$18.00	
8/2011	Margaret	Peacock	02/02/2011	1250	$2,497.05	
9/2011	Janet	Leverling	02/03/2011	1251	$45.00	
10/2011	Anne	Dodsworth	02/03/2011	1252	$70.50	
11/2011	Janet	Leverling	02/03/2011	1253	$2,683.82	
12/2011	Michael	Suyama	02/03/2011	1254	$2,497.05	

Figure 11-10 Group customer orders by month report

How To Check Or Edit Summary Fields

Sometimes reports will have more than two or three summary fields and you may not remember what each summary field is calculating. If a summary field is not producing the output that you think it should, it is possible that you selected an option that you should not have. If either of these is the case, all is not lost. You do not have to delete the summary field and start over.

You can right-click on the percentage summary field and select **EDIT SUMMARY**. You will see the dialog box shown in Figure 11-11. You can make any changes that are necessary.

The Edit Summary dialog box is almost identical to the Insert Summary dialog box. The difference is that you cannot change the location of the summary field.

If you need to move a summary field from one section of the report to another, you will have to do it manually.

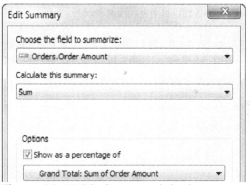

Figure 11-11 Edit Summary dialog box

Modify The Report

The report would look better if the following changes were made.

① Add a report title to the page header section.
② Create titles for the summary fields.
③ Create a grand total field and title for the order amount and count of orders summary fields.
④ Rearrange the fields in the details section so that the report is easier to read.

1. Create a report title and type `Orders By Month` in the object. Make the font size 16 and place the title above the field headings.

2. Delete the Last Name field heading. Change the First Name field heading to `Salesperson`. Center this title over the two name fields in the details section.

3. Format the Order ID field in the group 1 footer section to display as a whole number without a comma.

4. Copy the Order ID and Order Amount summary fields in the group 1 footer section and place the copies of both fields in the report footer section.

5. Add a line under the totals in the group 1 footer section. Change the size of the line to 0.5.

6. Create the field titles in Table 11-1 for the summary fields.

Summary Field	Section	Title
Order Amount	Group 1 Footer	Total order amount for the month -
Order ID Distinct Count	Group 1 Footer	Total # of orders for the month -
Order Amount Percent	Group 1 Footer	Percent of yearly sales -
Order Amount	Report Footer	Total order amount for the year -
Order ID Distinct Count	Report Footer	Total # of orders for the year -

Table 11-1 Field titles for Exercise 11.2

7. Copy the group 1 header field and place the copy in the group 1 footer section. Remove the bold from the field in the group 1 footer section.

8. Create a title in the group 1 footer section and type `Totals For:` in the object.
Create a title in the report footer section and type `Report Grand Totals:` in the object.

9. Arrange the fields so that they look like the layout shown in Figure 11-12. Save the changes and refresh the data. Leave the report open to complete the next part of the exercise.

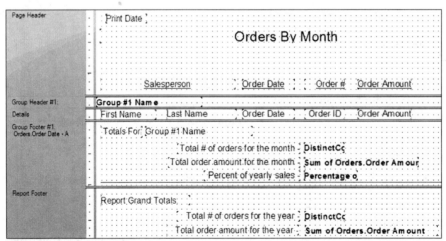

Figure 11-12 Report layout

When you preview the report you will see the months in the group tree section of the workspace. If you click on the 1/2011 group illustrated in Figure 11-13, you will see the orders that were placed in January. The Percent of yearly sales field lets you know that the orders in January represent 7.37% of the total sales in 2011.

E11.2 Group customer	Salesperson		Order Date	Order #	Order Amount
1/2011	Robert	King	01/25/2011	1229	$17.50
2/2011	Nancy	Davolio	01/25/2011	1230	$1,668.36
3/2011	Janet	Leverling	01/26/2011	1231	$2,524.05
4/2011	Anne	Dodsworth	01/27/2011	1232	$8,174.25
5/2011	Robert	King	01/27/2011	1233	$139.48
6/2011	Michael	Suyama	01/27/2011	1234	$1,723.22
7/2011	Anne	Dodsworth	01/27/2011	1235	$1,642.05
8/2011	Janet	Leverling	01/27/2011	1236	$989.55
9/2011	Robert	King	01/27/2011	1237	$998.35
10/2011	Robert	King	01/28/2011	1238	$1,024.01
11/2011	Robert	King	01/28/2011	1239	$101.70
12/2011	Robert	King	01/28/2011	1240	$3,635.34
	Robert	King	01/28/2011	1241	$4,849.86
	Michael	Suyama	01/29/2011	1242	$2,993.75
	Michael	Suyama	01/29/2011	1243	$128.20
	Janet	Leverling	01/30/2011	1244	$24.00
	Michael	Suyama	01/30/2011	1245	$3,419.25
	Margaret	Peacock	01/30/2011	1246	$3,884.25
	Margaret	Peacock	01/31/2011	1247	$36.00

Totals For: **1/2011**

Total # of orders for the month - **127**

Total order amount for the month - **$ 211,265.10**

Percent of yearly sales - **7.37%**

Figure 11-13 Third page of the Group customer orders by month report

How To Create A Custom Group Name

As you can see in Figure 11-14, the Order Date group name displays the month number and year. The report would look better if the group name displayed the actual month name (January, February, March, etc.).

	Salesperson		Order Date	Order #	Order Amount
1/2011					
	Anne	Dodsworth	01/01/2011	1121	$851.77
	Michael	Suyama	01/01/2011	1122	$1,025.40
	Janet	Leverling	01/02/2011	1123	$5,219.55

Figure 11-14 Order Date group name illustrated

The Format Editor has an option that is used to display the month name. You could create a formula to accomplish this task, but using the Format Editor is easier. The steps below show you how to create a custom group name using the Format Editor.

1. Right-click on the **GROUP 1 NAME** field in the group header section, then open the Format Editor. Click the **CUSTOMIZE** button on the Date and Time tab.

2. Open the **ORDER** drop-down list and select Date, as shown in Figure 11-15.

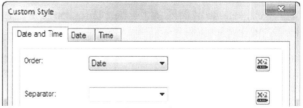

Figure 11-15 Date and Time tab options

3. On the Date tab open the Month drop-down list and select **MARCH**, then select **NONE** for the Day and Year options.

   Figure 11-16 illustrates the options that should be selected.

   Click OK twice, to close both dialog boxes.

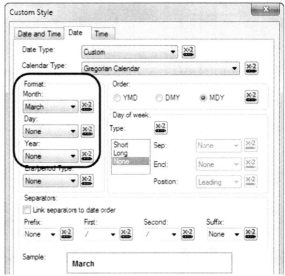

Figure 11-16 Date tab options illustrated

4. Format the Group Name field in the group footer section to have the same formatting as the one in the group header section.

5. Save the changes.

   Go to the last page of the report.

   The totals for December and the report grand totals should look like the ones shown in Figure 11-17.

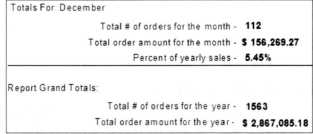

Figure 11-17 Last page of the Group customer orders by month report

Group Selection Criteria On Summary Fields

Group selection is similar to record selection. The difference is that group selection is done on summary fields, instead of fields in the details section. If a report is grouping the orders by state, each state would include an order total amount.

In Exercise 11.2 you created a report that grouped the orders by month. At the end of each month are summary calculations for the total number of orders and total order amount for the month. This section explains selection criteria on group summary fields. The report that you created in Exercise 11.2 displays data for every month in 2011. You could use the Select Expert to modify that report to only display months whose total monthly sales is greater than $250,000.

As shown in Figure 11-18, the first page of the report is for June. (The E11.2 report was modified to only display months with total orders over 250K for this figure.) Notice that all of the groups are still visible in the group tree. If you click on the 02/2011 option in the group tree, you will not see the data for February. That is because the monthly total for February is less than $250,000. I don't know about you, but I would prefer that the only options that appear in the group tree are the ones that meet the criteria. This happens because of the way Crystal Reports processes data, which currently cannot be changed. Remember that the group header information is processed before the totals for the summary calculations in the group footer are processed. This is why all of the months appear in the group tree.

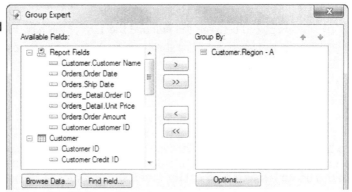

	Salesperson		Order Date	Order #	Order Amount
June					
Anne	Dodsworth		06/01/2011	1665	$161.20
Margaret	Peacock		06/01/2011	1666	$10,662.75
Robert	King		06/01/2011	1667	$959.70
Janet	Leverling		06/01/2011	1668	$1,138.09
Anne	Dodsworth		06/01/2011	1669	$8,945.25

Group tree: 1/2011, 2/2011, 3/2011, 4/2011, 5/2011, 6/2011, 7/2011, 8/2011, 9/2011, 10/2011, 11/2011, 12/2011

Monthly Total Orders Over $250,000

Figure 11-18 Monthly total orders over 250K

Using The Group Expert

All of the groups that you have created so far were created using the Insert Group dialog box. Groups can also be created using the Group Expert shown in Figure 11-19. Groups can also be reordered on this dialog box.

There are two ways to open the Group Expert, as explained below.

① Click the Group Expert button on the Expert Tools toolbar.
② Report ⇒ Group Expert.

Figure 11-19 Group Expert

 Memo fields cannot be used as a field to sort or group on from the Record Sort Expert or Group Expert dialog boxes. If you need to sort or group on a memo field, you have to create a formula.

The **OPTIONS** button will open the Change Group Options dialog box shown in Figure 11-20. It is the same as the Insert Group dialog box shown earlier in Figure 11-8.

One benefit of using the Group Expert is that you can create all of the groups for the report without having to re-open the dialog box to create each group.

Another benefit is if you need to see the data in a field, you can click the Browse Data button.

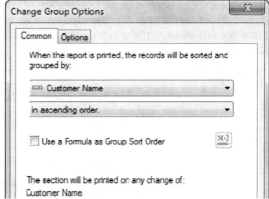

Figure 11-20 Change Group Options dialog box

User Defined Groups

In Exercise 11.2 you learned how to create a custom group name. Custom group names are used to rename existing group names. Custom groups must be based on a single field in the report. User defined groups are similar to custom group names. The major difference is that the user defined group name is free form. In addition to being able to create a free form group name, you can create custom groups. Below are examples of user defined groups.

① Orders placed between the first and the 15th of the month.
② Group customers based on their year to date sales (example Gold, Bronze and Silver levels).
③ Create sales territories and associate states to a territory (example Northeast, Southeast and Midwest).

The four steps to creating a user defined group are explained below.

Step 1: Select the field that you want to create the user defined group for, then select the option, **IN SPECIFIED ORDER** in the second drop-down list on the Common tab on the Insert Group dialog box. Once this option is selected, other tabs (the Specified Order and Others tabs) will appear on the dialog box.

Step 2: Type in the name for the first group name that you need in the **NAMED GROUP** drop-down list shown in Figure 11-21, then click the **NEW** button.

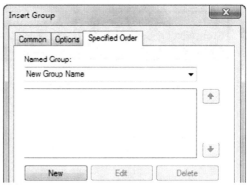

Figure 11-21 Specified Order tab options

Step 3: The **DEFINE NAMED GROUP** dialog box is similar to the Select Expert. One difference is that each tab on the Define Named Group dialog box is for the same field. User defined groups cannot use parameter fields and the formula cannot be modified. You would select the criteria for the user defined group, as shown in Figure 11-22.

Figure 11-22 Criteria for a user defined group

The other difference is that these filters or selection criteria use the **OR** operand, meaning that the detail record can meet the criteria for filter 1 or filter 2 or filter 3.

Step 4: Click OK and repeat steps 2 and 3 until you have created all of the user defined groups that the report needs.

 If checked, the **USE A FORMULA AS GROUP SORT ORDER** option on the Insert Group dialog box shown earlier in Figure 11-8 will not let you select a specified order that is based on a formula.

If you wanted to group orders by specific date ranges like 1/1/11 to 1/15/11, 2/1/11 to 2/15/11 and 3/1/11 to 3/15/11, you would create three named groups, for example, Jan 11, Feb 11 and Mar 11. For each named group you would select the Order Date field, the operator Is between and the date range for the named group. The report would show the three groups and the detail records that have an order date that falls into one of the three date ranges.

If one group or all groups need additional criteria, click on the New tab and add the next piece of criteria for the group. You can only add criteria for the same field.

For example, if you also wanted to see orders for 1/15/11 to 1/25/11, you would add this criteria on a new tab, as shown in Figure 11-23.

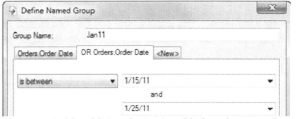

Figure 11-23 Additional criteria added to the named group

The criteria for each group name is joined using the **OR** operand. This means that as long as the record meets one of the sets of criteria for the group name, it will appear on the report.

The options on the Others tab, which you will learn about in the next exercise, are used to select what you want to do with the records that do not meet the criteria for any of the named groups.

Exercise 11.3: Create A User Defined Group Report

In this exercise you will modify the E10.1 report to include the following region user defined groups: CA, IL and PA.

1. Save the E10.1 report as E11.3 User defined groups.

2. Right-click in the group header section on the left and select **CHANGE GROUP**.

3. Select the **IN SPECIFIED ORDER** option in the second drop-down list. You should see the **SPECIFIED ORDER** tab.

4. Select CA, IL and PA in the **NAMED GROUP** drop-down list. Make sure that the states are in the order shown in Figure 11-24.

   If they are not in the order shown, use the up and down arrow buttons to put the states in the order shown.

Figure 11-24 Change Group Options dialog box

5. On the **OTHERS** tab, select the option **DISCARD ALL OTHERS**, as shown in Figure 11-25. Click OK twice to close both dialog boxes.

Selecting the Discard all others option means that records that are not in any of the groups listed on the Specified Order tab will not appear on the report.

The **PUT ALL OTHERS TOGETHER, WITH THE NAME** option, will put all of the records that do not meet the criteria on the Specified Order tab under a new group name that you enter on the field below the option. This group will appear at the end of the report.

Figure 11-25 Others tab options

6. Preview the report. You should only see the CA, IL and PA groups in the group tree, as shown in Figure 11-26. Save the changes and leave the report open to complete the next exercise.

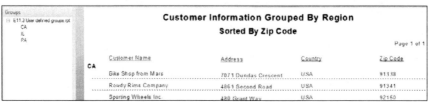

Figure 11-26 User defined groups report

Exercise 11.4: Create A Custom Group Name Report

In the previous exercise, the User defined groups report displayed the two character state name. In this exercise you will modify that report so that the state names are spelled out.

1. Save the E11.3 report as E11.4 Custom group name.

2. Right-click in the group header section and select **CHANGE GROUP**, then click on the Specified Order tab and delete all of the Named Groups.

3. Click the **NEW** button, then type
   California in the Group Name
   field.

   Open the drop-down list and select
   IS EQUAL TO, then select CA from the
   second drop-down list. Figure 11-27
   shows the options that should be selected.

   Click OK.

Figure 11-27 Define named group options for CA

4. Repeat the steps above for IL and PA. Leave the Change Group Options dialog box open when
   you are finished.

5. On the **OTHERS** tab select the option
   PUT ALL OTHERS TOGETHER, WITH THE NAME,
   then type Other States, as shown in
   Figure 11-28.

   Click OK and save the changes.

   The report should look like the one shown
   in Figure 11-29. Notice that the state
   names are spelled out in the group tree
   and on the report.

Figure 11-28 Others tab options

You should see a new group called **OTHER STATES** in the group tree, as illustrated in Figure 11-29.
This group contains all of the records that meet the selection options for the report, but are not in
CA, IL or PA.

Figure 11-29 Custom group name report

 If you find that the majority of the reports with groups that you create do not need the
group name field that is automatically added to the group header section, clear the
INSERT GROUP NAME WITH GROUP option on the Layout tab on the Options dialog box.

USING THE REPORT CREATION WIZARDS

In the last few chapters, all of the reports that you created were created from scratch. I figured that I would give you a break in this chapter from creating reports from scratch.

Chapter 4 provided an overview of how to create reports and charts using a wizard. In this chapter you will learn more about the wizards. After completing the exercises in this chapter you will be able to:

☑ Understand the options on the common wizard screens
☑ Know the types of reports that each wizard can create
☑ Create reports using the Standard report wizard
☑ Use the Mailing Label wizard

Overview

Now that you have used several report creation and modification features and were able to see the completed reports, many of the options on the wizard screens will hopefully make more sense. Selecting the wrong option in the wizard or not selecting an option that you need will cause you to have to fix the report manually. That's okay though, as wizards can be used as a starting point for a report that you can modify as needed.

I think that it is important to understand sorting, grouping and summary options before using a wizard to create a report. One reason that I think this is important is because many of the wizard screens are scaled down versions of an expert screen. This is one reason why this chapter comes after chapters that had you create reports that demonstrate how to sort, group and summarize records.

Table 12-1 explains the type of report that each wizard creates. As you learn to use each of the report wizards, you will see that they have a core set of common screens. Table 12-2 lists the common screens and the screens that are unique to a specific wizard.

Report Wizards

Wizard	Type Of Report That The Wizard Creates . . .
Standard	A variety of reports because it is the generic report wizard. It is similar to creating a report from scratch.
Cross-Tab	Reports that contain summary information. This wizard is covered in Chapter 21.
Mailing Label	Reports in a column layout, which can be used to create any size mailing label that you need.
OLAP Cube	Reports that display data in a summarized format, similar to the Cross-Tab wizard. The difference is that an OLAP data source is used.

Table 12-1 Report wizards explained

Screen	Standard	Cross-Tab	Mailing Label	OLAP
Data	X	X	X	
Link	X	X	X	
Fields	X		X	
Grouping	X			
Summaries	X			
Group Sorting	X			
Record Selection	X	X	X	
Chart	X	X		X
Template	X			
Cross-Tab		X		
Grid Style		X		
Label			X	

Table 12-2 Report wizard screens

Screen	Standard	Cross-Tab	Mailing Label	OLAP
OLAP Data				X
Rows/Columns				X
Slice/Page				X
Style				X

Table 12-2 Report wizard screens (Continued)

The Standard Report Wizard

This is the most used wizard because it is somewhat free form. Even though this wizard has more screens, depending on the options that you select, you may not see all of the screens checked in the Standard column in Table 12-2 above.

You should be familiar with many of the screens in this wizard because in Exercise 4.1 you created a report using this wizard and selected options on every screen. This was done to demonstrate all of the options in the wizard. The reports that you create with wizards in this chapter will be more focused. Many of the reports that you will create in this chapter are reports that you have already created from scratch earlier in this book. The reason for this is two-fold:

① So that you will be able to determine which method (by wizard or by scratch) is better suited for a specific type of report.
② So that you can decide which method you like best.

The wizards are designed to make what may seem like a complicated task, a little easier to complete. What you may not realize is that there is often more going on behind the scenes of a wizard then you realize. By that I mean, wizards can have default options that you may not be aware of. In Exercise 12.4 you will see an example of this.

Unless you are very familiar with the data that is being used to create the report, you or the person using the report may not know that the data on the report is not 100% accurate. I personally try not to use wizards because of this. I may reconsider using the wizards more if there was documentation that thoroughly explains the inner workings and defaults that are set on wizard screens that you can't see.

Common Report Wizard Screens

As you saw above in Table 12-2, several of the report wizards use the same screens. The majority of reports that you will create with a wizard will be created using the Standard wizard. This section explains the purpose and features of the screens that provide the foundation for many of the wizards.

Some of the wizard screens including the Record Selection, Chart and Cross-Tab have less functionality than the "Expert" that it was taken from. If you find that there is a task that you can't complete using the wizard, check the options on the Expert toolbar to see if there is an option that will help you complete the task.

I would like to have the ability to preview the report before the wizard dialog box closes. This would let you know how "close" you are to getting the output that you want. If you make a mistake or leave something out, you would not have to start all over again because you could click the Back button on the wizard screen and fix the mistake or add what you need, because you could see what the report would look like before clicking the Finish button.

Data Screen

Figure 12-1 shows the Data screen. This is the first screen that many wizards use. This screen is used to select the data sources that are needed to create the report. The Data screen provides the same functionality as the Database Expert.

Figure 12-1 Data screen

Fields Screen

Figure 12-2 shows the Fields screen. This screen is used to select the fields that are needed for the report.

The fields that you select on this screen will be placed in the details section of the report.

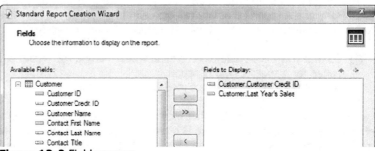

Figure 12-2 Fields screen

Grouping Screen

Figure 12-3 shows the Grouping screen. The options on this screen are used to select the fields to group on.

Creating groups is optional. If selected, the grouping options will create the group header and footer sections of the report. This screen is the equivalent of the Insert Group dialog box.

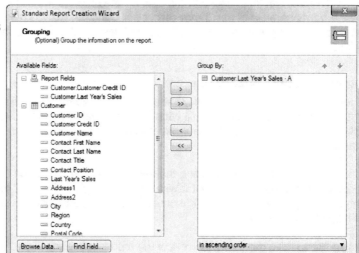

Figure 12-3 Grouping screen

Keep in mind that when you create a group using the wizard, the fields that are being grouped on, are automatically moved to the left most columns of the report. The fields do not stay in the order that you add them to the report on the Fields screen.

You cannot sort the detail records on this wizard screen. If you need to sort records in a report that does not have a group, you will have to do that through the Record Sort Expert after the report has been created with the wizard.

Summaries Screen

The Summaries screen is only available if at least one field is being grouped on. By default, the numeric fields that are selected on the Grouping screen are automatically added to the **SUMMARIZED FIELDS** list, as shown in Figure 12-4. This may not be what you want. You can remove the field from the Summarized Fields list if there is no need to create a total for it.

The fields in the Summarized Fields list will automatically have grand total fields created and placed in the report footer section of the report.

If you need to add a field to summarize on, select it here.

Figure 12-4 Summaries screen

Group Sorting Screen

The Group Sorting screen is only available if at least one field was selected on the Grouping and Summaries screens. Figure 12-5 shows the options that can be selected to change the order of the groups based on the value from the selection on the Summaries screen. The Group Sorting screen is a scaled down version of the Group Sort Expert.

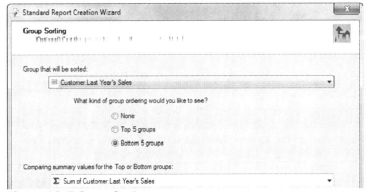

Figure 12-5 Group Sorting screen

There are three group ordering options that you can select from, as explained below.

① **NONE** This is the default group ordering option. This option will leave the group order the way it is. Most of the time, this is the option that you want.

② **TOP 5 GROUPS** This option will only select the five groups that have the highest value in the field that is being grouped on. The other groups will not appear on the report.

③ **BOTTOM 5 GROUPS** This option will only select the five groups that have the lowest value in the field that is being grouped on. The other groups will not appear on the report.

If the Top 5 groups or Bottom 5 groups option is selected, the **COMPARING SUMMARY VALUES FOR THE TOP OR BOTTOM GROUPS** option shown above in Figure 12-5 is enabled. This option is used to select the summarized field to base the sort on. The options available in the drop-down list come from the summary fields that you created on the Summaries screen.

Top and Bottom N reports, commonly known as Top N reports, are used to show the first N or last N records in a group. Instead of displaying all orders in a certain date range, you could only show the largest 10 orders in the date range. The wizard does not allow you to select the value of N. It always uses five. If you use the Group Sort Expert to create a Top or Bottom N report, you can select the value of N, by typing it in or using a parameter field to get the value of N each time the report is run. You can use the Group Sort Expert to edit a Top N report that is created with a wizard.

Chart Screen

The options shown in Figure 12-6 are used to add a chart to the report. Adding a chart is optional. In order to add a chart, the report has to have at least one group.

Compared to the Chart Expert, the options and chart types on the Chart wizard screen are limited, which means that most of the time you will have to modify the chart after the wizard creates it.

The other major drawback to creating a chart using a report wizard is that you have to create the chart from fields that will print on the report. The Chart Expert can create a chart with fields that will not be printed on the report. Once you select a chart type in the wizard, the three options explained below are available to help customize the chart.

① **CHART TITLE** The information that you enter in this field will be printed at the top of the chart.

② **ON CHANGE OF** This option defaults to a field that the report is being grouped on.

③ **SHOW SUMMARY** This option defaults to the summary field for the field that is in the On Change Of field.

Record Selection Screen

The options shown in Figure 12-7 are used to create selection criteria like you can do on the Select Expert. Selecting options on this screen is optional. As you learned, a formula is created when you use the Select Expert. A formula is created on the Record Selection screen if criteria is added. The difference is that you cannot see the formula that is created from the wizard screen.

You can view the formula after the report is created with the wizard by opening the Select Expert. This will let you edit the formula if necessary. Like the Select Expert, you can create as many filters as needed.

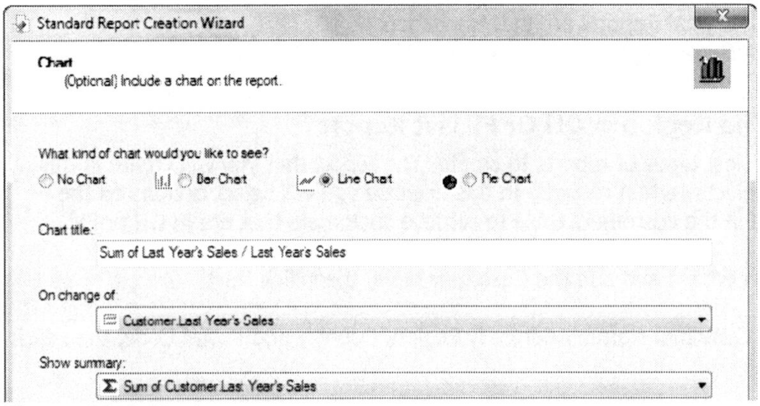

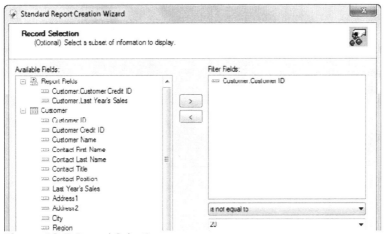

Figure 12-6 Chart screen

Figure 12-7 Record Selection screen

Template Screen

The options shown in Figure 12-8 are used to apply a template (a pre-formatted style) to the report.

Applying a template to a report is optional. You can also create your own templates.

If there is a template that you want to use that is not shown in the Available Templates list, click the **BROWSE** button. This will let you navigate to the location where the template is that you want to use.

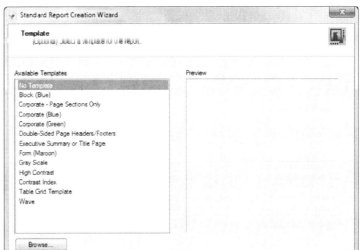

Figure 12-8 Template screen

The templates that come with Crystal Reports are in this location:
C:\Program Files (x86)\SAP Business Objects\Crystal Reports 2011\Templates\en

Exercise 12.1: Create The Region = OH Or FL List Report

List reports are one of the easiest types of reports to create. The report that you will create in this exercise is a list report that selects certain records. In this exercise you will select options on the wizard that will filter the data in the customers table to retrieve customers that are in OH or FL.

1. Open the Standard report wizard and add the Customer table, then click Next.

2. Add the following fields: Customer Name, Address1, Region, Country and Postal Code, then click Next.

3. Click Next on the Grouping screen because this report does not have any grouping requirements. Add the Region field to the **FILTER FIELDS** list on the Record Selection screen.

4. Open the drop-down list and select **IS ONE OF**, then open the next drop-down list and select **OH** or you can type it in.

5. Open the same drop-down list that you just used and select **FL** or you can type it in.

    Click the **ADD** button.

    Figure 12-9 shows the filter options that should be selected.

Figure 12-9 Record Selection screen options

6. The report does not require a template. Click **FINISH**. The report should look like the one shown in Figure 12-10. Notice that a date field was automatically added to the report. Save the report as `E12.1 Region = OH or FL list`. This report is similar to the one that you created in Exercise 9.2.

8/6/2011				
Customer Name	Address1	Region	Country	Postal Code
Bike-A-Holics Anonymous	7429 Arbutus Boulevard	OH	USA	43005
Wheels and Stuff	2530 Bute Avenue	FL	USA	34666
Uni-Cycle	1008 Kerr Street	OH	USA	43042
Extreme Cycling	1925 Glenaire Avenue	FL	USA	34638
Karma Bikes	1516 Ohio Avenue	OH	USA	43092

Figure 12-10 Region = OH or FL list report

Exercise 12.2: Create The Order Date And Order Amount Report

In this exercise you will create a report that uses data from three tables. You will create a filter that will select records that have an order date greater than or equal to 6/24/10 and has an order amount greater than 2499.99. This is the same report that you modified in Exercise 9.4.

1. Open the Standard report wizard and add the Customer, Orders and Orders Detail tables, then click Next. The default links between the tables are correct. Click Next.

2. Add the following fields: Customer Name, Order Date, Ship Date, Order Amount, Order ID and Unit Price, then click Next.

3. Click Next on the Grouping screen because this report does not have any grouping requirements. Add the Order Date field to the **FILTER FIELDS** list. Open the drop-down list and select **IS GREATER THAN OR EQUAL TO**, then type 6/24/2010 in the next field.

4. Add the Order Amount field to the **FILTER FIELDS** list, then open the drop-down list and select **IS GREATER THAN**.

5. Type 2499.99 in the next drop-down list, then click Finish.

6. Save the report as E12.2 Order Date and Order Amount. The report should look like the one shown in Figure 12-11.

Customer Name	Order Date	Ship Date	Order Amount	Order ID	Unit Price
Deals on Wheels	12/2/2010 12:00:00AM	12/2/2010 6:45:32AM	$5,060.28	1,002	$33.90
Deals on Wheels	12/2/2010 12:00:00AM	12/2/2010 6:45:32AM	$5,060.28	1,002	$1,652.86
Cyclopath	12/3/2010 12:00:00AM	12/3/2010 11:11:11PM	$14,872.30	1,010	$2,939.85
Cyclopath	12/3/2010 12:00:00AM	12/3/2010 11:11:11PM	$14,872.30	1,010	$2,645.87
Cyclopath	12/3/2010 12:00:00AM	12/3/2010 11:11:11PM	$14,872.30	1,010	$253.67
Piccolo	12/3/2010 12:00:00AM	12/5/2010 4:59:00PM	$10,259.10	1,012	$2,939.85

Figure 12-11 Order Date and Order Amount report

Exercise 12.3: Create A Group Summary Report

In this exercise you will create a report that groups records by the product that was ordered.

1. Open the Standard report wizard and add the Orders Detail and Product tables, then click Next. The reason that you are adding the Product table is so that you can print the name of the product instead of the Product ID number that is in the Orders Detail table.

2. Click Next on the Link screen because the link options do not need to be changed.

3. Add the following fields: Product Name, Quantity and Order ID, then click Next.

4. Add the Product Name field to the Group By list. The default sort order for the group will cause the Product Names to be sorted in ascending order. Click Next.

As you can see in Figure 12-12, two summary fields were automatically added to the Summarized Fields list. By default, numeric fields are automatically selected to be summarized on in the wizard. You should remove the fields in the Summarized Fields list that you do not need.

To count the number of orders for each product you can use the Order ID field or the Product Name field because each will print in the details section of the report.

The Quantity summary field is not needed.

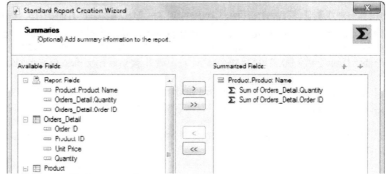

Figure 12-12 Group and summary options

5. Remove the Quantity summary field, then click on the Sum Order ID field.

6. Open the drop-down list and select Count. Click Finish. The report should look like the one shown in Figure 12-13.

If you look in the group tree section you will see a list of all of the products that were purchased by product name, instead of by Product ID number.

This makes it easy to find out how many orders were placed for a certain product.

Figure 12-13 Product summary report

7. Save the report as E12.3 Product summary.

Exercise 12.4: Create A Top N Report

In previous exercises you created reports that grouped the data. By default, the groups are sorted on the value in the group field. For example, orders would be grouped by the values (the actual customer names) in the summary customer name field.

There is another way to sort groups on a report. Just like you can filter detail records, you can filter groups. One way to explain Top N reports is that this sort method is sorting the groups on the value of a group summary field instead of the values in the group by field. Top N reports do not display all of the groups. They only display the groups that N has. Top N reports rank the groups based on the summary field values. For example, if N equals 7, only the seven highest groups based on the value of the summary field would be displayed on the report.

 The Group Sorting screen is used to limit the number of groups on the report to five, by selecting the Top 5 or Bottom 5 group option. No more or no less. The Group Sorting Expert does not have a group number limitation.

> The grand totals that appear on a report when the top five or bottom five group sorting option is used, are not the real totals for the detail records on the report. They are the totals for all records that meet the other report criteria before the top five or bottom five group sort option is applied. This happens when the **INCLUDE OTHERS** option on the Group Sort Expert dialog box is not checked. If you do not want to use the Include Others option, create a running total field instead of the summary grand total field.

In this exercise you will create a report that will display the top five days in June 2011 with the largest daily order totals. You will also create a pie chart that displays the top five order days.

1. Open the Standard report wizard and add the Customer and Orders tables, then click Next. Click Next on the Link screen.

2. Add the following fields: Customer Name, Order ID, Order Amount and Order Date, then click Next.

3. Add the Order Date field to the **GROUP BY** list, then click Next.

4. Remove the Order ID field from the Summarized Fields list, then click Next.

5. Select the **TOP 5 GROUPS** option on the Group Sorting screen, then click Next.

6. Select the Pie chart option on the Chart screen and type
   `Top 5 Order Days In June 2011` in the Chart Title field, then click Next.

7. Add the Order Date field to the Filter Fields list on the Record Selection screen. Open the drop-down list and select **IS BETWEEN**, then type `6/01/2011` in the next drop-down list. In the last drop-down list, type `6/30/2011`. Figure 12-14 shows the options that should be selected.

Figure 12-14 Record Selection options

8.   Click Finish. The report should look like the one shown in Figure 12-15. You will only see detail information for the top five order days.

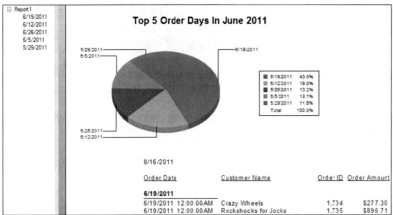

Figure 12-15 Top 5 order days in June 2011 report

As you can see, one of the dates in the group tree is in May. If you click on that link, you will see orders for June. No, I did not lead you astray. This is one of the features of the wizards that do not work as intended. There are options that are preset that you don't know about, that can produce unexpected results.

If you plan to use this wizard on a regular basis for something other then a basic report, hopefully you see how important it is to understand the data that the report should produce. That should lead you in the direction of how to fix any problem that the wizard creates.

9.   Save the report as E12.4 Top 5 order days in June 2011 and leave it open to complete the next exercise.

Exercise 12.5: Fix The Top 5 Order Days Report
When I looked at the data in the E12.4 report, I noticed that each of the five groups actually had more than one days worth of data. Each group actually had a weeks worth of data, even though I was expecting to only see data for one day in each group. Because the data is grouped on the Order Date field, I realized that the wizard must have the group default set to weekly. I opened the Group Expert (which is a different expert then the Group Sort Expert) and sure enough, the option was set to weekly.

This is an example of how a wizard can produce unexpected results. What scares me is that I get the feeling that because the majority of people that use wizards use them without questioning the results, this is something that could easily be missed. What would be helpful on the wizard would be if the Group Sorting wizard screen had an option that is used to select how you want the data to be grouped, by day, week, month, year etc. After looking at the options on the Group Sort Expert, I noticed that it did not have this option either, so because the Group Sorting wizard screen is a subset of the Group Sort Expert, it made a little sense.

Even though the wizard produces results that you may not want, I do not know about you, but I can do without this type of "help" from a wizard. The best advice that I can give you if you insist on using a wizard, is after the wizard creates the report, open each corresponding expert for a screen that you selected options on in the wizard and look at the options. While this is good advice, if you think for a minute, you will realize that even that advice would not have helped you detect this error because options from the Group Expert are not used in this wizard. The good news is that this report can be fixed by following the steps below.

1. Save the E12.4 report as `E12.5 Fixed Top 5 order days in June 2011 report`.

2. Report ⇒ Group Expert, then click the **OPTIONS** button. You will see the Change Group Options dialog box. In the last drop-down list you will see that the option **FOR EACH WEEK** is selected. Open **THE SECTION WILL BE PRINTED** drop-down list and select **FOR EACH DAY**. As you can see, knowing about this option would allow you to create a variety of reports just by changing this option. Click OK twice to close both dialog boxes.

3. Refresh the data and preview the report. It should look like the one shown in Figure 12-16. You should now see five days in June (opposed to four as shown above in Figure 12-15) in the group tree. All of the detail records in each group should have the same order date. Save the changes.

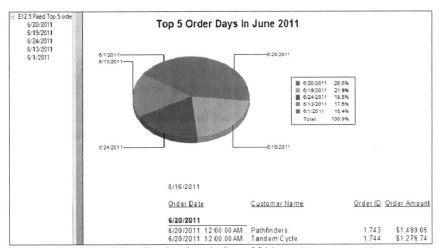

Figure 12-16 Fixed Top 5 order days in June 2011 report

Exercise 12.6: Use The Mailing Label Wizard

This wizard is used to create a column layout report which many people use to print labels. You can use this wizard to create other types of columnar reports besides mailing labels. In this exercise you will learn how to create a report that can be used to print labels. The report will print shipping labels for customers that placed an order in June 2011, that are in the US. Many of the screens in this wizard are the same as the ones that you used in the Standard report wizard.

1. Open the Mailing label report wizard and add the Customer and Orders tables, then click Next. Click Next again, because the links are correct.

2. Add the following fields: Customer Name, Address1, Address2, City, Region and Postal Code, then click Next.

3. Open the **MAILING LABEL TYPE** drop-down list and select Avery 5163.

   Figure 12-17 shows the options that should be selected.

   The Mailing Label type drop-down list has the **USER-DEFINED LABEL** option, which is used to create a custom size label.

Figure 12-17 Label screen options

After you select all of the options for the labels, look in the **NUMBER OF LABELS** section in the lower right corner of the dialog box to make sure that the selections that you made work with the labels that you will print.

4. Click Next, then add the Country field to the Filter Fields list. Open the drop-down list and select **IS EQUAL TO**, then open the next drop-down list and select **USA** or you can type it in.

5. Add the Order Date field to the Filter Fields list. Open the drop-down list and select **IS BETWEEN** and type 6/01/2011 in the first drop-down list, then type 6/30/2011 in the last drop-down list. Click Finish. The report should look like the one shown in Figure 12-18. The report should have 108 records.

Because the date criteria was for a month, you see duplicate customer names.

More than likely, the labels would be printed daily, which means that you would not see duplicate customer names in the labels unless a customer placed more than one order on the same day.

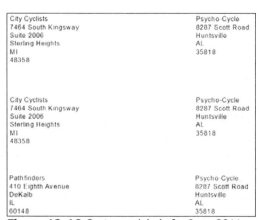

Figure 12-18 Customer labels for June 2011 report

 This label report uses two address lines. What many people do is modify the label layout and put both address fields on the same line and put the city, state and zip code on the same line. That is not a requirement for this exercise.

6. Save the report as E12.6 Customer labels for June 2011.

PRINTING AND EXPORTING REPORTS

Overview

You have created and modified a lot of reports in the previous chapters. So far, the reports that you have created have not been printed.

After completing the exercises in this chapter you will be able to use the following printing and exporting options:

☑ Page Setup dialog box
☑ Diagnose printing problems
☑ Set print date and time
☑ Preview Sample
☑ Report Options dialog box
☑ Export reports to a variety of file formats

CHAPTER 13

Printing Options

Crystal Reports has the majority of printing options for reports that you have already used in word processing and other software packages. Most people that will run the reports that you create will not have Crystal Reports installed. Therefore, you should select the appropriate printing options so that the report will print as you intended it to. The first part of this chapter covers the printing options that are available.

Page Setup Options

As shown in Figure 13-1, there are several options that you can select from to change the printed page layout to what is best suited for the report. The options shown are the defaults that are set when Crystal Reports is installed. The graphic in the bottom right corner of the dialog box will change as the options are changed.

Table 13-1 explains the options on the Page Setup dialog box (File ⇒ Page Setup), that you may not be familiar with.

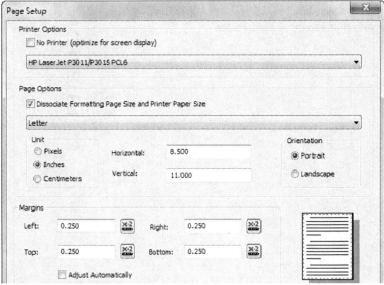

Figure 13-1 Page Setup dialog box

Setup Option	Description
No Printer	Select this option if the report will not be printed. This option will optimize the report to be viewed on a screen. No printer driver will be saved with the report. It can also be used to resolve printing problems, as you will learn later in this chapter.
Dissociate Formatting Page Size . . .	Select this option if you need complete control over how the report will print on the page.
Adjust Automatically	This option causes the margins to change automatically, when the paper size or orientation is changed.

Table 13-1 Page Setup dialog box options explained

Page Orientation

As shown above in Figure 13-1, the default orientation is **PORTRAIT**. You can fit more fields across the page if the orientation is **LANDSCAPE**. Some reports that you create may have a field hanging off of the right side of the report. When you preview the report, all of the data in the last field would not be displayed. If this happens you can make some of the fields smaller, create additional sections to put fields in or select the Landscape orientation option. The orientation can also be changed for a section of the report. This means that a report can have some sections in portrait and some sections in landscape. [See Chapter 16, Paging Tab]

Page Margins

If you have the need to change the margins based on a condition met in the report or from a condition set by a parameter field, click the Formula button next to the margin that you need to control, as shown above in Figure 13-1 in the **MARGINS** section and type in the formula.

Paper Size

As shown earlier in Figure 13-1, the default paper size is **LETTER**. Some reports, in particular financial reports, may need to be printed on legal paper.

To change the paper size, open the Page Setup dialog box, then select the paper, envelope or post card size that you need, as shown in Figure 13-2.

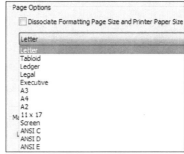

Figure 13-2 Page options

Using The Adjust Automatically Option

You have read how to change the paper size, orientation and margins manually. When you change the paper size or orientation, the margins do not change. If you need to make the margins change automatically when the paper size is changed from letter size to legal size for example, open the Page Setup dialog box and check the **ADJUST AUTOMATICALLY** option, then click OK and save the changes. Now when the paper size of the report is changed, the margins will change automatically.

While this feature sounds like it will resolve a margin problem, there are two issues that using this option can cause, as explained below. To avoid these problems it is best to set the report margins manually on the Page Setup dialog box.

① If you print a report on a printer that has default margins that are less than the margins saved with the report, the objects on the report automatically shift to the left side of the report.

② If you print a report on a printer that has default margins that are greater than the margins saved with the report, the objects on the right side of the report may get cut off.

Printer Options

The Print Setup dialog box shown in
Figure 13-3 is used to select a printer
and its options. These are the same
options that you have probably used
in other software packages.

File ⇒ Print, will open this dialog box.

If you have more than one printer
installed, the default printer that you
have selected in Windows will appear
in the **NAME** drop-down list shown in
Figure 13-3.

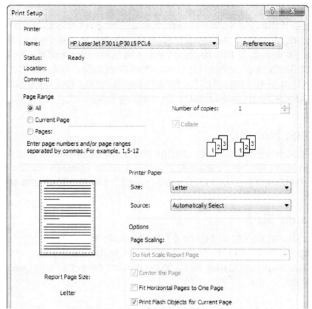

Figure 13-3 Print Setup dialog box

If the printer shown is not the one
that you want to use, open the
drop-down list and select the
printer that you want.

The **PREFERENCES** button is used to
select additional options for the
printer that is selected.

Figure 13-4 shows the options for
my default printer.

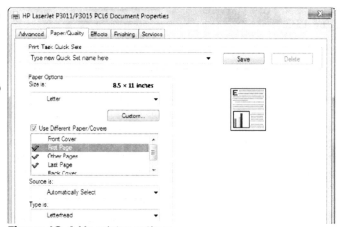

Figure 13-4 My printer options

Printing Problems

If you have an ink jet printer and have opened a document that was created by someone that has a
laser jet printer, you may have noticed that sometimes the spacing is off. If so, the topics discussed
in this section will be helpful. If you have experienced formatting issues (when it comes to printing a
document) using other software, many of those problems are also found in Crystal Reports, as
explained below.

While the reports that you create may look good on your computer screen and look good when
you print them, that may not be the case when the reports go into production. This is because
information like printer drivers and screen resolution come from the options that are on the computer

that the reports are created on. Technical people tend to install printer and video driver updates, while end-users do not. This can cause reports to print differently even if you have the same model printer as the person printing the report.

Printer information is saved with the report. This is why someone that does not have the same exact settings on their computer and the same printer driver as you do, will sometimes get different printed or visual screen results when they run the report. The list below discusses several printing concepts that you should be aware of that can effect how the reports that you create look on a computer screen and how they look when printed.

① Crystal Reports uses information from the default printer driver when the report was created (meaning the one on your computer). The printer driver determines the character width and height of the information printed on a report.
② The video driver resolution and operating system used when the report was created can also effect the report when it is viewed on a different computer.
③ Some of the layout options of reports that you create come from the default options on the Page Setup dialog box. An example is the page margins.
④ The length of the report page comes from the type of printer that is selected, which is usually your default printer. This is important to know because each printer model has limits on how close to the edge of the paper that it can print.

Okay, I can imagine that the information that you just read is cause for concern. The suggestions below will help resolve many of the printing problems discussed above.

① Set the margins for the report instead of using the default printer driver margins.
② Install the latest printer drivers.
③ Use the **CAN GROW** option for fields that contain a lot of data, like memo fields. Putting memo fields in their own subsection of the report would also be helpful.
④ Select the computer screen video resolution that most of the people that will view the report have. If this is not possible, consider exporting the report to PDF format, so that more people can view and print the report as intended.
⑤ Selecting the **NO PRINTER** option shown earlier in Figure 13-1 is best if the report will be printed on several different printer models. Doing this helps keep the formatting generic enough so that the report can be printed on a variety of printers.
⑥ Use common True Type fonts like Arial, Garamond and Times New Roman that come standard on Windows based computers. Crystal Reports will replace fonts that it does not recognize, which will often cause the printed report to not look as you intended. If you need to use a non standard font, you should export the report to PDF format because this file format can be viewed as intended on any computer that has the free Adobe Reader installed.

Exercise 13.1: Use The Set Print Date And Time Options

The Set Print Date and Time options are useful when you use the Print Date or Print Time special fields on a report and have the need to override these dates when the report is printed. The options on the dialog box are used to set these fields to a date or time, other then the current date or time.

1. Save the E8.5 report as E13.1 Set print date. Notice the date in the **DATE THE REPORT WAS PRINTED** field. It should be today's date.

2. Report ⇒ Set Print Date and Time.

    Select the **OTHER** option, then type
    1/1/2010 in the Date field,
    as shown in Figure 13-5.

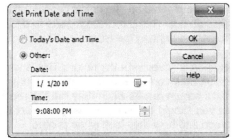

Figure 13-5 Set Print Date and Time dialog box

3. Click OK and save the changes. You should see 1/1/2010 in the Date the report was printed field, as shown in Figure 13-6.

Date the report was printed:	Date the report was last saved: 8/16/2011	Date the data was last refreshed: 8/16/2011
1/1/2010	Time the report was last saved: 9:10:41PM	Time the data was last refreshed: 9:10:52PM
		Date the report was designed: 8/4/2011

Figure 13-6 Set print date report with the print date changed

4. Close the report. The 2010 date will print every time this report is run, until you remove the date from the Set Print Date and Time dialog box.

Exercise 13.2: Use The Preview Sample Option

If the report has hundreds or thousands of records and you do not want to see all of them when you are creating and testing the report, you can specify the number of records that you want to see on the report. The default for this is **ALL RECORDS**, which is why all of the records that meet the criteria have appeared in every report that you have created so far.

1. Save the Chapter 11 Group orders by shipping method report as E13.2 Preview sample option. Notice that there are 1,562 records.

2. View ⇒ Preview Sample. Select the **FIRST** option, then type 525 in the **RECORDS** field.

    Figure 13-7 shows the options that should be selected.

    Click OK.

    The report will automatically re-open in the preview tab. Notice that there are 525 records being displayed in the report.

Figure 13-7 Preview Sample options selected

If you look in the group tree section, you will see that only two shipping methods are included in the report, as shown in Figure 13-8. If you look at the group tree section in the original report shown in Figure 13-9, you will see that six shipping methods are on the report. The Preview Sample option will stay in effect until it is removed.

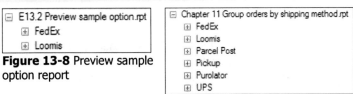

Figure 13-8 Preview sample option report

Figure 13-9 Chapter 11 Group orders by shipping method report

Keep in mind that when you select to preview a sample number of records, that they may not be the same first **N** number of records that will appear when you view all of the records. (N is the number that you enter on the Preview Sample dialog box shown earlier in Figure 13-7.) In the exercise above, 525 records were selected to be previewed. If you preview the original report, some or all of the records that you see at the beginning of the report could be different.

3.   Save the changes.

Report Options Dialog Box

The settings on the Options dialog box are global report options that are set. They are automatically applied to every report that you create. [See Chapter 2, Options Dialog Box]

There are also options that you can set on a report by report basis, as shown in Figure 13-10. (File ⇒ Report Options)

The options that are checked are the default report options. Many of the default options on this dialog box come from options that are selected on the Options dialog box.

Some options on this dialog box are not on the Options dialog box.

Figure 13-10 Report Options dialog box

The Role Of The Report Options Dialog Box
Changes that you make on the Reporting tab on the Options dialog box will change the default options on the Report Options dialog box, shown above. The options selected on the Report Options dialog box override the corresponding option on the Options dialog box (when applicable), for the active report. This means that the options on the Report Options dialog box will always be applied to the report, while the options on the Options dialog box will only be applied if there is no corresponding option on the Report Options dialog box.

Below are some options that you may find helpful.

RESPECT KEEP GROUP TOGETHER ON FIRST PAGE If checked and the Keep Group Together option on the Format Editor is checked, the first group will start printing on the second page if it will not fit on the first page. If this option is not checked, the first group will start printing on the first page, even if the Keep Group Together option is selected.

SAVE LOCK REPORT DESIGN Is used to password protect the report to keep any one from changing it. If they make changes, they will have to save it with a new file name.

PROMPT FOR HYPERLINKS If the report has a link that points to a file on your computers hard drive, you will see a message that lets you know that the file will be opened.

Report Export Overview

A report designer is not only responsible for creating and modifying reports, they can also be responsible for distributing the reports. There are several ways that an end-user can access and run the reports that you create, as explained below.

① Purchase and install Crystal Reports for every end-user that needs to run a report. This is probably not the best solution especially if there are hundreds or thousands of people in the company that need to run reports. This option could cost tens of thousands of dollars in hardware upgrades, software purchases, training and technical support.

② Hire someone to run reports all day, print them and send them via inter-office mail or email to end-users. This may sound good until you realize that end-users may not get the reports in a timely manner.

③ If the reports are part of an application that is being developed in a software package like Visual Basic or C++, the reports can be added to menu options or be attached to forms in the application. If this is the case, that's great, because your job is done.

④ Save the reports to a SAP Crystal Server or to a SAP Business Objects Enterprise.

⑤ Put the reports on www.crystalreports.com.

⑥ Use the free Crystal Reports viewer.

⑦ If none of the options discussed above are appropriate, all is not lost. There is another option. Exporting reports is cost effective and is something that a report designer can set up. The DBA would have to create a script that runs the exported report and place the exported report on a server. The only downside to this solution is that the reports probably will not have the most current data. If this is a problem, you will have to select one of the options above that gives users access to the live data (any option except 2, 6 or 7).

Export Format Options

Crystal Reports supports over 20 formats that reports can be exported to. Some export formats save the report in a better format then others in terms of the formatting and layout. Other export formats are better suited for data. Many of the formats are installed when Crystal Reports is installed. Exporting reports is a two step process, as explained below.

① Select the **EXPORT** format. This option is used to select the file format that the exported report will be saved in.

② Select the **DESTINATION**. This option is used to select where the exported file will be saved.

There are two ways to open the Export dialog box shown in Figure 13-11, as explained below.

① Click the **EXPORT** button on the Standard toolbar.

② File ⇒ Export ⇒ Export Report.

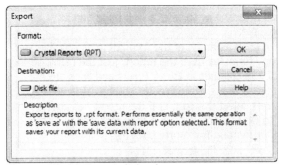

Figure 13-11 Export dialog box

Figure 13-12 shows the export format options. You may see the same or different options, then those shown.

Reports can be exported to more than one format if needed. Some export formats are better suited for certain types of reports then others. For example, some Word and Excel export format options are better suited for reports that may need to be edited by the end-user.

Table 13-2 explains the export format options. Some of the formats in the table do a better job of duplicating the report then others. I have noticed that sometimes reports that are exported to Excel get shifted a little. If the data does not need to be edited by the person using the exported report, the best format to use is PDF because it retains all of the formatting that you see when the report is viewed in Crystal Reports.

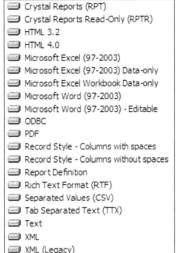

Figure 13-12 Export options

Format	Select This Format If You Want To . . .
Crystal Reports (RPT)	View the report with the current data in Crystal Reports or the Crystal Reports viewer.
𝕹𝕰𝖂 Crystal Reports Read-Only (RPTR)	View the report with a Crystal Reports viewer. The difference between this export format and the one above is that this file format is read only and cannot be opened in Crystal Reports. This file format prevents the layout of the report from being modified.
HTML 3.2	Display the report on the Web in a browser that does not support HTML 4.0 or higher. It does not maintain the exact layout that the report has. By today's standards, browsers that cannot use anything higher than HTML v3.2 are considered obsolete. (1) (2)

Table 13-2 Export format options explained

Format	Select This Format If You Want To . . .
HTML 4.0	Display the report on the Web. This format can be read by web browsers that use HTML v4.0 or higher. This format has better formatting capabilities then the HTML v3.2 format because it preserves the formatting by using DHTML. (1) (2)
MHTML	Send an HTML file in an email message or to save a web page and its objects like pictures in a single file.
Excel (97-2003)	Export the report to Excel and keep as much of the formatting as possible. This format will not include any formulas from the report, just the result of the formulas. It has a limit of 256 columns in Excel. Boxes and lines are not exported in this format. (3) (4)
Excel (97-2003) Data-Only	Export the report to Excel. Don't select this format if the report has charts or maps that you also need to export. Any data that is suppressed will not be exported. The majority of formatting is exported. (3) (4)
𝙽𝙴𝚆 Excel Workbook Data Only (.xlsx)	Save the report in the Excel 2007 .xlsx file format. (3) (4)
Word (97-2003)	Create an RTF document. Report objects are placed in text frames. The majority of formatting is retained. RTF stands for Rich Text Format.
Word (97-2003) - Editable	Create an RTF document. It allows the user to edit the report in Microsoft Word. Text formatting is retained. All of the layout may not be retained. (3)
ODBC	Export the report to any ODBC compliant database.
PDF	Create a PDF file, which is one of the most popular export formats because it can be read by both PC and MAC computers. If you want the report to retain its formatting and layout after it is exported, select this format. True Type fonts are embedded. (3) (5)
Record Style - Columns with spaces	Export the report data to an ASCII fixed length format like text, with spaces between columns. (3) (6)
Record Style - Columns without spaces	Export the report data to an ASCII fixed length format like text, without spaces between columns. (3) (6)
Report Definition	Create a report that contains a description of the reports design. This includes the sections, selection criteria, object formats, groups and more. This export format is usually for technical people. It does not export the data in the report. It exports information about the report.
Rich Text Format (RTF)	Export the report to RTF format, which retains the formatting of the report including graphics. Select this option if the report will be opened in a word processor other than Word.
Separated Values (CSV)	Create a comma delimited file. CSV stands for Comma Separated Values. This format is similar to the two Record Style formats discussed above. The difference is that in this format the fields are separated by a comma. This is often called a "Comma Delimited" file. Reports with any of the following cannot be exported to this format: Subreports in the page header or footer section, cross-tab or OLAP grids. (3) (7)
Tab Separated Text (TTX)	Export the report in text format and keep the layout. This format is similar to the Separated Values format because it separates the fields. The difference is that the fields are separated by tab spaces. (7)
Text	Create a plain text file. (3) (7)

Table 13-2 Export format options explained (Continued)

Format	Select This Format If You Want To . . .
XML	Create an XML file from the data in the report using the Crystal XML Schema for the data exchange. Style sheets can be applied to the XML file so that the data can be used in another application or on the web. XML stands for Extensible Markup Language. (3)
XML (Legacy)	Use an older Crystal Reports XML Schema to produce an XML file. The XML option above should be used.

Table 13-2 Export format options explained (Continued)

(1) Left justified is the only justification that will work.
(2) This export file format creates more than one file if the report has images.
(3) This export file format has the ability to save the report export options selected with the report. Doing this means that the person running the report does not have to select any export options. [See Default Export Options later in this chapter]
(4) This export file format does not merge cells. Some summary functions like SUM and COUNT are exported.
(5) The drill down feature and hyperlinks will not work with this report format.
(6) This export format is often used to move data into older applications. Only data from the details and group sections are exported.
(7) This export format does not retain any formatting like bold, italic or underline.

Export Destination Options

In addition to selecting an export format, a destination for the report also has to be selected. The destination refers to where the exported file will be viewed or saved. The options that are available by default are explained in Table 13-3. Some of the options may not be installed on your computer. You may have other options in addition to the ones in the table.

Option	Description
Application	Select this option when the export format is the Adobe Reader or a Windows based application like Word or Excel. Selecting this option causes the application that is associated with the export format to open after the report is exported. Exported files that use this destination option are automatically saved in the TEMP directory. You can move the file to another location. If you want to change the default location, you have to modify the path of the ExportDirectory key in the registry. The path to this key is HKEY_CURRENT_USER\Software\SAP Business Objects\Suite XI 4.0\Crystal Reports\Export, as illustrated in Figure 13-13.
Disk File	Is used to select a folder, either on a hard drive or on a server (which is also known as a network drive), where the exported report will be placed. This destination option does not automatically open the application associated with the export file.
Exchange Folder	Allows the exported report to be placed on a public or private Exchange mail server, which allows the report to be shared.
Lotus Domino	Exports the report to a Lotus Domino database. This requires that the form already be created in the Lotus database before the export is run. (8)
Lotus Domino Mail	Uses Lotus Domino Mail to export the report via email. (8)
MAPI	This option is used to send the exported report as an attachment to a MAPI (Microsoft) compliant email. To use this option, email software like Outlook or Exchange has to be installed and configured on your computer.

Table 13-3 Export destination options explained

(8) To use this option, the appropriate Lotus mail client software must be installed and configured on your computer.

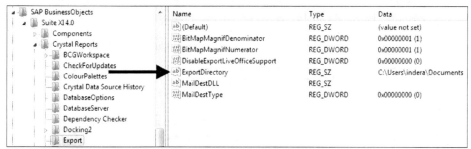

Figure 13-13 Path in the registry to change the default application export folder

Export Formatting Tips

I have found that by making sure that the export format tips listed below are followed, the exported file, regardless of the format, will look more like the report does in Crystal Reports.

① Make sure that all of the data fields in the same column have the same alignment (left or right). This is especially important for number and currency fields. If the fields in the same column have a different alignment option, some fields may appear in a different column in the exported report.
② All objects in the same column should be attached to the same guideline.
③ Remove any space that is not needed in each section of the report by moving all of the objects in each section up, as much as possible.

Default Export Options

If you know that the majority of times a report is exported that it will be exported to the same format, you can set default export options on the dialog box shown in Figure 13-14.

File ⇒ Export ⇒ Report Export, opens this dialog box.

Notice that the list of export options that can be saved in a report are fewer than the list of export options shown earlier in Table 13-2.

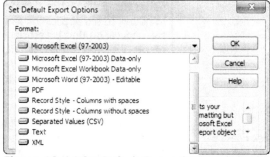

Figure 13-14 Set Default Export Options dialog box

Report Export Formats

The remaining exercises in this chapter show you how to create some of the more popular report export formats. To demonstrate the differences between the export format output options, you will use the same report to create all of the export formats covered in this chapter.

The E11.2 Group customer orders by month report is the report that you will use to create all of the export reports. You should open this report and then open the Export dialog box shown earlier in Figure 13-11, prior to starting each export exercise, unless instructed otherwise. Save each exported report in the folder that you created for this book.

Exercise 13.3: Create A PDF Export File

This export file type will create a PDF (Portable Document Format) file of the report. End-users that need to open reports in this file type will need to have the Adobe Reader installed. The Adobe Reader software is free and can be downloaded from http://get.adobe.com/reader/.

You do not have to download any of the other software that is on the web page for the Adobe Reader software to work. This file type can also be opened and viewed with Adobe Acrobat, which is the full version of the software that is used to create PDF files.

1. Select the PDF format, then open the Destination drop-down list and select **DISK FILE** if it is not already selected. Click OK.

> If you select the **APPLICATION** destination option, you will get the same PDF export file. The difference is that the Application option will not let you select where the export file will be saved initially. Once the report is exported you can save it to a different location. The exported file will automatically be stored in this location:
> C:\Users\{username}\AppData\Local\Temp\
> Usually the files are not automatically deleted from this folder so you may want to check this folder from time to time and delete the files.

The dialog box shown in Figure 13-15 is used to select whether you want to include all or some of the pages from the report in the PDF export file that you are about to create.

If you were going to send each sales rep their stats for the month from the report, you would enter the corresponding page numbers in the From and To fields on the dialog box. If the report has **PARAMETER FIELDS**, you would not have to do this to get a specific sales reps stats.

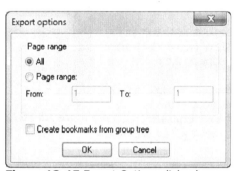

Figure 13-15 Export Options dialog box

The **CREATE BOOKMARKS FROM GROUP TREE** option will create bookmarks (similar to hyperlinks) in the PDF file for each group. This will make it easier for the person reading the PDF version of the report to find specific information.

2. Check the Create bookmarks from group tree option.

    Click OK to include all of the pages. You will see the dialog box shown in Figure 13-16.

    This dialog box is used to select where you want to save the export file.

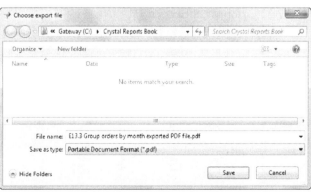

Figure 13-16 Choose Export File dialog box

3. Navigate to your folder, as shown above in Figure 13-16, then type

   `E13.3 Group orders by month exported PDF file` as the file name.

   Press Enter or click the Save button.

   You will see the dialog box shown in Figure 13-17. It displays that the export file is being created and how many records will be exported.

Figure 13-17 Exporting Records dialog box

When the export is complete, you can open the PDF file in either the Adobe Reader or Adobe Acrobat.

The exported PDF file should look similar to the one shown in Figure 13-18.

The bookmarks shown on the left side of Figure 13-18 are the groups on the report.

Like the report, you can click on the group in the PDF file and the corresponding section of the report will be displayed.

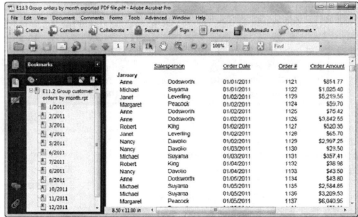

Figure 13-18 Group orders by month exported PDF file

Exercise 13.4: Create An Excel (97-2003) Export File

This export file type copies the data in the report to an Excel spreadsheet. To view this exported file type, Microsoft Excel needs to be installed. As you read in Table 13-2, there are three Excel export formats. The Excel export format options provide a slightly different output of the data.

1. Select the first Excel (97-2003) format, then open the Destination drop-down list and select **APPLICATION**.

   Figure 13-19 shows the options that should be selected.

   Click OK.

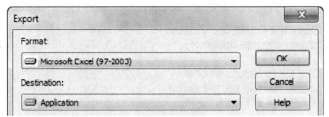

Figure 13-19 Export format options

You will see the dialog box shown in Figure 13-20.

These options are used to select how the data will be formatted in Excel.

Table 13-4 explains the options.

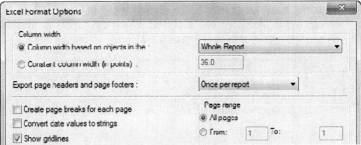

Figure 13-20 Excel (97-2003) Format Options dialog box

Option	Description
Column Width	These options are used to select the column width in Excel. ① The **COLUMN WIDTH BASED ON OBJECTS IN THE** option is used to select the column width in Excel based on a section in the report. ② The **CONSTANT COLUMN WIDTH (IN POINTS)** option is used to select a free form column width.
Export page headers and page footers	The options in this drop-down list determine where the page header and page footer information will be placed in the Excel file. ① **NONE** prevents the page header and footer sections from being exported. ② **ONCE PER REPORT** causes the page header information to be placed at the top of the first page and the page footer information to be placed at the bottom of the last page. ③ **ONCE PER PAGE** causes the page header and footer information to print on each page of the spreadsheet.
Create page breaks for each page	Adds page breaks to the spreadsheet in the same place they would appear in Crystal Reports. This may cause the report to break someplace other then at the end of the printed page in Excel. If you want the page breaks to happen automatically in Excel, do not check this option.
Convert date values to strings	Keeps the date formatting in Crystal Reports when the report is exported to Excel. If this option is not checked, the formatting for the date fields will come from the date formatting options in the copy of Excel that the exported file is opened in. This means that if different people have different date settings in their copy of Excel, the dates in the spreadsheet will appear differently.
Show Gridlines	This option forces gridlines to appear in the spreadsheet.
Page range	These options are used to select how many pages of the report will be exported.

Table 13-4 Excel (97-2003) export format options explained

2. Select the **SHOW GRIDLINES** option shown above in Figure 13-20, then click OK. You will see the records being processed and exported. When the export is complete, Excel will open and you will see the report shown in Figure 13-21.

	AF3228		*fx*				
A	B	CDEFGH	I	JK	L	M O P	Q
1							
3	8/16/2011						
4							
5		Salesperson		Order Date	Order #		Order
6	**January**						
8	Anne	Dodsworth		01/01/2011	1121		$851.77
10	Michael	Suyama		01/01/2011	1122		$1,025.40
12	Janet	Leverling		01/02/2011	1123		$5,219.55

Figure 13-21 Group orders by month exported Excel file

3. Scroll down to the row that has the Total # of orders for the month for January and click in the cell illustrated in Figure 13-22. If you look in the formula bar, you will not see the summary calculation (formula).

	O263		*fx*	127	←	**Formula Bar**
	A	B	CDEFGH	I	JK	L	M	O	P
261	Totals For:	January					
263			Total # of orders for the month -	127	
264			Total order amount for the month -	$211,265.10	
265			Percent of yearly sales -	7.37%	

Figure 13-22 Formula Bar illustrated

One reason to use this export format is if you do not want the end-user to be able to change or see the formulas. For other end-users, it would be helpful if the formulas that are used in the report were also exported.

4. Save the exported file as E13.4 Group orders by month exported file.

NEW Exercise 13.5: Create An Excel Workbook Data Only Export File

In this exercise you will export the report to an .xlsx file, which is the format that Excel 2007 and 2010 supports.

1. Select the Excel Workbook Data-Only format, then select the Application Destination option. Click OK. You will see the dialog box shown in Figure 13-23. The typical and minimal options pre-select some options on the bottom portion of the Excel Format Options dialog box for you. Table 13-5 explains the Excel format options.

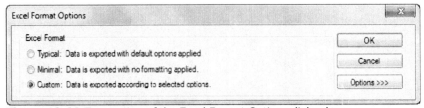

Figure 13-23 Top section of the Excel Format Options dialog box

Format	What Is Pre-Selected . . .
Typical	The most common options in the bottom section of the dialog box, which are shown in Figure 13-24.
Minimal	The basic options shown in Figure 13-25, to export the report without any formatting.
Custom	This option lets you select the export options.

Table 13-5 Excel Format Options dialog box options explained

Changing an option after selecting the typical or minimal option changes the format to custom.

The pre-selected options shown in Figures 13-24 and 13-25 can be used as a starting point. You can select one of these options and then add or remove options as needed.

This may be helpful if one of these export formats has a few of the options already selected that you need. Selecting one of these options and then making changes to it may save you some time.

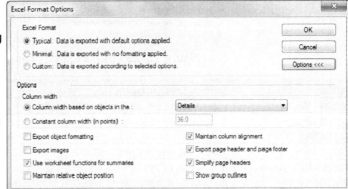

Figure 13-24 Typical format pre-selected default options

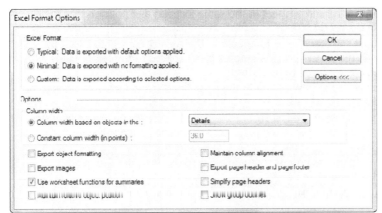

Figure 13-25 Minimal format pre-selected default options

2. Click the **OPTIONS** button. You will see the options shown in Figure 13-26.

   Table 13-6 explains the options.

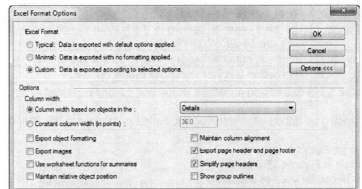

Figure 13-26 Custom format pre-selected default options

Option	Select This Option . . .
Column Width	[See Table 13-4 earlier in this chapter]
Export object formatting	To export as much of the formatting that is in the report as possible.
Export images	To export any images that are in the report.
Use worksheet functions for summaries	If you want Crystal Reports to try and convert summary fields to Excel functions. If a matching function is not found, the summary field will be exported as a number without the formula.
Maintain relative object position	If you want Crystal Reports to add rows and columns as needed to keep objects in the spreadsheet in the same location and position that they are in the report.
Maintain column alignment	To force summary fields to appear in the correct column in Excel. By default, the export process ignores blank spaces to the left of fields, which causes fields to be shifted.
Export page header and page footer	If you want the information in the page header and footer sections to be exported.
Simplify page headers	If you only want the last row of the page header section to be exported. Usually the last row of the page header section contains the field headings.
Show group outlines	If the report has groups that you want to use with the Group and Outline features in Excel.

Table 13-6 Excel data only export options explained

3. Check the option **USE WORKSHEET FUNCTIONS FOR SUMMARIES**, then click OK.

4. Make columns A through H wider in the spreadsheet.

5. Scroll down and click in cell F130, then look in the Formula Bar. You will see the equivalent of the summary calculation that was created in the report, as illustrated in Figure 13-27.

F130		f_x =SUM(E3:E129)			
A	B	C	D	E	F
127 Michael	Suyama	01/30/2011	1245	$3,419.25	
128 Margaret	Peacock	01/30/2011	1246	$3,884.25	
129 Margaret	Peacock	01/31/2011	1247	$36.00	
130 Totals For:	January	Total # of orders for t	127	Total order am	$211,265.10
131 February					

Figure 13-27 Summary calculation in the Formula Bar illustrated

6. Save the exported file as `E13.5 Orders by month in xlsx format`.

Exercise 13.6: Create A Separated Values (CSV) Export File

In this exercise you will export the report to a csv file.

1. Select the **SEPARATED VALUES (CSV)** format, then open the Destination drop-down list and select Application. Click OK.

The options on the dialog box shown in Figure 13-28 are used to select how you want the data from the report to be exported. The options that you select depend on how the data will be used.

The **ISOLATE REPORT/PAGE SECTIONS** option will export the report and page header and footer sections of the report as separate records.

The **ISOLATE GROUP SECTIONS** option will export the group header and footer sections of the report as separate records.

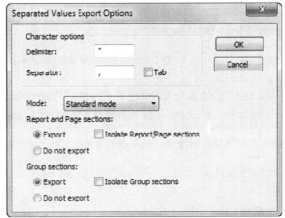

Figure 13-28 Separated Values Export Options dialog box

2. For this exercise, the default options on the dialog box shown above in Figure 13-28 are fine. Click OK. Because the Application destination option was selected, the .csv file will be opened in Excel, unless you have another software package associated with .csv files.

3. Any columns with the pound signs means that the column is not wide enough for the data that it contains.

   To make the column wider, double-click on the line after the column that you want to widen, as illustrated in Figure 13-29.

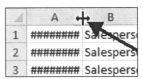

Figure 13-29 Mouse pointer in position to widen the column

After the column is made wider, the spreadsheet should look like the one shown in Figure 13-30. Notice that some of the columns (B, C and D for example) don't have data. They have field titles. That's because everything is exported. You can delete the columns that aren't needed.

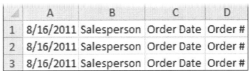

Figure 13-30 CSV exported file with Column A made wider

4. File ⇒ Save As. Type `E13.6 Exported CSV file` as the file name. You will see the message shown in Figure 13-31. This message is asking if you want to keep the formatting. For this exercise, click Yes.

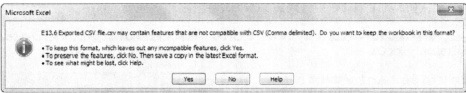

Figure 13-31 Excel formatting message

5. Close Excel. You will be prompted to save the file again. Save it with the same file name.

NEW Exercise 13.7: Create A Crystal Reports Read-Only File

In this exercise you will learn how to create a read only (.rptr) report file.

1. Select the Crystal Reports Read-Only format, then select the Disk File option. Click OK.

2. Save the report as `E13.7 Read only file`.

ODBC Export Format

If you select the ODBC export format, the destination option is not enabled on the Export dialog box. This is because the ODBC format exports the data from the report to a table. When you click OK on the Export dialog box, you will see the dialog box shown in Figure 13-32. You may be prompted to install a dll file. Select the ODBC format that you want to export the report to, then click OK. You will then see the dialog box shown in Figure 13-33. Select the database, then enter the name for the table that you will export the data to. Click OK. The table will be created in the ODBC format that you selected and the report data will be exported to it.

Figure 13-32 ODBC database format options

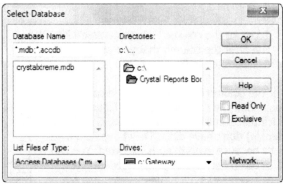

Figure 13-33 ODBC table name options

Text Export Format

This export format will prompt you to select the **CHARACTERS PER INCH** and the **NUMBER OF LINES PER PAGE** that you want for the exported file, as shown in Figure 13-34.

To me, the characters per inch option is similar to selecting the font size.

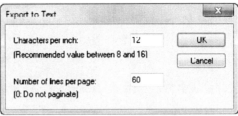

Figure 13-34 Export To Text dialog box

XML Export Format

This export format is similar to the HTML export format that you read about earlier in this chapter, because it is also web based. Like the HTML export format, the XML export format requires you to create a folder to store the XML files in. XML uses **TAGS** that will format the data or content for the report. Figure 13-35 shows the XML options.

To view a report in XML format, software that recognizes XML files is needed.

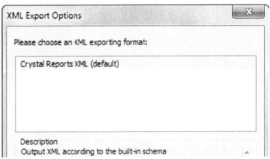

Figure 13-35 XML Export Options dialog box

File ⇒ Export ⇒ Manage XML Exporting Formats, opens the dialog box shown in Figure 13-36. Use this dialog box when you need to customize or add an XML export format.

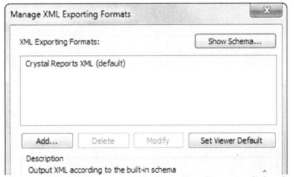

Figure 13-36 Manage XML Exporting Formats dialog box

Crystal Reports Viewer

This viewer can be used to view reports that were created in Crystal Reports. On the Resources tab on the Start Page is a link for the Crystal Reports Viewer. If that link doesn't work, you can try this web page. www.businessobjects.com/forms/crystalreports/viewer/

At the time this book went to print, the current viewer is the 2008 version, which cannot open .rptr (read-only) files. The 2011 version of the viewer will be available at some point.

FORMULAS AND FUNCTIONS

Overview

After completing the exercises in this chapter you will be able to:

- ☑ Understand the difference between formulas and functions
- ☑ Know what the formula (syntax) rules are
- ☑ Select a Syntax Editor
- ☑ Use the Formula Workshop
- ☑ Use the Workshop Tree
- ☑ Customize the Formula Editor
- ☑ Understand the formula evaluation order
- ☑ Create numeric formulas
- ☑ Create string formulas
- ☑ Use functions in string formulas
- ☑ Use date functions
- ☑ Use the Truncate function

Overview

Formulas and functions are some of the most powerful features in Crystal Reports. Ironically, many people that are first learning Crystal Reports think that formulas and functions are one of the most dreaded features because there is math and logic involved <smile>. If you fall into this category, hopefully this chapter will help you overcome some of the fear.

As part of the report design process, you learned that not all fields that are needed for a report exist in tables. You learned how to create summary fields which are not stored in tables. While summary fields provide a quick way to create totals, that is about as far as they go.

For example, summary fields will not let you add two fields together, nor can you multiply a field in a table by a constant value, like calculating the sales tax for an order. When you have exhausted all other math related options, it is time to turn to formulas and functions. Formulas are created in the Formula Workshop, which you use later in this chapter.

Actually, you have two options for creating formulas: The Formula Workshop and writing SQL Expressions. This type of field is what would be placed in the SQL Expression Fields section of the Field Explorer. If you are already freaking out about creating formulas, don't worry because this book does not cover SQL. The focus of this book is using the Formula Workshop because you would need to learn the version of SQL that works with the database that you are using for the reports.

The benefit that SQL Commands have over formulas is that they can process the data on a database server, which is usually more efficient then processing the data through the Crystal Reports engine, when the report is run, which is how formulas created in the Formula Workshop are evaluated. While creating SQL Commands is more efficient than creating formulas in the Formula Workshop, SQL Commands are evaluated (processed) on the server and sent back to Crystal Reports. By efficient, I mean that the records are retrieved faster and are not subject to as much of a performance hit, as it would be if the same number of records were processed locally on your computers hard drive. The syntax for SQL Commands can vary depending on the type of database.

The SQL for some types of databases is limited and can have fewer options than Crystal Reports has. For example, if you have to create a formula that needs to process or refer to (as in lookup) a record, other than the current record, you would have a problem if the database does not have any analytical functionality. I'm not saying this to scare you away from learning SQL, merely pointing out something that you may not be aware of.

What Is The Difference Between Formulas And Functions?

This is one of the questions that I am asked a lot. Formulas are calculations or some type of data manipulation that you create. Functions are built-in formulas or procedures that have already been created. If there is a built-in function that meets your needs, use it because there is no point to reinventing the wheel, as they say. If you have created or used formulas or functions in spreadsheet software, you are already familiar with the basics of using them in Crystal Reports.

Formulas

Formulas are used to create new fields. If you need to include data on a report that is not stored in tables, many times you will need to create a formula to get the data. An example of this would be the line item total on an order report. Line item information is not stored in an Order Detail table, but the price and quantity ordered are stored in the table. These are the fields that you would use to create the formula to calculate the line item total. A line item total is sometimes referred to as the

EXTENDED PRICE. Formulas allow you to create the following types of calculations, comparisons, manipulations and much more.

    ① Solve math problems

    ② Convert data from one format to another

    ③ Compare or evaluate data

    ④ Combine two or more text fields into one field

    ⑤ Combine text and data fields

You may be thinking or asking why all of this information is not stored in tables. There are many reasons including the following, why data that falls into these categories is not stored in tables.

    ① It would take a lot of hard drive or server space to store all of the data for these fields.

    ② Applications that share data have slightly different data needs, which means that some tables would have empty fields.

    ③ Some data is only needed once or the data changes constantly, so it is more efficient to calculate it when it is needed.

    ④ The more data that has to be written (added or changed) to a table in a database, the slower the application will run. This "slowness" is often referred to as a performance issue.

Syntax Rules

Formulas have rules (also known as syntax rules) that have to be followed. Basically, the rules require that items be placed in a certain order, so that the formula will work. Table 14-1 provides the rules for Crystal Syntax, that if followed will make learning how to write formulas easier. The items listed below are the parts of the formula.

Item	Syntax
//	The double slash is used to add comments to a formula. This is helpful when you need to document the formula. Comments should be added to formulas to explain the purpose of the formulas and to provide documentation. If the comment needs more than one line, each line must start with two slashes, otherwise Crystal Reports will treat the line as part of the formula, which will generate a syntax error. You may think that you will remember what the formula does six months from now, but it may take you a minute or so to remember. I have learned that it is easier to add comments to formulas and give them a descriptive name when you first create them.
Case Sensitive	Formulas are not case sensitive.
Hard Returns	Pressing the Enter key to continue the formula on the next line to make the formula easier to read is acceptable. The one time that this will cause an error is if there is a hard return between quotation marks in a formula.
Operators	Placing a space before or after an operator is acceptable, but is not required. Many people include spaces to make the formulas easier to read. The spaces are ignored when the formula is executed. The operators are similar to the ones that you learned about in Chapter 9. The difference is that symbols are used in formulas instead of words. = < > + - are some of the operators that you can use when creating formulas.
Fields	They must be surrounded by braces. For example, {Table Name.Field Name}.

Table 14-1 Syntax rules explained

Item	Syntax
Functions	Each function requires at least one argument. Each argument must be followed by a comma, except the last one. Arguments must be entered in this format: FunctionName (Argument 1, Argument 2).
Numbers	Numbers must be entered without any formatting. 5600 and 56000 is correct. 5,600 and 56,000.00 is not correct.
Text	Text must be entered inside of quotation marks. Examples: "Help" would be printed as Help. ' "Help" ' would be printed as "Help". Notice the difference in the output when different types of quotes are used.

Table 14-1 Syntax rules explained (Continued)

Functions

Functions are prewritten, built-in formulas or procedures. The functions that Crystal Reports provides have been thoroughly tested and from what I can tell, they are error free. However, this does not mean that if there is bad data in a table that you won't have a problem with the function. If you do not follow the syntax rules or fill in the arguments correctly when using the function, an error will be generated.

Crystal Reports comes with over 300 functions that you can use. Sum, Average, Count and Distinct Count are functions that you have already learned how to use. Many of the Special Fields that you have learned about are also functions, as are the Document Properties that you learned about. You can also create your own functions. This chapter covers some of the more popular functions that you may have a need to use.

Functions are one area where you may find the help file useful. Pressing the F1 key will open the help file. You can search for a particular function that you want to know more about or you can click on the Index tab on the Help window and type the word `functions`. Double-click on the Functions topic on the Topics Found dialog box. Doing this will display a list of the function categories on the right side of the Help window, as shown in Figure 14-1. From here you can scroll through the list and click on the category of functions that you want to learn more about.

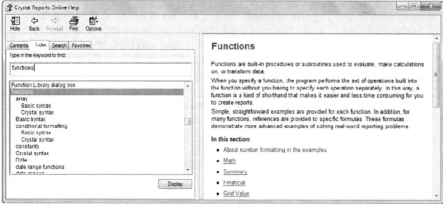

Figure 14-1 Functions in the Help window

Syntax Language And Editors

You can select the syntax language that you want to use. If you are already familiar with one, by all means continue to use it. If you have used a previous version of Crystal Reports, you may already be familiar with Crystal Syntax. You can create formulas and incorporate functions in both languages and both can be used in the same report. The good thing is that you do not have to be a programmer to create formulas or use functions in the Formula Workshop. Each language has its own rules for control structures, functions and other syntax. In order to create a formula in Crystal Reports, you need to select one of the following languages:

① **CRYSTAL SYNTAX** This language has been included in every version of Crystal Reports and is the default language that is selected when Crystal Reports is installed. The formulas that you viewed at the bottom of the Select Expert dialog box are written in Crystal Syntax, unless you changed the default language to Basic Syntax prior to working on the exercises in this book. Some say that Crystal Syntax is more user-friendly than Basic Syntax.

② **BASIC SYNTAX** If you have developed applications in Visual Basic, you will find this syntax language familiar. The main difference that you will notice between Visual Basic and Basic Syntax is that the Basic Syntax language has extensions for creating reports. Figures 14-2 and 14-3 show the same formula using different syntax editors.

```
// This formula combines the Supplier ID and Supplier Name fields
ToText ({Supplier.Supplier ID},0 )+ " - " +{Supplier.Supplier Name}
```
Figure 14-2 Formula using Crystal Syntax

```
'This formula combines the Supplier ID and Supplier Name fields
formula = ToText ({Supplier.Supplier ID},0)+ " - " + {Supplier.Supplier Name}
```
Figure 14-3 Formula using Basic Syntax

The benefit that Crystal Syntax and Basic Syntax have over SQL expressions is that formulas that cannot be created in SQL can be created using Crystal Syntax or Basic Syntax.

> The exercises in this book use Crystal Syntax because many features like record selection use this syntax language.

Statements

Depending on the environment that you work in, you may hear the term "Statement" and have a different interpretation of what a statement is then the context that I will present it in. That's fine, I just don't want you to think that either interpretation is incorrect. You may have also heard the term **EXPRESSION**. I believe that the terms statement and expression mean the same thing, but some will argue that there is a difference. Formulas in Crystal Reports consider a statement a combination of fields, operators, functions and other variables that provide an answer or value. I think of statements in Crystal Reports as sentences. Formulas have at least one statement.

Control Structures

This is how Crystal Reports processes a formula. The process starts at the beginning of the formula and moves from one statement to the next. Control structures evaluate expressions or conditions. The result of this evaluation is known as the **RETURN VALUE**. Formulas must return a value. The result of the last statement executed in the formula contains the result value. It is important to note that the last statement executed may not be the last physical line of code in the formula. Types of control structures include **WHILE DO/DO WHILE**, **SELECT CASE** and **IF STATEMENT**, which is also known as an If Then Else statement.

Formula Workshop

The window shown in Figure 14-4 is the tool that you will use to create and manage formulas. You can also work with record and group selection formulas in the Formula Workshop. Notice that it does not have any menus. Depending on how you open the Formula Workshop, you will either see the Formula Editor or the Formula Expert. If you do not like the toolbars at the top of the window, you can move them. Each section of the Formula Workshop is explained below.

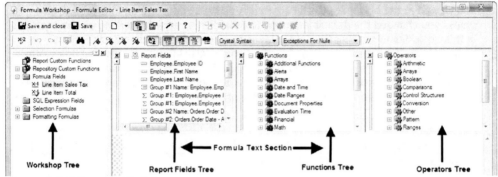

Figure 14-4 Formula Workshop

General Toolbar

Figure 14-5 shows the General toolbar. Table 14-2 explains the buttons on the toolbar.

Figure 14-5 General toolbar

Button	Description
1	Closes the Formula Workshop after prompting you to save changes if necessary. (1)
2	Saves the formula and leaves the Formula Workshop open. (1)
3	The New button is used to create a new formula based on the category selected from the drop-down list shown in Figure 14-6. If a formula is open prior to clicking this button, the syntax is checked and the current formula is saved.
4	The Show/Hide Workshop Tree button displays or hides the Workshop Tree.
5	The Toggle Properties Display button toggles between displaying the Custom Function Editor and the Custom Function Properties dialog box. Custom functions and formulas (when possible) are displayed in the selected mode until this button is clicked again.
6	The Use Expert/Editor button toggles between the Formula Editor and the Formula Expert. Use the Formula Expert to create a formula based on a custom function. This button is not available when creating a custom function.
7	Opens the online help file for the Formula Workshop, Formula Editor or Formula Expert, depending on which is currently displayed or where the insertion point is.

Table 14-2 General toolbar buttons explained

(1) When you save the changes, the formula, custom function or SQL Expression is checked for errors.

New Button Options

The **RECORD SELECTION FORMULA** option is used to create a formula to select data that will appear on the report based on records. (2)

The **GROUP SELECTION FORMULA** option is used to create a formula to select which groups will appear on the report. (2)

The **SAVED DATA SELECTION FORMULA** option is used to create a formula to filter the data that has already been saved with the report.

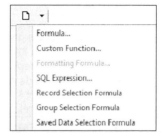

Figure 14-6 New button options

(2) This type of formula cannot be created using the Basic Syntax language.

Expression Editor Toolbar

Figure 14-7 shows the Expression Editor toolbar. Table 14-3 explains the buttons on the toolbar.

Figure 14-7 Expression Editor toolbar

Button	Description
1	The Check button tests the syntax of the formula or custom function and identifies syntax errors.
2	The Undo button undoes the last action made to the formula.
3	The Redo button redoes the last action made to the formula.
4	The Browse Data button is used to view the data in a field in the Report Fields window. (3)
5	The Find or Replace dialog box shown in Figure 14-8 searches the formula, fields, functions or operators for words or expressions. You can also replace text in formulas using this dialog box.
6	The Bookmark button inserts a bookmark in the current line of the selected formula. Click the button again to remove the bookmark. Bookmarks are used to mark a line of code in the formula as important. The bookmark feature is helpful in long formulas when you have to go from one part of the formula to another.
7	The Next Bookmark button places the insertion point at the next bookmark in the formula.
8	The Previous Bookmark button places the insertion point at the previous bookmark in the formula.
9	The Clear All Bookmarks button deletes all bookmarks in the current formula.
10	Sorts the options in the Report Fields, Functions and Operators trees in alphabetical order or returns them to their original order.
11	Displays or hides the Report Fields tree. (3)
12	Displays or hides the Functions tree.
13	Displays or hides the Operators tree.
14	Displays or hides the formula search results window shown in Figure 14-9.

Table 14-3 Expression Editor toolbar buttons explained

Button	Description
15	Is used to select **CRYSTAL SYNTAX** or **BASIC SYNTAX** as the formula syntax editor.
16	This option is used to select **EXCEPTIONS FOR NULLS** or **DEFAULT VALUES FOR NULLS** as the method for dealing with null values in the data. Fields in a formula that have a null value will return invalid data or generate an error. Selecting the Default values for nulls option will replace data that has a null value with the default value for the field type. String fields are changed to an empty string. Numeric fields are changed to zero. If you do not know how or do not want to create a formula to test for nulls or check for errors, select the Default values for nulls option.
17	Is used to add comments to a formula. Commented lines are not evaluated as part of the formula. I type the // into the Formula Text section when typing the formula because I find that faster then clicking this button.

Table 14-3 Expression Editor toolbar buttons explained (Continued)

(3) This button is not available for custom functions.

The **SEARCH** options on the Find dialog box change depending on the field type or object that is selected prior to clicking the Find and Replace button.

Figure 14-8 Find dialog box

Formula ▲	Line	Matches for "{Employee.Birth Date}"
Age	2	Truncate ((CurrentDate - {Employee.Birth Date})/365)
Test	1	{Employee.Birth Date} - 10

Figure 14-9 Find Results window (from the Find In Formulas option)

How To Open The Formula Workshop

Like many other tools in Crystal Reports, there is more than one way to open the Formula Workshop, as explained below.

① Click the **FORMULA WORKSHOP** button on the Expert Tools toolbar.

② Report ⇒ Formula Workshop.

③ Right-click on a formula or SQL Expression field on the design (or preview) tab, then select Edit.

④ Right-click on a formula or SQL Expression field on the Field Explorer, then select New or Edit.

⑤ Click on a formula or SQL Expression field, then click the **NEW** button on the Field Explorer toolbar.

⑥ Click the **FORMULA** button on any tab of the Format Editor dialog box.

⑦ Open the Select Expert, click the Show Formula button, then click the **FORMULA EDITOR** button.

Workshop Tree

This section of the Formula Workshop contains the following: All of the formula types that you can create or modify, the formulas that are in the report and the formulas that are in the repository that can be used in the report.

As you saw earlier in Figure 14-4, the Workshop Tree contains several sections called **NODES** or **CATEGORY** folders that formulas can be saved in. In addition to being able to create formulas, you can also rename and delete formulas, just like you can in the Field Explorer. Each of the category folders in the Workshop Tree are explained below.

① **REPORT CUSTOM FUNCTIONS** If you create a function or copy a function from the repository into the report, this is where it would be stored. The functions in this folder can be used by any formula in your report. Custom functions are used just like the built-in functions that come with Crystal Reports.

② **REPOSITORY CUSTOM FUNCTIONS** The functions in this folder are actually stored in the SAP Business Objects Enterprise or on a Crystal Reports Server. Functions in this folder can be used with any report. To use a repository custom function, it has to be added to the report so that it will become a report custom function.

③ **FORMULA FIELDS** The formulas in this folder are the same ones that are in the Field Explorer in the Formula Fields, Parameter Fields, Running Total Fields and Group Name Fields sections.

④ **SQL EXPRESSION FIELDS** The formulas in this folder are the same expression fields that are in the SQL Expression Fields section of the Field Explorer. If you create a new expression or modify an existing expression in this folder, the SQL Expression Editor will open in the Formula Workshop instead of the Formula Editor. The options in the Report Fields Tree, Functions Tree and Operators Tree will change and display the options that are available for the type of database that the report is using. It has been reported that the SQL Expression Editor may not reflect all of the operators and functions that are really available for certain database types.

⑤ **SELECTION FORMULAS** The formulas in this folder are the formulas that are created when you use the Select Expert or the selection formula options on the Report menu. You can also create selection formulas in the Formula Workshop. If you click on the Group Selection option, the **GROUP SELECTION FORMULA EDITOR** will open. If you click on the Record Selection option, the **RECORD SELECTION FORMULA EDITOR** will open. If you click on the Saved Data option, the **SAVED DATA SELECTION FORMULA EDITOR** will open. The only difference that you will notice with these editors is that the title bar of the Formula Workshop shown earlier in Figure 14-4, will display the name of the editor.

⑥ **FORMATTING FORMULAS** This category has a folder for each section of the report. All of the objects from each section of the report are listed here. Formatting formulas like changing the color, font, font size for objects in the report or conditional formatting are stored in this folder. Formulas in this folder come from formulas that you create using the Format Editor or the Report Section Expert.

Workshop Tree Toolbar

Figure 14-10 shows the Workshop Tree toolbar. Table 14-4 explains the buttons on the toolbar.

Figure 14-10 Workshop Tree toolbar

Button	Description
1	Duplicates the formula selected in the Formula Fields section of the Workshop tree.
2	Renames the selected formula, custom function, or SQL Expression.
3	Deletes the selected formula, custom function, or SQL Expression.
4	Expands the selected nodes in the Workshop Tree.
5	The Show Formatting Formulas button displays or hides all of the report objects in the Formatting Formulas folder or only the objects that have a formatting formula.
6	The Add To Repository button opens the Add Custom Function To Repository dialog box so that you can select the repository to add the custom function to.
7	The Add To Report button adds the selected repository custom function to the report.

Table 14-4 Workshop Tree toolbar buttons explained

Formula Editor

The Formula Editor is in the Formula Workshop. The contents of each of the trees in the Formula Editor change to show the options that are available for the type of formula that you are creating. The Formula Editor is used to create formulas by double-clicking on the functions, operators and fields that you need to include in the formula. The Formula Editor can create at least 90% of the formulas that you need. It contains the three trees explained below. You may want to open some of the categories (nodes) in each tree to become familiar with the options.

① The **REPORT FIELDS TREE** displays all of the fields that are on the report, including groups, summary fields, running totals, parameters, formulas and the tables that the report uses. This tree is similar to the Field Explorer. You can use any of these fields in a formula.

② The **FUNCTIONS TREE** contains the built-in functions. The functions are divided into categories, which should make it easier to find the function that you need.

③ The **OPERATORS TREE** contains the operators (logical and mathematical) that you can use to create formulas. The operators are grouped by type to make them easier to find. Operators in the Formula Editor use symbols instead of words like the Select Expert uses. It is usually easier to type in the operator then to select it from this tree.

> When you first open the Formula Workshop, you will not see the Formula Editor. You can do either of the following to open the Formula Editor.

① Select an option in a folder under the Formula Fields, SQL Expression Fields or Selection Formulas in the Workshop Tree.

② Select one of the formula or function options on the New button drop-down list shown earlier in Figure 14-6.

> If you open the Formula Editor using the **FORMULA EDITOR** button on the Select Expert, Crystal Syntax is the only programming language that you can use.

Formula Text Section

In addition to the three trees, the empty section below the trees is called the Formula Text section. This is where you type in the formula. Depending on the field selected in the Workshop Tree, the Formula Editor can change to a different editor because each formula type has its own editor. By default, the font is automatically color coded as follows:

① Green is used for comments that you type in.
② Blue is used for reserved words like functions.
③ Black is used for constants and variables.

Formula Editor Shortcut Keys

Like word processors, the Formula Editor has shortcut key functionality including the following:

- ☑ Ctrl+C Copy the formula.
- ☑ Ctrl+X Delete the selected content.
- ☑ Ctrl+V Paste the selected content.
- ☑ Ctrl+A Select all of the content in the Formula Text section.
- ☑ Ctrl+S Save the formula and close the Formula workshop.

Using Auto Complete

You can use the **AUTO COMPLETE** feature in the Formula Text section by typing in the first few letters of the function that you need, then press the **CTRL+SPACE BAR** keys.

You will see a list that has functions that start with the letters that you typed in, as shown in Figure 14-11.

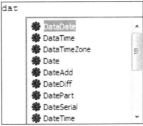

If you type in enough letters to only display the function that you want, the drop-down list will not be displayed. Instead, the function will be filled in for you. If you press the CTRL+Space bar keys before typing any letters, you will see all of the functions in the list.

Figure 14-11 Auto complete list of functions in the Formula Text section

To view a list of tables, type a {, as shown in Figure 14-12.

Figure 14-12 Auto complete list of tables in the Formula Text section

Customizing The Formula Editor

You can customize the Formula Editor by doing any or all of the following:

① You can resize any of the tree sections by dragging the bar illustrated in Figure 14-13.
② Close a tree by clicking on the ☒ button to the left of the section that you want to close.
③ Expand a tree by clicking on the ⬛ button to the left of the section that you want to expand.
④ Make the Formula Text section longer or shorter by dragging the section bar above it, up or down.

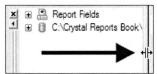

Figure 14-13 Mouse pointer in position to resize a tree

SQL Expression Editor

At the beginning of this chapter you read that SQL Commands could be used to create formulas. There is another SQL option called **SQL EXPRESSIONS**. SQL Expressions are formulas that are evaluated by the database server. The main difference between them and SQL Commands is that they can be used with reports that are created from tables, stored procedures and views. SQL Expressions can only use a subset of the operators and functions that Crystal Reports supports.

As shown in Figure 14-14, the SQL Expression Editor looks similar to the Formula Editor shown earlier in Figure 14-4. The largest difference that you will notice is that the Report Fields tree only displays fields from a database. Formula fields and parameter fields are not displayed in the SQL Expression Editor because they cannot be used to create SQL Expressions. This is because expressions are evaluated on a database server.

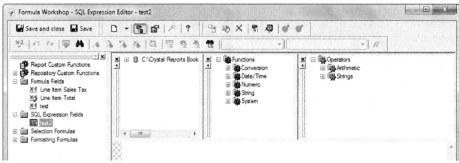

Figure 14-14 SQL Expression Editor

Formula Expert

The Formula Expert shown in Figure 14-15 is used to create and modify custom functions. The functions that you create in the Formula Expert can be used in other reports if they are saved in the SAP Business Objects Enterprise Repository. By design, the Formula Expert will help you create a formula without having to use the Crystal Reports syntax programming language. While this may sound appealing to those that are new to Crystal Reports or do not want to write code, the Formula Expert only creates formulas that use one custom function. You cannot use the math operators or the Crystal Reports syntax programming language in the Formula Expert.

Extracting A Custom Function

You just read that the Formula Expert is used to create formulas which use built-in functions. The Formula Extractor works just the opposite. It is used to create custom functions from formulas. The options on the dialog box shown in Figure 14-16 are used to create a custom function from an existing formula. Formulas created on this dialog box can be used on reports and can be added to the repository so that they can be used in other reports. To open this dialog box, right-click on the Report Custom Functions node in the Workshop Tree and select New. Type in a name for the function, then click the **USE EXTRACTOR** button.

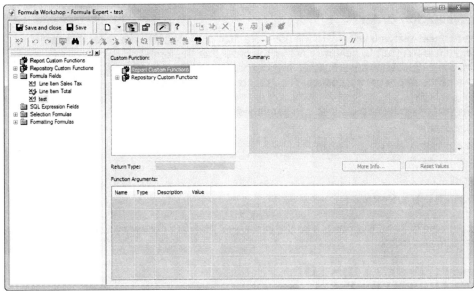

Figure 14-15 Formula Expert

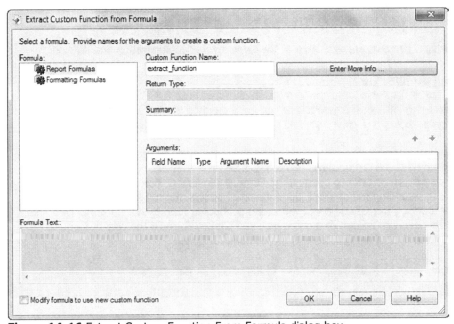

Figure 14-16 Extract Custom Function From Formula dialog box

Formula Editor vs Formula Expert

The main difference between the two is that formulas created in the Formula Editor are saved with the report that they are created in and can only be used in that report. Formulas created in the Formula Expert can be saved as a CUSTOM FUNCTION in the repository and can be used in any report. If you find yourself creating the same formula in several reports, copy it to the Formula Expert and save it as a custom function. Creating custom functions and using the repository are beyond the scope of this book.

Formula Evaluation Order

Many of the formulas that you will create will use more than one operator. The order that the formula is written in from left to right may not be the order that the formula is calculated or evaluated in. Some operations are processed first, regardless of where they are in the formula. This is known as the **ORDER OF PRECEDENCE**. The formula evaluation order is:

① The portion of the formula that is in parenthesis.
② Exponential
③ Multiplication and division (4) (5)
④ Integer division
⑤ MOD
⑥ Addition and subtraction (4)

(4) If the operators in 3 and 6 above are on the same level, they are evaluated from left to right. See the examples below.

Example #1 $3 + 4 / (2 + 19) = 3.19$
Example #2 $3 + (4 / 2) + 19 = 24$

The first example calculates (2+19) first, then divides that by 4 and then adds 3.
The second example calculates (4/2) first, then adds 3 and then adds 19.

(5) In Crystal Syntax, percents are evaluated at the same level as multiplication and division.

Creating Formulas Tip
You may find it helpful to write the formula on paper and use data in the tables to test the formula to see if you get the results that you are expecting from the formula. As you saw in the examples above, the same data and operators can produce different results.

I have noticed in the workplace and in classes that I have taught that this is one area where many people have a lot of trouble. I think this is because they are not willing to write out the formula and test it prior to opening the Formula Workshop. Yes, I am fully aware that doing this takes more time up front, but experience shows that the more time that you spend "preparing", the less time you will spend debugging reports in the future. Trust me, a year from now, you will not remember why you wrote a formula the way that you did <smile>. Keep the following in mind when creating formulas:

① Formulas must have an equal number of left and right parenthesis.
② Arguments must be the same data type.

Formula Naming Conventions

The naming conventions for formulas is free form. Formula names can be up to 256 characters. You should use as descriptive a name as possible, one that will make sense to you a year from now. The name that you select is what you will see when the formula field is added to the report. You can use upper and lower case letters, spaces and the underscore. You should not use characters like the slash, dollar or percent sign in the formula name.

The company that you work for may have naming conventions. You should check to find out. One convention that many companies have is that they do not want spaces in object names. When this is the case, most people use the underscore in place of spaces in object names.

Create Numeric Formulas

The exercises in this section teach you how to create numeric formulas.

Exercise 14.1: Create A Formula Field

The report that you will modify in this exercise displays an order total per customer. As you will see, the order total is not correct. You will create a formula that will calculate the amount for each item. This is known as the line item amount. The formula is Unit Price * Quantity. This will allow the report to have the correct total amount.

1. Save the Chapter 14 Orders by sales rep report as `E14.1 Formula field for line item totals`.

2. Click on the **FORMULA FIELDS** option in the Field Explorer, then click the **NEW** button on the Field Explorer toolbar.

3. Type `Line Item Total` in the dialog box shown in Figure 14-17, then click OK.

Figure 14-17 Formula Name dialog box

4. In the Report Fields tree, double-click on the Unit Price field in the Orders Detail table.

   You should see the field in the Formula Text section in the Formula Editor, as shown at the bottom of Figure 14-18.

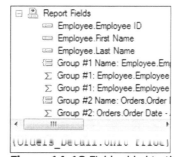

Figure 14-18 Field added to the Formula Text section

 In addition to double-clicking on a field you can also drag the field to the Formula Text section.

5. Type a * after the Unit Price field, then double-click on the Quantity field.

 You can use the **MULTIPLY** arithmetic operator illustrated in Figure 14-19 instead of typing in the operator.

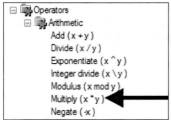

Figure 14-19 Multiply arithmetic operator illustrated

6. Add a blank line above the formula, then type the following comment.
   `// This formula calculates the Line Item Total.`
   The formula should look like the one shown in Figure 14-20.

```
// This formula calculates the Line Item Total
{Orders_Detail.Unit Price}*{Orders_Detail.Quantity}
```

Figure 14-20 Line Item Total formula

 Notice that the comment line is a different color then the formula line. This is one way to know that you have entered the comment correctly. Comments do not have to go above a formula.

7. Click the **(x+2)** button on the Expression Editor toolbar. You should see the message shown in Figure 14-21.

   If you do not see the message, there is an error in your formula. Check to make sure that your formula looks like the one shown above in Figure 14-20.

Figure 14-21 No errors found message

 The message shown above in Figure 14-21 means that Crystal Reports did not find a syntax error. This does not mean that the formula will produce the results that you are expecting. For example, you could have added the wrong field to the formula.

 Using the **(x-2)** button is optional because the syntax is automatically checked when you exit the Formula Editor.

Figure 14-22 shows one error message that you could see.

If there is an error, the flashing insertion bar will be in the location in the formula where Crystal Reports thinks the error is. The part of the formula where the syntax checker stopped understanding the formula will also be highlighted, as illustrated in Figure 14-22.

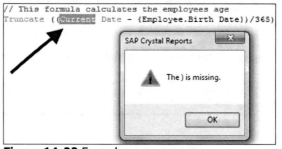

Figure 14-22 Formula error message

You are not required to fix the error immediately. You can save the formula as is and work on something else. Just don't forget to come back and fix it.

8.   Click the **SAVE AND CLOSE** button.

 If you need to work on another formula, click the **SAVE** button instead of the Save and close button. Doing this will leave the Formula Workshop open. When you save a formula it becomes a field that you can add to the report or use in another formula.

Using Formula Fields In Reports

You can use formula fields in reports, just like you use fields from a table. Formula fields can be placed in any section of the report. You can create counts and summary fields that are based on formula fields. You can also use formula fields as selection criteria.

Add The Line Item Formula Field To The Report

In this part of the exercise you will add the formula field that you just created to the report.

1.   Delete the Order Amount field, then move the four fields after the Order Amount field over to the left.

2.   Add the Line Item Total formula field to the report. The report should look like the one shown in Figure 14-23. Save the changes and leave the report open to complete the next part of the exercise.

Salesperson		Order Date	Order ID	Customer #	Product #	Unit Price	Quantity	Line Item Total
1	Nancy Davolio							
2/14/2010								
30								
		02/19/2010	1310	30	1101	$14.50	3	$43.50
		02/19/2010	1310	30	1104	$14.50	1	$14.50
	Total order amount for customer -	**$ 116.00**						
75								
		02/19/2010	1312	75	302162	$479.85	1	$479.85
		02/19/2010	1312	75	401001	$267.76	1	$267.76
		02/19/2010	1312	75	2202	$41.90	1	$41.90
	Total order amount for customer -	**$ 2,368.53**						

Daily Totals   # of Orders for the day - **2**

Total amount of sales for the day 8,9,404.53

Figure 14-23 Line item total field added to the report

Modify The Total Fields

As you can see, the total order amount for each customer is still not correct. That is because the Total Order Amount field is adding the values in the Order Amount field. The Total Order Amount field should be adding the values in the Line Item Total formula field because the Line Item field calculates the total for each item on the order.

1.   Modify the Total order amount for customer, Total amount of sales for the day, Total amount of sales for salesperson and Total amount of sales fields to use the Line Item Total field for the summary, instead of the Order Amount field as shown in Figure 14-24. (**Hint:** Use the Edit Summary option on the shortcut menu.) The report should look like the one shown in Figure 14-25. Compare the totals illustrated to those shown above in Figure 14-23.

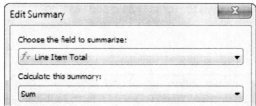

Figure 14-24 Edit summary options

Salesperson		Order Date	Order ID	Customer #	Product #	Unit Price	Quantity	Line Item Total
1	Nancy Davolio							
2/14/2010								
30								
		02/19/2010	1310	30	1101	$14.50	3	$43.50
		02/19/2010	1310	30	1104	$14.50	1	$14.50
	Total order amount for customer - **$ 58.00** ←							
75								
		02/19/2010	1312	75	302162	$479.85	1	$479.85
		02/19/2010	1312	75	401001	$267.76	1	$267.76
		02/19/2010	1312	75	2202	$41.90	1	$41.90
	Total order amount for customer - **$ 789.51** ←							
Daily Totals		# of Orders for the day - **2**						
	Total amount of sales for the day - **$ 847.51** ←							

Figure 14-25 Modified report

Exercise 14.2: Create A Sales Tax Formula

Many items that you buy require sales tax to be collected. This exercise shows you how to create a sales tax formula. You will create a formula that calculates 6% of the line item total. If all items were taxable, you could create a sales tax formula that used the order total times the sales tax rate. In this exercise, you will modify a customer order report and create a sales tax formula that will use the Line Item Total field instead of the Order Total field.

 In the real world, the product table would have a field that is used to signify if a product is taxable or not. In that case, you would have to create a conditional formula that checked the field to see if the product is taxable. If it is taxable, then calculate the sales tax for that product.

1. Save the E14.1 report as E14.2 Sales tax formula.

2. Create a formula field and name it Line Item Sales Tax.

3. Double-click on the Line Item Total field in the Report Fields tree, then type *.06 at the end of the field. Check the formula to make sure that the syntax is correct. The formula should look like the one shown in Figure 14-26. Save the formula and close the Formula Workshop.

```
{@Line Item Total}*.06
```
Figure 14-26 Line Item Sales Tax formula

4. Move all of the fields except for the Salesperson field to the left, then add the Line Item Sales Tax field to the end of the details section.

5. Change the field title for the Line Item Sales Tax field to Sales Tax. The report should look like to the one shown in Figure 14-27. Save the changes and leave the report open to complete the next part of the exercise. Keep in mind that currently on this report, the total order amount for the customer does not include the tax field that you just added to the report.

Salesperson	Order Date	Order ID	Customer #	Product #	Unit Price	Quantity	Line Item Total	Sales Tax
1	Nancy Davolio							
2/14/2010								
30								
	02/19/2010	1310	30	1101	$14.50	3	$43.50	$ 2.61
	02/19/2010	1310	30	1104	$14.50	1	$14.50	$ 0.87
	Total order amount for customer - **$ 58.00**							
75								
	02/19/2010	1312	75	302162	$479.85	1	$479.85	$ 28.79
	02/19/2010	1312	75	401001	$267.76	1	$267.76	$ 16.07
	02/19/2010	1312	75	2202	$41.90	1	$41.90	$ 2.51
	Total order amount for customer - **$ 789.51**							
Daily Totals	# of Orders for the day - **2**							
	Total amount of sales for the day - **$ 847.51**							

Figure 14-27 Sales tax formula report

Create A Summary Formula

All of the summary fields that you created so far in this book were based off of fields in a table. In this part of the exercise you will create a summary field that is based off of a formula field.

1. Right-click on the Line Item Total formula field, then select Insert ⇒ Summary. Select the Average summary type, then select the Group 2 Orders Date option, as the section to place the field in. Click OK.

On the preview tab you will see the average amount for the daily totals, as illustrated in Figure 14-28.

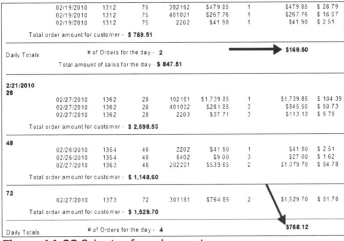

Figure 14-28 Sales tax formula report

2. If you want, you can create a title for the field so that the person reading the report knows what the number is. Save the changes.

Exercise 14.3: Create A Weekly Salary Formula

In this exercise you will create a formula that will calculate each employees weekly salary.
The annual salary field is stored in the Employee table. You will use this field to calculate the weekly salary.

1. Save the Chapter 14 Employee list report as
   E14.3 Employee list with weekly salary formula.

2. Create a formula field and name it Weekly Salary.

3. Double-click on the Salary field in the Employee table and then drag the **DIVIDE (X/Y)** Arithmetic operator to the Formula Text section.

4. Type 52 after the slash. Check the formula to make sure that the syntax is correct. The formula should look like the one shown in Figure 14-29. Save the formula and close the Formula Workshop.

{Employee.Salary}/52

Figure 14-29 Weekly Salary formula

5. Delete the Region field, then add the Weekly Salary formula field before the Salary field. The report should look like the one shown in Figure 14-30. Save the changes and leave the report open to complete the next part of the exercise.

First Name	Last Name	Address1	Weekly Salary	Salary
Steven	Buchanan	14 Garrett Hill	$961.54	$ 50,000.00
Robert	King	Edgeham Hollow	$711.54	$ 37,000.00
Anne	Dodsworth	7 Houndstooth Rd.	$673.08	$ 35,000.00
Michael	Suyama	Coventry House	$576.92	$ 30,000.00

Figure 14-30 Employee list with weekly salary formula report

Use A Formula Field As Selection Criteria

Earlier you learned that you can use a formula field as selection criteria. In this part of the exercise you will use the Weekly Salary formula field to only display employees that have a weekly salary between $500 and $750.

1. Create the selection criteria for the Weekly Salary formula field.

2. The report should look like the one shown in Figure 14-31. There should be five records on the report. Save the changes.

First Name	Last Name	Address1	Weekly Salary	Salary
Robert	King	Edgeham Hollow	$711.54	$ 37,000.00
Anne	Dodsworth	7 Houndstooth Rd.	$673.08	$ 35,000.00
Michael	Suyama	Coventry House	$576.92	$ 30,000.00
BC				
Margaret	Peacock	4110 Old Redmond Rd.	$673.08	$ 35,000.00
Janet	Leverling	722 Moss Bay Blvd.	$634.62	$ 33,000.00

Figure 14-31 Formula field used as selection criteria

Create String Formulas

The exercises in this section teach you how to create formulas that use string fields or literals. The most used string formulas are used to convert date and numeric fields to text, select specific portions of a field and trim fields. A common string formula that is used is one that will concatenate (combine) the first and last name fields. Names are usually stored in two or more fields in a table. There are several string formula operators and functions that you can use, as explained in Tables 14-5 and 14-6.

String Operators

Operator	Description
+ or &	These are known as concatenation operators. They are used to combine text fields. The plus sign operator requires that all arguments be string fields. The plus sign operator allows for custom formatting. Crystal Reports will automatically convert every argument to a string when the ampersand (&) operator is used. This means that you can combine fields with different data types if you use the ampersand.
[ ]	Subscript operators are used to select specific characters from a text field.
" " or ' '	Quotes will treat the text inside of them as a literal. If a string or text field contains numeric data and you need to use it in a formula, you have to put the numeric data in quotes.
If Then Else	This operator allows different actions to be taken based on a condition.

Table 14-5 String operators explained

> Date/Time literals must be in one of these formats: #6/24/2011# or #June 24, 2011#.

> Keep in mind that while the + (plus sign) operator is used to join text and data fields, it does not add a space between the fields that are being joined. You have to type + " " + to add a space between the fields that you are joining. There is a space between the quotes in the syntax above.

String Functions

Function	What The Function Does . . .
Is Null	Checks to see if a field has a value. It is often used with the If...Then... Else statement. If the function is used alone, it returns a value of True or False (Boolean).
Length (str)	Counts the number of characters in a string. It is used to determine if the value in a field is a certain length.
Lower Case (str)	Converts the text to all lower case letters. Use LOWERCASE for Crystal Syntax. Use LCASE for Basic Syntax.
Picture (str, picture)	Formats a string field. This is similar to the "mask" feature found in some databases.
To Text	Converts non text fields like date, number and currency to a text field. This function can have multiple arguments, as shown in Figure 14-32. The only argument that requires a value is X. Unless being used on a parameter field, it is better not to use this function to convert a numeric field.

Table 14-6 String functions explained

Function	What The Function Does . . .
Trim (str)	Removes spaces before and after the data in a string argument. Use **TRIMLEFT** if you only want to remove spaces to the left of the string argument. Use **TRIMRIGHT** if you only want to remove spaces to the right of the string argument.
Upper Case (str)	Converts the text to all upper case letters. Use **UPPERCASE** for Crystal Syntax. Use **UCASE** for Basic Syntax.

Table 14-6 String functions explained (Continued)

```
⊟ ToText
    ToText (x)
    ToText (x, y)
    ToText (x, y, z)
    ToText (x, y, z, w)
    ToText (x, y, z, w, q)
```

Figure 14-32 To Text functions

Exercise 14.4: Combine Two String Fields

Earlier in this chapter you modified an employee report. That report would look better if the employee first and last names were closer together. This produces the same result as dragging one field into another. One reason that you would create a formula is to combine the name fields is if you only needed to combine fields when a certain condition was met. Another reason to create a formula is to combine fields is if there is a possibility that at least one of the fields is null.

1. Save the E14.1 report as `E14.4 Combine string fields`.
2. Create a formula field and name it `Employee Name`, then add the First Name field from the Employee table to the Formula Text section.
3. Click after the First Name field, then type `+ " " +`. This will add a space after the First Name field. Make sure that there is a space between the quotes, then add the Last Name field to the formula.
4. Add a blank line above the formula, then type `// This formula combines 2 fields`. Check the formula for errors. The formula should look like the one shown in Figure 14-33. Save the formula and close the Formula Workshop.

```
// This formula combines 2 fields
{Employee.First Name}+" "+{Employee.Last Name}
```

Figure 14-33 String formula

Add The Employee Name Formula Field To The Report

1. Delete the First and Last name fields in the group 1 header section, then add the Employee Name formula field in place of the two fields that you just deleted.
2. Create a field heading. Type `Employee` in the field, then underline it. Place it above the Employee Name field. The report should look like the one shown in Figure 14-34. Save the changes and leave the report open to complete the next exercise.

Employees	Order Date	Order ID	Customer #	Product #	Unit Price	Quantity	Line Item Total
1 Nancy Davolio							
2/14/2010							
30							
	02/19/2010	1310	30	1101	$14.50	3	$43.50
	02/19/2010	1310	30	1104	$14.50	1	$14.50
Total order amount for customer - **$ 58.00**							

Figure 14-34 Combine string fields report

Exercise 14.5: Use The Subscript Operator

The subscript operator is used to extract specific characters in a field based on their position in the field. In Exercise 14.4 you learned how to combine the first and last name fields. If you needed to modify that formula to only display the first letter of the first name, you would use the subscript operator. The subscript [3] means to select the third character in the field from the left. In this exercise you will add the subscript operator to an existing formula.

1. Save the E14.4 report as `E14.5 Subscript`.

2. Modify the Employee Name formula so that it looks like the one shown in Figure 14-35.

```
// This formula combines 2 fields and only uses the first letter
// of the First Name field
{Employee.First Name}[1]+" "+{Employee.Last Name}
```

Figure 14-35 Subscript formula

3. Save the changes. The report should look like the one shown in Figure 14-36.

   Notice that only the first letter of the first name is displayed.

Employees	Order Date
1 N Davolio	
2/14/2010	
30	
	02/19/2010
	02/19/2010
Total order amount for customer - **$**	

Figure 14-36 Subscript report

Exercise 14.6: Combine A Text And Numeric Field

In the reports that you have created with totals, you created a text object for the title of the summary field. If you had trouble either getting the text object and total field to line up or getting the two fields to be close together, this exercise shows you how to combine these fields using a formula, which means that you will not have to align the field and text object.

 If the numeric field that you will use needs to be formatted, you should not combine it with a text field because text fields cannot be formatted with numeric formatting options.

1. Save the E10.1 report as `E14.6 Combine text and numeric fields`.

2. Create a formula field and name it `Total Field`.

3. Add the comment `This formula combines text with a numeric field`.

4. Type `"Total # of customers in region - "` in the Formula Text section.

5. Open the **STRINGS** operators node, then drag the **CONCATENATE (X&Y)** operator illustrated on the right in Figure 14-37 to the Formula Text section.

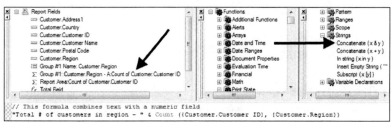

Figure 14-37 Group 1 Customer ID field added to the formula

6. Add the Group 1 Customer ID field illustrated above in Figure 14-37 to the formula, then check the formula for errors. Save the formula and close the Formula Workshop.

Add The Total Field To The Report

1. Delete everything in the group footer section.

2. Add the Total Field formula field to the group footer section. The report should look like the one shown in Figure 14-38. Notice that there is a decimal point in the number. Save the changes.

Customer Information Grouped By Region
Sorted By Zip Code

Page 1 of 19

Customer Name	Address	Country	Zip Code
Abu Dhabi			
UAE Cycle	Post Box: 278	United Arab Emirates	3453

Total # of customers in region - 1.00

AL			
Psycho-Cycle	8287 Scott Road	USA	35818
The Great Bike Shop	1922 Beach Crescent	USA	35857
Benny - The Spokes Person	1020 Oak Way	USA	35861

Total # of customers in region - 3.00

Figure 14-38 Combine text and numeric fields report

Use Functions In String Formulas

You may have the need to combine data that is stored in fields that have different data types or format data differently then it is stored in the table. The next two exercises show you how to incorporate functions in string formulas.

Exercise 14.7: Use The Picture Function

The phone numbers in the Supplier table are stored in the format shown in Figure 14-39.

Notice that there are also international phone numbers in the table. When you want to print US phone numbers, they will look better if they are printed like this **(704) 555-5555**.

In this exercise you will use the Picture function to format phone numbers in the Supplier table.

Figure 14-39 Phone numbers stored in the table

1. Create a new report. Add the Supplier table, but do not add any fields to the report. Save the report as E14.7 Picture function.

2. Create a formula field and name it Supplier Phone, then add the comment
   This formula formats the Phone Number field.

3. Open the Report Fields tree, then open the Supplier table.

4. Open the **ADDITIONAL FUNCTIONS** category in the Functions tree, then open the **SAMP1** category and double-click on the **PICTURE** function illustrated in Figure 14-40.

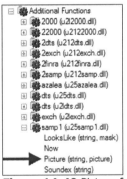

Figure 14-40 Picture function illustrated

5. Double-click on the Phone field in the Report Fields tree, then click after the comma in the formula and type "(XXX)XXXXXXX". The formula should look like the one shown in Figure 14-41. Save the formula and leave the Formula Workshop open to complete the next part of the exercise.

```
// This formula formats the Phone Number field
Picture ({Supplier.Phone},"(XXX)XXXXXX" )
```
Figure 14-41 Phone number formula

 The brackets { } in a formula are used for data fields. The parenthesis ( ) are used to control the order that the formula is evaluated in.

In Figure 14-39 shown earlier, you saw the phone numbers that are stored in the Supplier table. All of the phone numbers will not work with the mask that you just created in the formula. In order to be able to accommodate international phone numbers, the formula would have to be modified to also use the **LENGTH** function and have another mask to accommodate phone numbers of a different length. This is known as conditional formatting, which you will learn about in the next chapter.

Use The ToText Function

The ToText function is one of the more popular functions. It is used to convert dates, numbers and more to a string field. In this part of the exercise you will combine the Supplier ID and Supplier Name fields. In order to combine a numeric and string field, you have to convert the numeric field to text. The ToText function is used to do this.

1. Create a formula field and name it `Supplier ID & Name`, then add the comment `This formula combines the Supplier ID and Supplier Name fields.`

2. Open the Strings category in the Functions tree, then double-click on the ToText (x,y) function.

3. Click inside of the parenthesis and add the Supplier ID field.

4. Click after the comma in the formula and type a zero. The zero means that the number should not display any decimal places, if there are any in the field.

5. Click outside of the formula on the right and type + " - " +, then add the Supplier Name field. The formula should look like the one shown in Figure 14-42. Save the formula and close the Formula Workshop.

```
// This formula combines the Supplier ID and Supplier Name fields
ToText ({Supplier.Supplier ID},0 )+" - "+{Supplier.Supplier Name}
```
Figure 14-42 Supplier ID and Name formula

6. Add both of the formula fields to the details section of the report.

   The report should look like the one shown in Figure 14-43.

   Save the changes.

Supplier ID & Name	Supplier Phone
1 - Active Outdoors	(503) 555-9931
2 - Triumph	(313) 555-5735
3 - Guardian	(81)3 3555-5011
4 - InFlux	(81)6 431-7877
5 - Craze	(604) 681 3435
6 - Roadster	(44)171 555-2222
7 - Vesper	(514) 555-9022

Figure 14-43 Picture function report

Using The Ampersand To Concatenate Strings
In the exercise that you just completed, you used the ToText function and the plus sign operator to concatenate string fields. The benefit of using the ToText function with the plus sign operator is that you can control the formatting. If you do not need to control the formatting, use the ampersand operator instead of the plus sign operator.

Formatting Strings With A Mask

In Exercise 14.7 you formatted a phone number field with the Picture function, which used a mask to format the field. Masks use characters including x, d, m and y as placeholders for the data. These characters determine how the data will be formatted when it is converted to a string.

Table 14-7 lists some of the mask characters that are used the most for date fields. Table 14-8 provides mask examples for the date 6/1/11.

Character	Description
d	Day of the month in numeric format without a leading zero.
dd	Day of the month in numeric format with a leading zero if necessary.
dddd	Name of the day spelled out.
M	Month in numeric format without a leading zero.
MM	Month in numeric format with a leading zero if necessary.
MMMM	Name of the month spelled out.
y	Last two digits of the year.
yyyy	Four digit year.

Table 14-7 Mask character options explained

Mask	Displays
dd, MM, yy	01, 06, 11
MMMM dd yyyy	June 01 2011
dddd MMMM d, yyyy	Wednesday June 1, 2011
M, d, yy	6, 1, 11

Table 14-8 Mask examples

Using Date Functions

Table 14-9 provides an overview of some of the date functions. The exercises in this section show you how to create some of the more popular date formulas using functions.

Function	What It Does . . .
ChrW(x)	Returns the character that represents the Unicode value of (x).
CurrentDate	Uses the system date on your computer.
DateAdd	Increments a date field by intervals, including days, weeks, months and years.
DateDiff	Calculates the difference between the start and end dates in the function. (6)
Day	Extracts the day from a Date or Date/Time field and returns a whole number.
Month	Extracts the month from a Date or Date/Time field and returns a whole number.
ToText	Formats any or all parts of a date field. This function is also used to convert a date field to a text value.
Year	Extracts the year from a Date or Date/Time field and returns a whole number.

Table 14-9 Date functions explained

(6) **DateDiff Function**
The DateDiff function has arguments that are used to determine how to calculate the difference between two date fields. Three of the most used arguments are explained below.
D will calculate the difference in days.
M will calculate the difference in months.
yyyy will calculate the difference in years.

Exercise 14.8: Create A Date Formula To Calculate The Order Processing Time

In this exercise you will create a formula to find out how long it is between the day an order is placed and when the order was shipped. This is known as the order processing time.

1. Save the E9.3 report as E14.8 Calculate order processing time.

2. Create a formula field and name it Order processing time.

3. Expand the **DATEDIFF** function folder, then double-click on the first DateDiff function.

4. Type "d" before the first comma in the formula.

5. Add the Order Date field to the formula after the first comma, then add the Ship Date field to the formula after the second comma. The formula should look like the one shown in Figure 14-44. Check the formula for errors, then save the formula and close the Formula Workshop.

```
DateDiff ("d",{Orders.Order Date} ,{Orders.Ship Date} )
```
Figure 14-44 Order processing time formula

Add The Order Processing Time Formula Field To The Report

1. Remove the time from the Order Date and Ship Date fields. Make these fields smaller, then move the fields starting with the Ship Date field to the left.

2. Add the Order processing time formula field to the report and format it so that it does not have any decimal places. The report should look like the one shown in Figure 14-45. Save the changes.

Customer Name	Order Date	Ship Date	Order ID	Unit Price	Quantity	Order processing time
City Cyclists	12/02/2010	12/10/2010	1	$41.90	1	8
Deals on Wheels	12/02/2010	12/02/2010	1,002	$33.90	3	0
Deals on Wheels	12/02/2010	12/02/2010	1,002	$1,652.86	3	0
Warsaw Sports, Inc.	12/02/2010	12/05/2010	1,003	$48.51	3	3
Warsaw Sports, Inc.	12/02/2010	12/05/2010	1,003	$13.78	3	3
Bikes and Trikes	12/02/2010	12/02/2010	1,004	$274.35	3	0
SAB Mountain	12/03/2010	12/03/2010	1,005	$14.50	2	0

Figure 14-45 Calculate order processing time report

 A zero in the Order processing time field means that the order was shipped within 24 hours of when it was placed. Depending on the time an order was placed and shipped, the Ship Date could be the next day and still have a zero in the Order processing time field because the order was shipped in less than 24 hours. Remember that the fields used in this formula are Date/Time fields.

Exercise 14.9: Calculate The Employee Age

One of the more popular date functions is used to calculate a persons age if you have their date of birth. In this exercise you will create an employee birthday list report. You will create a formula to calculate the age of the employees. Earlier in this chapter, I listed four reasons why certain types of data are not saved in a table. A persons age is a good example of the type of data that should not be stored in a table. The reason is because the age changes every year. This would mean that the field would have to be updated once a year on each persons birthday. This is why it is best to calculate the age, each time the report is run.

1. Create a new report and add the following fields from the Employee table: Position, Birth Date and Hire Date.

2. Remove the time from the Birth Date and Hire Date fields, then save the report as `E14.9 Calculate age formula.`

3. Create a formula field to combine the first and last name fields. Save the formula field as `Employee Name.`

4. Create another formula field and save it as `Age.`

5. Add the Current Date function from the Date and Time category to the Age formula, then type a – (minus sign).

6. Add the Birth Date field to the formula, then check the formula for errors. Save the formula and close the Formula Workshop.

Modify The Report

1. Add the Employee Name formula field to the beginning of the details section, then add the Age formula field to the report after the Birth Date field.

2. Sort the report in ascending order by the Last Name field. The report should look like the one shown in Figure 14-46.

Employee Name	Position	Birth Date	Age	Hire Date
Justin Brid	Marketing Director	10/08/1977	12,400.00	01/01/1994
Steven Buchanan	Sales Manager	03/04/1975	13,349.00	09/13/1992
Laura Callahan	Inside Sales Coordinator	01/09/1974	13,768.00	01/30/1993
Nancy Davolio	Sales Representative	12/08/1972	14,165.00	03/29/1991

Figure 14-46 Age field added to the report

Modify The Age Formula

As you can see, the formula did not return the age in the format that you expected. The age shown on the report is in days, not years. This is because the Current Date function calculates in days. The formula needs to be modified so that the age is displayed in years.

1. Right-click on the Age formula field and select Edit.

You may be thinking that the only thing that you have to do is click after the Birth Date field and type /365 and the age would be converted to years. Just adding this to the formula will not calculate the age in years. Instead, you will see the message shown in Figure 14-47.

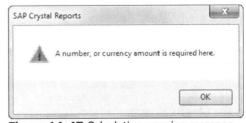

Figure 14-47 Calculation warning message

The reason that you see this message is because you are trying to divide the Birth Date field which is a Date/Time field by 365, which is a numeric field. As you learned earlier, arguments must be the same data type to use them in a formula. That is not the case in this formula.

Another reason that this formula will not work is because of the formula evaluation order. The evaluation order must be forced in this formula. The way to force it is by adding parenthesis around the portion of the formula that has to be evaluated first. The order needed is to force the Birth Date to be subtracted from the Current Date **BEFORE** the division takes place.

2. Type parenthesis around the formula, then type /365 after the last parenthesis and check the formula.

Use The Truncate Function

When you previewed the report you saw that the age field has a decimal place. The decimal place represents part of the year. This is not what you want. The Truncate function will remove that portion of the field.

1. Add the comment This formula calculates the employees age.

2. Expand the Math function node, then expand the Truncate function node.

3. Click at the beginning of the formula, then double-click on the Truncate (x) function.

 TRUNCATE(X) shortens a field. **TRUNCATE (X, #PLACES)** determines how many decimal places to keep before truncation occurs.

4. After the truncate function, you will see parenthesis. Delete the right parenthesis and add it to the end of the formula. The formula should look like the one shown in Figure 14-48. Check the formula for errors, then save and close the formula.

```
// This formula calculates the employees age
Truncate ((CurrentDate - {Employee.Birth Date})/365)
```
Figure 14-48 Age formula

5. Format the Age field so that it does not have any decimal places. The report should look like the one shown in Figure 14-49.

Employee Name	Position	Birth Date	Age	Hire Date
•		•		
•		•		
•		•		
Robert King	Sales Representative	05/29/1972	39	11/29/1992
Janet Leverling	Sales Representative	08/30/1971	39	02/27/1991
Xavier Martin	Marketing Associate	11/30/1975	35	01/15/1994
Caroline Patterson	Receptionist	09/11/1979	31	05/15/1993
Margaret Peacock	Sales Representative	09/19/1973	37	03/30/1992
Laurent Pereira	Advertising Specialist	12/09/1970	40	02/01/1994

Figure 14-49 Calculate age formula report

You may see a different age for some or all of the employees. This will happen if you run the report after an employees birthday has past. For example, I ran the report shown above in Figure 14-49 in early August 2011. I ran the report shown in Figure 14-50 towards the end of September 2011. Notice that the age for some of the employees has changed. That is because some people had a birthday since I ran the report shown above.

Employee Name	Position	Birth Date	Age	Hire Date
•		•		
•		•		
•		•		
Robert King	Sales Representative	05/29/1972	39	11/29/1992
Janet Leverling	Sales Representative	08/30/1971	40	02/27/1991
Xavier Martin	Marketing Associate	11/30/1975	35	01/15/1994
Caroline Patterson	Receptionist	09/11/1979	32	05/15/1993
Margaret Peacock	Sales Representative	09/19/1973	38	03/30/1992
Laurent Pereira	Advertising Specialist	12/09/1970	40	02/01/1994

Figure 14-50 Calculate age formula report run over a month later

 If you need to use the same formula in more than one report, you can copy it from one report and paste it in another report.

Run-Time Errors

No one likes to talk about errors, but they do happen. Earlier in this chapter you learned about syntax errors and that if a formula passes the syntax checker, errors can still occur. These errors occur when the report is run (previewed). Run-time errors usually occur when the data type being used is not what the formula expected.

Examples of run-time errors include null values in a field or formula that returns zero (Divide By Zero). You can debug these errors using the **CALL STACK**. If you get a run-time error, you will see the error message in the Formula Workshop, which will display the formula that triggered the error.

The call stack shown on the left of Figure 14-51 shows the formula that has the error. You will also see all of the fields in the formula and the values in the field of the record that was being processed when the run-time error occurred.

The value in the field is displayed after the field name, as illustrated. Being able to see the data may help you figure out what caused the error.

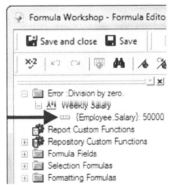

Figure 14-51 Run-time error call stack illustrated

CONDITIONAL FORMATTING

Overview

After completing the exercises in this chapter you will be able to use the following tools and techniques to format fields and sections in a report.

☑ The Highlighting Expert
☑ Apply conditional formats to fields
☑ Create If Then Else formulas
☑ Suppress fields and sections

CHAPTER 15

Overview

In Chapter 7 you learned basic formatting techniques. In Chapter 14 you learned that data could be formatted or manipulated using formulas and functions. The techniques covered in those two chapters will handle a large percent of your report formatting needs. What you may have noticed is that the formatting that you have learned to create so far is applied to every detail (or group) record. There will be times when the report does not need or require the same formatting to be applied to every detail record.

Conditional Formatting Tips

As you will learn, you may not always need to apply the formatting that you create. There are formatting techniques that apply the formatting only if a condition is met. This is known as **CONDITIONAL FORMATTING**. Examples of conditional formatting include the following:

① Highlighting records when the data in one field is greater than a constant value.
② Highlighting records with a specific color that have data missing in a field.
③ Check the value or length of a field and apply different formatting, depending on the value or length of the field.
④ Print a background color on every other detail record on the report.
⑤ Formatting one field with a border based on the value in another field.

The options on the Format Editor and Section Expert turn on what is known as **ABSOLUTE FORMATTING**, which means that the format will be applied to all values in the field. Absolute formatting is not on if the option is not checked. This also applies to drop-down lists and text fields on these dialog boxes.

The formatting techniques that you learned in Chapter 7 are known as absolute formatting because they are applied to every occurrence of the object. Conditional formatting starts off as absolute formatting, but goes a step further by setting up criteria to determine when the formatting should be applied.

 Conditional formatting is created using the Format Editor. Conditional formatting overrides absolute formatting that is created with the Format Editor. You can set the "on" and "off" properties conditionally.

There are two types of properties that conditional formatting can be applied to. The property type determines the type of conditional formula that has to be created. When you create a formula for an option, this is known as conditional formatting because the formula will turn the option on and off. Boolean formulas are used for on-off options in conditional formatting. When creating conditional If...Then...Else statements, keep the following in mind.

① **ON-OFF** properties like the Can Grow option or any option that has a check box on the Format Editor. On-off properties require **BOOLEAN** formulas. Check box formatting options are either on or off. This means that you do not have to type the entire If...Then...Else statement. Crystal Reports will turn the format option on if the test returns a true value. If the formula returns a false value, the formatting is not turned on.
② **MULTIPLE CHOICE** properties like the border line style option, which is a drop-down list on the Line tab of the Format Editor. Multiple choice properties require If Then Else or Select Case statements. Drop-down list and Text Box formatting options can have more than one choice. For this type of conditional formatting you have to type the entire If...Then...Else statement to specify what you want to happen if the test is true and if the test is false.

Highlighting Expert

The Highlighting Expert shown in Figure 15-1 is used to create and apply font, background and border conditional formatting to fields on a report without having to create a formula. It is a scaled down version of the Format Editor. The downside is that it does not provide a lot of options like the Formula Workshop has. The Highlighting Expert is similar to the Select Expert. One difference that I noticed is that the Highlighting Expert does not have as many operators as the Select Expert.

An example of when to use the Highlighting Expert would be if you wanted to highlight the order amount if it is more than $1,000. The Highlighting Expert is used to bring attention to certain values on the report by changing at least one of the following: Font style, Font color, Background color or Border style.

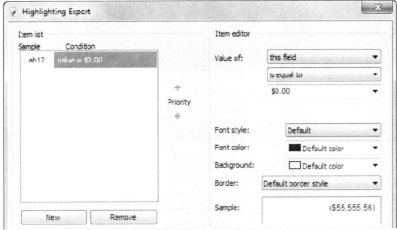

Figure 15-1 Highlighting Expert dialog box

 Conditional formatting that is created by the Highlighting Expert cannot be modified in the Formula Editor.

 The Highlighting Expert does not work with **PARAMETER FIELDS**. The Highlighting Expert can only compare data in a table to set the conditional formatting.

There are three ways to open the Highlighting Expert dialog box, as explained below.

① Right-click on the field that needs to meet a condition and select Highlighting Expert.
② Click the Highlighting button on the Experts toolbar.
③ Format ⇒ Highlighting Expert.

As shown above in Figure 15-1, the Highlighting Expert has the following two sections:

① **ITEM LIST** Displays the conditional formatting formulas created by the Highlighting Expert for the field that is selected. The **CONDITION** column displays the formula that will create the formatting.
② **ITEM EDITOR** Is used to create and view the conditional formatting formulas. The **SAMPLE** area displays the highlighting that will be applied.

Item List Section Options

① The **PRIORITY** buttons are used to change the order that the highlighting will be applied. Priority is important when there are multiple conditions set for the same field. For example, if you want to set the background color of a date field to green if it is greater than 1/1/09 and another condition to place a border around the same date field if the date is greater than 6/24/10. If the date is 1/24/11, which of the two formatting conditions should be applied to the date field? If the greater than 1/1/09 is the first condition, all of the records that are greater than 1/1/09 would have a green background applied, even if the date is greater than 6/24/10. In some instances, multiple conditions can conflict. This is why setting a priority is important. Setting a priority is how Crystal Reports resolves the conflicts.

② The **REMOVE** button will delete the highlighting criteria that is displayed in the Item List.

Item Editor Section Options

① The **VALUE OF** drop-down list contains the fields, formulas and functions that are on the report or that are connected to the report, as shown in Figure 15-2.

These are the fields that you can use to create the conditions for.

Figure 15-2 Field selection drop-down list

The **THIS FIELD** option in the Value Of drop-down list uses the field that was selected before the Highlighting Expert was opened. Selecting a different field then the one that was selected prior to opening the Highlighting Expert means that you want to apply the formatting to the field selected prior to opening the Highlighting Expert, but you want the condition to be set based on the value in a different field.

The last option in the drop-down list, **OTHER FIELDS** opens the Choose Field dialog box. This dialog box is used to select another field from any data source connected to the report to use to create highlighting criteria for.

② The **COMPARISON** drop-down list is the second field in the Item Editor section. It contains the selection criteria operators shown in Figure 15-3.

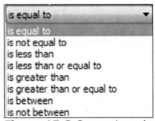

You can use these operators to select which records will be highlighted.

Figure 15-3 Comparison drop-down list operators

③ The **COMPARE TO** drop-down list is the third field from the top. It displays the values in the field that you select in the Value Of drop-down list. This is like the Browse Data dialog box. You can also type in the value that you want.

Create Reports That Highlight Data

The first two exercises in this chapter show you how to highlight data using the Highlighting Expert.

Exercise 15.1: Use The Background Highlighting Option

In this exercise you will modify a report to highlight the background of the Order processing time field for orders that were not shipped two days after the order date.

1. Save the E14.8 report as
   E15.1 Highlight the order processing time conditionally.

2. Right-click on the Order processing time formula field and select **HIGHLIGHTING EXPERT,** then click the **NEW** button on the Highlighting Expert dialog box.

3. Open the Comparison drop-down list and select **IS GREATER THAN OR EQUAL TO,** then type a 3 in the next field.

4. Select **GRAY** as the background color.

   Figure 15-4 shows the options that should be selected.

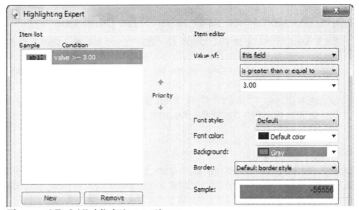

Figure 15-4 Highlighting options

5. Click OK, then save the changes. The report should look like the one shown in Figure 15-5.

Customer Name	Order Date	Ship Date	Order ID	Unit Price	Quantity	Order processing time
City Cyclists	12/02/2010	12/10/2010	1	$41.90	1	
Deals on Wheels	12/02/2010	12/02/2010	1,002	$33.90	3	0
Deals on Wheels	12/02/2010	12/02/2010	1,002	$1,652.86	3	0
Warsaw Sports, Inc.	12/02/2010	12/05/2010	1,003	$48.51	3	
Warsaw Sports, Inc.	12/02/2010	12/05/2010	1,003	$13.78	3	0
Bikes and Trikes	12/02/2010	12/02/2010	1,004	$274.35	3	0
SAB Mountain	12/03/2010	12/03/2010	1,005	$14.50	2	0
Poser Cycles	12/03/2010	12/05/2010	1,006	$16.50	1	2
Poser Cycles	12/03/2010	12/05/2010	1,006	$33.90	1	2
Poser Cycles	12/03/2010	12/05/2010	1,006	$14.50	1	2
Spokes	12/03/2010	12/03/2010	1,007	$16.50	3	0
Clean Air Transportation	12/03/2010	12/07/2010	1,008	$726.61	2	
Clean Air Transportation	12/03/2010	12/07/2010	1,008	$431.87	1	
Clean Air Transportation	12/03/2010	12/07/2010	1,008	$329.85	1	
Extreme Cycling	12/03/2010	12/10/2010	1,009	$14.50	2	

Figure 15-5 Report with conditional field background highlighting

Exercise 15.2: Use One Field To Highlight Another Field And Set A Priority

More than one highlighting condition can be created for a field. You can also use one field to highlight another field. In this exercise you will create two conditions for the same field and set a priority for the conditions. You will create the following conditions:

① Make the quantity bold if it is greater than or equal to three.
② Italicize the quantity if the unit price is greater than $500.

Create The Quantity Is Greater Than Condition

1. Save the E14.8 report as E15.2 Use multiple conditions to highlight a field.

2. Right-click on the Quantity field and select the Highlighting Expert option, then click the New button.

3. Open the Comparison drop-down list and select **IS GREATER THAN OR EQUAL TO**, then type 3 in the next field.

4. Select the bold font style. Leave the Highlighting Expert dialog box open to complete the next part of the exercise.

Create The Unit Price Is Greater Than Condition

1. Click New, then open the Value Of drop-down list and select the Unit Price field.

2. Open the Comparison drop-down list and select **IS GREATER THAN**, then type 500 in the last field.

3. Select the bold italic font style, then select red as the font color. Leave the Highlighting Expert dialog box open to complete the next part of the exercise.

Set The Priority

There could be a lot of records that meet both of the conditions that you just created. Unless it does not matter which order the conditions are applied to the field, you should set a priority. In this exercise, the most important criteria is for the Unit Price field.

1. Click on the Unit Price condition in the **ITEM LIST**, then click the (Priority Up) button.

   Figure 15-6 shows the options that should be selected.

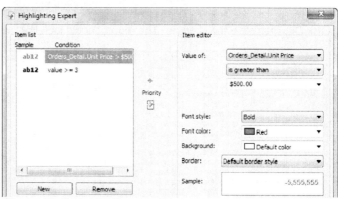

Figure 15-6 Highlighting conditions

2. Click OK and save the changes. The report should look like the one shown in Figure 15-7.

Customer Name	Order Date	Ship Date	Order ID	Unit Price	Quantity	Order processing time
City Cyclists	12/02/2010	12/10/2010	1	$41.90	1	8
Deals on Wheels	12/02/2010	12/02/2010	1,002	$33.90	3	0
Deals on Wheels	12/02/2010	12/02/2010	1,002	$1,652.86	3	0
Warsaw Sports, Inc.	12/02/2010	12/05/2010	1,003	$48.51	3	3
Warsaw Sports, Inc.	12/02/2010	12/05/2010	1,003	$13.78	3	3
Bikes and Trikes	12/02/2010	12/02/2010	1,004	$274.35	3	0
SAB Mountain	12/03/2010	12/03/2010	1,005	$14.50	2	0

Figure 15-7 Use multiple conditions to highlight a field report

Highlighting Expert Limitations

Despite being relatively easy to use, the Highlighting Expert is one feature in my opinion that could be improved. You should be aware of the following two facts about the Highlighting Expert.

① Formulas created by the Highlighting Expert override formulas in the Formula Editor.
② Formulas created by the Highlighting Expert are not stored in the Formula Editor. This means that you cannot see the formulas created by the Highlighting Expert and can easily forget that they exist.

 Any formula that you can create with the Highlighting Expert can be created in the Formula Editor. For me, it is easier to maintain formulas if they are all in the same place. Take from this what you will.

If...Then...Else Statements

This is one of the most used lines of programming code. This statement is used to set different options based on what you need to happen when the data is evaluated. The syntax below is for an If Then Else statement.

If **EXPRESSION/CONDITION** Then **TRUE STATEMENTS**
Else
FALSE STATEMENTS

Parts Of The If Then Else Statement Explained

① The **EXPRESSION/CONDITION** must evaluate to true or false.
② The **TRUE STATEMENTS** will execute if the Expression/Condition is true.
③ The **ELSE** part of the statement is optional. If the Else clause is not included and the Expression/Condition is false, nothing will happen, which may be what you want. By "nothing happens", I mean that the If statement will default to the value for the data type. For example, If Field A is greater than 95, then textfield5 = "Great Job". If the variable "textfield5" was not declared to have a specific default value, the default value for a text field data type is " " (null), which is what would be displayed if Field A is not greater than 95. The rule of thumb is to use the Else keyword to avoid problems like these.
④ The **FALSE STATEMENTS** will execute if the Expression/Condition is false.

The plain English translation of an If Then Else statement is: **IF** Choice A meets this condition, **THEN** do X, **ELSE** do Y. Walk through the examples in Table 15-1 to gain a better understanding of If Then Else statements. Fill in the column on the right based on the numbers in the Choice A column.

If Choice A is greater than 25, then Field B = 100, else Field B = 0.

Choice A	What Does Field B=
26	
1	
25	

Table 15-1 If Then Else examples

It may help to understand If...Then...Else statements if you think of them as a true or false test question. In the example above, the test question can be worded as "Is Choice A greater than 25?" There are two possible answers:

① Yes it is (True). If it is, Field B would be set to 100.

② No it isn't (False). If it isn't, Field B would be set to 0.

How Did You Do?

Table 15-2 contains the answers for the second column in Table 15-1. The third column in the table explains the answer.

Choice A	Field B=	Reason
26	100	The answer is 100 because 26 is greater than 25.
1	0	The answer is 0 because 1 is less than 25.
25	0	The answer is 0 because 25 is not greater than 25.

Table 15-2 Answers for Table 15-1

To complicate If statements even more, there can be multiple true and false statements in the same If Then Else statement. When this is the case, they have to be enclosed in parenthesis, otherwise Crystal Reports will stop processing the statement after the first semi-colon, which often will produce a syntax error. Statements with multiple true and false statements are known as **NESTED IF STATEMENTS**.

 Each statement except the last one in an If Then Else statement must end in a semi-colon.

Conditional Formatting Warnings

You should be aware of the following when creating conditional formatting:

① If a field has formatting that is created with the Highlighting Expert and with conditional formatting, the Highlighting Expert formatting takes precedence. If the conditional formatting does not change the formatting created by the Highlighting Expert, the conditional formatting will be applied.

② Conditional formatting overrides absolute formatting even if the result of the conditional formatting is false.

③ Crystal Reports does not require the "Else" part of an If Then Else statement.

④ If absolute and conditional formatting are applied to a field and the If Then Else statement for the conditional formatting does not have an Else clause and the conditional formatting does not return a "True" value, neither the conditional formatting or the absolute formatting is applied.

⑤ In addition to If Then Else statements you can also use **SELECT CASE** statements, as long as the formatting property is in the Functions tree.

As you can see, it can be difficult to apply both absolute and conditional formatting to the same field. Even with the best intentions and formulas, you can get unexpected results. There are two things that you can do to help ensure that you get the output that you need when you have to combine absolute and conditional formatting. I have found the second option below to be more effective, but if the first option fits your needs, you should use it.

① Use the "Else" clause on If statements or the **DEFAULT** clause on Select Case statements.

② Use the "Else" clause with the **DEFAULTATTRIBUTE** function. To do this, select the default (absolute) option on the Format Editor dialog box and use the DefaultAttribute as the Else part of the If statement. For example, if you need to set the default value for a field to green on the Format Editor, use the following If Then Else statement.

        If {Employee.Salary}/52 <= 750
           Then crRed
              Else
                 DefaultAttribute

This formula will display weekly salaries that are less than or equal to $750 in red and the other salaries in green if the salary field is set to green on the Format Editor.

 Formulas are created because the report needs an action to be taken based on the result. Sometimes you always need an action to be taken, regardless of the outcome of the formula. In those cases, you would put what you want to happen in place of the DefaultAttribute in the formula. Use the Default Attribute function when you do not want to change the property. It is not a requirement to use this function.

 Unless stated otherwise, when instructed to open a category in an exercise, the category is in the Functions tree.

IsNull Function

The formula shown in Figure 15-8 is often used to combine two address fields. This formula is fine as long as there is data in both address fields. Unless the fields are required to be filled in on a data entry form, you cannot be 100% sure that they will contain data. The second address field is an example of a field that can have null values because all addresses do not require two fields.

```
{Employee_Addresses.Address1} + " " +{Employee_Addresses.Address2}
```
Figure 15-8 Address fields combined

While the Employee Addresses table in the Xtreme database only has a few records, you could manually check to see if both address fields contained data before creating the formula. If the table had two million records, checking them manually is probably not a good idea and could be quite time consuming. There are two options explained below that you can use to prevent a formula from failing, if a field is null (empty).

① The **ISNULL** function is used to test a field to see if it is empty. If it is, you can make a decision on what to do. To make this decision you need to use the If Then Else statement with the IsNull function.

② Turn on the **CONVERT DATABASE NULL VALUES TO DEFAULT** option on the Options dialog box Enabling this option will convert null values to zero for numeric fields or blank for string fields. "Blank" is different than Null.

 While Crystal Reports supports the **CONVERT DATABASE NULL VALUES TO DEFAULT** option, not all databases support it. If you want to use this option, you need to make sure that the database that you are using supports it. If you can't or don't want to confirm whether or not a database supports this feature, you can use the **ISNULL** function. I personally find it easier to use the IsNull function all the time, so that I can "see" what is going on.

Exercise 15.3: Use The If Then Else Statement And IsNull Function

In this exercise you will create a formula that will combine the two employee address fields and check the Address2 field to see if it is null. The majority of the time, the second address field will be the one that will not have data. On the rare occurrence that the first address field is null, you would want the formula to fail so that the field would be blank on the report. Hopefully, people reading the report will notice this and fix the data. You can also create a formula that will print a message in the combined address field if either of the address fields is empty.

 The **ISNULL** function has to be placed inside the If Then Else statement because the check that it will perform on the Address2 field is the first part (the test question) that the If Then Else statement evaluates. In "plain" English, the formula that you will create is:
If the Address2 field does not have any data
then set the Full Address field (the name of the formula) to only use the Address1 field
else set the Full Address field to use the Address1 field and the Address2 field.

1. Save the Chapter 14 Employee list report as E15.3 If Then Else statement.

2. Create a formula field named Full Address.

3. Open the **CONTROL STRUCTURES** category in the Operators tree, then double-click on the **IF X THEN Y ELSE Z** statement illustrated in Figure 15-9.

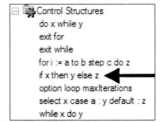

Figure 15-9 If Then Else statement illustrated

4. Open the **PRINT STATE** category in the Functions tree, then double-click on the **ISNULL** function illustrated in Figure 15-10.

Figure 15-10 IsNull function illustrated

5. With the flashing insertion point between the parenthesis in the formula, double-click on the Address2 field in the Reports Field tree. This is the question part of the **IF** statement.

6. Click after the word **THEN** in the formula and double-click on the Address1 field, then press Enter. The word **ELSE** should be on the next line. This is the "true" part of the question, meaning that this is what you want to have print if the Address2 field is null.

7. Click after the word **ELSE** and add the Address1 field, then type + " " +.

8. Add the Address2 field. If you want to add a comment to the formula, you can. Check the formula for errors. The formula should look like the one shown in Figure 15-11.

```
// This formula checks to see if the Address2 field is null
if IsNull ({Employee_Addresses.Address2}) then{Employee_Addresses.Address1}
else{Employee_Addresses.Address1}+" "+{Employee_Addresses.Address2}
```

Figure 15-11 If Then Else and IsNull formula

9. Delete the Address 1 field from the report. Add the Full Address field and change the title.

10. Save the changes. The report should look like the one shown in Figure 15-12. You will now see data in the Address field. Compare this to the report shown in Figure 15-13, that does not have the If Then Else statement.

First Name	Last Name	Address	Region	Salary
Steven	Buchanan	14 Garrett Hill		$ 50,000 00
Robert	King	Edgeham Hollow		$ 37,000 00
Anne	Dodsworth	7 Houndstooth Rd		$ 35,000.00
Michael	Suyama	Coventry House		$ 30,000.00
Bas-Rhin				
Justin	Brid	2 impasse du Soleil	Bas-Rhin	$ 75,000.00
Xavier	Martin	9 place de la Liberté	Bas-Rhin	$ 50,000 00
Laurent	Pereira	7 rue Nationale	Bas-Rhin	$ 45,000 00

Figure 15-12 If Then Else statement report

First Name	Last Name	Address	Region	Salary
Steven	Buchanan			$ 50,000.00
Robert	King	Edgeham Hollow		$ 37,000.00
Anne	Dodsworth			$ 35,000.00
Michael	Suyama			$ 30,000.00
Bas-Rhin				
Justin	Brid		Bas-Rhin	$ 75,000.00
Xavier	Martin		Bas-Rhin	$ 50,000.00
Laurent	Pereira		Bas-Rhin	$ 45,000.00

Figure 15-13 Report without the If Then Else statement report

Exercise 15.4: Using Nested If Statements In Formulas

In this exercise you will create a Nested If statement to give customers a different discount on their next order based on the total amount of their last order.

1. Save Chapter 15 Customer discount report as `E15.4 Nested If statement`.

2. Create a formula field and name it `Order Discount`, then add the If Then Else statement to the Formula Text section.

3. Add the Order Amount field, then type `>=10000`.

4. Click after the word **THEN** and type `"10% discount"`.

5. Copy the formula and paste it twice.

6. Change the middle Order Amount line of code to `>=5000`, then change the discount to 15%.

7. Change the last Order Amount line of code to `>=2500`, then change the discount to 20%.

8. Click after the last **ELSE**, press Enter, then type `"25% discount"`. The formula should look like the one shown in Figure 15-14.

```
if {Orders.Order Amount} >=10000 then "10% discount" else
if {Orders.Order Amount} >=5000 then "15% discount" else
if {Orders.Order Amount} >=2500 then "20% discount" else
"25% discount"
```

Figure 15-14 Order Discount formula

9. Save the formula and close the Formula Workshop. Add the Order Discount formula field to the report after the Ship Via field. The report should look like the one shown in Figure 15-15. Save the changes.

Customer Discount Report					

Customer Name	Order ID	Order Date	Order Amount	Ship Via	Order Discount
City Cyclists	1	12/02/2010	$41.90	UPS	25% discount
Deals on Wheels	1002	12/02/2010	$5,060.28	Pickup	15% discount
Deals on Wheels	1002	12/02/2010	$5,060.28	Pickup	15% discount
Warsaw Sports, Inc.	1003	12/02/2010	$186.87	UPS	25% discount
Warsaw Sports, Inc.	1003	12/02/2010	$186.87	UPS	25% discount
Bikes and Trikes	1004	12/02/2010	$823.05	Pickup	25% discount
SAB Mountain	1005	12/03/2010	$29.00	Loomis	25% discount

Figure 15-15 Nested If statement report

Because the Order Discount field is evaluated for each record, it will only match one of the If statements when the statement is set up correctly. If the order amount is $3,000, the formula will stop processing after the third statement. If the order amount is $6,500, the formula will stop processing after the second statement.

The order that you place the criteria values in is very important. If the statements were in a different order, the formula would not return the correct result because it is possible that the order amount would meet the criteria of another statement. For example, if the >=2,500 portion of the statement was above the >=10,000 portion of the statement and the order amount is $6,500, the formula would stop processing after the first If statement because $6,500 is >=2,500. That is not the outcome that you want though. You really want the $6,500 order to receive a 15% discount.

The rule of thumb is to put the criteria in high to low order. The option after the last else statement is the "catch all" statement. Sometimes you may need to print a message on the report because the data is outside of the range of data that you need to report on. In the example above, the customer would receive a 25% discount off of their next order if their last order was less than $2,500. In this example, the company is going to offer larger discounts to customers that placed smaller orders in hopes of having them place a larger order the next time that they order.

Suppressing Fields And Sections

There are times when there is no need to print the same data over and over on a report. Sometimes not repeating the same data makes the report easier to read. There are also times when you will need to suppress a section of the report. Like the Highlighting Expert, fields and sections in a report can be suppressed based on a condition. These conditions are created using Boolean formulas.

Exercise 15.5: Suppressing Fields

In this exercise you will learn how to suppress fields by creating a conditional formula for a field that has a salary greater than $50,000.

. . . .

1. Save the Chapter 14 Employee list report as `E15.5 Suppress salary GT 50000`.

2. Right-click on the Salary field and select Format Field.

   On the Common tab, check the **SUPPRESS** option illustrated in Figure 15-16.

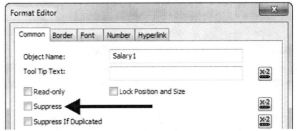

Figure 15-16 Common tab on the Format Editor

 As you see in Figure 15-16 above, most of the options have the button shown in Figure 15-17. This button will open the **FORMAT FORMULA EDITOR**. The default color for the Formula button is blue, which means that the option does not have a formula. If the button is red, it means that the option does have a formula. You will also notice that the pencil on the button is in a different position when the option has a formula, as shown in Figure 15-18. Formatting formulas that you create with the Section Expert or Format Editor will be applied whether or not the property option that it is attached to is checked. As long as the Formula button is red, which means that the property has a formula, the formula will be applied.

Figure 15-17 Blue formula button

Figure 15-18 Red formula button

3. Click the **FORMULA** button across from the Suppress option on the Format Editor. Create a formula to suppress the salary if it is greater than $50,000. Add a comment that explains what the formula does. Save the changes and close the Formula Workshop.

4. Notice that the button across from the **SUPPRESS** option is red. Click OK. Notice that the Salary field is not enabled on the design tab. This means that the value in this field will not always print because of the suppression criteria. The report should look like the one shown in Figure 15-19. If your report does not look like the one shown, make sure that the formula looks like the one in Figure 15-20. You can refer to the Chapter 14 Employee list report to see what it looks like without the conditional formatting. Save the changes.

First Name	Last Name	Address1	Region	Salary
Steven	Buchanan	14 Garrett Hill		$ 50,000.00
Robert	King	Edgeham Hollow		$ 37,000.00
Anne	Dodsworth	7 Houndstooth Rd		$ 35,000.00
Michael	Suyama	Coventry House		$ 30,000.00
Bas-Rhin				
Justin	Brid	2 impasse du Soleil	Bas-Rhin	⬭
Xavier	Martin	9 place de la Liberté	Bas-Rhin	$ 50,000.00
Laurent	Pereira	7 rue Nationale	Bas-Rhin	$ 45,000.00
BC				
Andrew	Fuller	908 W. Capital Way	BC	⬭
Albert	Hellstern	13920 S.E. 40th Street	BC	⬭

Figure 15-19 Suppress salary GT $50000 report

```
// This formula will suppress the salary if it is > 50000
{Employee.Salary} >50000
```
Figure 15-20 Suppression formula

Comparison Conditional Formatting

You can use one field for the comparison criteria and a different field to apply the conditional formatting to. You will learn how to do this in the next three exercises.

Exercise 15.6: Compare Customer Averages

The report that you will modify currently prints the average order amount for each customer and the average order amount for all of the customers on the report. In this exercise you will modify the report to display a message if a customers average order amount is greater than the average order amount for all customers on the report. If the average order amount is less, no message will print. In order to print a message based on a condition, the formula has to use the **DISPLAY STRING** option on the Format Editor.

 If you open the Formula Workshop from the Format Editor dialog box, you cannot create a different type of formula. You also cannot modify or delete existing formulas.

1. Save the Chapter 15 Customer order averages report as E15.6 Display string conditional formatting.

2. Right-click on the Average Order Amount field in the group footer section and select Format Field.

3. On the Common tab click on the Formula button across from the **DISPLAY STRING** option, then add the If Then Else statement to the Formula Text section.

4. After the word **IF**, add the Group 1 Avg of Orders field, then type >= after the field.

5. Add the Report Area.Avg Of Orders field, then press Enter.

6. Click after the word **THEN** and add the ToText(x) function. (It's under the Strings category.)

7. Add the Group 1 Avg of Orders field inside of the ToText(x) function. Click outside of the parenthesis and type + " ** Above report average", then press Enter.

8. Copy the ToText portion of the formula up to the plus sign and paste it after the **ELSE** clause, then type + " " at the end of the formula. The formula should look like the one shown in Figure 15-21.

```
if Average ({Orders.Order Amount}, {Customer.Customer Name}) >=Average ({Orders.Order Amount})
then ToText (Average ({Orders.Order Amount}, {Customer.Customer Name}))+" ** Above report average"
else ToText (Average ({Orders.Order Amount}, {Customer.Customer Name})) +" "
```
Figure 15-21 Customer average comparison formula

9. Save the changes and close the Formula Workshop, then click OK to close the Format Editor.

10. Make the Average Order Amount field in the group footer section longer, then preview the report.

    The first page of the report should look like the one shown in Figure 15-22.
    The last page of the report should look like the one shown in Figure 15-23. Notice that there is no message next to these averages. This is because the customer average amount is less than $5,625.32, which is the average order amount when the report was run.

    Save the changes and leave the report open to complete the next exercise.

 If the average amount field is not lined up, this is one of the rare times that I will modify a report on the preview tab. To line up the Average Order Amount field, left align it and then drag it in the direction needed to line it up with the field above.

	Order Date	Ship Date	Order Amount	Order #	Unit Price
Alley Cat Cycles					
	01/08/2011	01/08/2011	$5,879.70	1151	$2,939.85
	09/28/2011	09/30/2011	$2,559.63	2157	$313.36
	09/28/2011	09/30/2011	$2,559.63	2157	$539.85
	10/27/2011	11/06/2011	$2,699.55	2272	$899.85
	01/31/2012	02/03/2012	$9,290.30	2664	$2,792.86
	01/31/2012	02/03/2012	$9,290.30	2664	$455.86
	02/19/2012	02/22/2012	$8,819.55	2735	$2,939.85
	02/19/2012	02/22/2012	$8,819.55	2735	$2,939.85
Total # of orders -8	Total $ amount of orders -		$ 49,918.21		
	Average order amount for customer -		$6,239.78 ** Above report average		
Aruba Sport					
	06/05/2011	06/08/2011	$5,879.70	3079	$2,939.85
Total # of orders -1	Total $ amount of orders -		$ 5,879.70		
	Average order amount for customer -		$5,879.70 ** Above report average		

Figure 15-22 First page of the report

Yue Xiu Bicycles					
	06/20/2011	06/20/2011	$2,939.85	3148	$2,939.85
Total # of orders -1	Total $ amount of orders -		$2,939.85		
	Average order amount for customer -		$2,939.85		

Total # of customers on this report - 102

Grand Total # of orders - 1,142

Grand Total $ amount of all orders - $ 6,424,118.58

Average order amount for all customers - $ 5,625.32

Figure 15-23 Last page of the report

Exercise 15.7: Font Color Conditional Formatting

In the previous exercise you compared the customer average order amount to the average order amount for the report. Detail records that are below the report average order amount were not formatted. It may be helpful to change the color of customer order amounts that have an average less than the report average.

1. Save the E15.6 report as E15.7 Font color conditional formatting.

2. Right-click on the Average Customer Order Amount field in the group footer section and select Format Field. On the Font tab, click on the Formula button across from the COLOR option.

| The comments that you see in the formula section are colors that you can use. |

The formula that you need to create to change the font color is the opposite of the formula that you created in the previous exercise. Rather than type the formula in again, you can copy the formula that you created in the previous exercise and change it as needed.

3. Open the **FORMATTING FORMULAS** folder in the Workshop Tree. Under the Avg Of Order Amount1 section, you should see the **DISPLAY STRING** formula illustrated in Figure 15-24.

    Click on the Display String formula and select (highlight) the formula up to the first ToText function, then press the **CTRL+C** keys.

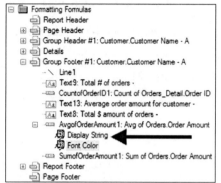

Figure 15-24 Formatting Formulas folder

4. Click on the Font color formula in the Workshop Tree, then scroll to the end of the comments and paste the formula in by pressing the **CTRL+V** keys.

5. Change the >= to <=, then type crRed after the word **THEN**. Save the changes and close the Formula Workshop. Click OK to close the Format Editor.

6. Go to the last page of the report. You should see the customer average dollar amounts in red. If you do not see the color red on the last page of the report, compare your font color formula to the one shown in Figure 15-25. Save the changes.

```
if Average ({Orders.Order Amount}, {Customer.Customer Name}) <=Average ({Orders.Order Amount})
then crRed
```

Figure 15-25 Font color formula

Exercise 15.8: Suppress Currency Formatting

Every detail record on the E15.6 report prints the dollar sign for the Order Amount field. The report may look better if the dollar sign only printed for the first detail record for the customer. In this exercise you will create conditional formatting to suppress the dollar sign on records other then the first one for each customer.

1. Save the E15.6 report as E15.8 Suppress currency formatting.

2. Right-click on the Order Amount field in the details section, then select Format Field. Click the Customize button on the Number tab. Click on the **CURRENCY SYMBOL** tab.

3. Click the Formula button across from the **ENABLE CURRENCY SYMBOL** option, then add the If Then Else statement to the Formula Text section.

4. Click after the word **IF** and add the **ONFIRSTRECORD** function, which is under the Print State category. Press the space bar. Type the word or, then press the space bar.

5. Add the Customer Name field, then type `<> Previous`. Add the Customer Name field again, then press Enter.

6. Delete the word **ELSE**, then add the **CRFLOATINGCURRENCYSYMBOL** function. (**Hint:** You can copy this function from the comments above the formula.)

7. Type two left parenthesis in front of the first Customer Name field and one parenthesis after the field.

8. Type two left parenthesis in front of the second Customer Name field and three after the field. You can add a comment to the formula.

9. Save and close the formula. Click OK twice to close both dialog boxes. The report should look like the one shown in Figure 15-26.

   As you can see, the dollar sign for the Order Amount field only prints on the first detail record for each customer. If your report does not look like the one shown, compare your formula to the one in Figure 15-27. Save the changes.

	Order Date	Ship Date	Order Amount	Order #	Unit Price
Alley Cat Cycles					
	01/08/2011	01/08/2011	$5,879.70	1151	$2,939.85
	09/28/2011	09/30/2011	2,559.63	2157	$313.36
	09/28/2011	09/30/2011	2,559.63	2157	$539.85
	10/27/2011	11/06/2011	2,699.55	2272	$899.85
	01/31/2012	02/03/2012	9,290.30	2664	$2,792.86
	01/31/2012	02/03/2012	9,290.30	2664	$455.86
	02/19/2012	02/22/2012	8,819.55	2735	$2,939.85
	02/19/2012	02/22/2012	8,819.55	2735	$2,939.85
Total # of orders - 8		Total $ amount of orders -	$ 49,918.21		
		Average order amount for customer -	$6,239.78 ** Above report average		

Figure 15-26 Suppress currency formatting report

```
// This formula will suppress the dollar sign on all detail records
// in each group, except for the first record
if OnFirstRecord or (({Customer.Customer Name}) <> Previous (({Customer.Customer Name})))
then  crFloatingCurrencySymbol
```

Figure 15-27 Dollar sign suppression formula

Formula Wrap Up

So how did you do creating If Then Else statements? Hopefully, you did okay. The reason that I am asking is because if you can understand and create If Then Else statements, you are on your way to becoming a Crystal Reports power report writer. If you are curious about other statements that you can use, check out the following in the Help file: For Loop and my favorite, the Select Case statement.

Select Case Statement

The Select Case statement is similar to the If Then Else statement. I personally find Select Case statements easier to read and understand, especially easier then Nested If statements. For example, in Exercise 15.4 you created a nested If statement. The following Select Case statement provides the same logic as the Nested If statement shown earlier in Figure 15-14. For whatever reason, I find this easier to read and understand.

```
Select {Orders.Order Amount}
    Case Is >= 10000: "10% discount"
    Case Is >= 5000: "15% discount"
    Case Is >= 2500: "20% discount"
    Default: "25% discount";
```

Exercise 15.9: Use The Select Case Statement

In this exercise you will modify the Select Case statement shown above to change the font color of the Order Amount field on the report.

1. Save the E15.4 report as `E15.9 Select Case statement`.

2. Right-click on the Order amount field, then select Format field.

3. On the Font tab, click the formula button for the Color field, then type the formula below.

```
Select {Orders.Order Amount}
Case 0 To 2500: crGreen
Case 2501 To 5000: crRed
Case 5001 To 9999: crTeal
Case is > 9999: crPurple;
```

4. Save and close the formula. Close the Format Editor dialog box.

5. Save the changes. The values in the Order Amount field should have different colors.

Boolean Formulas

You learned that Boolean fields have values of true/false or yes/no. **BOOLEAN EXPRESSIONS** return a value of true or false. In Chapter 7 you learned how to format a Boolean field. Earlier in this chapter I said that one way to understand If Then Else statements is to think of them as a true or false question. A Boolean formula is the test question portion of an If Then Else statement. Boolean formulas do not have to be created on Boolean fields. The value that a Boolean formula returns is either true or false. You can then format the result of the Boolean formula like you did in Exercise 7.7.

In Exercise 15.5 you created a formula that would suppress the salary if it was greater than $50,000. A Boolean formula could have been used to accomplish the same result. Figure 15-20 shown earlier shows the formula. The difference would be the values printed in the salary field in the E15.5 report.

Instead of printing the salary for some records and leaving the field blank for other records, as shown earlier in Figure 15-19, the values **TRUE** or **FALSE** would have printed, as shown in Figure 15-28.

First Name	Last Name	Address1	Region	Salary > 50K
Steven	Buchanan	14 Garrett Hill		False
Robert	King	Edgeham Hollow		False
Anne	Dodsworth	7 Houndstooth Rd.		False
Michael	Suyama	Coventry House		False
Bas-Rhin				
Justin	Brid	2 impasse du Soleil	Bas-Rhin	True
Xavier	Martin	9 place de la Liberté	Bas-Rhin	False
Laurent	Pereira	7 rue Nationale	Bas-Rhin	False
BC				
Andrew	Fuller	908 W. Capital Way	BC	True

Figure 15-28 E15.5 report using a Boolean formula

USING THE SECTION EXPERT

Overview

After completing the exercises in this chapter you will be able to use the Section Expert to format fields and sections in a report. You will also learn the following techniques:

- ☑ Create page breaks
- ☑ Reset page numbers
- ☑ Suppress a section of the report
- ☑ Use the row color formula
- ☑ Create odd and even page headers

CHAPTER 16

The Section Expert

So far, all of the formatting techniques that you have used changed individual objects on the report. You can use the Section Expert to format an entire section of the report, similar to how the Format Editor is used to format fields. You can also create formulas for many of the options on the Section Expert, which is shown in Figure 16-1.

Figure 16-1 Section Expert

With section formatting, you can make the following types of changes to a report:

① Force each group to start on a new page.
② Change the line spacing in the details section to something other than single spacing.
③ Create page breaks.
④ Conditionally suppress a section of the report.

How To Open The Section Expert

① Right-click on the section name on the left side of the design tab and select Section Expert.
② Click the Section Expert button on the Experts toolbar.
③ Report ⇒ Section Expert.

 The advantage to using the first option above to open the Section Expert is that the section will already be selected on the left side of the Section Expert dialog box when it is opened. Table 16-1 explains the formatting section options on the Common tab. The options on this tab are available for most sections. Table 16-2 explains the options on the Paging tab. The options on this tab are used to select the orientation, format page numbers and page breaks. Table 16-3 explains the options on the Common tab that are only available for a specific section of the report. Table 16-4 explains the options on the Layout tab, which is only available when the **FORMAT MULTIPLE COLUMNS** option for the details section is selected.

Merging And Deleting Sections

In addition to being able to create more sections with the Section Expert, you can also delete sections. In Figure 16-1 above, you see the Delete and Merge buttons enabled. **MERGING SECTIONS** combines the objects in two section into one section. Merging moves the objects in the lower section up. In Figure 16-1 above, the objects in the Details c section would be moved up to the Details b section.

To delete a section, select it on the Section Expert, then click the Delete button. You can also right-click on the section that you want to delete in the design window and select Delete section. Keep in mind that when you delete a section, everything in the section is deleted.

Common Tab

Option	Description
Hide (Drill-Down OK)	Hides the section when the report is printed. The section can be viewed on the preview tab. If the section that this option is applied to is part of a higher level group and the group is drilled-down on, the objects in the section will be visible on the drill-down tab. This option is not available for subsections.
Suppress (No Drill-Down)	The section that this option is applied to will not be printed, does not allow drill-down and cannot be viewed on the preview tab, even if a higher level section is drilled-down on. This option is also available for subsections.
Print at Bottom of Page	Forces the section to be printed as close to the bottom of the page as possible, even if the detail records stop printing half way down the page.
Keep Together	Keeps the data for a record in the detail section together on the same page when printed. The exception is if the detail section has a memo or multi-line field. This option is sometimes confused with the Keep Group Together option on the Group Expert dialog box. These options produce different results.
Suppress Blank Section	Prevents the section from printing when all of the objects in the section are blank. This option saves space on the page.
Underlay Following Sections	Causes the section to print in the same location that the section below it will print. This option will allow charts or images to print next to the section that follows.
Read-Only	Prevents any formatting to the section. This option is similar to the **LOCK FORMAT** and **LOCK SIZE AND POSITION** options on the Format Editor and Formatting toolbar.
Relative Positions	Locks an object next to another object like a cross-tab or OLAP grid. If the cross-tab grows, the object will be repositioned so that it remains aligned with the grid object.
Background Color	This option is on the Color tab. It is used to select a color for the background of the section. This is different then the formatting that objects in the section have. You learned how to use this option in Exercise 8.2.

Table 16-1 Common tab section formatting options explained

Paging Tab

Option	Description
New Page Before	Forces a page break before the section. This option is not available for the report header and page header sections. (1)
Reset Page Number After	Resets the page number back to one after the section has printed. This option also resets the Total Page Count special field.
New Page After	Forces a page break after the section or after a specific number of records have printed. (1)
Orientation	Is used to select the orientation (portrait or landscape) for a section of the report, as shown in Figure 16-2. Figure 16-3 shows the options on the Paging tab for the details section. The orientation option is not available for the page header and footer sections.

Table 16-2 Paging tab options explained

(1) This option is often used to force each group to start on a new page.

Formatting options that are not available for the section of the report that is selected are not enabled.

For example, in Figure 16-2, the **NEW PAGE BEFORE** option is not enabled for the report header section.

Figure 16-2 Paging tab options for the report header section

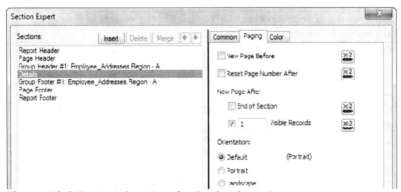

Figure 16-3 Paging tab options for the details section

The New Page After option shown above in Figure 16-3, for the details section, has the following options:

The **END OF SECTION** option forces a page break after the section is printed.
The **VISIBLE RECORDS** option is used to select the number of records that will print (in the details section) before the page break for the group occurs.

. . . .

Section	Option	Description
Page Footer	Clamp Page Footer	This option removes white space from the bottom of the report. If the page footer section is empty, selecting this option removes the white space from the page footer, which will provide more space on the page for the other sections of the report. This option is also helpful when a report is viewed online.
Page Footer	Reserve Minimum Page Footer	Select this option to reduce the space set aside for the page footer section on reports that have more than one page footer section. This provides more space for other data on the printed page.
Details	Format With Multiple Columns	Displays data in columns similar to a newspaper layout. When checked, a tab named **LAYOUT** will open, as shown in Figure 16-4. The options on the Layout tab are used to select the size of the columns, as explained in Table 16-4.

Table 16-3 Section specific common tab formatting options explained

 If all of the detail sections have the Hide or Suppress option checked, the result is a summary report.

Layout Tab

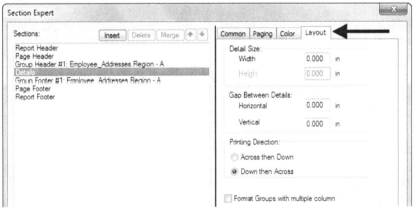

Figure 16-4 Layout tab options

Option	Is Used To . . .
Detail Size	Select the height and width size of each column in the details section.
Gap Between Details	Select the amount of space between the rows and columns. The **HORIZONTAL** option is for the space between columns. The **VERTICAL** option is for the space between rows.
Printing Direction	Select how the rows and columns in the details section are printed. The **ACROSS THEN DOWN** option prints row by row. The **DOWN THEN ACROSS** option prints column by column.
Format Groups with multiple column	Apply the same options (as those selected above in this table) to the details section of groups that have multiple columns.

Table 16-4 Layout tab options explained

Exercise 16.1: Create Page Breaks

Page breaks are one of the most used section formatting techniques. While the concept appears straight forward, it can be tricky and can produce unexpected results. In this exercise you will add a page break to a report that prints orders by month. The objective is to force a page break when the month of the order date changes in the group header section of the report.

1. Save the E11.2 report as `E16.1 Report with a page break`.

2. Open the Section Expert, then click on the group header section option. On the Paging tab check the **NEW PAGE BEFORE** option.

3. Preview the report. You should notice that the first page of the report is blank. More than likely, having the first page break occur before the detail records for the first group are printed on the report is not what you had in mind. Save the changes and leave the report open to complete the next exercise.

Using Page Breaks With More Than One Group

In reports that have two or more groups, the page break options work differently, as illustrated below.

1. Save the E11.1 report as `E16.1A Page break with two groups`.

2. Apply the New Page Before option to the group header #1 section. Save the changes and leave the report open to complete the next exercise.

You should see that the first page of the report is blank. More than likely, having the first page break occur before the detail records for the first group are printed on the report is not what you had in mind. If you applied the New Page Before option to the group header 2 section, the first page displays the page header information and the group name, but no detail records.

Exercise 16.2: Conditionally Format The Page Break

As you saw in the previous exercise, selecting the **NEW PAGE BEFORE** option did not accomplish what you thought it would. In this exercise you will fix this problem. The problem with only selecting this option is that it causes a page break before any data prints.

Hopefully you are asking yourself what is different about the first group of data. You may have looked through the functions to see if there is a function that you can use. If you have looked for a function, you won't find any that are specifically for sections on a report or for page breaks. You could create your own formula, but what would you write? You may have to think outside of the box on this one.

In case you are thinking that you could use the **NEW PAGE AFTER** option for the group header section, this option would cause the detail records to start on a different page, but the group header information would remain on the previous page, as shown in Figure 16-5.

Figure 16-5 New Page After option turned on for the group header 2 section of the E16.1A report

I know what you are thinking: Use the **NEW PAGE AFTER** option on the group footer section. That will give you the desired output of having each group start on a new page. The downside is that if the report has data in the report footer section, it will not print on the same page as the last group footer section of information. The information in the report footer section will be forced to a new page.

If the report that you are creating does not have data in the report footer section or you want the information in the report footer section to print on a page by itself, using the New Page After option on the group footer section will work. If you are going to use the New Page After option with the group footer section, you should create a formula using the **ONLASTRECORD** function so that a new page will not be created after the last record is printed. Not doing this could cause a blank page to appear at the end of the report.

In Exercise 15.8 you used a function called **ONFIRSTRECORD**. You could create a formula to see if the group contains the first record in the report. If it does, do not force a page break. This will work because only one group per report will contain the first record on the report. It just so happens that the first record is in the first group, which is the group that currently has a page break before it. Creating a formula to not force a break on the first record will cause the formatting (in this case a page break) to be turned off, on the first group. This is what you want to have happen.

1. Save the E16.1 report as `E16.2 Conditional page break`.

2. Open the Section Expert, then click on the group header section. On the Paging tab click on the Formula button across from the New Page Before option.

3. Type `Not` and press the space bar, then add the OnFirstRecord function, or you can type the function in. Save and close the formula, then click OK to close the Section Expert. Preview the report. Save the changes.

The first group (January), should be on the first page of the report instead of on the second page, like it was in the previous exercise. If you look at the last page of the report, you will see that the report footer information is not on a page by itself.

> **Using The New Page After Option To Format A Page Break**
> Earlier, the idea of using the New Page After option was discussed as a way to force a page break. Adding the **NOTONLASTRECORD** function to the New Page After option on the group footer section will force each group to start on a new page, just like the exercise that you just completed.

Exercise 16.3: Resetting Page Numbers

Depending on the type of report that you create, you may have the need to have the page number reset after a certain condition has been met. A report that you may need this for is one that will be distributed to more than one person. An example of this would be a monthly order by sales rep report. Resetting the page number to one when orders for a different sales rep prints would allow the report to be distributed to each rep and have the page numbers make sense to each sales rep. Can you imagine receiving a report that started on page 75? You may think that the report was missing pages. Using the **RESET PAGE NUMBER** section formatting option would prevent that from happening. In this exercise you will learn how to use this option.

1. Save the Chapter 16 Monthly orders by sales rep report as `E16.3 Reset page number`.

2. Create a page break formula that does not cause a page break on the first record of the report, for the group header section.

3. Check the **RESET PAGE NUMBER AFTER** option for the group footer section. The first page of the report should start on page 1. The page number is at the top of the report.

4. In the group tree, click on Group 3. You will see that the page number is 1. If you go to the next page, it will be page 2. This is what should happen. Save the changes and leave the report open to complete the next exercise.

Suppress The Page Footer Section On The First Page Of The Report
Depending on the type of the report, you may not want the content in the page footer section to print on the first page of the report. For example, the page header of the E16.2 report contains the current date and page number, but you do not want this information to print of the first page of the report. If this is the case, you can follow the steps below to suppress the page footer section on the first page of the report.

1. Open the report that has the page footer section that you want to suppress.
2. Open the Section Expert, then click on the Page Footer option.
3. On the Common tab, click the formula button for the Suppress (No Drill-Down) option.
4. Type this formula. `PageNumber=1`
5. Save the changes. When you view the report, the first page will not display the content in the page footer section.

Exercise 16.4: Use The Change Group Options Dialog Box

If you look at the second page for any group in the E16.3 report that you just modified, you will notice that the group header information (the Salespersons name) only prints on the first page of each group. Figure 16-6 shows the second page of the first group. The report would look better if the group name printed on every page. Options on the **CHANGE GROUP OPTIONS** dialog box are used to force the group header information to print on every page.

Salesperson	Order Date	Order ID	Product ID	Unit Price	Quantity
	11/18/2011	2376	201161	$832.35	2
	11/17/2011	2362	103171	$899.85	3
	11/17/2011	2362	303221	$329.85	2

Figure 16-6 Second page of the first group on the E16.3 report

1. Save the E16.3 report as E16.4 Repeat group header option.

2. Right-click on the group header section on the left side of the design tab, then select **CHANGE GROUP**.

3. On the Options tab check the **REPEAT GROUP HEADER ON EACH PAGE** option shown in Figure 16-7.

   This option will cause the group header information to print on every page of the report.

   Click OK. If you go to any page after the first page of a group, you will see the group header information, just like it is on the first page of each group. Save the changes and leave the report open to complete the next part of this exercise.

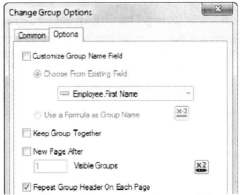

Figure 16-7 Change Group Options dialog box

How The Change Group Options Work

The **CUSTOMIZE GROUP NAME FIELD** option is used to create the name for the group as you want it to appear in the group header section, or a different section if you copy or move the group header field to it.

 Do not check this option if you only want to display the data that is in the field that is being grouped on.

The **USE A FORMULA AS GROUP NAME** option is used to create a formula that will control what appears in the Group Name field. This option is very helpful if you need to change what prints in the group name field based on data that appears in the report or data in a table that is connected to the report. This option is often used to create a formula that combines the data from two or more fields.

The **NEW PAGE AFTER VISIBLE GROUPS** option is used to control the number of page breaks after a specific number of groups have printed. If you wanted a page break to occur after every three groups, enter a 3 in this field.

The **REPEAT GROUP HEADER ON EACH PAGE** option will cause the group header section to be printed at the top of each page. This will let you know which group the detail records and totals are for.

 The purpose of the **KEEP GROUP TOGETHER** option shown above in Figure 16-7 is to force all records that are in the same group print on the same page. If this option is checked and the first group on the report does not fit on the first page, the group will start printing on the second page and the first page of the report will be blank. If this happens, clear the **RESPECT KEEP GROUP TOGETHER ON FIRST PAGE** option on the Report Options dialog box. In my opinion, it is best to only use the Keep Group Together option if the groups do not contain a lot of detail records.

The Keep Group Together option will cause all of the group sections (the group header, group footer and detail section for the group) to be printed on the same page. If all three sections will not fit on the current page, they will start printing on the next page. This is different then the **KEEP TOGETHER** option on the Section Expert, which only causes the section that the option is applied to, to print on the same page. [See Table 16-1, earlier in this chapter] These options are best suited for reports that do not have a lot of detail records in each group. Groups that have a lot of detail records may require more than one page, which may result in the report having breaks in unexpected places.

Exercise 16.5: Using The InRepeatedGroupHeader Function

Prior to changing the group options in the previous exercise, it was easy to tell which was the first page for each group in the report. For this report, that is not exactly true because each group starts on page 1, but pretend that the page numbers are not reset. To help make reading the report easier, adding text to every page that the group header is printed on would resolve this issue.

The **INREPEATEDGROUPHEADER** function is used to add conditional formatting to a group header or footer section when the group prints on more than one page.

1. Save the E16.4 report as E16.5 Use the InRepeatedGroupHeader function.

2. Add a text object to the right of the Last Name field in the group header section, then type (Continued) in the object. Change the font size of the text object to 8.

3. Right-click on the text object and select Format Text, then click the Formula button across from the Suppress option. Type Not InRepeatedGroupHeader in the Formula Text section.

4. Save the changes. Go to the second page of the report. You should see (Continued) next to the salespersons name, as shown in Figure 16-8.

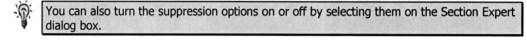

	Salesperson	Order Date	Order ID	Product ID	Unit Price	Quantity
1	Nancy Davolio	(Continued)				
		11/18/2011	2376	3305	$21.90	1
		11/18/2011	2367	401002	$281.85	2
		11/18/2011	2376	202221	$485.87	2

Figure 16-8 Second page of the Repeat group header report

Exercise 16.6: Suppress A Section Of The Report

There will be times when you need to permanently hide a section of a report. Often, this is done (on a second copy of an existing report) when you do not want some users to see certain information on a report. An example that comes to mind is the monthly orders by sales rep report that you modified in Exercise 16.3. Because the goal of that report is to distribute the sections of the report to the appropriate sales rep, there is no reason to display the Report Total information in the report footer section. You will learn how to suppress a report section in this exercise.

1. Save the E16.3 report as E16.6 Report footer section suppressed.

2. Right-click in the report footer section on the left and select **HIDE (DRILL-DOWN OK)** on the shortcut menu.

> You can also turn the suppression options on or off by selecting them on the Section Expert dialog box.

3. On the last page of the report you should not see the report totals at the end of the report. Save the changes.

Use The Suppress (No Drill-Down) Option

Earlier in this book you learned how to add subsections to a report. In the exercise that you just completed, you learned how to suppress a section of the report.

If you have the need to create a report that uses more than one address field, often each address field is placed in separate rows in the details section.

The second address field is often blank, which means that a blank row will print for the records when the second address field is blank, as illustrated in Figure 16-9.

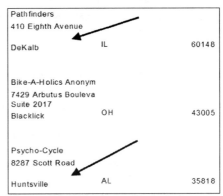

Figure 16-9 Blank row illustrated

When combined, the Suppress (No Drill-Down) option and adding a section with conditional formatting will allow you to suppress a section of the report based on a condition. You can combine these options and place the second address field in a section by itself, they conditionally hide the section if the second address field is blank. Remember that if you suppress a field in a section that has other objects, the entire section will be suppressed if the condition is true. Often, this is not what you want.

If you move the second address field to its own section of the report as shown in Figure 16-10, you can suppress the section if the address field is empty. This will cause the report to print like the one shown in Figure 16-11, instead of the one shown above in Figure 16-9.

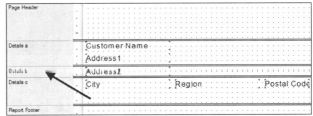

Figure 16-10 Address 2 field in a section by itself

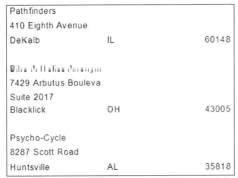

Figure 16-11 Report with the Address 2 field suppressed if empty

Exercise 16.7: Suppress A Group

Depending on the amount of data that is displayed on a report, not all users may need to view all of the records. In this exercise you will modify a report to only print groups of data that meet specific criteria. You will modify a customer average report to only print groups that have a group total average amount that is less than $2,500.

Modify The Existing Record Selection Criteria And Total Fields

1. Save the Chapter 15 Customer order averages report as `E16.7 Suppress a group`.

2. Delete the Order Amount record selection criteria.

3. Change the Order Date selection criteria to only include orders in 2011.

4. Change the Total # of orders field in the group footer section to Distinct count.

5. Change the Grand Total # of orders field in the report footer section to Distinct count.

6. Change the format on the two distinct count summary fields that you just modified to be whole numbers with no cents.

Add The Suppression Criteria

1. Open the Section Expert and add the formula shown in Figure 16-12 to the Suppress (No Drill-Down) option for the group header, details and group footer sections. (**Hint**: You can paste the formula after you type it once.)

```
// This formula will suppress groups on the report where the
// average order amount of the customer is less than $2,500
//
// This formula is used on the Group Header, Details
// and Group Footer report sections
Average ({Orders.Order Amount}, {Customer.Customer Name}) <2500
```
Figure 16-12 Suppress group formula

Notice that the Formula Workshop displays the format option Suppress (No Drill-Down) in the Title Bar, as shown in Figure 16-13.

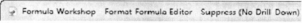
Figure 16-13 Formula Workshop Title Bar

2. Save the formulas and close the Section Expert. The report should look like the one shown in Figure 16-14. Some of the groups (customers) that you should not see are AIC Children's, Alley Cat Cycles and Belgium Bike Company.

	Order Date	Ship Date	Order Amount	Order #	Unit Price
Aruba Sport					
	06/05/2011	06/08/2011	$5,879.70	3079	$2,939.85
Total # of orders -1	Total $ amount of orders -		$ 5,879.70		
	Average order amount for customer -		$ 5,879.70		
Athens Bicycle Co.					
	06/08/2011	06/18/2011	$8,819.55	3097	$2,939.85
Total # of orders -1	Total $ amount of orders -		$ 8,819.55		
	Average order amount for customer -		$ 8,819.55		
Backpedal Cycle Shop					
	02/08/2011	02/09/2011	$3,544.20	1279	$12.00

Figure 16-14 Suppress group report

Figure 16-15 shows the grand totals for the report. The report has suppression criteria to not display a group if the average customer order amount is less than $2,500.

Total # of customers on this report - 256
Grand Total # of orders - 1,562
Grand Total $ amount of all orders - $ 5,830,030.25
Average order amount for all customers - $ 2,228.60 ◄───

Figure 16-15 Report totals on the last page

Remember that records that are suppressed are still included in the total fields on the report. Some people consider this a flaw so to speak, of how data is processed. To correct this problem, running total fields should be used instead of summary fields in the group and report footer sections. Chapter 22 will explain how to fix this report so that the customers whose averages are less than $2,500 are not counted in any total amount field on the report.

Exercise 16.8: Use The Color Tab Section Expert Options

One of the more popular uses of the Color tab on the Section Expert is to add a background color to every other detail record on the report. If you have ever seen what is known as "green bar" computer paper, you already know the color effect that you will create in this exercise.

1. Save the Chapter 15 Customer discount report as `E16.8 Add color to rows`.

2. Open the Section Expert. Click on the details section, then click on the Color tab.

3. Click the Formula button, then type the formula shown at the bottom of Figure 16-16.

   You can change this formula to create a background pattern different then every other row as you will see in the examples in the next section.

```
// This formula will print a silver background for all
// even number rows in the details section of the report.
//
// RecordNumber mod 2 will return 0 for even row numbers
// and 1 for odd row numbers
//
// DefaultAttribute is the default row color
//

If RecordNumber mod 2=0
  then crSilver
  Else DefaultAttribute
```

Figure 16-16 Row color formula

4. Save the changes. The report should look like the one shown in Figure 16-17.

Customer Discount Report				
Customer Name	Order ID	Order Date	Order Amount	Ship Via
City Cyclists	1	12/02/2010	$41.90	UPS
Deals on Wheels	1002	12/02/2010	$5,060.28	Pickup
Deals on Wheels	1002	12/02/2010	$5,060.28	Pickup
Warsaw Sports, Inc.	1003	12/02/2010	$186.87	UPS
Warsaw Sports, Inc.	1003	12/02/2010	$186.87	UPS
Bikes and Trikes	1004	12/02/2010	$823.05	Pickup

Figure 16-17 Add color to rows report

 Some of the options on the Format Editor and Section Expert will be displayed with comments when they are opened in the Formula Workshop, as shown in Figure 16-18. The comments that you see are for the four line style options for the Border tab on the Format Editor. The options in the comments let you know what values you can use in your formula. The row color formula that you just created had a list of colors at the top of the formula that you could select from to use as the background color.

```
// This conditional formatting formula must return one of the following Line Style Constants:
//
// crSingleLine
// crDoubleLine
// crDashedLine
// crDottedLine
// crNoLine
//
```

Figure 16-18 Default comments for the line style option

How The Row Color Formula Works

Now that you have created a row color formula, knowing how it works will be helpful because you can modify the formula to create other color patterns.

RECORDNUMBER is a special field that counts records in the details section.

MOD divides one number by another number and returns the remainder, instead of the result of the division.

The formula **IF RECORDNUMBER MOD 2=0** means to divide the record number by 2. If the remainder is zero, meaning that if the record number is evenly divisible by two, the background color is applied to the detail row.

If the report section that you are applying the background row color formatting to also has background color formatting for objects, you should use **NOCOLOR** for the Else clause for the background color row formatting instead of using the color white because NoColor produces a result that is similar to being transparent, which is what you want. Using the color white will cause the background color applied to individual fields to produce results that are not always visually appealing.

If the report section does not have any fields with background color formatting, using the **DEFAULT ATTRIBUTE** is acceptable for the background color row formatting, as shown in Figure 16-21.

Row Color Examples

Example #1 The formula, If RecordNumber mod 5=0 will shade every fifth row, as shown in Figure 16-19.

Customer Name	Order ID	Order Date	Order Amount	Ship Via
City Cyclists	1	12/02/2010	$41.90	UPS
Deals on Wheels	1002	12/02/2010	$5,060.28	Pickup
Deals on Wheels	1002	12/02/2010	$5,060.28	Pickup
Warsaw Sports, Inc.	1003	12/02/2010	$186.87	UPS
Warsaw Sports, Inc.	1003	12/02/2010	$186.87	UPS
Bikes and Trikes	1004	12/02/2010	$823.05	Pickup
SAB Mountain	1005	12/03/2010	$29.00	Loomis
Poser Cycles	1006	12/03/2010	$64.90	Purolator
Poser Cycles	1006	12/03/2010	$64.90	Purolator
Poser Cycles	1006	12/03/2010	$64.90	Purolator
Spokes	1007	12/03/2010	$49.50	Parcel Post
Clean Air Transportation	1008	12/03/2010	$2,214.94	Purolator
Clean Air Transportation	1008	12/03/2010	$2,214.94	Purolator
Clean Air Transportation	1008	12/03/2010	$2,214.94	Purolator
Extreme Cycling	1009	12/03/2010	$29.00	Loomis
Cyclopath	1010	12/03/2010	$14,872.30	UPS

Figure 16-19 Result of the mod 5=0 formula

Example #2 The formula, If RecordNumber mod 3 in [1,2] will shade the first two rows out of every three rows, as shown in Figure 16-20.

Customer Name	Order ID	Order Date	Order Amount	Ship Via
City Cyclists	1	12/02/2010	$41.90	UPS
Deals on Wheels	1002	12/02/2010	$5,060.28	Pickup
Deals on Wheels	1002	12/02/2010	$5,060.28	Pickup
Warsaw Sports, Inc.	1003	12/02/2010	$186.87	UPS
Warsaw Sports, Inc.	1003	12/02/2010	$186.87	UPS
Bikes and Trikes	1004	12/02/2010	$823.05	Pickup
SAB Mountain	1005	12/03/2010	$29.00	Loomis
Poser Cycles	1006	12/03/2010	$64.90	Purolator
Poser Cycles	1006	12/03/2010	$64.90	Purolator

Figure 16-21 shows the formula.

Figure 16-20 Result of the mod 3 in [1,2] formula

```
If RecordNumber mod 3 in [1,2]
then crSilver
Else DefaultAttribute
```

Figure 16-21 Mod 3 in [1,2] formula

Example #3 The formula, If RecordNumber mod 10 in [3,5] will shade the third and fifth rows out of every ten rows, as shown in Figure 16-22.

Customer Name	Order ID	Order Date	Order Amount	Ship Via
City Cyclists	1	12/02/2010	$41.90	UPS
Deals on Wheels	1002	12/02/2010	$5,060.28	Pickup
Deals on Wheels	1002	12/02/2010	$5,060.28	Pickup
Warsaw Sports, Inc.	1003	12/02/2010	$186.87	UPS
Warsaw Sports, Inc.	1003	12/02/2010	$186.87	UPS
Bikes and Trikes	1004	12/02/2010	$823.05	Pickup
SAB Mountain	1005	12/03/2010	$29.00	Loomis
Poser Cycles	1006	12/03/2010	$64.90	Purolator
Poser Cycles	1006	12/03/2010	$64.90	Purolator
Poser Cycles	1006	12/03/2010	$64.90	Purolator

Figure 16-22 Result of the mod 10 in [3,5] formula

Use The Suppress And Record Number Options

Earlier in this chapter you learned how to use the Suppress (No Drill-Down) option to suppress a section of the report. You also learned that the Record Number special field can be used to control when the formatting is applied. When used together, these two features can be used to conditionally add blank lines to a report. The steps below show you how to conditionally print a blank line in the details section after every third detail record.

1. Save the E16.7 report as E16.8A Suppress and Record Number options, then add another details section. Make sure the data for the details section is in the first details section.

2. On the Section Expert, select the second details section.

3. Check the Suppress (No Drill-Down) option, then click the Formatting button.

4. Type the formula Remainder(recordumber, 3) <>0, then save the changes.

5. If you view the data for the Back Pedal Cycle Shop, you will see a blank line after every third record, as illustrated in Figure 16-23.

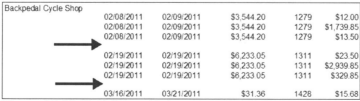

Backpedal Cycle Shop					
	02/08/2011	02/09/2011	$3,544.20	1279	$12.00
	02/08/2011	02/09/2011	$3,544.20	1279	$1,739.85
	02/08/2011	02/09/2011	$3,544.20	1279	$13.50
	02/19/2011	02/19/2011	$6,233.05	1311	$23.50
	02/19/2011	02/19/2011	$6,233.05	1311	$2,939.85
	02/19/2011	02/19/2011	$6,233.05	1311	$329.85
	03/16/2011	03/21/2011	$31.36	1428	$15.68

Figure 16-23 Blank lines added to report

Exercise 16.9: Create Odd And Even Page Headers

As more and more word processing mail merge documents are being converted to reports, the need for odd and even page headers and footers in reports is becoming more popular. Some word processing and mail merge documents have header and footer information similar to the pages in this book are often printed on printers that support duplex printing.

In the previous section you learned that the MOD function can be used with a special field to determine an action based on the current record number. Creating odd and even page headers is similar. The difference is that for the page header, you need two page header sections on the report and each one requires its own conditional MOD formula. These formulas are for the page number to determine if the current page number is odd or even. Each page of the report only needs the odd page header information or the even page header information. Therefore, each page header section has to be suppressed when the other page header section prints.

 Even page numbers have a remainder of zero. Odd page numbers have a remainder of one.

1. Open a new report and add the Customer Name and Address fields from the Customer table to the report.

2. Add another page header section, then delete the print date field.

3. In the first page header section add a text object, then type `This is the right page header and should have an odd page number` in the object.

4. Add the Page Number field to the right corner of the Page Header a section, then place the text object to the left of the page number field.

5. Copy everything in the Page Header a section to the Page Header b section. Make sure that the field headings in both page header sections are lined up with the fields in the details section.

6. In the second page header section change the text object to `This is the left page header and should have an even page number`. Move the Page Number field to the left corner, then place the text object to the right of the page number field. The report layout should look like the one shown in Figure 16-24.

PHa	This is the right page header and should have an odd page number Page
	Customer Name Address1 Address2 City Postal Code
PHb	Nu This is the left page header and should have an even page number
	Customer Name Address1 Address2 City Postal Code
D	Customer Name Address1 Address2 City Postal Code

Figure 16-24 Report layout

7. Add the following formula `PageNumber mod 2=0` to the Page Header a Suppress (No Drill-Down) option on the Section Expert. You are adding this to the right page header section so that the left page header section will be suppressed when the right page header information is printed. Because the report does not have any groups, you do not have to check the Suppress (No Drill-Down) option.

8. Add the following formula `PageNumber mod 2=1` to the Page Header b Suppress (No Drill-Down) option on the Section Expert.

9. Save the report. Type `E16.9 Odd even page headers` as the file name. The report should look like the one shown in Figures 16-25 and 16-26.

This is the right page header and should have an odd page number 1				
Customer Name	Address1	Address2	City	Postal Code
City Cyclists	7464 South Kingsway	Suite 2006	Sterling Heights	48358
Pathfinders	410 Eighth Avenue		DeKalb	60148

Figure 16-25 Odd page header of the report

2 This is the left page header and should have an even page number				
Customer Name	Address1	Address2	City	Postal Code
Bike Shop from Mars	7071 Dundas Crescent	Suite 1730	Newbury Park	91338
Feel Great Bikes Inc.	3015 Delta Place	Suite 2601	Eden Prairie	55367

Figure 16-26 Even page header of the report

CREATING CHARTS

 Overview   Crystal Reports has an expert for creating charts. There are 16 types of charts that you can create, including pie, bar and line. In this chapter you will learn how to create the majority of the chart types.

Overview

In addition to being able to format data in reports, charts are used to present data in a graphical format which often makes the data easier to understand because the relationship between the data is visually displayed. Charts also allow data to be presented in formats that text-only reports cannot do as well. For example, charts can show trends over time, relationships or how one set of data compares to another set of data.

In previous chapters you created basic charts using a report wizard. As you saw, the chart options were very limited. When you need to create or modify charts that require more detail than the wizards provide, you should use the Chart Expert. It is very easy to get carried away when creating charts. Try to create charts that present the data in a meaningful way. Remember that sometimes, less is more.

There are four ways to open the Chart Expert, as explained below.

① Click the **INSERT CHART** button on the Insert Tools toolbar.
② Insert ⇒ Chart.
③ Right-click on an existing chart and select Chart Expert.
④ Click on an existing chart, then Format ⇒ Chart Expert.

Chart Considerations

There are two areas that need to be addressed before you start to create the chart: The chart type and the source of the data for the chart. You will select the chart type on the Type tab on the Chart Expert, which is explained below. Changing the chart type is easy. If you are not sure which chart type is the most appropriate, with a few mouse clicks, you can try out a few chart types and variations to see which chart type is the best one for the data.

Charts should enhance the ability to understand the data and make it easy to see the differences. While a report can have more than one chart, keep in mind that charts are memory intensive. The data source for the chart comes from one of the following: Records in the details section of the report, a cross-tab, an OLAP grid or summary data.

I use to teach a technical writing class and one of the assignments had students create three charts to visually present data. Overall, the students did a good job on the charts. However, it was easy to tell which students had never created a chart before, for at least one of the reasons listed below.

① The wrong chart type was selected. Newsflash: Bar charts are not the best option for all types of data, especially data that shows trends or needs to show how data has changed over time.
② The values on the X and Y axes are backwards. Dollar amounts, quantity and percents usually go on the Y axis and time, dates and categories usually go on the X axis.
③ Not understanding the data that the chart will use.

The Chart Expert

This tool is used to create and edit charts. It has wizard like characteristics because you click on the tabs to accomplish different tasks associated with creating and editing a chart. The biggest benefit of using the Chart Expert instead of the chart options on a wizard is that you have a lot of the chart options available from the beginning and the chart does not have to be based on data that will be printed on the report, like the wizards require. The options on each tab are covered in detail in this chapter. Not understanding what all of the options are or not knowing where they are, will take you longer to create a chart. You will probably gain a better understanding of the options if you have the Chart Expert open.

The tabs on the Chart Expert (Type, Data, Axes, Options, Color Highlight and Text) contain options for a variety of features that you can use to make the chart as effective as possible. Keep in mind that not all of these tabs are available for all chart types. The tabs and options are explained below.

 You do not have to create a chart from an existing report when you use the Chart Expert. You can select the fields that you need on the Chart Expert.

Type Tab

The options on this tab are used to select what the chart will look like. There are 16 chart types that you can select from, as shown on the left side of Figure 17-1. Many of these chart types also have variations that you can select, which gives you more chart options. Each chart type is explained later in Table 17-1.

There are additional chart types, which Crystal Reports refers to as templates.

You will learn about the other chart types in the next chapter.

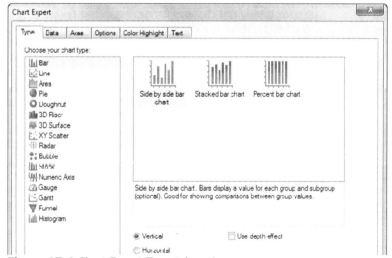

Figure 17-1 Chart Expert Type tab options

In previous chapters you created a pie and bar chart using a wizard. If you have created charts in spreadsheet software, you are probably familiar with many of the chart types in Crystal Reports. When selecting the chart type, the most important consideration should be to select the chart type that will best display the data that will be presented in the chart. This is the first thing that you have to do. When you select the chart type on the left side of the dialog box you will see variations of the chart on the right. Click on the chart style (variation) on the right that you want to use. Under the chart variations you will see a description of the chart type.

Chart Type Options

At the bottom of the Type tab shown above in Figure 17-1, you will see the first two options explained below for the bar, line, area and histogram chart types. Most chart types also have the third option below.

① **VERTICAL** This is the default option. The elements will start at the bottom of the chart, as shown on the percent bar chart on the right side of Figure 17-1 above.

② **HORIZONTAL** This option changes the direction of the elements on the chart. The bars will start on the left, instead of the bottom, as shown in Figure 17-2.

③ **USE DEPTH EFFECT** This option displays the chart in 3D format, as shown in Figure 17-3.

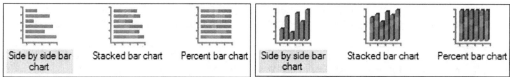

Figure 17-2 Horizontal bar chart options   **Figure 17-3** Use depth effect option

Chart Types

Chart Type	This Chart Type . . .
Bar	Shows differences between items and relationships between multiple groups of data, as shown in Figure 17-4. This is probably the most used chart type. Stacked bar charts show each item as a percent of the total.
Line	Shows trends and changes for groups over a period of time. The markers on the bottom three line chart types on the Chart Expert indicate the exact values. In Figure 17-5, the data is represented with lines. A good use of **3D LINE CHARTS** is when the data lines cross each other often. This makes a line chart easier to read. (1)
Area	Shows how the data has changed over a period of time. Figure 17-6 shows how four types of income (mail order, store, kiosk and Internet) make up the total income and how the income changes over the months. Area charts are almost identical to stacked line charts. The difference is that area charts are filled in below the trendline. Area charts are probably best suited for a few groups of data. (1)
Pie	Only displays data for one point in time. Figure 17-7 shows various types of income for July. Each slice of the pie represents the percent for the item. The Multiple pie chart type will create a chart for each group. (2)
Doughnut	Is similar to pie charts. The difference is that there is a hole in the center, which contains the grand total of the data presented in the chart. (2)
3D Riser	Is the 3D version of bar charts that shows extreme data values side by side, separately or stacked. It can display several groups of data in shapes like a pyramid or octagon.
3D Surface	Is the 3D version of area charts. This chart type uses three sets of data. The surface of the chart has a curve and shows trends in relation to time.
XY Scatter	Shows how two values are related (like month of year and order amount) and how a change in one value affects the other value, as shown in Figure 17-8. This chart type is used to show the correlation between the items. The X and Y axis must display numeric data. If data like dates or months can be converted to numeric data, it can be used in this chart type.
Radar	Compares sets of data relative to a center point and shows how far the data value is from the standard (the center point value). The values that are often used are group subtotals. The data from the X axis is usually plotted in a circle and the Y axis values are plotted from the center of the circle out.
Bubble	Is similar to XY Scatter charts because it plots individual points. The difference is that bubble charts use different size plot points (bubbles) based on the data value. The larger the data value, the larger the size of the bubble.

Table 17-1 Chart types explained

Chart Type	This Chart Type . . .
Stock	Is similar to bar charts. The difference is that the bars in stock charts do not have to touch the bottom of the chart. This type of chart is often used to display the minimum and maximum of stock prices, where each bar represents a different stock. Stock charts plot the first and last trade of the day or the high and low values for each element.
Numeric Axis	Does not use a fixed X axis value or interval like many other chart types do. You can use a date/time field or numeric field for the X axis (the On change of field). This chart type is another way to create bar, line and area charts.
Gauge	Looks like a gauge in a car, as shown in Figure 17-9. The needle in the chart points to the value that is being represented. The value is usually a percent. If there is more than one value or group being represented, a gauge chart is created for each value or group. Multiple needles in one gauge means that there is more than one "On change of" value.
Gantt	Is often used to display project management data in a horizontal bar chart like the start and end dates of tasks on a project plan. Gantt charts only work with date and date/time fields. For example, the vertical axis would display the project tasks and the horizontal axis would display the time frame.
Funnel	Is similar to stacked bar charts because each bar on the funnel shows each item as a percent of the total. The difference is that the bars are in the shape of a funnel. The height of the bar represents the percent of the data. The width of the bar does not represent anything.
Histogram	Displays the frequency of a data element in a data set. This chart places the data into buckets (which are range intervals on the x axis) and displays a count of the records in each bucket, as shown in Figure 17-10. Usually, you will not see more than eight bars on a histogram chart, regardless of how many ranges (buckets) there really are.

Table 17-1 Chart types explained (Continued)

(1) This chart type requires at least two sets of data.
(2) This chart type only uses one value because it shows how the whole (100%) is divided.

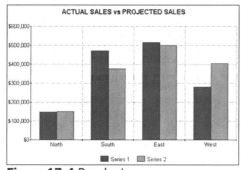

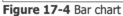

Figure 17-4 Bar chart

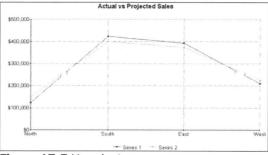

Figure 17-5 Line chart

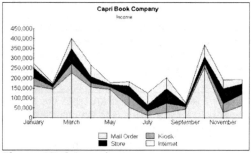

Figure 17-6 Area chart

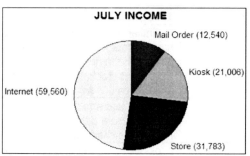

Figure 17-7 Pie chart

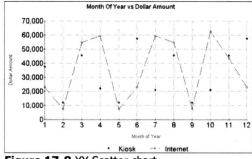

Figure 17-8 XY Scatter chart

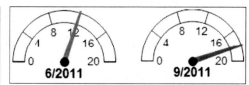

Figure 17-9 Gauge chart

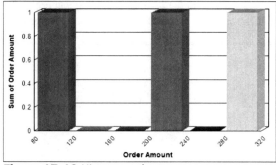

Figure 17-10 Histogram chart

It would be very helpful and a big time saver to me if at least one of the tabs on the Chart Expert would display the chart with the options that are selected, similar to what you see when you use the Chart Options dialog box to modify the chart. You will learn about the Chart Options dialog box in the next chapter.

Data Tab

The options on this tab are used to select the data for the chart. This is the second area that needs to be addressed before you create the chart. Data selection is based on the selected chart type and the section of the report that the chart is in. There are four ways (called layout options) to chart data, as explained below. Depending on the chart type that is selected, not all of the data layout options are available.

Each layout type works independently of the others. You can only select one layout type for a chart. If you select one and make changes on that screen, then select a different layout type and make changes, the only information that will be saved will be the layout that you changed last. All of the layout options have the **ON CHANGE OF** drop-down list. The options in this list are how you select when a new element (bar, slice of pie, point on a line, etc) will be added to the chart. This option lets Crystal Reports know that when the value in the fields listed below this option changes, you want a new element of the chart to be created.

Advanced Layout Options

This layout option is always available and is used to create a chart based on specific values. This is probably the most complex layout option because it can be used to create a chart that is not based on data that will print on the report. If you created a report using the Blank Report option and have not added any fields to the report, the options on this tab are used to select the fields for the chart. This is how you would create a report that only has a chart or a chart that is not based on groups and is not a cross-tab chart.

If you need to a create a chart based on records in the details section of the report, click on the Advanced layout option on the Data tab.

You will see the options shown in Figure 17-11.

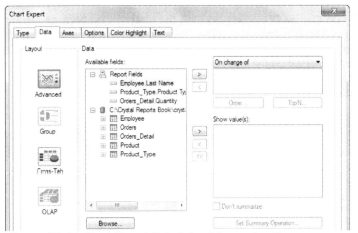

Figure 17-11 Chart Expert Data tab - Advanced options

 When you are working on exercises that use the options on the Advanced tab, you will see this instruction: **ADD THE FIELD TO THE FIRST LIST BOX.** This means to add the field to the list that is under the On Change Of option.

 If the report already has groups defined, you can still create an advanced chart because the options on this tab are not affected by the groups that are on the report.

The **AVAILABLE FIELDS** section on the Advanced layout screen contains the fields that are already on the report, including the summary and running total fields, as well as, all of the fields in the tables connected to the report. Select the fields to go on the X and Y axis. This section is only available if the On Change of option is selected in the drop-down list on the right.

 Summary and running total fields can only be added to the **SHOW VALUE(S)** list.

The **ON CHANGE OF** option is used to select up to two fields to group the data in the chart on. This group is not a real group like the ones that you learned how to create earlier in this book. When the value in the field changes, a new element is created. Each element on the chart represents one group. There can only be one field in the Show Value list if there are two fields in the On Change Of list.

If you wanted to create a chart that displayed the orders by sales rep, you would add the sales rep (Employee Last Name) field to the list box below this drop-down list.

The Order Amount field would be added to the Show value(s) list to get a total for each sales rep. Figure 17-12 shows this report. [See the Chapter 17 Sales reps orders chart by last name report]

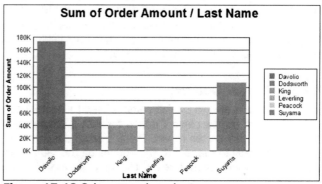

Figure 17-12 Sales rep orders chart

The On Change Of option works like the group option because it summarizes the values in the group. The difference is that the groups in the chart do not have an effect on the report. If you select multiple fields to group on, the data from each group will be displayed side by side or stacked, based on the chart type that is selected. If the order date was added to the Evaluate option, as shown in Figure 17-13, the report would look like the one shown in Figure 17-14. [See the Chapter 17 Sales reps orders chart by order date report]

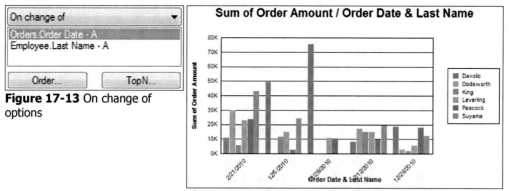

Figure 17-13 On change of options

Figure 17-14 Sales rep orders chart with additional options

The first field below the On change of drop-down list is the primary group and determines how the data is grouped. The second field below the drop-down list creates the elements in the primary group. In the example shown above in Figure 17-13, the Order Date field is the primary group. The Employee Last Name field is the secondary group. Putting the fields in this order groups the records by date. Each element in the date group is a different sales rep.

The **FOR EACH RECORD** option in the On change of drop-down list will cause a new element to be added to the chart for every record that would print on the report. If this option is selected, only one field can be added to the box below this drop-down list. If there is not a lot of data in the table for the field that you select, it is okay to select this option because the chart will be legible. If there are a lot of records, more than likely it would be hard to read the chart if this option is selected. If this option is selected, fields that are added to the **SHOW VALUE(S)** list will not be summarized, the actual value in the field is what will appear in the chart.

You can reduce the records that are used to create the chart by using the Select Expert. If you realize that you need to do this, you can create the selection criteria after the chart has been created.

 Gantt charts have to use the **FOR EACH RECORD** option. A start and end date field must be added to the Show value(s) list.

The **FOR ALL RECORDS** option creates a chart with only one element, which is a grand total for all of the records that are on the report. You cannot add any fields to the box below the On change of drop-down list if this option is selected.

The **SHOW VALUE(S)** list contains the fields that the chart will create a summary for. The default calculation type is SUM. The actual value or the value from the summary calculation will be used as an element on the chart. Which value is used is determined by the option selected in the Evaluation option drop-down list.

Table 17-2 explains the type of summary value that each evaluation option creates. If you add more than one field to this list, the chart will plot a separate line or bar for example, for each field in this list. Each chart type allows at least one field in the Show value(s) list. In the Orders by sales rep example, if you add the Order Amount field to the Show value(s) list, a total (summary) for each sales rep would be created.

Option	Show Value Summary Type
On change of	Summary for each group.
For each record	Actual value of each record.
For all records	One summary value for the entire report.

Table 17-2 Evaluation options explained

Summary Calculations

Table 17-3 explains the default type of summary calculations that are applied to different field types. You can change the type of calculation as needed.

Field Type	Default Calculation Type
Number	Summary
Currency	Summary
All others	Count

Table 17-3 Default summary calculations

You can change the summary calculation type by following the steps below.

① Click on the field that you want to change the calculation for, in the Show value(s) list.
② Click the **SET SUMMARY OPERATION** button shown earlier at the bottom of Figure 17-11. You will see the Edit Summary dialog box.
③ The options in the **CALCULATE THIS SUMMARY** drop-down list are the ones that are available for the data type of the field that you are changing. Select the type of calculation that you want.

The **DON'T SUMMARIZE** option is only available if a formula or running total field is in the Show Value(s) list. Select this option if the formula field already has the value that you want displayed on the chart.

The **ORDER** button on the Advanced layout screen opens the dialog box shown in Figure 17-15.

The options on this dialog box work the same way that the options on the Insert Group dialog box work. These options are used to select the sort order for the element in the chart.

Figure 17-15 Chart Sort Order dialog box

Group Sort Expert

In the orders by sales rep example, if you selected the Order Amount field and then clicked the Order button you would be able to select how you wanted the total order amount for each rep to be displayed. If you were creating a bar chart and wanted to see the sales reps in order from high to low based on sales, you would select **DESCENDING**.

The **TOP N** button on the Advanced layout screen opens the Group Sort Expert shown in Figure 17-16.

The options on this dialog box are similar to the ones on the **OTHERS** tab on the Change Group Options dialog box. If you only wanted to include the top or bottom N records, groups or percents, you would select the options here.

Figure 17-16 Group Sort Expert

The options selected above in Figure 17-16 will display the five sales reps that had the lowest dollar amount of sales.

If you want to include groups that are not part of the group sort, you can by checking the appropriate **INCLUDE** option on the right side of the Group Sort Expert dialog box. The **INCLUDE TIES** option will include groups that have the same summarized value if they meet the other selection criteria. Notice that you can also create formulas for options on the Group Sort Expert dialog box if the chart requires it. [See Chapter 22, The Group Sort Expert]

Group Layout Options

This is the default layout, but has less functionality than the Advanced layout. The primary reason is because advanced charts do not require a summary or group field, like the group layout does. The group layout options create a chart that is based off of fields in a group header or footer section of the report. This chart layout type is only available if the following conditions explained below are met.

① The chart must be placed in the report header or footer section or in a group header or footer section that is on a higher level then the data in the group that the chart will be based on.
② If the report has more than one group and you want to create a chart by group, the chart has to go in the group 1 section. Placing the chart in the group 2 section disables the group layout options.
③ The report has to have one group that has a summary or total field.

The options shown in Figure 17-17 are used to select how the data in the group will be displayed in the chart. The options are explained below.

Figure 17-17 Chart Expert Data tab - Group options
(On Change Of options for the two groups below the chart)

The options below the **ON CHANGE OF** drop-down list are the fields (that have a summary or total field) that are in a lower level then the section of the report that the chart has been placed in. This option is used to select the group that the chart will be based on.

A sample Orders by shipping method report has two groups: The Ship Via group and the Customer Name group. Both of these groups have summary fields. If you put the chart in the report header or footer section, the On Change Of drop-down list will have the options shown above in Figure 17-17.

If the report has three groups with a summary or total field and you place the chart in the first group section, you would see the summary or total fields for the two groups below it. Just by looking at the options in Figure 17-18, you do not know if the chart is in a report or group section.

If you put the chart in the first group header or footer section or the report header or footer section and there is only one group below it that has a summary or total field, you would only see one option in the On Change Of drop-down list, as shown in Figure 17-18.

Figure 17-18 On Change Of options for one group below the chart

These are the summary fields in the group header or footer section in the report. The fields in the **SHOW** drop-down list are the summary and subtotal fields in the group that is selected in the On Change Of field. This is how you select the summary field in the group that will be used in the chart.

Cross-Tab Layout Options

This layout option is only available if the report has a cross-tab object in the same or corresponding section of the report that the chart is placed in. This layout option displays relational data in rows and columns in summary format.

By corresponding section, I mean if the cross-tab that the chart will be based on is in the Group 2 footer section, the chart can be placed in the Group 2 header or footer section.

The options shown in Figure 17-19 are used to create a chart based on the summary data in the cross-tab.

Figure 17-19 Chart Expert Data tab - Cross-Tab options

Earlier you learned that cross-tab charts cannot be placed in the details section. If you move the cross-tab object to a different section after a cross-tab chart has been created, the report will automatically be moved to the new section also.

 If the report has more than one cross-tab object, you have to select the cross-tab object that you want to create the chart for before you open the Chart Expert.

The options in the **ON CHANGE OF** drop-down list are the first fields in the Rows and Columns sections of the Cross-Tab Expert or Wizard, regardless of how many fields each of these sections have. The field selected in this drop-down list is the first (or only) element that will be used as the primary X axis value.

Selecting a field in the **SUBDIVIDED BY** drop-down list is optional, which is why the default option is **NONE**. The only field that is available in the Subdivided By drop-down list is the one that was not selected in the On Change Of drop-down list. Selecting a field will create a second X value, which will add a second series of data to the chart. This will let you create a chart that does a side by side comparison.

Figure 17-20 shows a line chart with the first field in the Row section and the first field in the Column section from the cross-tab selected.

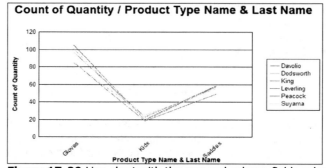

Figure 17-20 Line chart with the row and column fields selected

The options in the **SHOW** drop-down list are the fields that are in the Summary Fields section of the Cross-Tab tab on the Cross-Tab Expert. They are the fields that you select from to summarize the report on, like the Show Value list on the Advanced Layout screen.

OLAP Layout Options

Creating a chart that is based on data in an OLAP cube is very similar to creating a chart that is based on data in a cross-tab. The major difference is that charts that are based on data in an OLAP cube do not use summary fields. Another difference is that OLAP grids display multidimensional OLAP data. This layout option is only available if the report has data from an OLAP cube in the same or corresponding section that the chart is placed in, just like charts that are based on cross-tab data. The options shown in Figure 17-21 are used to create a chart based on the data in an OLAP cube.

 If the report has more than one OLAP cube, you have to select the OLAP cube that you want to create the chart off of before you open the Chart Expert.

The **CHART OFF ENTIRE GRID** option will use all of the options that the OLAP grid used to create the report, to create the chart. Selecting this option causes the other data options on the window to become disabled. The only time that you would use the other options shown in Figure 17-21 is if you need to change the dimensions of the data that the chart will be created from.

The default **ON CHANGE OF** option is the first **DIMENSION** on the Rows/Columns tab on the OLAP Expert or Wizard.

The drop-down list contains the other dimension options that you can select to use as the data for the X axis.

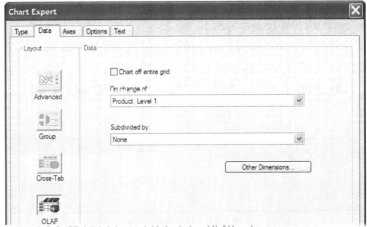

Figure 17-21 Chart Expert Data tab - OLAP options

 When creating a chart based on OLAP data, some chart types require multiple dimensions to be selected.

Selecting a field in the **SUBDIVIDED BY** drop-down list is optional. The default for this field is None. Selecting a field will divide the data in the On Change Of option. The only field that is available in this drop-down list is the one that was not selected in the On Change Of drop-down list. Selecting a field from this list will cause a second series of data to be added to the chart. Figure 17-22 shows a bar chart with only one dimension selected (the field in the On Change Of drop-down list). Figure 17-23 shows a 3D Riser chart with two dimensions selected.

If you move the OLAP grid from a report section to a group section, the chart will move to the corresponding group section. Data in an OLAP grid will not change if it is moved from the report header or footer section to a group header or footer section, which means that the data in the chart will not change if the chart is moved.

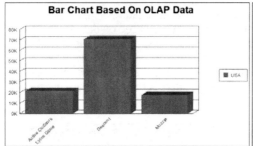

Figure 17-22 Bar chart with only one dimension selected

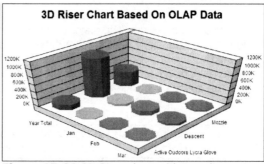

Figure 17-23 3D Riser chart with two dimensions selected

The **OTHER DIMENSIONS** button opens the Format Other Dimensions dialog box shown in Figure 17-24. The options on this dialog box are used to limit the values in the dimensions that will be displayed on the chart.

This is the equivalent of filtering the records that will be used to create the chart. For example, if you want to limit the products that appear in the chart to one product, click the **SELECT A MEMBER VALUE** button. You will see the Member Selector window. Select the product that you want.

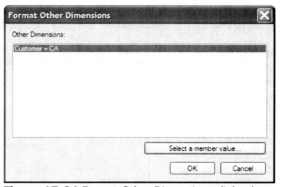

Figure 17-24 Format Other Dimensions dialog box

Axes Tab

Depending on the chart type that is selected, you may not see the Axes tab shown in Figure 17-25.

You will see this tab if the chart type selected uses the X and Y axis. For example, bar, line and area charts use the X and Y axis. Pie, Doughnut and Gantt charts do not.

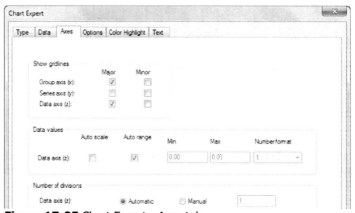

Figure 17-25 Chart Expert - Axes tab

The options on this tab are used to select how the chart will display the data values that you see across the bottom of the chart (the X axis) and on the left side of the chart (the Y axis). **X** and **Y Axis** represent the horizontal (X) axis and vertical (Y) axis of the chart. The X axis often represents quantities or percents.

If you are creating a 3D chart, you can also select the data values for the Z axis. If the chart that you are creating needs to display order totals by month, the months would be placed on the X axis because the report is grouped by month and the totals would be placed on the Y axis because they represent the quantity, as shown in Figure 17-26. If you were creating the same chart but selected a 3D layout, the chart would look like the one shown in Figure 17-27, which also includes the data axis (the Z axis).

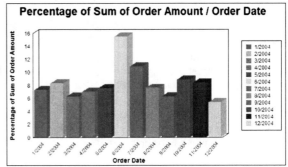

Figure 17-26 Bar chart with X and Y axis data

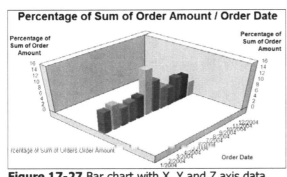

Figure 17-27 Bar chart with X, Y and Z axis data

Show Gridlines Options Gridlines make the chart easier to read if the values are close in range. You can have horizontal and vertical gridlines. You will see two or three axis options in this section of the Axes tab, depending on whether the chart is two or three dimensional.

The **GROUP AXIS** option corresponds to the **ON CHANGE OF** field on the Advanced layout screen.
The **SERIES AXIS** option will only appear for three dimensional chart types.
The **DATA AXIS** option corresponds to the **SHOW** field on the Advanced layout screen.

 Some chart types will have a gridline on the Group axis whether you select the option or not.

The major and minor options will add gridlines to the chart.

The **MAJOR** option will place the gridlines (with labels) on the axis, as shown in Figure 17-28.

The **MINOR** option can only be used with numeric labels and will place the gridlines between the labels on the axis.

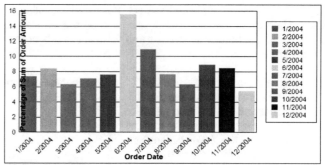

Figure 17-28 Bar chart with major gridlines

Data Values Options The options in this section of the Axes tab are used to customize the number ranges displayed on the chart.

The **AUTO RANGE** option is the default and uses the chart values to set the starting and ending values for the Data Y axis. If you want to customize the values, clear this option, then enter the Min, Max and Number formats that you want. If you change the data value options and then recheck this option, the changes that you made will still be in effect, even though the options are not enabled.

MIN is the lowest value that you want on the Y axis. Usually this is zero, but you may have the need to use a different starting value.

MAX is the highest value that you want on the Y axis. This value is usually larger than the largest value of the data on the axis.

 The danger in changing the Max value in my opinion is that you would be basing the change on the current values being displayed on the chart. If the report is run later and for whatever reason has a larger value than the value that you entered in the max field, the chart would not display the largest value.

The **NUMBER FORMAT** option is only available if the Auto Range option is not checked.

The options in the drop-down list shown in Figure 17-29 are used to select the format for the numbers that will be displayed on the chart.

Number format:

$1

1
1.0
1.00
1K
1M
$1
$1.00
$1K
$1M
100%
100.0%
100.00%

Figure 17-29 Number format options

The **AUTO SCALE** option is used to select the starting numeric value that the chart will use. The scale shows the unit of measurement. The scale range is taken from the data that is displayed on the report. The scale is automatically created for you, but you can change it. Crystal Reports uses the Auto Scale and Auto Range options on the Chart Expert Axes tab to create the scale.

Number Of Division Options The options in this section are used to customize the number of gridlines (intervals) and labels that the X data axis will have. Select the **MANUAL** option if you want to set the intervals.

. . . .

Options Tab

Figures 17-30 to 17-32 show various versions of the Options tab. The options are different depending on the chart type that is selected.

The options on this tab are used to customize the chart color, legend, data points and more.

The **AUTO-ARRANGE** option resets the chart to its original size and position.

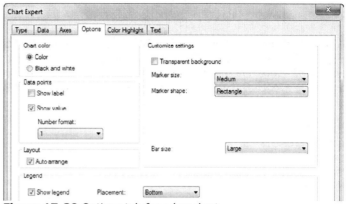

Figure 17-30 Options tab for a bar chart

The options in the **CUSTOMIZE SETTINGS** section are used to select the size and shape for the legend in some chart types or the shape of the markers for bar and line charts.

The **MARKERS** are the points on a chart that are connected by lines. This option is often used in line charts, as shown earlier in Figure 17-5.

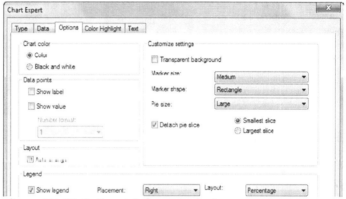

Figure 17-31 Options tab for a pie chart

The last size option in this section is used to select the size of the element. For example, the size of a slice of the pie chart or the size of the bar, as shown in Figures 17-31 above and Figure 17-32.

The options in the **DATA POINTS** section are used to select whether or not labels and values (the actual data) are displayed with the elements.

Each element (slice) in the pie chart shown earlier in Figure 17-7 has a label and value. The value is in parenthesis for illustration purposes.

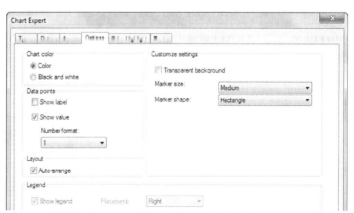

Figure 17-32 Options tab for a histogram chart

The options in the LEGEND section are used to display or hide the legend, as well as, select where you want the legend placed. The legend is used to help make the chart easier to read. Legends are color coded representations of different data elements on the chart.

The area chart shown earlier in Figure 17-6 has the legend at the bottom of the chart. In Figure 17-31 shown earlier, the legend will be placed on the right side of the chart. Notice in Figure 17-32 above that the legend options are not enabled. That means that the chart type cannot have a legend. There are also times when a chart looks better without a legend.

Color Highlight Tab

The options on this tab are used to conditionally format the colors for the elements (like a slice of a pie chart) on a chart.

The options shown in Figure 17-33 should look familiar because they are similar to the options on the Highlighting Expert.

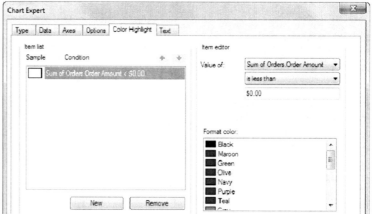

Figure 17-33 Color Highlight tab options

Differences Between The Color Highlight Tab And The Highlighting Expert

Conditional formatting on the Highlighting tab is not available for all of the chart types. The difference is that the Highlighting Expert works with objects on the report and the options on the Color Highlight tab work with elements on a chart. The options shown above in Figure 17-33 will change the color of the field to Teal if the percent of sales for the quarter is less than 20%.

To display conditional formatting using the Color Highlight tab, line charts have to have data markers. Area charts have to have two "On Change Of" values to display conditional formatting.

 The conditional formatting that you apply (using the Color Highlighting tab) to an element does not change if the data for that element changes. For example, if you apply conditional formatting to the bottom section (for example, the mail order section) of the area chart shown earlier in Figure 17-6 and the data changes and the mail order element is no longer on the bottom, the formatting for the mail order element does not change. The new data that is in the bottom section of the area chart will change. I think that conditional formatting usually looks better on charts that are using data that is grouped.

Text Tab

The options on this tab are used to add titles to a chart. As shown in Figure 17-34, the AUTO TEXT option is checked for all of the title fields and the text fields are not enabled. This is because Crystal Reports automatically creates many of the titles based on the field names that the chart is being created from. You saw this when you created charts with the wizard in Chapter 12.

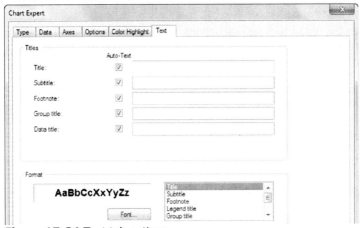

Figure 17-34 Text tab options

To change a title, clear the check mark next to the title that you want to change and type in the title that you want. It is not a requirement to have titles. You can change the font of a title by clicking on the title that you want to change in the **FORMAT** section and then click the Font button. You will see the Font dialog box. [See Chapter 2, Figure 2-35]

Parts Of A Chart

Charts can contain all or any of the options illustrated in Figure 17-35. These options can be added or deleted as needed. Many of the parts of a chart that have already been explained in this chapter.

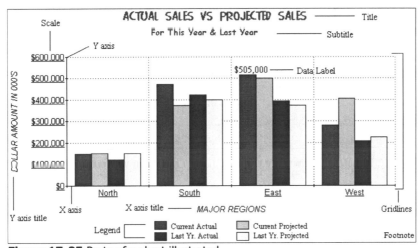

Figure 17-35 Parts of a chart illustrated

Adding A Chart To A Report

When the Insert ⇒ Chart option or Insert Chart button option is selected, you will see a shadow box like you see when you add an image to a report. Click in the section of the report that you want to place the chart in. If you select a section that the chart cannot be placed in, the mouse pointer will change to a circle with a line through it. If this happens, you have to start the insert chart process over. Once you select a section of the report where the chart will be placed, one of two things will happen:

    ① The Chart Expert will automatically open.

    ② A bar chart will be added to the report with several options already selected. If this happens and the default options are not what you need, right-click on the chart and select Chart Expert on the shortcut menu to change the options.

The way that the above options are determined is not random. The scenarios below explain under what conditions the Chart Expert will or will not automatically open.

    ① If a chart is added to the report header or footer section of a report that has a group with a summary field, a bar chart based on the group will automatically be added to the report. The Chart Expert will not automatically open.

    ② If a chart is added to the report header or footer section of a report that does not have a group or a group that does not have a summary field, the Chart Expert will open automatically.

    ③ If a report has a cross-tab or OLAP object and it is not selected prior to inserting a chart, the Chart Expert will automatically open.

    ④ If a report has a cross-tab or OLAP object selected prior to inserting a chart, a bar chart based on the data in the cross-tab or OLAP object will be added to a new section of the report.

Like summary fields on the report, the section of the report that a chart is placed in determines the data that will be used to create the chart. If the chart is placed in the report header or footer section, the chart will contain data from the entire report. If the chart is placed in the group header or footer section, the chart will only contain data for the group.

> Unless stated otherwise, if the exercise does not create a new report, place a chart object in the report header section of the report and open the Chart Expert after step 1 in each exercise.

> When you view a chart on the design tab, you may see fields that you did not select. The chart on the design tab does not represent data in the tables that the chart is using. I am telling you this because I do not want you to think that you are losing your mind when you see a chart on the design tab that doesn't display what you may be expecting. You will see real data on the preview tab.

Exercise 17.1: Create A Bar Chart

1. Save the E12.5 report as `E17.1 Bar chart.`

2. Delete the existing chart. Select the Side by side bar chart type, then select the Group data layout option on the Data tab, if it is not already selected.

3. Select the Order Date field from the On Change Of drop-down list if it is not already selected, then select the Order Amount field in the Show drop-down list.

4. On the Axes tab, add a major gridline to the Group axis option.

5. On the Options tab, select the Show value Data Points option, then change the Number format to $1.

6. Place the legend at the bottom of the chart.

   Figure 17-36 shows the options that should be selected.

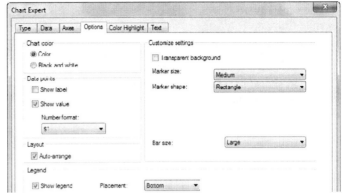

Figure 17-36 Options for the bar chart

7. On the Text tab, change the Title to Bar Chart.

   Save the changes. The chart should look like the one shown in Figure 17-37.

   The chart looks good, but with a few changes it would look better. In the next chapter you will learn how to modify a chart.

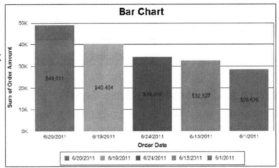

Figure 17-37 Bar chart

Exercise 17.2: Create A Line Chart

In this exercise you will create a line chart that displays order totals by month.

1. Save the E11.2 report as E17.2 Line chart.

2. Create selection criteria to only display order totals for 2011.

3. Select the Line chart type with markers at data points, then select the Group layout option.

4. Select the Sum Order Amount field in the Show drop-down list.

5. Place the legend on the right side of the chart. Select the large MARKER SIZE and the TRIANGLE Marker shape.

6. Change the Title to
   Line Chart.

   Save the changes.

   The chart should look like the
   one shown in Figure 17-38.

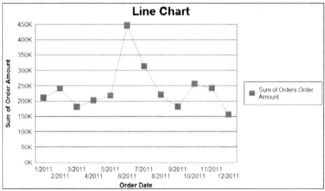

Figure 17-38 Line chart

 Marker Shape Option
As you can see, the markers are not triangle shaped. This option does not work on the
Chart Expert. You will learn another way to select a marker shape in the next chapter.
The chart module is a third-party application, which means that SAP cannot fix this issue.

Exercise 17.3: Create An Area Chart

As mentioned earlier, you can add a chart to a report that does not have any data. You will learn
how to do that in this exercise by creating a report that charts the sum of last years sales by region.

1. Create a new report and add the Customer table, then save the report as E17.3 Area
   chart.

2. Place a chart object in the report header section. The Chart Expert should open automatically.
   Select the Stacked Area chart type, then check the Use depth effect option.

3. Add the Region and Customer Name fields to the On change of list box on the Data tab, then
   add the Last Year's Sales field to the Show value(s) list. Figure 17-39 shows the options on the
   Data tab that should be selected.

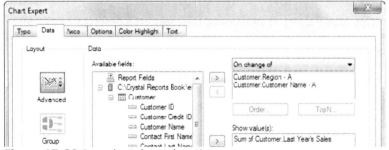

Figure 17-39 Area chart data tab options

4. Add a major gridline to the Group axis option, then change the option to show the legend at
   the bottom of the chart.

5. Change the Subtitle to Area chart. Delete the Group title, then click OK.

Add The Selection Criteria

In addition to being able to create a report that does not have any other information besides a chart, you can also select the records that you want the chart to be based on.

1. Open the Select Expert, select the Region field.

2. Select the **IS ONE OF** value, then add the following regions: CA, NY, PA and BC.

   Click OK and save the changes.

   The chart should look like the one shown in Figure 17-40.

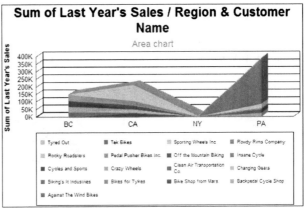

Figure 17-40 Area chart

Exercise 17.4: Create A Pie Chart

In this exercise you will create a pie chart that displays the order totals for 2011, by quarter.

1. Save the Chapter 17 Orders by quarter report as `E17.4 Pie chart`.

2. Select the Pie chart type, then check the Use depth effect option.

3. Check the Show label and Show value options. Change the Number format to 1. Select **BOTH** for the Legend layout option.

4. Change the Title to `Pie Chart`.

   Add the Footnote `Orders By Quarter`, then make the footnote italic.

   Click OK twice to close both dialog boxes and save the changes.

   The chart should look like the one shown in Figure 17-41. The number under the date on each slice of the pie is the number of orders for that quarter.

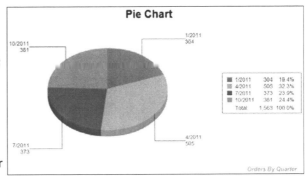

Figure 17-41 Pie chart

Exercise 17.5: Detach A Slice Of A Pie Chart

One way to emphasize a slice of a pie chart is to pull it away from the rest of the chart. This is sometimes referred to as "Exploding" a slice of a pie chart.

1. Save the E17.4 report as E17.5 Explode a slice of the pie chart.

2. Open the Chart Expert. On the Options tab, check the option **DETACH PIE SLICE**, then select the **LARGEST SLICE** option.

3. Change the Title to Explode a slice of a pie chart.

   Save the changes.

   The chart should look like the one shown in Figure 17-42.

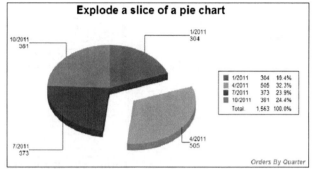

Figure 17-42 Explode a slice of the pie chart

Exercise 17.6: Create A Doughnut Chart

In this exercise you will modify the pie chart that you created in Exercise 17.4 so that it will be a doughnut chart.

1. Save the E17.4 report as E17.6 Doughnut chart.

2. Select the Doughnut chart type.

3. Change the Title to Doughnut Chart.

   Save the changes.

   The chart should look like the one shown in Figure 17-43.

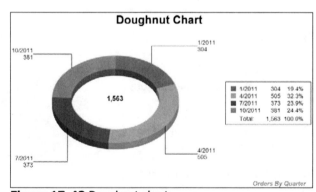

Figure 17-43 Doughnut chart

 You can detach a slice of a doughnut chart, just like you can in a pie chart.

Exercise 17.7: Create A 3D Riser Chart

In this exercise you will create a chart that shows last years sales for three states that are over a certain dollar amount. In order to do that, the report will need selection criteria.

1. Save the E17.3 report as E17.7 3D Riser chart.

2. Use the Select Expert to create the criteria shown in Figure 17-44, then refresh the data.

> {Customer.Region} in ["MA", "PA", "WI"] and
> {Customer.Last Year's Sales} >= $35000.00

Figure 17-44 Selection criteria

3. Select the 3D Riser bar chart type.

4. Display major gridlines for all axes. Show minor gridlines for the Data axis. Clear the Auto Scale option.

5. Change the Title to 3D Riser Chart.

   Change the Subtitle to Last Year's Sales >= 35,000.

   Save the changes.

   The chart should look like the one shown in Figure 17-45.

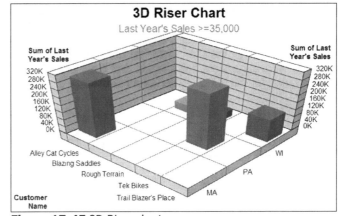

Figure 17-45 3D Riser chart

Exercise 17.8: Create An XY Scatter Chart

In this exercise you will create a chart that plots the number of orders in 2011 by month and total dollar amount.

1. Save the E11.2 report as E17.8 XY Scatter chart.

2. Select the XY Scatter chart type, then select the Advanced layout option.

3. Add the Order Date field to the first list box, then add the Order ID and Order Amount fields to the Show value(s) list.

4. Change the summary type of the Order ID field to Distinct count.

5. Change the Marker shape to **TRIANGLE**.

6. Change the Title to
XY Scatter Chart.

Add the Subtitle Orders By
Month.

Save the changes.

The chart should look like the
one shown in Figure 17-46.

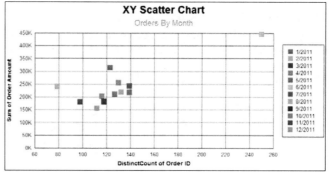

Figure 17-46 XY Scatter chart

Exercise 17.9: Show The Bottom 20% Of Orders Chart

In the exercise that you just completed, the chart plotted the data for all 12 months. If the
marketing department wanted to create a campaign to increase sales in the months that had the
lowest number of sales, it could be difficult to tell which months fall into that category. If the chart
was modified to only display the months that are in the bottom 20% of sales based on the total
order amount by month, the chart would be easier to know which months had the lowest number
of sales. You have already created a report that displayed the top five order days for a month.
Creating a report for the bottom 20% is very similar.

1. Save the E17.8 report as E17.9 Bottom 20 percent chart.

2. On the Chart Expert click on the Data tab. Click on the Order Date field on the top list on the
right, then click the **TOP N** button.

3. Open the Group Sort drop-down list and select **BOTTOM PERCENTAGE**. Change the Percentage
field to 20, then check the **INCLUDE TIES** option.

The options selected in
Figure 17-47 will display the
months that are in the bottom
20%, based on the number of
orders placed that month.

Click OK.

Figure 17-47 Group Sort Expert options

4. Change the Title to
   `Bottom 20% of Orders.`

   Delete the Subtitle.

   Change the Group title to
   `Number of orders.`

   Change the Data title to
   `Total monthly order
   amount.`

   The chart should look like the
   one shown in Figure 17-48.

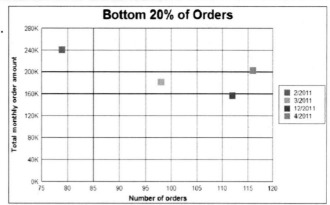

Figure 17-48 Bottom 20% of orders chart

 If you create a Top N report and do not add the records on the report that do not meet the Top N criteria to the "Others" group option, any grand total fields that are placed in the report footer will include totals for all records that meet the report criteria, whether or not they appear on the report. This means that if the records that do not meet the Top N criteria are not added to the "Others" option, the report grand totals will not be accurate because they will include amounts for detail records that are not on the report. This may not be what you want. If you only want the grand totals to include records that print on the report, in this case the Top N records, you have to create running total fields and place them in the report footer instead of summary fields. [See Chapter 22, Running Total Fields]

Exercise 17.10: Create A Radar Chart

In this exercise you will create a chart that plots the order totals in 2011 by quarter.

1. Save the Chapter 17 Orders by quarter report as `E17.10 Radar chart.`

2. Select the Radar chart type, then select the Group layout option, if it is not already selected.

3. Select the Sum of Orders.Order Amount field from the Show drop-down list.

4. Check the Show value option, then select the circle Marker shape.

5. Change the Title to
   `Radar Chart.`

   Add the Subtitle
   `Sum of orders by
   quarter.`

   Save the changes.

   The chart should look like the
   one shown in Figure 17-49.

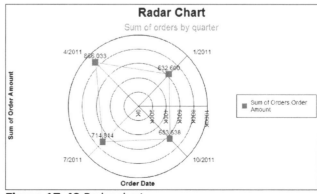

Figure 17-49 Radar chart

Exercise 17.11: Create A Bubble Chart

In this exercise you will create a chart that plots the orders between 6/1/2011 and 6/15/2011. Even though the Bubble chart is similar to the XY Scatter chart, the Bubble chart requires three fields in the Show value(s) list.

1. Save the E12.2 report as E17.11 Bubble chart.

2. Change the Order Date selection criteria to between 6/1/2011 and 6/15/2011, then delete the Order Amount criteria and refresh the data.

3. Change the chart type to Bubble.

4. On the Data tab, add the Order Date field to the first list box, then add the Order Amount field to the Show value(s) list.

5. Add the Order ID field to the Show value(s) list, then change the summary type to Count.

6. Add the Order Amount field to the Show value(s) list again, then change the summary type to Average.

7. Add a major gridline to the Group axis option.

8. Change the Title to Bubble Chart.

    Add the Subtitle For orders between 6/1/2011 and 6/15/2011.

    Save the changes and refresh the data.

    The chart should look like the one shown in Figure 17-50.

Figure 17-50 Bubble chart

Exercise 17.12: Create A Stock Chart

The stock report that you will create in this exercise will display the average order amount for five regions and the largest order in each region. Stock charts plot minimum and maximum values. The average value will be used as the minimum value and the largest order amount will be used as the maximum value.

The reason that I am using the average value for the minimum is because the lowest value would touch the bottom of the chart which defeats the purpose of the exercise of showing you how a stock chart really does look different then a bar chart.

Create The Selection Criteria

1. Create a new report, then add the Customer and Orders tables to the report.

2. Click on the Links tab. The tables should be joined on the Customer ID field. If they aren't, create the link by dragging the Customer ID field in the Orders table to the Customer ID field in the Customer table. To make sure that link is correct, right-click on the link between the tables and select **LINK OPTIONS**. You will see the dialog box shown in Figure 17-51. Make sure that the link is exactly like the one illustrated. Click OK, then click Finish.

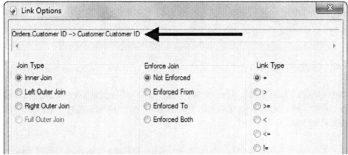

Figure 17-51 Link Options dialog box

3. Create selection criteria for the Region field in the Customer table to only include customers in the following regions: MA, PA, AL, ID, WI.

4. Save the report as `E17.12 Stock chart.`

Create The Chart

1. Add a chart object to the report header section, then select the High-Low stock chart.

2. Add the Region field to the first list box on the Advanced layout screen.

3. Add the Order Amount field to the Show value(s) list, then change the summary type to Maximum.

4. Add the Order Amount field to the Show value(s) list again, then change the summary type to Average.

5. Check the Show value option. Do not display a legend.

6. Change the Title to `Stock Chart.`

Add the Subtitle `Avg & Max order amounts for 5 states.`

Save the changes.

The chart should look like the one shown in Figure 17-52.

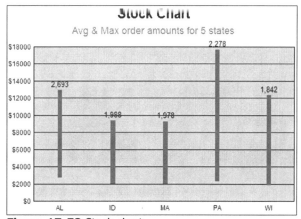

Figure 17-52 Stock chart

Exercise 17.13: Create A Numeric Axis Chart

In this exercise you will create a chart that displays the sum of orders for one company during a specific date range. You will use the options on the Chart Sort Order dialog box to select the frequency of the On Change Of option.

Create The Report

1. Save the E17.12 report as E17.13 Numeric Axis chart.

2. Delete the chart and record selection criteria.

3. Create selection criteria for the Order Date field. The order date should be between 11/1/2011 and 11/30/2011, then create selection criteria that limits the report to only display information for the customer, To The Limit Biking Co.

4. Add the Order Date and Order Amount fields to the details section. Delete the date field from the page header section, if it's there.

5. Change the format of the Order Date field to MM/DD/YYYY, then sort the Order Date field in ascending order.

Create The Chart

1. Add a chart object to the report header.

2. Select the Numeric Axis - Date axis bar chart type, then select the Use depth effect option.

3. On the Data tab, add the Order Date field to the first list box. Click on the field, then click the **ORDER** button. Make sure the last option on the Chart Sort Order dialog box is set to **FOR EACH DAY**, then click OK.

4. Add the Order Amount field to the Show value(s) list.

5. Add a minor gridline to the Data axis option.

6. Check the Show value option, then select the $1 Number format.

7. Change the Title to Numeric Axis Chart.

    Add the Subtitle To The Limit Biking Co - Nov 2011.

    Save the changes.

    The chart should look like the one shown in Figure 17-53.

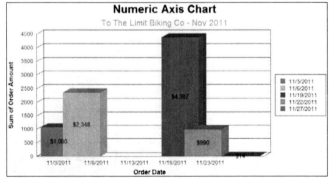

Figure 17-53 Numeric Axis chart

Exercise 17.14: Create A Gauge Chart

Earlier in this book you read how to create a report that displayed the words True or False in a Boolean field based on the employees salary. This was done to keep the employees actual salary private. In this exercise you will create a chart that will plot how many employees salaries are greater than 50K.

1. Save the Chapter 17 Boolean suppression formula report as E17.14 Gauge chart.

2. Select the Gauge chart type. Select the Advanced Data layout.

3. Add the **BOOLEAN_STYLE** formula field to the first list box, then add the Employee ID field to the Show value(s) list. Change the summary type to Count.

4. Change the Title to Gauge Chart. Add the Subtitle Employee salary over 50K.

Save the changes.

The chart should look like the one shown in Figure 17-54.

The company has 15 employees. If you look at the needles on the chart, you will see that when added together they equal 15.

Figure 17-54 Gauge chart

Exercise 17.15: Create A Gantt Chart

In Chapter 14 you created a report that calculated how many days it took to process customer orders. Gantt charts require a start and end date. In this exercise you will use the order date as the start date and the ship date as the end date.

The E14.8 Calculate order processing time report currently only has criteria that the order date is greater than or equal to a specific date. The Gantt chart would not be readable if all of the records that are currently on the report were displayed on the chart. To make the chart readable, you will select a few Order ID numbers to display on the chart.

1. Save the E14.8 report as E17.15 Gantt chart.

2. Create selection criteria that limits the report to the following Order ID numbers from the Orders Detail table: 1, 1015, 1020, 1069 and 1090.

3. Add a chart object to the report header section. Select the Gantt chart layout and the Use depth effect option.

4. Select the **FOR EACH RECORD** option from the drop-down list on the Data tab, then add the Customer Name field to the first list box.

5. Add the Order Date and Ship Date fields to the Show value(s) list.

6. Add the Title `Gantt Chart`.

   Add the Subtitle
   `Order processing time`.

   Save the changes.

   The chart should look like the
   one shown in Figure 17-55.

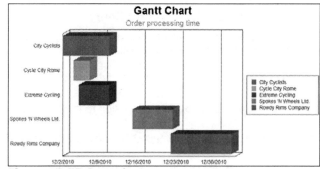

Figure 17-55 Gantt chart

Exercise 17.16: Create A Histogram Chart

In this exercise you will create a chart that shows how many orders per day were placed in 2011.

1. Save the Chapter 16 Monthly orders by sales rep report as `E17.16 Histogram chart`.

2. Select the Histogram chart type, then select the Advanced layout option.

3. Add the Order Date field to the first list box. Add the Order ID field to the Show value(s) list, then change the summary type to Distinct Count.

4. On the Options tab, check the Show value option and change the Number format to 1.

5. Change the Title to `Histogram Chart`.
   Change the Subtitle to `Count of orders per day`.
   Change the Data title to `Number of orders`.

   Save the changes. The chart should look like the one shown in Figure 17-56. As you learned earlier, a histogram chart does not display all of the data.

A problem that I have noticed is
that it is often difficult to know
what data is actually being
displayed.

For example, order dates are
across the bottom of the chart.
By looking at the chart, you don't
know what month the order dates
are for.

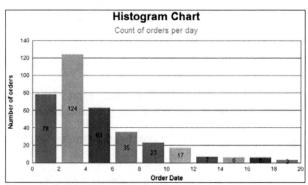

Figure 17-56 Histogram chart

Exercise 17.17: Create A Color Highlighting Chart

In this exercise you will create a chart that will change the color of the bars on the chart to red, if the order processing time is greater than or equal to seven days or yellow if the order processing time is between four and six days. To reduce the number of order days to something that will make the chart readable, you will add selection criteria to the report.

. . . .

1. Save the E14.8 report as `E17.17 Highlighted chart`.

2. Create selection criteria so that only orders with an order date between 12/02/2010 and 12/05/2010 will appear on the report.

3. Create selection criteria to only display orders that have an order processing time greater than or equal to two.

4. Select the Side by side bar chart type and the Use depth effect option.

5. Add the Order ID field to the first list box, then add the Order processing time formula field to the Show value(s) list.

6. Change the Title to `Color Highlighting Chart`.
   Add the Subtitle `Yellow = 4-6 day delay, Red = 7+ day delay`.
   Add the Footnote `Orders between 12/2/2010 & 12/5/2010`.
   Change the Group title to `Order Number`.
   Change the Data title to `Order processing time`.
   Leave the Chart Expert open to complete the next part of the exercise.

Add The Color Highlighting To The Chart

In this part of the exercise you will create the criteria that will change the colors of the bars on the chart to red or yellow depending on the value in the Order processing time field.

1. On the Color Highlight tab, click the New button.

2. Open the first drop-down list and select the Order processing time field. Open the second drop-down list and select Is greater than or equal to. Type a 7 in the last field.

3. Select Red as the Format color, then click the New button.

4. Open the first drop-down list and select the Order processing time field, then open the second drop-down list and select Is between. Type a 4 in the first field and a 6 in the last field.

5. Select Yellow as the Format color.

   Click OK, then save the changes.

   The chart should look like the one shown in Figure 17-57.

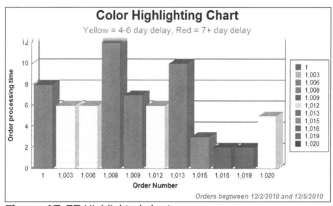

Figure 17-57 Highlighted chart

FORMATTING AND EDITING CHARTS

In this chapter you will learn basic chart formatting and editing techniques.

CHAPTER 18

Overview

There are a variety of techniques available to format and edit charts as a whole or individual parts of a chart, like the legend or axis titles. The majority of these options are on the Chart Options dialog box or the Format Series dialog box. Other options are on the Chart menu. Some of the formatting techniques that you will learn about are resizing a chart, adding color to the background of a chart and how to apply a template to a chart.

Zooming In And Out

Depending on the level of formatting intricacy, you may find it helpful to zoom in or out on the chart while you are modifying it. There are two ways to access the Zoom In option from the preview tab, as explained below. Once you select the Zoom In option, the mouse pointer will change to a magnifying glass with a plus sign.

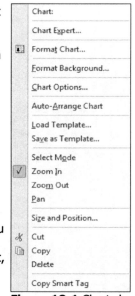

① Right-click on a blank space on the chart and select Zoom In, as shown in Figure 18-1.
② Click on a blank space on the chart, then Chart ⇒ Zoom In.

The zoom option for charts does not work the same way in Crystal Reports that it does in other software packages where you can click on the chart to zoom in or out. Instead, once you select the Zoom In option, you have to draw a box on the portion of the chart that you want to zoom in on. To zoom out, right-click on the chart, select Zoom Out, then click anyplace on the chart.

Figure 18-1 Chart shortcut menu

When you are finished zooming in or out, you have to select the option **SELECT MODE** from the shortcut menu or from the Chart menu. Doing this will change the mouse pointer back to the default, so that you can continue working.

 The Zoom options only work with bar and line charts.

 After changing the mouse pointer back to the default, I was expecting the chart to go back to its original size. I didn't find that to be the case. To put the chart back to its original size, I clicked the Undo button once for each time that I zoomed in on the chart.

The **PAN** option shown above in Figure 18-1 is only available when a chart has been zoomed in on. This option is used to scroll left or right on the chart.

The **FORMAT BACKGROUND** option shown above in Figure 18-1 opens the dialog box shown later in Figure 18-30. It is used to select options to change the background.

Resizing Charts

Charts and objects have the same resize handles that images have. Like images, you can drag the chart to another section of the report or to a different location in the section that it is currently in. You can resize the chart manually or you can use the options on the Size and Position dialog box. There are two ways to open the Size and Position dialog box, as explained below.

① Right-click on a blank space on the chart and select **SIZE AND POSITION**.

② Click on a blank space on the chart, then Format ⇒ Size and Position.

There are two options for resizing charts. You can resize the entire chart or you can resize individual elements on the chart. When you want to resize the entire chart, make sure that individual elements on the chart are not selected. If the default size of the chart is too small or too large, you can resize the chart by following the steps below.

1. Open the report that has the chart that you want to resize.

2. Click on a blank space in the chart, then place the mouse pointer in the lower right corner of the chart and drag the border down and to the right to make the chart larger or drag the border up and to the left to make the chart smaller.

 You can place the mouse pointer anyplace on the highlighted border of the chart to resize the chart in any direction that you need.

Exercise 18.1: Use The Chart Expert Preview Tab Shortcut Menu Options

If you right-click on a chart in a group section on the preview tab, then select the Chart Expert option, you will see the shortcut menu shown in Figure 18-2.

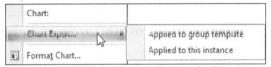

Figure 18-2 Chart Expert preview tab shortcut menu options

The **APPLIED TO GROUP TEMPLATE** option is used to apply the changes that you are about to make on the Chart Expert to all charts in all of the groups in the report.

The **APPLIED TO THIS INSTANCE** option is used to only apply the changes that you are about to make to the group chart that is selected. Remember that the preview tab displays every occurrence of a chart that is in a group section.

Add Charts To The Report

The report that you will modify already has one group for the months. You need to create another group so that you can see how the options on the Chart Expert shortcut menu work. The group that you will create will be for the sales reps.

1. Save the E11.2 report as `E18.1 Group chart changes`.

2. Insert ⇒ Group. Open the first drop-down list, select the Employee Last Name field, then click OK.

3. Copy the three summary fields and headings in the group footer 1 section to the group footer 2 section, then save the changes.

Add Two Charts To The Report

1. Add a bar chart to the group header 1 section, as shown in Figure 18-3.

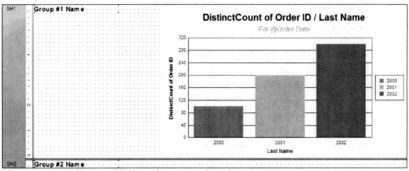

Figure 18-3 Chart added to the group header 1 section

2. Make the Group 1 Name field smaller, then make the chart smaller. Move the chart closer to the Group 1 Name field.

3. Open the Chart Expert and select the side by side bar chart if it is not already selected.

4. Change the Title to Monthly Order Amount By Order Date.
    Delete the Subtitle. Change the Group title to Sales rep.

5. Change the Data title to Number of sales.

    Save the changes.

    The chart should look like the one shown in Figure 18-4.

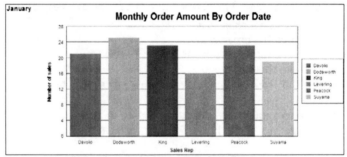

Figure 18-4 Monthly orders by order date chart

6. Add a side by side horizontal bar chart with depth effect to the group header 2 section.

7. Add the Last Name field to the first list box on the Data tab.
    Add the Order ID field to the Show value(s) list, then change the summary type to distinct count. Add the Order Amount field to the Show value(s) list.

8. On the Options tab, check the Show value option.

9. Add the Title Sales Rep Totals By Order Date.

10. Make the Group 2 Name field smaller, then make the chart smaller.

Move the chart closer to the Group 2 Name field.

Save the changes. The chart should look like the one shown in Figure 18-5.

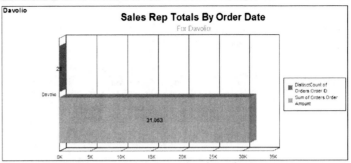

Figure 18-5 Sales rep totals by order date chart

Modify The Group Header 1 Chart

In this part of the exercise you will modify one of the group charts on the preview tab and apply the change to all charts in the group.

1. Right-click on the chart for January in the group header 1 section, then select Chart Expert ⇒ Applied to group template.

2. Change the location of the legend to the left of the chart. Click OK, then save the changes. When you look at all of the charts in the group header 1 section (the charts for January, February, March etc.), you will see that the legend is now to the left of the chart.

Modify The Group Header 2 Chart

In this part of the exercise you will modify the chart for a particular sales rep from the preview tab.

1. Right-click on the chart for the sales rep whose last name is Dodsworth on page 2. Select Chart Expert ⇒ Applied to this instance.

2. On the Options tab, check the Show label option, then change the **BAR SIZE** to small.

Save the changes.

The chart for Dodsworth should look like the one shown in Figure 18-6.

Figure 18-6 Modified chart for Dodsworth

Notice the values on the bars and the size of the bars. The chart for Davolio should still look like the one shown earlier in Figure 18-5. This chart was not changed.

More Chart Types

There are more chart types in addition to the ones on the Type tab on the Chart Expert. If you want to apply a different chart type, follow the steps below.

1. Right-click on the chart in a report that you want to change and select **LOAD TEMPLATE**.

   You will see the dialog box shown in Figure 18-7.

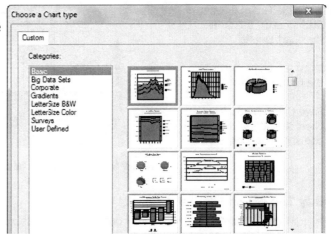

Figure 18-7 Choose A Chart Type dialog box

 You will not see the Load Template option if the **CUSTOM CHARTING** option was not installed when Crystal Reports was installed. If this is the case, you can run the Crystal Reports setup again and install this option.

2. Click on a category on the left to view the chart types, then select the chart type that you want to use on the right and click OK. Customize the chart as needed.

Trendlines

Trendlines are added to a chart to better illustrate trends in data. They are often applied to bar charts. To add trendlines to a bar chart, select one of the options below. You will see the Trendlines dialog box shown in Figure 18-8.

Select the type of trendline that you want from the **AVAILABLE TYPES** list, then add it to the Show Trendlines list.

All trendline types are not available for every chart type.

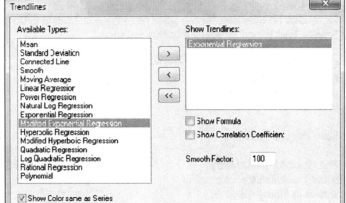

Figure 18-8 Trendlines dialog box

How To Add A Trend Line

① Right-click on a bar in the chart and select Trendlines.
② Click on a bar in the chart, then Chart ⇒ Trendlines.

Exercise 18.2: Use The Underlay Following Sections Option

This option is used to place the content in one section of the report next to the content in the section below it. In this exercise you will apply this option so that the chart will print next to the data that it represents. This is often used with charts that are in the group header section of a report so that the records in the details section will print next to the chart.

The **UNDERLAY FOLLOWING SECTIONS** option on the Section Expert is better suited for reports that do not have a lot of fields in the details section. If you cannot get the chart and the fields (in the details section) to fit, you can select the landscape print option to have more space across the page. You will modify a report and apply the Underlay option to the group header section.

1. Save the Chapter 18 Chart in group footer report as `E18.2 Chart with underlay option`.

2. Delete the group name field in the group header 1 section.

3. Drag the chart in the group footer 1b section up to the group header 1 section and place it as far left as possible.

4. Resize the chart so that it ends at the 3.5 inch mark on the ruler.

5. Change the chart title to `Chart With Underlay Option`.

6. Move the fields in the details and group footer 1a sections over to the right so that they start to the right of the chart, as shown in Figure 18-9.

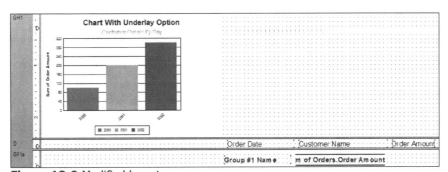

Figure 18-9 Modified layout

 Keeping Objects From Moving
A few months from now you may not remember why the layout is the way that it is. This would be a good use of the **LOCK POSITION AND SIZE** option on the Format Editor. [See Chapter 7, Figure 7-12]

7. Open the Section Expert and apply the **UNDERLAY FOLLOWING SECTIONS** option to the group header 1 section.

    Delete the group footer 1b section. Save the changes. The report should look like the one shown in Figure 18-10.

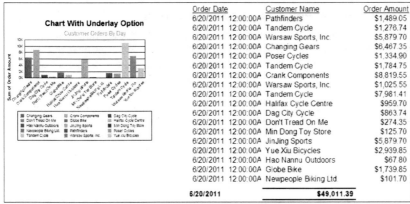

Figure 18-10 Chart with the Underlay option applied

 If there is information in the group header section that you do not want to include in the underlay, place the chart in a new group header section, as shown in Figure 18-11. You would still apply the underlay option to the group header section with the chart. The report would look like the one shown in Figure 18-12. Notice that the information in the first group header section (the Group #1 Name field) did not move.

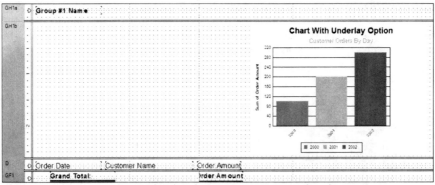

Figure 18-11 Report layout for the chart in its own group header section

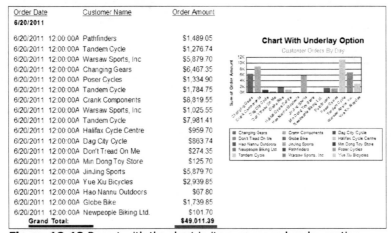

Figure 18-12 Report with the chart in its own group header section

Chart Options Dialog Box

The options on this dialog box pick up where the options on the Chart Expert leave off. I would like to see the following dialog boxes added to the Chart Expert: Chart Options, Choose A Chart, Series options and Chart Format. I think that would make creating and modifying charts easier because all of the chart options would be in one place.

Depending on the chart type, you will see slightly different options on the Chart Options dialog box. The options are used to change the overall look of the chart. What I like most about the Chart Options dialog box is that you can see what your changes will look like without having to preview the report. This is very helpful when you need to experiment with several options. To open the Chart Options dialog box, right-click on the chart and select Chart Options.

 If you click on the Help button on any tab on the Chart Options dialog box, you will see detailed information for all of the options on the tab.

Many of the settings on the Chart Options dialog box are the same as the ones on the Chart Expert. One difference that you will notice is that the options have more settings on the Chart Options dialog box then they do on the Chart Expert.

Appearance Tab

The options on this tab are used to modify the general look of the chart.

Figures 18-13 to 18-15 show the appearance options for three types of charts.

USE DEPTH This option will display the chart in 3D format.

DIRECTION This slider is used to change the direction of the bars on the chart.

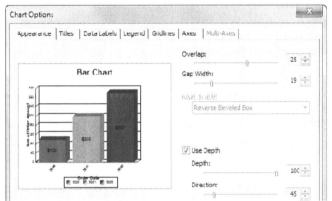

Figure 18-13 Bar chart appearance tab options

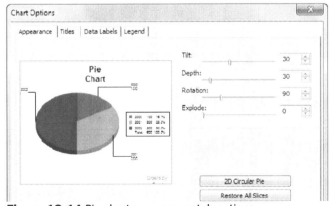

Figure 18-14 Pie chart appearance tab options

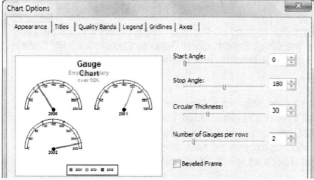

Figure 18-15 Gauge chart appearance tab options

 How To Change The Markers Shape
In Exercise 17.8 you created an XY Scatter chart and were expecting the markers to have a triangle shape. If you want to change the markers shape, open the report, then open the Chart Options dialog box and select Triangle from the Shape drop-down list on the Appearance tab.

Titles Tab

The options shown in Figure 18-16 are used to add or modify the titles on the chart.

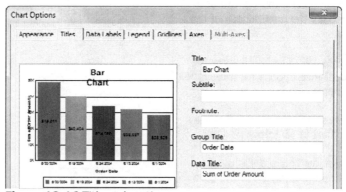

Figure 18-16 Titles tab options

Data Labels Tab

The options shown in Figure 18-17 are used to add data labels to the chart, change the location of the labels and what the label will display.

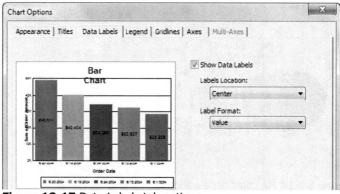

Figure 18-17 Data Labels tab options

Legend Tab

The options shown in Figure 18-18 are used to modify the legend, add a frame around the legend, change the color of the items and swap the series and group names.

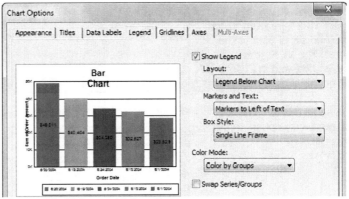

Figure 18-18 Legend tab options

Gridlines Tab

The options shown in Figure 18-19 are used to add and remove major and minor gridlines for the group and data axis on the chart.

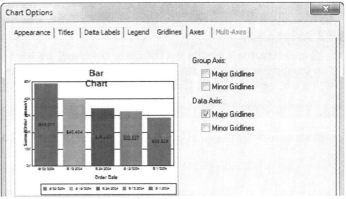

Figure 18-19 Gridlines tab options

Axes Tab

The options shown in Figure 18-20 are used to select how the group axes (X axis) and data axis (Y axis) lines will be displayed on the chart. The options on this tab vary depending on the chart type.

The axis line may not be visible on the report after selecting the option if it is the same color as the frame of the chart.

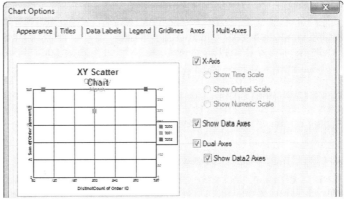

Figure 18-20 Axes tab options

Multi-Axes

The options shown in Figure 18-21 are used to add a second set of data to the report. The XY Scatter chart that you created in Chapter 17 will enable these options.

To enable this tab, check the **DUAL AXES** option on the Axes tab.

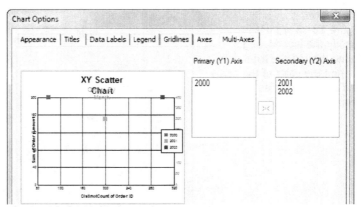

Figure 18-21 Multi-Axes tab options

This chart is currently plotting data for only one year. If you want to plot data for another year, select the second year from the Secondary (Y2) Axis list.

Edit X Axis Labels

If the labels across the X axis (at the bottom of the chart) are hard to read, right-click on the specific label on the preview tab, then select the **EDIT AXIS LABEL** option shown in Figure 18-22. You will see the dialog box shown in Figure 18-23. Make the changes to the label, then click OK.

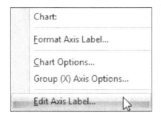

Figure 18-22 Axis label shortcut menu

Figure 18-23 Label Aliasing dialog box

Modify Parts Of The Chart Manually

So far, almost all of the chart modification techniques that you have learned have been selecting or changing options on a dialog box. You can also move or resize elements like the title or legend on the chart manually. Doing this allows you to have greater control over what the chart will look like.

If you make changes to the chart and then decide that you do not like them, you can use the **AUTO ARRANGE CHART** option. This option will reset the chart to its default size, formatting and placement settings. You have to select the entire chart, not a specific element, for this option to appear on the chart shortcut menu.

Exercise 18.3: Move Labels On A Chart

In many of the charts that were created in the previous chapter, one or all of the axis labels are displayed on top of the values for the axis. Moving the axis labels would make the charts easier to read. In Exercise 17.8 you learned that the marker option on the Chart Expert does not work. You will learn another way to change the markers in this exercise.

Moving labels is easier to do on the preview tab because you can see the live data in the chart.

1. Save the E17.8 report as E18.3 Move labels on a chart.

2. Select the Sum of order amount label on the left and drag the label to the left so that there is a little more space before the numbers.

3. Right-click on the chart title and select Chart Options, then click on the Titles tab.
   Change the Title to Move Labels On A Chart.
   Change the X-Axis to Number of orders.
   Change the Data title to Total monthly order amount.

4. On the Appearance tab, change the **SIZE** to 50, then change the **SHAPE** to Triangle.

   Save the changes.

   The chart should look like the one shown in Figure 18-24.

   Compare this chart to the one shown in Exercise 17.8. The markers now have a triangle shape.

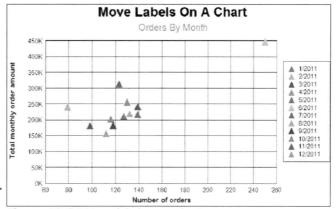

Figure 18-24 Move labels on a chart

Customizing 3D Charts

The Appearance tab options are used to tilt and rotate 3D charts. If you want or need more 3D chart formatting options, right-click on a chart like the 3D Surface or 3D Riser chart and select **3D VIEWING ANGLE**. You will see the dialog box shown in Figure 18-25.

You can scroll through the list of viewing angles to find one that you like. If clicked, the **ADVANCED OPTIONS** button displays additional options that are used to customize the viewing angle even more, as shown in Figure 18-26.

You can also view the Preset Viewing Angles on the left by clicking on the forward and backward (VCR style) buttons that are to the left of the Duplicate button. Another way to view the preset viewing angles is by opening the drop-down list under the chart thumbnail (illustrated in Figure 18-26). The options on the **ROTATE**, **PAN**, **WALLS** and **MORE** tabs are used to customize additional 3D options.

 If you make any manual changes to a viewing angle, you will be prompted to save the changes with a new viewing angle preset name when you click OK. Entering a name on this dialog box is used to save a new viewing angle or replace an existing one. You do not have to save the changes that you have selected on the Choose a Viewing Angle dialog box to apply them. If you want to apply the changes to the chart without saving them as a viewing angle, click the Cancel button on the **ENTER 3D VIEWING ANGLE PRESET NAME** dialog box and the changes will still be applied to the chart.

 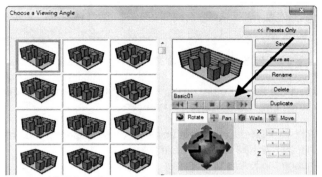

Figure 18-25 Choose A Viewing Angle dialog box   **Figure 18-26** Advanced viewing angle customization options

Customizing Individual Elements On A Chart

Each element on a chart can be customized. For example, you can change the color of the report title or change the color of individual bars or slices of the chart. Earlier in this book you learned about the Format Editor and how you can use it to customize fields on the report. Each of the elements on a chart also has a Format dialog box that has additional formatting options.

Figures 18-28, 18-30 to 18-32, 18-34 to 18-37 show the Format dialog boxes for some of the more popular chart elements. You can open these dialog boxes by selecting either of the options explained below.

① Right-click on the chart element that you want to modify and select the Format option on the shortcut menu shown in Figure 18-27.

The **TRENDLINES** option opens the dialog box shown earlier in Figure 18-8.

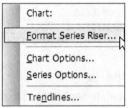

Figure 18-27 Bar element shortcut menu

 The name after the word Format on the shortcut menu will change depending on the type of element that is selected.

② Click on the chart element that you want to modify, then Chart ⇒ Format.

The **GRADIENT** button will open the dialog box shown in Figure 18-29.

The options on the Fill tab are used to format the charts background.

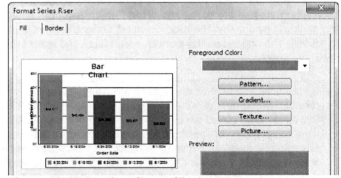

Figure 18-28 Bar chart format fill tab options

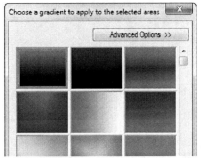

Figure 18-29 Bar chart gradient options

Selecting the options on the border tab shown in Figure 18-30 will place a dotted border around the chart.

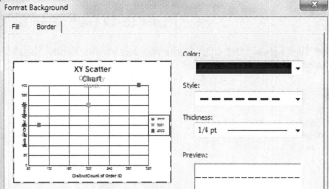

You have to select a color. I think the Color option should default to black instead of transparent, like it does on the Format Gridlines dialog box shown in Figure 18-31.

Figure 18-30 XY Scatter chart format border tab options

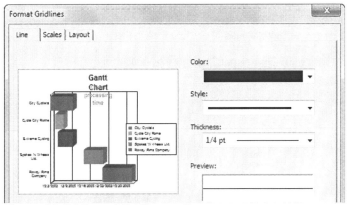

Figure 18-31 Format Gridlines options

Right-click on a marker in the chart and select Format Series Marker.

You will see the dialog box shown in Figure 18-32. The border options are the same as those shown earlier in Figure 18-30.

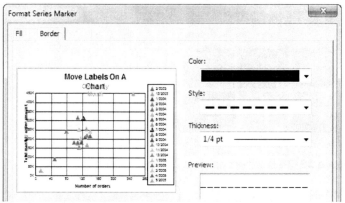

Figure 18-32 Chart marker border tab options

Figure 18-33 shows the chart frame shortcut menu. Figure 18-34 shows the options to format the frame of a chart.

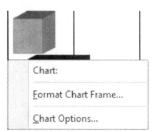

Figure 18-33 Chart frame shortcut menu

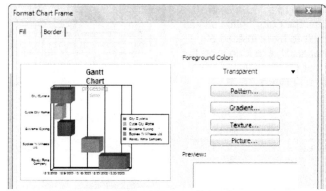

Figure 18-34 Format Chart Frame dialog box

To open this dialog box, right-click on a data label on the chart and select **FORMAT DATA LABEL**.

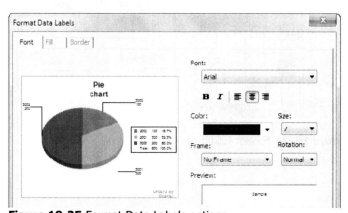

Figure 18-35 Format Data Labels options

Figure 18-36 shows the options to modify the Y axis options. There is a similar dialog box for the X axis.

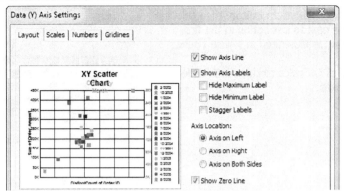

Figure 18-36 Data (Y) Axis Settings dialog box

The **LAYOUT** tab has general axis formatting options.
The **SERIES** tab has scale options for the axis.
The **NUMBERS** tab has formatting options for the numbers on the axis.
The **GRIDLINES** tab has formatting options for the gridlines on the axis.

Figure 18-37 shows the appearance options that are available to modify a data series on the chart.

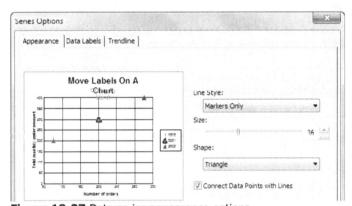

Figure 18-37 Data series appearance options

Exercise 18.4: Apply Color To Chart Elements

This is probably one of the most used formatting options. In this exercise, you will apply color to parts of a chart.

1. Save the E18.1 report as E18.4 Add color to charts.

2. Click on the second bar from the top (so that it is selected) on the chart in the group header 2 section, then right-click on it and select Format Series Riser. Change the **FOREGROUND** color to Yellow. (It's on the first row.)

3. Click the Pattern button, then select the next to last option in the first row, as illustrated in Figure 18-38.

   Click OK twice to close both dialog boxes.

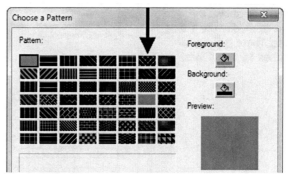

Figure 18-38 Pattern option illustrated

4. Change the chart in the group header 1 section to a pie chart.

5. Open the Chart Options dialog box for the pie chart and make the following appearance changes: Tilt 45 and Explode 15, then click OK.

6. Right-click on the pie chart and select Format Background.

7. Click the Gradient button, then select the fourth option in the first column. (It's yellow) Click OK twice to close both dialog boxes.

 If you click the **ADVANCED OPTIONS** button on the **CHOOSE A GRADIENT TO APPLY TO THE SELECTED AREAS** dialog box that you used in step 7 above, you will see options that are used to create your own gradients, as shown in Figure 18-39. Compare this to the default options that were shown earlier in Figure 18-29.

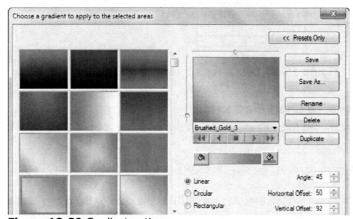

Figure 18-39 Gradient options

8. Save the changes.

The pie chart should look like the one shown in Figure 18-40.

The bar chart should look like the one shown in Figure 18-41.

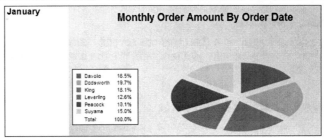

Figure 18-40 Format options applied to a pie chart

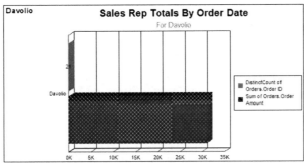

Figure 18-41 Format options applied to a bar chart

Modifying Charts On The Preview Tab

 If you modify a chart in the preview tab, in particular, a chart that is in the group header or footer section, by default the changes that you make will only be applied to that instance of the chart. This does not happen when a chart is modified on the design tab. Changes made to charts on the design tab will be applied to all instances of the chart.

In Exercise 18.2 you modified a chart that was in the group header section that displays data for the top five order days in June. Because the chart is grouped by order date, the chart in the group section will appear five times on the report, once for each of the order date groups.

If you selected the chart for the second order date and made changes to it from the preview tab, the changes that you make would only be applied to that instance of the chart. The charts for the other four dates would not be changed. If you decide that you do want to apply the changes that you made to the one instance of the chart, to all of the charts in the same group, select one of the two options listed below. They work the same as the Applied to group template option that you learned about earlier in Exercise 18.1.

① Right-click on the chart that you made changes to on the preview tab, then select Apply Changes To All Charts.
② Click on the chart that you made changes to on the preview tab, then Chart ⇒ Apply Changes To All Charts.

Chart Templates

If you have formatted a chart that has several options that you would like to use on other charts, you can save the options as a template, like the ones you saw earlier on the Choose A Chart Type dialog box.

Save A Chart As A Template

You can save a chart as a template by selecting one of the options below, then type in a name for the template.

① Right-click on the chart and select Save As Template.

② Click on the chart, then Chart ⇒ Save As Template.

To apply the template to another chart, click on the **USER DEFINED** category on the Choose A Chart Type dialog box shown earlier in Figure 18-7.

> Chart templates that you create are saved in the following location on your computers hard drive: C:\Program Files (x86)\SAP Business Objects\Crystal Reports 2011\ChartSupport\Templates\User Defined folder.
>
> If you want to change the location that the chart templates that you create are saved in, you can change the ChartSupportPath registry key, which is in this location in the registry. HKEY_LOCAL_MACHINE\Software\SAP Business Objects\Suite XI 4.0\Crystal Reports\

PARAMETER FIELD BASICS

Overview

Parameter fields add interaction between the person running the report and the report. Parameter fields are used to customize reports to better meet the users needs. In this chapter you will learn how to do the following:

- ☑ Use the Create Parameter Field dialog box
- ☑ Create a list of static values for a parameter field
- ☑ Use parameter fields with the Select Expert

Overview

The reports that you have learned to create so far in this book did not require any input from the people that would run them. You also learned that different users may need slightly different versions of the same report. Based on the report creation techniques that you have learned so far, especially the Select Expert, if one group of people needed to see a customer report for a specific date range and another group of people need to see the same report for specific customers, you would have to create two reports. This is the largest downside to only using the Select Expert to create selection criteria. Using parameter fields to pass data to the Select Expert is a much better solution.

Think about this. If a user requested a report to only show data for one year, the date range would be entered as the criteria on the Select Expert. Now, the same user or a different user needs the same report, but for a different date range and specific customers. The easiest thing to do based on the report techniques that you have learned so far is to open the existing report and save it with a new file name and change the selection criteria to the new date range and add customer criteria. As you can see, this could get out of hand quickly. If the original report used parameter fields to get the criteria from the person running the report, the report could be used for any date range and any customer. Another thing to think about is maintaining all of these reports. If a field needs to be added, you would have to add the field to more than one report.

If you created two parameter fields for the report, one for a date range and another one to select customers, both groups of people could use the same report. A popular type of parameter field is one that passes data to the Select Expert. In addition to being able to pass data to the Select Expert, a parameter field can also pass data to conditional and other types of formulas. This allows the person running the report to have control over the records that will appear on the report without having to know how to use the Select Expert or how to create formulas. The reports that you created that have criteria on the Select Expert can be enhanced by using parameter fields in place of specific (hard coded) values from a table or the value that you type in the second drop-down list on the Select Expert. This would give reports a lot more flexibility.

To help the person that will run a report that has parameter fields, you can include features like default values and drop-down lists. For example, if you were creating a parameter field that needed to allow the user to select a country, you could set a default country if the report is often run using a specific country. You could also create a drop-down list field that contains all of the countries and let the user select the country that they wanted to run the report for. In the workplace you may hear the drop-down list referred to as a PICK LIST when referencing a parameter field. There are different types of pick lists and you will learn about them in this chapter.

An example of a pick list and how to combine existing reports (which means less reports for you to create or maintain) would be the reports that you created in Exercises 9.1 and 9.2. The report in Exercise 9.1 used the Select Expert to only display customers in one region. The report that you created in Exercise 9.2 displayed customers in two regions. These reports could easily be combined with the use of a parameter field. What would you do if the user needed to run the reports that you created in Exercise 9.1 or 9.2 for different regions next week? Someone, probably you, would have to save the current report with a new name and change the selection criteria for the new regions.

Parameter fields that contain a record or group selection formula do not have to be placed on a report. Parameter fields can be configured to be optional when the report is run.

How Do Parameter Fields Work?

When a report is run that has a parameter field, it prompts the user to select options, which creates all or part of the criteria that is needed to run the report. The information that is gathered from parameter fields is passed to various components of the report like the Select Expert or a formula. The data in the parameter field is used to run the report.

Like the Select Expert, parameter fields ask questions that will determine what data will be retrieved for the report. Using parameter fields, the following questions can be answered: Which three months do you want to see the sales reps totals for? Which country do you want to see sales for? Which customers ordered hats in December?

In addition to using parameter fields to gather the report selection criteria, parameter fields can be used to customize and format the report. For example, parameter fields can be used to select the sorting or grouping options or highlight records that meet a certain condition. If a report has confidential information, one of the parameter fields can require the person running the report to enter their User ID. Based on the User ID, parts of the report would be hidden.

While parameter fields are a good way to get input from the person running the report, they may not be the best solution because they can lack functionality that you may need. If you are a programmer, you can create a form in Visual Basic or Visual C++ for example, to get user input. This also allows you to create more input validation rules then are available parameter fields.

The Create New Parameter Dialog Box

Now that you know what parameter fields are, how useful they are and how they work, it is time to learn about the dialog box shown in Figure 19-1, which is used to create parameter fields. Tables 19-1 and 19-2 explain the options on the Create New Parameter dialog box. Reports can and often do have more than one parameter field.

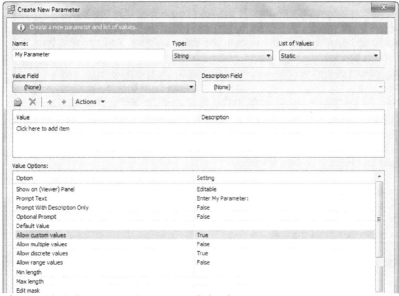

Figure 19-1 Create New Parameter dialog box

Option	Description
Name	Is used to give the parameter field a name. The name is how you reference the parameter field. Try to use as descriptive a name as possible, while keeping the name as short as possible. You can use the name of the field in the table that the parameter field will query. You can also use the name of an existing formula. (1)
Type	Is used to select the data type for the parameter field. You should select the same data type as the field or data that the parameter field will be compared to. (1)
List of values	If you want to provide values for the parameter field, there are two types of values: Static values that do not change and dynamic values, which can change each time the report is run.
Value Field	The options in this field are the fields from the tables that are connected to the report. This field has two purposes: To select the field for the comparison for the parameter field or select the field that will be used to import values for a static or dynamic list.
Description Field	Is used to specify text or another field that will be displayed next to the Value Field in the list. This is helpful when the value field option is an ID field. Often, the person running the report will not understand the values in an ID field. For example, you may need to use the Customer ID field, but display either the Customer ID field and the Customer Name field or display the Customer Name field by itself. The Customer Name field contains data that the person running the report understands.
Insert	Clicking this button will retrieve the data that is in the field selected in the Value Field, explained above.
Actions	The options on the drop-down list shown in Figure 19-2 are used to create a list of values or export values.
Value/Description	These two columns function like a table and are used to select specific data from the field that is selected in the Value Field. Filling in the Description column is optional. If the field name that is in the Value column is not descriptive enough, you can enter text in the Description column to better explain the data in the Value column. You can also type values in this list.
Value Options	The options in this section are used to customize the parameter field. The options will change depending on the data type that is selected. Table 19-2 explains the options in this section if the string data type is selected. These options were shown above in Figure 19-1.

Table 19-1 Create New Parameter dialog box options explained

(1) This is a required option to create a parameter field.

The **APPEND ALL DATABASE VALUES** option adds (imports) all unique values from the table.

The **CLEAR** option removes all values from the list.

The **IMPORT** option imports the values for the parameter field.

Figure 19-2 Actions drop-down list options

The **EXPORT** option copies the values for the parameter field to a file.

Option	Description
Show On (Viewer) Panel	Is used to select whether or not the parameter field will be displayed on the Parameters Panel. It has the following three settings: ① The **DO NOT SHOW** setting hides the parameter field on the Parameters Panel. This is the default option. ② The **EDITABLE** setting allows the parameter field values to be changed when the report is run without refreshing the data. (2) ③ The **READ ONLY** setting allows the parameter field values to be viewed, but not changed. To change the values, press the F5 key or click the Refresh button. (2)
Prompt Text	Is used to enter text that will let the person running the report know what to enter or select for the parameter field.
Prompt with description only	Is used to select whether the parameter field is displayed with just the prompt text or the prompt text and description.
Optional Prompt	Is used to select whether or not the parameter field is required to have a value. If required, the report will not run until the parameter field has a value.
Sort Order	Is used to select the order that the values in the parameter field are sorted in. This option is only available for dynamic parameter fields.
Default Value	Is used to select a default value for the parameter field.
Allow custom Values	Is used to select whether or not the person running the report can enter any value or if a value has to be selected from the values available for the field.
Allow multiple values	If this option is set to true, the person running the report can select or enter more than one value in the field.
Allow discrete values	Limits the parameter field to only accepting one value.
Allow range values	Requires the person running the report to enter start and end values.
Min Length	Is used to select the minimum length for the value in the parameter field.
Max Length	Is used to select the maximum length for the value in the parameter field.
Edit mask	Is used to enter an edit mask instead of a range of values for the string field. [See Chapter 20, Edit Masks]

Table 19-2 Value options explained

(2) This option allows the parameter field to be displayed on the Parameters Panel.

There are four ways to open the Create New Parameter dialog box, as explained below.

① Click on the Parameter Fields category in the Field Explorer, then click the **NEW** button on the Field Explorer toolbar.
② Right-click on the Parameter Fields category in the Field Explorer, then select **NEW**.
③ Click the Field Explorer button on the Standard toolbar to open the Field Explorer, then follow one of the options above.
④ View ⇒ Field Explorer, then follow option one or two above.

Data Types

The data type that you select determines how the parameter field will be used in the report. For example, you cannot select a string data type to use in a comparison with a date/time field. Number, currency and string data types do not have the limitations that date, date/time and Boolean data types have. The data types are explained below.

Number and **Currency** data types can only use the numbers zero to nine and the minus sign. Any other values will generate an error message.

String data types can use all of the number data type options, plus letters and special characters.

Date and **Time** Date fields may be the most used data type to limit the data that appears on a report. When you use the Select Expert to create criteria for a date field, you have several options including "Is greater than", "Is greater than or equal to" and "Is between". The Create New Parameter dialog box does not have the same options in terms of their names. The following three options are used to specify how to use dates on a parameter field. Figure 19-3 shows the options available for date/time parameter fields when the report is run.

Figure 19-3 Date/Time parameter field options

① **INCLUDE THIS VALUE** If checked, this option will include the date that is entered in the parameter field as part of the selection process. Checking this option on the Start of Range field is the equivalent of the "Is greater than or equal to" operator. Checking this option on the Start and End of Range fields is the equivalent of the "Is between" operator.
② **NO LOWER VALUE** If checked, the value in the Start of Range field will not be used. (3)
③ **NO UPPER VALUE** If checked, the value in the End of Range field will not be used. (3)

(3) You cannot select both of these options at the same time. If you type 1/1/10 in the Start of Range field and 6/1/10 in the End of Range field and clear the No lower value option, all records that have a value that is less than the value in the End of Range field will be included on the report, even though a date was entered in the Start of range field. If the No upper value option is checked, all records that have a date greater than 1/1/10 will be included in the report.

If you need to create a date range you have to set the **ALLOW RANGE VALUES** option to True on the Create New Parameter dialog box. By default, this option is set to False because the **ALLOW DISCRETE VALUES** option is set to True. These two options are mutually exclusive, meaning that only one of them can be set to True for the parameter field.

Boolean Parameter Fields

Boolean parameter fields are very similar to the Boolean formulas. Like Boolean formulas, Boolean parameter fields are used with a Boolean field in a table, which has one of two values: True or False.

Figure 19-4 shows the value options that are available for Boolean parameter fields. In addition to being able to select a default value of true or false for the Boolean parameter field, you can enter a description for the true and false options.

The description should help the person running the report decide which option is appropriate for the records that they want to appear on the report.

Value Options:	
Option	Setting
Show on (Viewer) Panel	Editable
Prompt Text	Enter My Parameter:
Prompt With Description Only	False
Optional Prompt	False
Default Value	
Boolean group #	
Exclusive group	False

Figure 19-4 Boolean parameter field options

The **BOOLEAN GROUP #** option is used to add the Boolean parameter field to a group of other Boolean parameter fields. Creating a Boolean group will remind you of a group of radio buttons that you have probably seen on dialog boxes in other applications, like the print range options on the dialog box shown in Figure 19-5.

Figure 19-5 Radio button group example

The number that you enter in the field is the Boolean group that the parameter field that you are creating or editing should be associated with. If the report has five Boolean fields and two are needed to create one Boolean group, you would enter the same number in this field for these two parameter fields. You would enter a different number for the other three Boolean parameter fields so that they would be grouped together. The three print options shown above in Figure 19-5 would have the same Boolean group number.

This is similar to how summary fields appear on the Data tab of the Chart Expert, as shown in Figure 19-6.

Notice how there are three fields that are in the Group 1 section and three fields in the Group 2 section. That would be the equivalent of two Boolean groups.

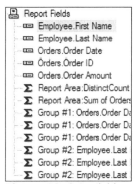

Figure 19-6 Available group fields in a chart

The **EXCLUSIVE GROUP** option shown earlier in Figure 19-4 works with the Boolean groups on the report. This option is used to select whether or not only one option in the Boolean group can be selected. Selecting **TRUE** for this option will only allow one option in the group to be selected. That option will be set to true and the other options will return a value of false.

Figure 19-5 shown earlier is an example of this because you can only select one of the print options. Selecting **FALSE** for the Exclusive Group option will allow more than one option in the group to be selected. Each option selected will be set to true and the other options will be set to false.

Using Parameter Fields With The Select Expert

This combination may be the most used parameter field option. Many of the reports that you have created in this book used the Select Expert to specify which records appear on the report.

In programming terminology, these reports are known as "hard coded" because all of the options needed to run the report are coded into the report. After you create the parameter fields, open the Select Expert and select the parameter field instead of the actual values in the table. For example, in Exercise 9.2 you created the criteria shown in Figure 19-7.

Figure 19-7 Select Expert criteria

Instead of selecting the specific states (regions) FL and OH, which is the hard coding that I am referring to, you would select the parameter field from the drop-down list. That is how the value in the parameter field is passed to the Select Expert.

 What you will find is that you cannot always use the same operator (Is greater than, Is between, etc) with parameter fields that you would when selecting actual values from a field. The majority of the time you will use the "Is equal to" operator with parameter fields on the Select Expert even when the parameter field will be used for a range of values like "Is between 1/1/11 and 1/31/11" or when the parameter field is used to select multiple values like "Is one of FL or OH".

 When creating a parameter field, you do not have to press F5 after selecting the parameter field on the Select Expert. The Enter Values dialog box will open automatically.

When you open the drop-down list on the Select Expert shown in Figure 19-8, you will see all of the parameter fields that have the same data type as the field from the table. Parameter fields are always at the top of the drop-down list.

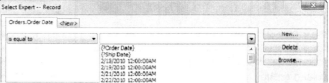

Figure 19-8 Select Expert with parameter field options

 If you do not see the parameter field that you are looking for when you open the drop-down list on the right of the Select Expert, it usually means one of two things:

① That you selected the wrong data type when you created the parameter field.

② You associated the parameter field with the wrong field. Open the Edit Parameter dialog box, change the data type or field that the parameter field is associated to, then re-open the Select Expert.

 You will see the terms "pick list", "list of values" and "prompt". Depending on who wrote the article or documentation, these words when used in conjunction with parameter fields can be used interchangeably. To me, the first two mean the same thing, but prompt, refers to the questions asked on the Enter Values dialog box that you saw earlier in Figure 19-3.

When a report with parameter fields is refreshed, you will see the dialog box shown in Figure 19-9. The options are used to select whether you want to use the parameter values that were selected the last time the report was run or if you want to select new values.

If the **USE CURRENT PARAMETER VALUES** option is selected, the report will run with the existing parameter values and you will not see the Enter Values dialog box.

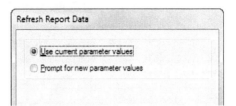

If the **PROMPT FOR NEW PARAMETER VALUES** option is selected, the Enter Values dialog box that you saw earlier in Figure 19-3 will appear so that new parameter values can be selected.

Figure 19-9 Refresh Report Data dialog box

When the Enter Values dialog box opens, it will display the values that were selected the last time that the report was run. You only have to select values that you want to change. I tend to always select this option because it is a good way to double check to make sure that you have the options that you want to use when the report is run.

Enter Values Dialog Box

This dialog box contains all of the parameter fields for the report, as you saw earlier in Figure 19-3. If there is more than one parameter field on the dialog box at first, you may only be able to select options for the first prompt. Once you select an option for the first prompt, you will be able to select an option for the next prompt. The reason this happens is because sometimes the values in the next prompt are dependant on what was selected in the previous prompt. This is known as **CASCADING PROMPTS**. For example, if the first prompt is used to select a country and the second prompt is used to select a state, the only values that will appear in the state drop-down list are states that are in the country that is selected in the first prompt.

Parameter fields appear on the Enter Values dialog box in the order that they are created. You can change the order by right-clicking on a parameter field in the Field Explorer or on the Parameter Fields Category and selecting **SET PARAMETER ORDER**. The Enter Values dialog box can be customized. You can change the color, fonts and more, as you will learn in the next chapter.

> **Tips For The Parameter Field Exercises**
> ① After saving the existing report with a new report name in step 1, open the Create New Parameter dialog box unless instructed otherwise.
> ② When you see the instruction "Press F5", after doing so, you should select the second option, **PROMPT FOR NEW PARAMETER VALUES** on the Refresh Report Data dialog box shown above in Figure 19-9, then click OK or press Enter.

Exercise 19.1: Create An Is Equal To Parameter Field

In this exercise you will enhance the E9.1 Region = CA report by creating a parameter field that will prompt for the state that will be used to run the report.

1. Save the E9.1 report as E19.1 Is Equal To parameter field.

2. Type Region in the Name field, then change the Type to String, if it is not already selected. Notice that the **PROMPT TEXT** value option at the bottom of the dialog box has the name that you just entered. Click OK.

3. Open the Select Expert. Open the second drop-down list. At the top of the list you will see the parameter field that you just created, as illustrated in Figure 19-10. Select the Region parameter field, then click OK. You will see the dialog box shown in Figure 19-11, when you preview the report. This dialog box is automatically created and displays the parameter fields that the report has.

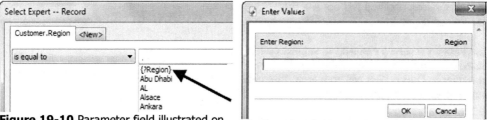

Figure 19-10 Parameter field illustrated on the Select Expert

Figure 19-11 Enter Values dialog box

4. Type CA in the Region field on the Enter Values dialog box, then press Enter or click OK. You should see six records on the report.

Unless the parameter field has an edit mask, string fields are not case sensitive, which means that you can type "CA" or "ca" and get the same results. When prompted to refresh the data, at this point it does not matter if you refresh the data because you refreshed it a minute or so ago. However, if you were running this report against live data, I would refresh the report every time it is run to make sure that I had the most current data.

 Reports that have a parameter field will not automatically refresh when you switch from the design tab to the preview tab. You have two options: press the F5 key or click the **REFRESH** button on the Navigation Tools toolbar.

5. Click the Refresh button on the toolbar or press the F5 key. You will see the Refresh Report Data dialog box shown earlier in Figure 19-9. Select the second option, then click OK. As you can see, the value that you entered last is still there.

6. Type your first name in the Region field, then press Enter. Save the changes.

Unless your first name is a region in the table, you will not see any data on the report. This isn't what you want to happen. Reports are usually created to retrieve data, not produce empty reports. If this report used a list of values for the region field, you would have been able to select a region from a list instead of typing it in. That is a better solution.

Parameters Panel

The options shown in Figure 19-12 make it easier for people running reports with parameter fields to change the parameter values. The options are on the left side of the preview tab and are activated by default when a report is run or refreshed that has a parameter field. The Parameters toolbar buttons are explained in Table 19-3.

You can change one of the parameter filter options by double-clicking in the space below the parameter that you want to change. For example, if you wanted to change the date range, double-click on the 2/18/2010 date. The Enter Values dialog box would open with the prompt to change the date range.

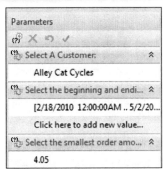

Figure 19-12 Parameters Panel options

Parameters Panel Toolbar Buttons

Button	Description
Prompt for parameters	Opens the Enter Values dialog box.
Remove Value	Deletes the last value that was added to the Parameters Panel.
Revert all changes	Deletes all of the parameter changes since the last time the report was run.
Apply changes	Runs the report with the current parameter options.
Enter {Value}	Toggles displaying the last value entered for the parameter field on the Enter Values dialog box. (These buttons are shown above in Figure 19-12.)

Table 19-3 Parameters Panel toolbar buttons explained

Exercise 19.2: Create An Is Greater Than Or Equal To Parameter Field

In this exercise you will enhance the E9.3 report by creating a parameter field that will prompt for the Order Date that will be used to run the report.

1. Save the E9.3 report as E19.2 Is Greater Than or equal to parameter field.

2. Type Order Date in the Name field, then change the Type to Date and click OK.

3. Open the Select Expert, then open the second drop-down list.

Notice that you do not see the parameter field that you just created at the top of the list. That is because the Order Date field is a date/time field. I did this to demonstrate that Crystal Reports does try to help you as much as possible.

4. Close the Select Expert and reopen the parameter dialog box by right-clicking on the Order Date parameter field in the Field Explorer and selecting Edit. Change the Type to Date Time, then click OK.

5. Open the Select Expert. Select the Order Date parameter field in the second drop-down list, then click OK. Save the changes.

6. Press F5, then select the prompt for new parameter values. You will see the Enter Values dialog box.

Calendar Control

There are two options for entering a date. The date can be typed in or it can be selected from the calendar control. If you entered data in a parameter field that isn't valid, the report would run, but not return any records, which would cause the report to be empty. This is why it is a good idea that parameter fields have a list of values or a way to select data as often as possible. All fields on the Enter Values dialog box are not required. I have noticed that if you leave some types of fields empty and click OK, you will see an error message that says "The value is not valid".

 Notice the icon at the end of the Order Date field shown in Figure 19-13. If you click on this icon you will see the calendar shown in Figure 19-14. Instead of typing in the date, you can use the calendar to select the date.

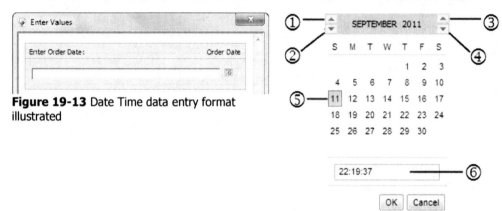

Figure 19-13 Date Time data entry format illustrated

Figure 19-14 Calendar control

 Date Parameter Fields
Crystal Reports 2008 and earlier automatically added a line of text to the Enter Values dialog box for date fields that had the date/time format that dates and times had to be entered in. This has been removed.

Calendar Control Options

Navigating in this calendar is similar to other electronic calendars that you may have used. If you need a date in the month and year that is currently displayed on the calendar, click on the date in the calendar. The options illustrated above in Figure 19-14 are explained below.

① Displays the next month.

② Displays the previous month.

③ Displays the next year.

④ Displays the previous year.

⑤ This is the current day. The current day is highlighted in the calendar.

⑥ Is used to type in a time in HH:MM:SS format.

7. Select June 24, 2010 in the calendar.

   You should see the date and time on the dialog box, as shown in Figure 19-15 when you run the report.

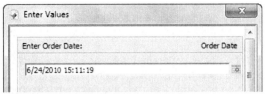

Figure 19-15 Order Date entered

 If you do not type 00:00:00 in the minutes field, you may not get all of the records for the date or date range that you select.

8. Click OK. The report should have 3,602 records like the report in Exercise 9.3.

   Save the changes and leave the report open to complete the next exercise.

   After the report is run once, you can select a different date from the Parameters section shown in Figure 19-16 by double-clicking on the date shown. Once you select the date, click the Apply Changes button on the Parameters toolbar.

Figure 19-16 Calendar in the Parameters Panel

Exercise 19.3: Set A Default Date For A Parameter Field

If you know that the majority of times that a report is run that a certain value will be selected, you can set that value as the default. Setting a default value will still let another value be selected when the report is run. Default values are usually created to save time. In this exercise you will set a default date for the parameter field in the E19.2 report.

1. Save the E19.2 report as E19.3 Parameter field with a default value.

2. Open the parameter dialog box for the Order Date field. In the Value Options section of the Edit Parameter dialog box, click in the Setting column for the DEFAULT VALUE option and type 6/24/2010, as illustrated in Figure 19-17.

Option	Setting
Show on (Viewer) Panel	Editable
Prompt Text	Enter Order Date:
Prompt With Description Only	False
Optional Prompt	False
Default Value	6/24/2010 12:00:00 AM

Figure 19-17 Default Value option illustrated

3. Click OK. Save the changes, then press F5. You will see the default date that you just added to the parameter field.

4. Select the date 7/15/2011 in the calendar, then click OK. The report should have 1,977 records. If you see a different number of records, run the report again and type 00:00:00 as the time. Save the changes.

There isn't much use in saving the data with a report that has a parameter value, unless the report will be exported. Reports with parameter fields usually refresh the data.

The remaining parameter field exercises in this chapter and the next one should not save the data with the report. After completing step 1 in the exercises, open the Report Options dialog box and clear the **SAVE DATA WITH REPORT** option.

List Of Values

As you learned in Exercise 19.1, if a parameter field does not have a default value or a drop-down list with values, it is possible that the person running the report will type in the values incorrectly. As much as possible, you should avoid creating parameter fields that allow this to happen. Instead, you should provide a list of values for the parameter field. There are three list of value types that you can create for parameter fields, as explained below.

① **STATIC PROMPT** The values are stored in the report.

② **DYNAMIC PROMPT** The values are not stored in the report, they are stored in a database.

③ **CASCADING PROMPT** The values are not stored in the report, they are stored in a database.

A list of values is the data that the person running the report will select from. You can use the same list of values for different prompts in the same report. For example, if the report prompted for a customer "Bill to" state and a "Ship to" state, you could use the same list of states for both parameter fields.

List Of Value Categories

There are two list of value categories, as explained below.

① **UNMANAGED LISTS** are stored in the report file. This type of list can use report fields or commands as the data source. If you are not going to publish the reports to the SAP Business Objects Enterprise, you can use an unmanaged list of values.

② **MANAGED LISTS** are stored in the SAP Business Objects Enterprise. Managed list of values are based on a Business View, even if the report is not based on a Business View.

Static And Dynamic List Of Values

As you learned in the exercises that you have completed earlier in this chapter, you can create parameter fields that require the person running the report to type in the data when prompted. You also saw that this type of parameter field can cause errors to be generated or produce empty reports. This is not the best solution. You can create a static or dynamic list of values to use for the parameter field. Depending on the data, one type of list of values may be better suited then another. It is easy to get carried away and create all dynamic lists, but if a static list is better suited for the parameter field, you should use it. In addition to static and dynamic list of values, you can also create a cascading list of values, which is a type of dynamic list.

 The dynamic and cascading list of values exercises that you will complete in the next chapter are not for reports that are published on the Crystal Reports Server or the SAP Business Objects Enterprise.

Static List Of Values

Out of the three types of list of values, static lists are the easiest to create. They are best suited for values that do not change or for data that is not stored in a field. An example of a static list of values would be a list of states. Keep in mind that static lists do not change unless you change them. This is the biggest drawback of a static list of values. I personally only use a static list of values if the list is small because the values are stored in the report which makes the report file size larger. The benefit of static lists is that they are retrieved faster.

There are three ways to create a static list of values, as explained below. You can use any combination of these options to create the list that you need.

    ① Import the values from a field in a table.
    ② Type the list of values in manually.
    ③ Import the list of values from a text file.

> If the static list of values needs to be used for more than one report, it is more efficient to import the values, then it is to manually enter the values for each report.

Adding Values Manually

There are two ways to add values manually on the Create (or Edit) Parameter dialog box, as explained below.

    ① Click on the **CLICK HERE TO ADD ITEM** option in the Value column.
    ② Click the **INSERT** button.

Exercise 19.4: Create A Static List Of Values Manually

In this exercise you will create a static list of values manually. In Exercise 9.2, the report was limited to two regions: OH and FL. In this exercise you will limit the regions to five, but the person running the report will be able to select which of the five regions will appear on the report from a drop-down list.

1.   Save the E9.2 report as `E19.4 Manual static list of values`.

2.   Type `Region` in the Name field.   *Create New Parameter Box*

3.   Select one of the ways explained above to add a value and type `OH` in the first row in the Value/Description section of the dialog box, then type `Ohio` in the Description column.

If the data in the Value column contains an ID number, abbreviation or other data that the person running the report may not be familiar with, you should enter a brief explanation in the Description column. The information that you enter in the Description column will appear in the drop-down list next to the content in the Value column. The description is only used for display purposes.

> You do not have to enter a value in the Description column for every option in the list, only those that you think the person running the report may not understand.

If you have entered a description for every value in the list, you can change the **PROMPT WITH DESCRIPTION ONLY** option at the bottom of the dialog box to True. If you do this, the only values that will appear in the drop-down list on the Enter Values dialog box will be the values in the Description column.

If there is data in a report that you do not want everyone to see, you can create a list of values that will prevent everyone from seeing all of the data. For example, you may not want all sales reps to see sales outside of their region. In this example, you would create a parameter field that lists the regions that you want the sales reps to be able to view. You can create this type of list of values with static or dynamic lists.

4. Add the following regions to the Value column: CA, PA, WI and FL.

5. Change the **ALLOW CUSTOM VALUES** option at the bottom of the dialog box to False.

    In this report, you are only going to allow the report to be run for one of the regions that you added to the static list of values.

    Figure 19-18 shows the options that should be selected.

Figure 19-18 Parameter field options for a static list of values

6. Click OK. Open the Select Expert and select the Region parameter field. Remove the other values from the list, then click OK.

You will see the Enter Values dialog box. If you open the drop-down list, you will see the values that you added to the static list of values, as shown in Figure 19-19. As you can see, the first option also displays the description that you entered.

If you try to type in this field you will see that you can't. That is because the **ALLOW CUSTOM VALUES** option is set to False, as shown above in Figure 19-18.

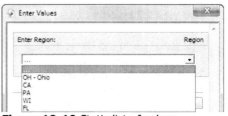

Figure 19-19 Static list of values

Also notice that the values are not in alphabetical order. They are in the order that they were added to the Value/Description table. In the next part of the exercise you will learn how to change the order of values in a static list of values.

If the **ALLOW CUSTOM VALUES** and **ALLOW MULTIPLE VALUES** options were set to True on the parameter dialog box shown earlier in Figure 19-18, you would see a field at the bottom of the Enter Values dialog box that would let you type in additional values, as illustrated in Figure 19-20.

The person running the report could select an option from the drop-down list or type in the value that they want. This would be useful if the static list contained the 10 most used options, which would keep the list small, while providing additional flexibility by allowing data to be entered manually.

Figure 19-20 Result of the Allow custom values option set to true

7. Select PA from the list and run the report. There should be five records on the report. Save the changes and leave the report open to complete the next part of the exercise.

Change The Sort Order Of A Static List Of Values

As you saw in the previous part of this exercise, the states are not in alphabetical order. Most lists are in alphabetical order because it is easier to find the value that you need. In this part of the exercise you will learn how to change the order of the items in the list.

> There are two ways to change the sort order of a list of values. The instructions in this section are best suited for a list that does not need a lot of changes or for a list that you do not necessarily want in alphabetical order, but just in a different order then the list is currently in.
>
> An example of this would be if you wanted to put a specific value at the top of the list because it is the most used option and then put the rest of the list in alphabetical order. You may have seen this on a web-based form for a country field. You would see "USA" at the top of the drop-down list because the company knows that most of their subscribers or customers are in the USA. Below that option, the rest of the countries are in alphabetical order.

1. Open the Edit Parameter dialog box for the Region field.

2. Click on the CA value, then click the Up button illustrated in Figure 19-21.

   Rearrange the other values in the column so that the entire list is in alphabetical order.

   Click OK.

Figure 19-21 Reorder buttons illustrated

3. Press F5. Select the second option, then click OK. When you open the drop-down list, the values will now be in alphabetical order. Save the changes.

How To Sort The Entire List At One Time

To sort the entire list at one time, click on the column heading (Value or Description) that you want to sort the list by. You will see an arrow, as illustrated in Figure 19-22. If the arrow is pointing up, the values will be sorted in ascending order.

Figure 19-22 Column sorting options illustrated

If the arrow is pointing up and you click on the arrow, the arrow will point down and the values will be sorted in descending order.

Importing A Static List Of Values

The list of values that you created manually in Exercise 19.4 was small, so it did not take a lot of time to set up. Often, that is not the case and you could have 50 or more values for a static list. If the data for the static list exists in a table or text document, it is easier to import the list. If you know that you do not need all of the values in the list that you will import, you have the two options explained below for removing the values that you do not need. You will have to evaluate which option is best, on a list by list basis.

   ① Import the list as is, then manually delete or change the options as needed on the parameter dialog box.
   ② Delete the values or make the changes to the list before importing it as a list of values. If the data that will be imported is in a table, it may not be possible or feasible to change the live data.

> If the list of values (static or dynamic) has a description, it will also be imported if all of the values are imported. If the values are added individually from a database, the Description column will not be imported.

Exercise 19.5: Create An Imported Static List Of Values

In this exercise you will import values from a field in a table to create a static list of values.

1. Save the E9.2 report as E19.5 Imported static list of values.

2. Type Region in the Name field.

3. Open the Value Field drop-down list and select the Region field.

4. Click the Actions button, then select the option **APPEND ALL DATABASE VALUES**.

You will now see all of the values from the Region field from the Customer table. If there were values in the list that you did not want or need, you can delete them by clicking on the value that you do not want and then click the Delete button (the X button above the list of values).

5. Change the Allow custom values option to False, then click OK.

6. Open the Select Expert and select the parameter field, then remove the other values from the list and click OK. When you open this parameter drop-down list you will see all of the values from the field in the table. If you changed any values, you will see the changes in the drop-down list. The data in the table was not changed. Save the changes.

CREATING DYNAMIC AND CASCADING PARAMETER FIELDS

Dynamic and cascading parameter fields add more functionality to the parameter fields that you learned how to create in the previous chapter. They filter the data in fields on the Enter Values dialog box. In this chapter you will learn how to do the following:

- ☑ Create a dynamic list of values for a parameter field
- ☑ Create cascading parameter fields
- ☑ Create formulas for parameter fields
- ☑ Create parameter fields for Top N reports
- ☑ Use parameter fields with the Section Expert
- ☑ Use parameter fields to highlight, sort and suppress data
- ☑ Print parameter fields on a report

CHAPTER 20

Dynamic List Of Values

In Chapter 3 you learned some basic report design techniques. You also learned that different groups of people may need similar reports. One of the ways that you can create one report that works for slightly different needs is by incorporating dynamic and cascading prompts. These prompts allow for greater flexibility when creating reports.

Unlike a static list of values that are not refreshed each time the report is run, dynamic and cascading list of values are refreshed each time the report is run. This means that if new values are added to the field in the table that the parameter field is getting the data from, the new values are also available in the parameter field. For example, if the dynamic parameter field is based on the product name field and 12 new products are added, those 12 products would also be available in the parameter field list. The opposite is also true. If values are deleted from the field in the underlying table, they would no longer be available in the parameter field list. Dynamic list of values are best suited for data that changes in a table, like new customers or a growing list of products.

> While you will not notice this completing the exercises in this book because the database is stored on your computers hard drive, dynamic and cascading lists take longer to be retrieved then static lists. Depending on the number of records in the table that the dynamic or cascading list is being retrieved from, you may notice a delay between the time that you open the drop-down list and the time that you actually see the values appear in the list.

Exercise 20.1: Create A Dynamic List Of Values

In Exercise 19.5 you imported regions from a table connected to the report. When a customer is added that is in a region that does not currently exist in the values for the parameter field, the E19.5 report would not include the new region on the report, meaning that the report will not contain up to date information because static lists are not automatically updated. In this exercise you will create a dynamic list of values for the region field.

1. Save the E9.2 report as E20.1 Dynamic region list of values.

2. Type Region in the Name field, then open the List of Values drop-down list and select **DYNAMIC**.

3. Click the Insert button.

    You will see a list of fields that are available for the dynamic list.

    Select the Region field.

    You should have the options shown in Figure 20-1.

Figure 20-1 Dynamic list of values options

The **EXISTING** option in the Data Source section is only available when the report already has a dynamic list.

The **DESCRIPTION** column works the same for dynamic lists as it does for static lists.

The **PARAMETERS** column is used when creating a dynamic cascading prompt. This is how you create the hierarchy between the fields that will be part of the cascading prompt.

4. Click OK. Open the Select Expert and select the parameter field, then remove the other values from the Region field.

5. Click OK. You will see that you can only select one value from the Region drop-down list. Save the changes.

> If this report was going to be put into production, it would probably be a good idea to change the operator to "Is equal to" so that when you read the formula, it will match the objectives of the report. Otherwise, it may be confusing later if you have to edit the report. If you leave it as it is, when the report is run, only one region can be selected from the drop-down list because the Allow multiple values parameter option is set to False.

Cascading Prompts And List Of Values

Cascading prompts are created like dynamic prompts. Unlike the dynamic list of values, cascading prompts contain related data and you must have at least two parameter fields to create cascading prompts. A cascading list of values will reduce the number of items to select from in at least one of the fields on the Enter Values dialog box.

The difference between dynamic and cascading prompts is that the option selected in the first prompt on the Enter Values dialog box is used to filter the values that will be displayed in the second prompt. An example of cascading prompts would be a list of suppliers and a list of products. The first prompt would be for the suppliers. Once a supplier is selected, the values in the second drop-down list would only contain products for the supplier that was selected in the first prompt.

> When you create cascading prompts, Crystal Reports will automatically change the name of the parameter field. It will be renamed to a combination of the name that you gave the field and the name of the field that it is connected to in the prompt group. You can rename the parameter field in the Field Explorer back to what you had originally named it.

Exercise 20.2: Create Cascading Prompts For Countries And Regions

In this exercise you will create two prompts. The first one is for the country, the second one is for the region. The region drop-down list will only show states (regions) that are in the country that is selected in the first prompt. The Chapter 20 Parameter fields report currently displays all countries and regions. The cascading prompts that you will create for this report will allow a specific country and specific region to be selected when the report is run.

1. Save the Chapter 20 Parameter fields report as
    E20.2 Cascading prompts for countries and regions.

2. Type Countries and Regions in the Name field, then select the Dynamic List of values option.

3. In the **PROMPT GROUP TEXT** field type `Select a country, then select a region:`.

4. Click the Insert button, then select the Country field. Click in the second row and select the Region field. Click OK.

5. Open the Select Expert, click on the Region field on the Choose Field dialog box, then click OK. In this step you have to select the last field that was added on the Create New Parameter dialog box.

6. Select the "Is equal to" operator, then select the Countries and Regions - Region parameter field and click OK.

    The Enter Values dialog box should look like the one shown in Figure 20-2. Notice that the Region field is not enabled. When a country is selected, the region field will be enabled.

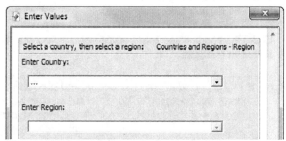

Figure 20-2 Dynamic cascading parameter options

7. Select USA, then select CA and click OK. There should be six records on the report. Save the changes.

Did you notice that the only states (regions) in the second drop-down list are for the USA? If you select a different country, you will only see regions in that country. This is the dynamic cascading (filtering) effect.

Exercise 20.3: Create Cascading Prompts For Customers And Their Orders

Many people in a company may have the need to view a particular customers orders. This is the type of report that dynamic cascading parameter fields were designed to handle.

1. Save the Chapter 20 Customer Orders report as `E20.3 Cascading prompts for customer orders.`

2. Type `Customer Orders` in the Name field, then select the Dynamic List of values option.

3. In the Prompt Group Text field type `Select a customer, then select the Order # that you want to view:`.

4. Select the Customer Name field in the Value column.

5. Change the **PROMPT TEXT** option to `Select A Customer:`, as illustrated in Figure 20-3.

6. Click in the second Value row and select the Order ID field, then change the Prompt Text option to `Select the order number that you want to view:`. Click OK.

7. Open the Select Expert, select the Order ID, then click OK.

8. Select the "Is equal to" operator, then select the Customer Orders - Order ID parameter field in the next drop-down list and click OK. Save the changes.

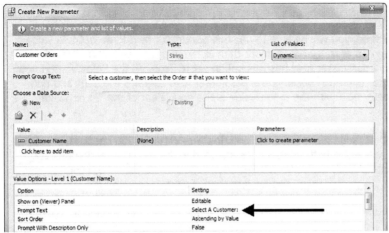

Figure 20-3 Options for the first parameter field

9. Run the report. Select the customer, Alley Cat Cycles, then select the order number 2300. The order numbers in the drop-down list are for the customer that is selected in the first drop-down list.

The dialog box should look like the one shown in Figure 20-4.

Click OK. You should see the data for order number 2300.

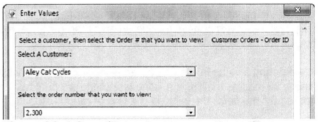

Figure 20-4 Cascading customer parameter options

 Editing Cascading Parameter Fields
What may not be obvious is that once you click OK on the Create New Parameter dialog box, you can't go back and edit cascading parameter field options. For that reason, I create each of the fields for the group separately and then put them in a group parameter field, which you will learn how to do. Doing this allows you to edit each of the fields in the parameter group if necessary.

Allow Range Values And Allow Multiple Values Options

The reports that you have created parameter fields for have added a lot of interactivity between the user and the report. This allows the person running the report to have more control over the records that will appear on the report. What you have probably noticed is that each parameter field that you have created only allows one option to be selected. In some instances this can limit the data that displays on reports in a way that is not best suited for the user.

The Create New Parameter dialog box has two options that will allow more flexibility. The **ALLOW RANGE VALUES** option allows the parameter field to accept high and low values, like the "Is between" Select Expert operator. A good use of this option would be for a date range. The **ALLOW MULTIPLE VALUES** option allows more than one value to be selected from the parameter field. A good use of this option would be if you need to select more than one value from the same field. An example is if you needed to select several products to see which ones are not selling.

Allow Range Values Option

When you set this option to **TRUE**, you will be able to use one parameter field to accept two values, a start of range value and an end of range value. More than likely, you will use this to allow date ranges to be entered. When a parameter field has this option set to True, on the Select Expert you have to select the "Is equal to" operator, because the parameter field contains the start and end values in one field. A parameter field with the range value is the equivalent of the "Is between" operator.

By default, the start and end of range fields have the **INCLUDE THIS VALUE** option checked. This means that the values entered in both fields will be included in the record selection process. If you clear this option for either field, the value will not be included in the record selection process. This is the equivalent of the "Is greater than" and "Is less than" Select Expert operators.

In the previous chapter you read about the **NO LOWER VALUE** and **NO UPPER VALUE** options. When the Allow range values option is set to True, these options are not checked. This means that only records that have a value between the start and end range values will be included in the record selection process. These options were also discussed earlier in conjunction with date fields. These options also work with non date field ranges. If either of these options are checked, the input field is disabled and you can't enter anything in the field. These options can also be used like the "Is greater than" and "Is less than" Select Expert operators.

Only entering a value in the Start of range input field and checking the No lower value option will retrieve all records that have a value greater than (or equal to, if the Include this value option is also checked for the field) the value in the Start of range field.

Only entering a value in the End of range input field and checking the No lower value option will retrieve all records that have a value less than (or equal to, if the Include this value option is also checked for the field) the value in the End of range field.

Exercise 20.4: Use The Allow Range Values Option With Dates

In Exercise 19.2 you created a parameter field that only allowed one date to be entered. In this exercise you will modify that parameter field to allow a date range to be entered.

1. Save the E19.2 report as E20.4 Date range parameter field.

2. Open the Order Date parameter dialog box. At the bottom of the dialog box, change the Allow range values option to True, then click OK.

3. Open the Select Expert. Change the Order Date operator to "Is equal to", then select the parameter field and click OK. Save the changes.

4. Refresh the data. Use the calendar control to select the start date 3/1/2011 and the end date 3/31/2011. You should have the options selected that are shown in Figure 20-5. Click OK. The report should have 159 records.

 You can also use the "Is not equal to" operator with range value parameter fields.

If you ran the report again and cleared the **INCLUDE THIS VALUE** option on the Start of Range field, there would be 139 records on the report. That means that 20 orders were placed on 3/1/2011. To verify that, check the Include this value option, then change the End of Range value to 3/2/2011. Clear the Include this value option on the End of Range field. The reason that I entered 3/2/2011 is

. . . .

to be able to account for the time portion of the date/time field. I find this easier then typing in the equivalent of 11:59:59 PM as the end time.

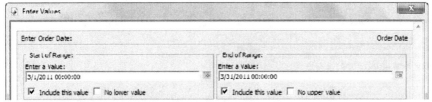
Figure 20-5 Date range parameter options

 If you wanted to run the report for one day, you would enter the same date in the start and end of range fields. You would have to include the equivalent of 11:59:59 PM on the End of Range field or you could enter the next day and use a time of 00:00:00.

 If you are running a monthly report and do not know if there are 30 or 31 days in the month, enter the first day of the next month that you are running the report for in the End of range field and clear the Include this value option. Doing this will include all records for the prior month.

Using Range Values For Non Date Data

A lot of the time, the range value parameter field is used for dates. You can use range parameter fields for other types of data. Two other uses that come to mind are to only print records in a zip code range. Another use is if you wanted to print a list of customers whose last name started with a specific letter or was in a range of letters, like customers whose last name started with A through D.

Long List Of Values

Parameter field drop-down lists that have a lot of values are separated into groups of 200 records by default. If the value that you are looking for is not in the first group of values, open the drop-down list shown in Figure 20-6 and select another level or click on the navigation buttons on either side of the drop-down list.

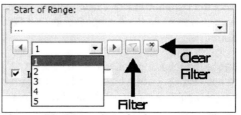
Figure 20-6 Long list of values options illustrated

The **FILTER** button is used to create a filter for the values in the entire list.

The **CLEAR FILTER** button removes the filter.

 How To Change The Default Long List Of Values Quantity For Parameter Fields
The information below explains how to change the number of items displayed in a parameter field drop-down list. The path to the registry key that you can change is: HKEY_CURRENT_USER\Software\SAP Business Objects\Suite XI 4.0\Crystal Reports\Report View. If the DWord value **PROMPTINGLOVBATCHSIZE** does not exist, as illustrated in Figure 20-7, create it, then enter the default value that you want to use, as shown in Figure 20-8. Select Decimal as the base value.

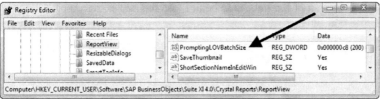

Figure 20-7 Registry key illustrated

Figure 20-8 New default value entered for the Long list of values

Exercise 20.5: Use The Allow Range Value Option With A Currency Field

In the previous exercise you used the Allow range values option with a date field. You can also use this option with numeric and currency fields. In this exercise you will use the option to find all orders that are within a certain dollar amount range.

1. Save the E17.1 report as `E20.5 Currency range parameter field`.

2. Type `Order Amount Range` in the Name field, then change the Type to Currency.

3. Select the Dynamic List of Values option. Type `Enter the order amount range for the report:` in the Prompt Group Text field, then add the Order Amount field to the Value column.

4. Change the following options, then click OK.
   Prompt Text `Select the order amount:`
   Change the Allow range values option to True.

5. Open the Select Expert and click on the **NEW** tab. Select the Order Amount field, then click OK. Select the "Is equal to" operator, then select the Order Amount Range parameter field and click OK. Save the changes.

6. Select the first order amount over $1,000 for the Start of Range value. Select the first order amount over $2,000 for the End of Range value.

7. Clear the Include this value option for the End of Range field. Doing this will only display orders that have an order amount between $1,000 and $2,000.

You should have the options shown in Figure 20-9.

Click OK. There should be 36 records on the report.

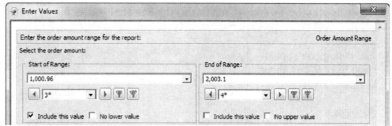

Figure 20-9 Currency range parameter options

Allow Multiple Values Option

When you set this option to **TRUE**, more than one value can be selected in the parameter field. This is the equivalent of the "Is one of" Select Expert operator. In Exercise 20.1 you created a dynamic list of values for the region field. When the report was run, only one region could be selected. You may often have a report request that requires that more than one value be included in the selection process. When the Allow multiple values option is set to True, you are creating what is called an **ARRAY**. This means that the field can contain more than one value.

 If the **ALLOW CUSTOM VALUES** and **ALLOW MULTIPLE VALUES** options are set to True, values can be added from the **AVAILABLE VALUES** list box and typed in manually if the values in the Available Values list box are from a static list. This cannot be done with dynamic and cascading lists of values.

Exercise 20.6: Use The Allow Multiple Values Option With A Static List Of Values

In Exercise 19.4 you created a static list of values by manually entering the values on the Create New Parameter dialog box. As you just learned, in addition to setting the Allow multiple values option to true, setting the Allow custom values option to true also, will allow the person running the report to select values from the static list and type in other values. In this exercise you will modify a parameter field to allow multiple values to be selected from the static list and allow other values to be entered.

1. Save the E19.4 report as E20.6 Customer multi value parameter field.

2. Open the Parameter dialog box for the Region field. Change the following options, then click OK.

   Prompt Text Select the regions or type them in below:
   Change the Allow custom values and Allow multiple values options to True.

3. Open the Select Expert. Select the "Is equal to" operator on the Region parameter field, then select the Region parameter field and click OK. If you see a warning message that says the array must be subscripted, click OK and save the changes.

4. Run the report. Select the FL and PA regions from the Available Values list and add them to the Selected Values list.

 If you hold down the **CTRL** key, you can click on multiple options in the Available Values list and then click the **ADD** button to add them to the Selected Values list box at the same time.

5. Manually add the TX and NY regions to the Selected Values list by typing one value in the Enter a Value field and then click the arrow button at the end of the field.

The dialog box should have the options shown in Figure 20-10.

Click OK.

There should be nine records on the report.

Save the changes.

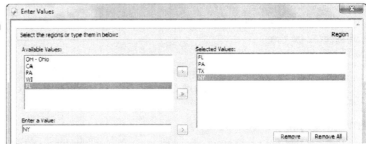

Figure 20-10 Multiple and custom value parameter options

Exercise 20.7: Use The Allow Multiple Values Option With A Dynamic List Of Values

With a dynamic list, there is usually no need to allow custom values. In this exercise, you will modify a report to be able to select the carriers that will appear on the report.

1. Save the Chapter 20 Shipping Info report as `E20.7 Dynamic multi value list.`

2. Type `Ship Via` in the Name field, then select the Dynamic List of Values option.

3. Type `Select the Ship Via options for the report:` in the Prompt Group Text field.

4. Add the Ship Via field to the Value column, then change the Allow multiple values option to True and click OK.

5. Open the Select Expert and change the Ship Via operator to "Is equal to", then select the Ship Via parameter field and click OK.

6. Run the report. Add the last three shipping options to the Selected Values list, as shown in Figure 20-11.

There should be 738 records on the report. The report may be easier to read if it was sorted on the Ship Via field.

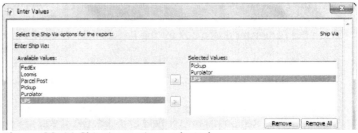

Figure 20-11 Shipping options selected

7. Sort the report on the Ship Via field in ascending order. The first shipping method on the report should be Pickup. Save the changes.

Combining Range And Multiple Values

What may not initially be apparent is that these two options can be combined on the same parameter field. Doing this allows for maximum flexibility and options when the report is run.

. . . .

On a report that uses a date parameter field, you can allow multiple date ranges to be entered. For example, if you wanted to be able to compare the orders for the first five days of three months, you could enter 1/1/11 to 1/5/11, 3/1/11 to 3/5/11 and 5/1/11 to 5/5/11 on the same parameter field. Another example would be if you wanted to see orders 1001 to 1050 and 1100 to 1124 on the same report. Setting the Allow range values and Allow multiple values options to true would allow you to create parameter fields for both of the examples just discussed.

Exercise 20.8: Combine Range And Multiple Values For A Date Field

In Exercise 20.4, the parameter field that you created only allowed one date range to be entered. In this exercise you will modify that parameter field to allow multiple date ranges to be entered.

1. Save the E20.4 report as E20.8 Multiple date range parameter field.

2. Open the Order Date parameter field dialog box.

3. Change the following options, then click OK.
   Prompt Text Enter the Order Date ranges:
   Change the Allow multiple values option to True.

4. Press F5 or click the Refresh button. After you add the End of Range date, click the **ADD RANGE** button, then add the next date range. Add the following date ranges to the Selected Values list. Don't forget to set the time to 00:00:00. 1/1/11 to 1/5/11, 3/1/11 to 3/5/11 and 5/1/11 to 5/5/11.

5. Figure 20-12 shows the options that should be selected. Click OK. There should be 95 records on the report. Save the changes.

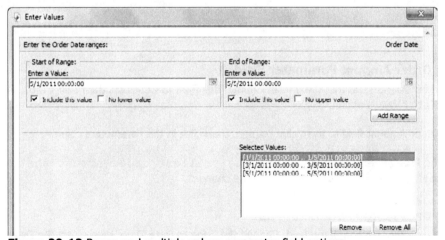

Figure 20-12 Range and multiple values parameter field options

Cascading Parameter Groups And Multi Value Parameter Options

Now that you have learned how to create cascading parameter groups and multi value parameter fields, the options that reports can have are almost endless. If you find that you cannot create the cascading parameter groups that you need, you can create individual parameter fields and add each one to the Select Expert and they will all appear on the Enter Values dialog box.

I prefer this method of one parameter field for each field that I need to query because I do not have to rename the parameter fields after I create them. This is also very helpful if you need to rearrange the order that the fields appear in on the Enter Values dialog box or if you need to add a new parameter field and place it between two existing parameter fields. This is what you will learn how to do in the next exercise.

Exercise 20.9: Create Dynamic Cascading Prompts For Customers And Their Orders

In this exercise you will create cascading prompts for three fields: Customers, Order Date and Order Amount. The E10.2 report displays the orders by customer. Creating cascading prompts will let the person running the report select a customer and only display orders that meet the date range and order amount that they select. For example, the prompts that you will create in this exercise will let you select all orders placed on or after 1/1/11 for a specific customer that has order amounts greater than $1,000.

Create The Customer Name Parameter Field

1. Save the E10.2 report as `E20.9 Cascading prompts for customer orders`.

2. Type `Customer Name` in the Name field, then select the Dynamic List of Values option.

3. Type `Select the customer, date ranges and minimum order amount:` in the Prompt Group Text field.

4. Add the Customer Name field to the Value column, then click in the Parameters column. This is what tells Crystal Reports that you want to use this field on the Enter Values dialog box as a cascading prompt field. It should have the same name as the one you typed in the Name field.

5. Change the Prompt Text option to `Select A Customer:`. Click OK, then save the changes.

Create The Order Amount Parameter Field

1. Type `Order Amount` in the Name field. Change the Type to Currency, then select the Dynamic List of Values option.

2. Add the Order Amount field to the Value column, then click in the Parameters column.

3. Change the Prompt Text option to `Select the smallest order amount that you want to see:`. Click OK, then save the changes.

Create The Date Range Parameter Field

1. Type `Date Range` in the Name field. Change the Type to Date Time, then select the Dynamic List of Values option.

2. Type `You have to select at least one date range. Once selected, click the Add Range button:` in the Prompt Group Text field.

3. Add the Order Date field to the Value column, then click in the Parameters column.

4. Change the following options, then click OK.
    Prompt Text Select the beginning and ending order dates from the drop-down lists:
    Change the Allow multiple values and Allow range values options to True.
    Save the changes.

Modify The Select Expert Options

1. Open the Select Expert and change the Order Amount operator to "Is greater than or equal to", then select the Order Amount parameter field.

2. Change the Order Date operator to "Is equal to", then select the Date Range parameter field.

3. Click on the New tab, then select the Customer Name field and click OK. Select the "Is equal to" operator, then select the Customer Name parameter field. The formula on the Select Expert should look like the one shown in Figure 20-13. Click OK.

> {Orders.Order Amount} >= {?Order Amount} and
> {Orders.Order Date} = {?Date Range} and
> {Customer.Customer Name} = {?Customer Name}

Figure 20-13 Select Expert formula

Test The Parameter Fields

1. Select the Alley Cat Cycles company, then select the Order Amount 100.4.

2. Select the first and last dates in 2011.

    This will return all of this customer's orders in 2011 that have an order total of $100.40 or more.

    You should have the options selected that are shown in Figure 20-14.

    Click OK.

    There should be 29 records on the report.

    Save the changes.

    Leave the report open to complete the next exercise.

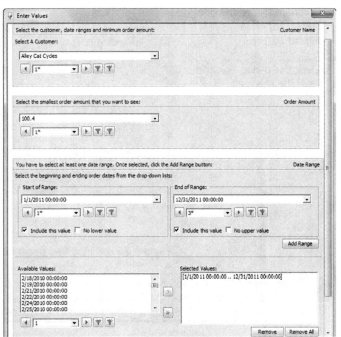

Figure 20-14 Report parameter options

Exercise 20.10: Rearrange The Parameter Fields Order

Earlier I mentioned that I think a benefit of creating individual parameter fields is that you can rearrange the order of the parameter fields on the Enter Values dialog box. In this exercise you will change the order of the parameter fields.

1. Save the E20.9 report as `E20.10 Rearrange the order of parameter fields`.

2. Right-click on the Parameter Fields option on the Field Explorer and select **SET PARAMETER ORDER**.

3. Click on the Order Amount parameter field, then click the down arrow button.

   The dialog box should look like the one shown in Figure 20-15.

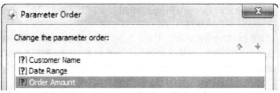

Figure 20-15 Parameter Order dialog box

4. Click OK, then click the Refresh button.

   The dialog box should look like the one shown in Figure 20-16.

   Compare this to the one shown earlier in Figure 20-14.

   Close the dialog box and save the changes.

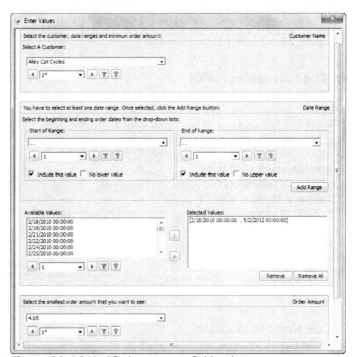

Figure 20-16 Modified parameter field order

 I don't know why, but you can only rename a parameter field from the Field Explorer. You cannot rename it from the Edit Parameter dialog box. The good thing is that if you rename a parameter field, it is renamed throughout the report.

Exercise 20.11: Allowing All Values In A Parameter Field

So far all of the parameter fields that you have created required specific information from the person running the report. For example, in Exercise 20.6 the region parameter field required at least one state to be selected. If the person running the report wanted all states, there was no way that it could be accomplished in that report without manually typing all of the states in.

In Chapter 9 you learned about wildcard characters. In this exercise you will learn how to incorporate the asterisk wildcard character into the region parameter field so that all regions can be selected.

1. Save the E20.6 report as `E20.11 Add Select All functionality to a parameter field`.

2. Open the Region parameter field. Add the following text to the end of the Prompt Text option as shown in Figure 20-17, then click OK. `or type * to select all regions.`

Option	Setting
Show on (Viewer) Panel	Editable
Prompt Text	Select the regions, type them in or type * to display all regions:

Figure 20-17 Modified prompt text

3. Report ⇒ Selection Formulas ⇒ Record.

    Change the formula to match the one shown in Figure 20-18.

    ```
    (If {?Region} = "*" Then True
    Else
    {Customer.Region} = {?Region};)
    ```
    Figure 20-18 Formula to select all regions

4. Save the changes and run the report. Remove all of the current selected values.

5. Type a * in the Enter a Value field, then add it to the Selected Values list, as shown in Figure 20-19. Click OK. You will see all of the regions on the report.

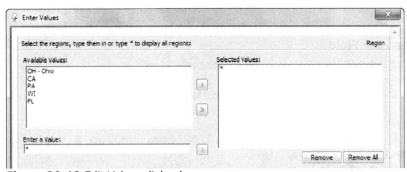

Figure 20-19 Edit Values dialog box

If you were really going to use this report, at the very least it should have a parameter field for the country and be sorted by region. If the report needed totals, it would need to be grouped.

Using Formula Fields In Parameter Fields

All of the formulas that you have created in this book so far have been static or hard coded, meaning that they do not change each time the report is run. There will be times when hard coded formulas will not produce the results that are needed. One way to tell is if you get requests for several reports that are very similar. This is often the case for reports that are used in what is known as "What-If" analysis.

For example, someone wants to see the potential revenue gain if they raise the price of the products by 5, 7 or 8%. Hard coded formulas would require you to create three reports, one for each of the potential percent increases. Creating a parameter field that prompted for the percent of increase means that only one report has to be created to accommodate any percent that the user needs.

A parameter field that is based off of a formula field will allow the user to be able to sort or group the report the way that best meets their needs. Instead of selecting a field name on the Record Sort Expert or the Insert Group dialog box, you would select the formula field.

In addition to using formula fields for What-If analysis, you can also base parameter fields off of formula fields that are used to conditionally format data. An example of this is the suppression of data shown in the E15.5 Suppress Salary GT 50000 report. Another example would be the conditional formatting that you created using the Highlighting Expert.

Top N Reports With Parameter Fields

In Exercise 12.4 you created a Top N report. Like other reports that have formulas, the options that you selected to create a Top N report are hard coded. You can create a conditional formula and use it with the parameter field to be able to run the Top N report with different **N** values.

Exercise 20.12: Create A Parameter Field For A Top N Report

In this exercise you will create a formula that will be used as the basis for a parameter field that will let the person running the report select the **N** value. You will also remove the hard coded date range and add a parameter field to allow a date range to be selected each time the report is run.

Create The Parameter Field

1. Save the E12.5 report as `E20.12 Top N parameter field`.

2. Type `Top N` in the Name field, then change the Type to Number.

3. Change the following options, then click OK.
    Prompt Text `Enter a number between 1 & 100 for the Top N value:`
    Change the Default Value option to 5.
    Change the Min Value option to 1.
    Change the Max Value option to 100.
    Figure 20-20 shows the options that should be selected. Save the changes.

 When you have to create a Top, Bottom or Percent N parameter field you can select the Default, Min and Max Values that you want. If you know that the majority of times the users will run the report and select a specific N number, set that number as the default. It is not a requirement to have Min and Max Values.

Option	Setting
Prompt Text	Enter a number between 1 & 100 for the Top N value:
Prompt With Description Only	False
Optional Prompt	False
Default Value	5
Allow custom values	True
Allow multiple values	False
Allow discrete values	True
Allow range values	False
Min Value	1
Max Value	100

Figure 20-20 Top N parameter field options

Create The Top N Formula

1. Open the Group Sort Expert, then click the Formula button.

2. Type {?Top N} as shown on the right side of Figure 20-21.

   Click the Save and close button.

Figure 20-21 Top N formula

3. Check the Include Ties option, then click OK to close the Group Sort Expert.

 If the **INCLUDE TIES** option is not checked and there are ties, only one of the tied groups will be displayed on the report. I could not find a way to specify which of the tied groups will appear on the report or no way to indicate that there is another group with the same number. Therefore, I think the best solution is to always check this option.

The report needs more changes. The current report title will not be accurate because the person running the report has the option of selecting the Top N number and the order date range. Later in this chapter you will learn how to add a parameter field to the report so that the criteria selected can be printed on the report.

Create The Order Date Range Parameter Field

In this part of the exercise you will remove the hard coded date range and replace it with a parameter field.

1. Open a new parameter field dialog box and type Order Date in the Name field, then change the Type to Date Time and select the Dynamic List of Values option.

2. Add the Order Date field to the Value column, then click in the Parameters column.

3. Change the following options and click OK.
   Prompt Text Select the date range that you want to see orders for:.
   Change the Allow range values option to True.

Modify The Select Expert Options And Parameter Field Order

1. Open the Select Expert. Select the "Is equal to" operator, then select the Order Date parameter field and click OK.

2. Open the Parameter Order dialog box.

   Put the parameter fields in the order shown in Figure 20-22, then click OK.

   Save the changes.

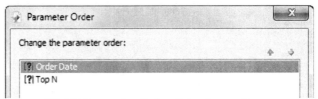

Figure 20-22 Parameter Order dialog box options

Test The Parameter Fields

1. Press F5.

   The dialog box should look similar to the one shown in Figure 20-23.

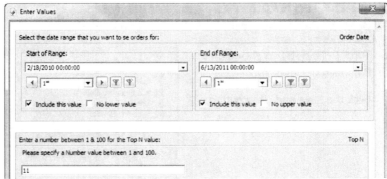

Figure 20-23 Top N parameter options

2. Run the report. If you select a high N number, the chart in this exercise will be difficult to read. More than likely, you would delete the chart from this report or reduce the Max value option for the Top N parameter field.

Using Parameter Fields To Highlight Data

In Exercise 15.1 you used the Highlighting Expert to conditionally format data when a certain condition was met. The report created in that exercise may be more helpful if an option existed to select the value, in this case, the threshold to use for applying the conditional formatting. The report currently highlights records if the value in the Order processing time field is greater than or equal to three.

Exercise 20.13: Create A Parameter Field To Highlight Rows Of Data

In this exercise you will modify the E14.8 report to prompt to select the order processing time. You will also add a date range parameter. The background color of the row will change to yellow if the record meets the condition.

Create The Order Date Range Parameter Field

1. Save the E14.8 report as E20.13 Highlight rows of data parameter field.

2. Type Date Range in the Name field. Change the Type to Date Time and select the Dynamic List of Values option.

3. Add the Order Date field to the Value column, then click in the Parameters column.

4.   Change the following options, then click OK.
     Prompt Text `Select the date range that you want to see orders for:`
     Change the Allow range values option to True.

Create The Highlight Rows Of Data Parameter Field

1.   Open a new parameter field dialog box. Type `Order processing time` in the Name field
     and change the Type to Number.

2.   Change the following options, then click OK.
     Prompt Text `Enter the minimum number of order processing days that
     you want to see:`
     Change the Default Value option to 3.
     Change the Min Value option to 1.
     Figure 20-24 shows the options that should be selected.

Option	Setting
Show on (Viewer) Panel	Editable
Prompt Text	Enter the minimum number of order processing days that you want t...
Prompt With Description Only	False
Optional Prompt	False
Default Value	3
Allow custom values	True
Allow multiple values	False
Allow discrete values	True
Allow range values	False
Min Value	1
Max Value	

Figure 20-24 Order processing days parameter field options

Create The Row Color Formula

In this part of the exercise you will create the formula that will change the background color to
yellow for the rows that have an order processing time greater than or equal to the number that is
entered on the parameter field that you just created.

1.   Open the Section Expert and click on the details section, then click on the Color tab.

2.   Click the Formula button and open the Report Fields tree.

Notice on the left side of the Formula Workshop that the conditional formatting formula that you are
creating is being applied to the background color option of the details section.

3.   Type `If` in the Formula Text section and press the space bar, then double-click on the Order
     processing time formula field in the Report Fields section.

4.   Press the space bar and type >=, then press the space bar.

5.   Double-click on the Order processing time parameter field in the Report Fields section, then
     press the space bar and type `Then crYellow Else crNoColor`. The formula should
     look like the one shown in Figure 20-25.

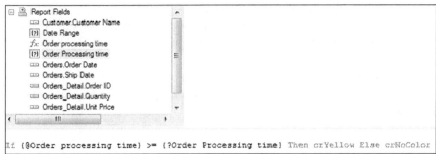

If {@Order processing time} >= {?Order Processing time} Then crYellow Else crNoColor

Figure 20-25 Parameter field formula

 If you did not add the crNoColor option, rows that did not meet the criteria would have a black background and you would not be able to see the text.

6.   Click the Save and close button. Click OK to close the Section Expert, then save the changes.

Add The Date Range Parameter Field To The Select Expert

If you look at the Parameter Fields section of the Field Explorer you will see that the Date Range field does not have a green check mark next to it. That is because the field is currently not being used on the report.

1.   Open the Select Expert and select the "Is equal to" operator for the Order Date field.

2.   Open the next drop-down list and select the Date Range parameter field, then click OK.

Test The Parameter Fields

1.   Save the changes, then refresh the report.

2.   Select the first date in 2011 for the Start of Range value, then select the last date in 2011 for the End of Range value. Notice that the default value that you set is in the Order processing time field. Figure 20-26 shows the options that should be selected.

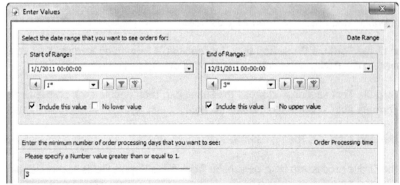

Figure 20-26 Order processing time parameter field options

3.   Click OK. The top of the first page of the report should look like the one shown in Figure 20-27. Every row that has a value of three or greater in the Order processing time field has a yellow background.

Customer Name	Order Date	Ship Date	Order ID	Unit Price	Quantity	Order processing time
Rough Terrain	01/01/2011	01/01/2011	1,121	$41.90	1	0
Rough Terrain	01/01/2011	01/01/2011	1,121	$809.87	1	0
Hooked on Helmets	01/01/2011	01/08/2011	1,122	$21.90	3	7
Hooked on Helmets	01/01/2011	01/08/2011	1,122	$479.85	2	7
Clean Air Transportation	01/02/2011	01/02/2011	1,123	$1,739.85	3	0
Off the Mountain Biking	01/02/2011	01/09/2011	1,124	$19.90	3	7
Road Runners Paradise	01/02/2011	01/03/2011	1,125	$19.71	2	1

Figure 20-27 Highlight rows of data parameter field report

Using Parameter Fields To Select The Sorting And Grouping Options

You have learned how to sort and group data by selecting options on the Record Sort Expert and Insert Group dialog boxes. There will be times when a report needs to be sorted or grouped in several different ways. Rather then hard code this information and have to create several reports, one for each field that the report needs to be sorted or grouped on, you can create a parameter field that will be used to select the field that the report will be sorted or grouped on. The value collected from the parameter field will be passed to the Record Sort Expert or the Insert Group dialog box.

Parameter fields cannot retrieve a formula or table name. Therefore you have to create a formula that uses the value in the parameter field as the field to sort or group on. The formula field is what you will select on the sorting or grouping dialog box.

Exercise 20.14: Create A Parameter Field To Sort The Records

In Exercise 5.1 you created a customer information report. As it is, the report is not sorted or grouped. In this exercise you will create a formula and parameter field that will allow the report to be sorted on one of the following three fields: Customer Name, Region or Country.

Create The Sort By Parameter Field

1. Save the E5.1 report as `E20.14 Sort records parameter field`.

2. Type `Sort By Field` in the Name field.

3. Type the values `Customer Name, Region` and `Country` in the Value column.
   Type `State` in the Description column of the Region value.

4. Change the following options, then click OK.
   Prompt Text `Select the field that you want to sort by:`
   Change the Allow custom values option to False.

Create The Sort Formula And Add It To The Parameter Field

1. Open the Formula Workshop and create a new formula. Type `SortBy` as the formula name.

2. Type the formula shown below, then click the Save and close button.

```
If {?Sort By Field} = "Customer Name" Then
{Customer.Customer Name}
Else
If {?Sort By Field} = "Region" Then {Customer.Region}
Else
{Customer.Country}
```

3. Open the Record Sort Expert, then add the SortBy formula field to the Sort Fields list box and click OK.

   Save the changes and preview the report. The Enter Values dialog box shown in Figure 20-28 will open.

Figure 20-28 SortBy field options

Test The Sort Parameter Field

1. Select the Customer Name option from the drop-down list, then click OK. The report should be sorted in Customer Name order.

2. Run the report again and sort the report by Region. Leave the report open to complete the next exercise.

Exercise 20.15: Create A Parameter Field To Group Data

In the previous exercise you learned how to sort the detail records using a parameter field. Selecting the field to group on via a parameter field basically works the same way. The difference is that you attach the formula field to the Insert Group dialog box instead of the Record Sort Expert.

In this exercise you will create a group for the customer information report from the previous exercise. One parameter field that you will create in this exercise will let you select which of the three fields; Customer Name, Region or Country to group on. You will create another parameter field that will be used to select the group sort order, ascending or descending.

Create The Group Sort Parameter Field

1. Save the E20.14 report as E20.15 Group data parameter field.

2. Type Group By Field in the Name field.

3. Type the values Customer Name, Region and Country in the Value column.

4. Change the following options, then click OK.
   Prompt Text Select the field that you want to group by:
   Change the Default Value option to Region. You can select it from the drop-down list.
   Change the Allow custom values option to False.

Create The Group Formula And Add It To The Parameter Field

1. Open the Formula Workshop and create a new formula. Type GroupBy as the formula name.

2. Click on the SortBy formula field under the Formula Fields node on the left of the Formula Workshop. Copy and paste the SortBy formula into the GroupBy formula.

3. Change the word "Sort" to Group in two places in the formula, then click the Save and close button.

Create The Group Sort Order Parameter Field

The parameter field that you will create in this part of the exercise will let the person running the report select the sort order of the group, either ascending or descending. Parameter fields are displayed on the Enter Values dialog box in the order that they were created in. The more logical order in this exercise would be to have the Sort By field last.

1. Open a new parameter field dialog box and type `Group Sort Order` in the Name field.

2. Type the options `Ascending` and `Descending` in the Value column.

3. Change the following options, then click OK.
    Prompt Text `Select the order that you want to sort the groups in:`
    Change the Default Value option to Ascending.
    Change the Allow custom values option to False.

4. Change the order of the parameter fields so that the Sort By field is last in the Field Explorer.

Create The Group And Add The Group Formula To The Insert Group Dialog Box

As you have noticed, the report that you are working on does not have any groups. In this part of the exercise you will create the group based on a formula field and sort the group based on a different formula field.

1. Click the Insert Group button on the Insert Tools toolbar.

2. Open the first drop-down list and select the GroupBy formula field.

3. Check the option, **USE A FORMULA AS GROUP SORT ORDER**, then click the Formula button and type the formula shown below.

    ```
    If {?Group Sort Order} = "Ascending" Then crAscendingOrder
    Else
    crDescendingOrder
    ```

4. Click the Save and close button, then click OK to close the Insert Group dialog box.
    Save the changes.

Test The Parameter Fields

1. Refresh the report.

    You should see the dialog box shown in Figure 20-29.

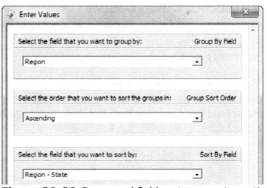

Figure 20-29 Group and field sort parameter options

2. Run the report a few times, selecting different options.

Boolean Parameter Fields

Boolean parameter fields, like Boolean formulas can only have two values: True and False. Like Boolean formulas, you do not have to display the options as true and false. If the Boolean parameter field is not a group, you can use the Description column to enter the text that you want to display in the drop-down list instead of the values, true and false.

Interestingly enough, you cannot use the Description column to change what is displayed in the drop-down list on Boolean group parameter fields. Instead, the name of the Parameter field is used. Therefore, make good use of the Name field.

Using A Parameter Field To Suppress Data

You have learned how to conditionally suppress data on a report. Suppression is often done with a Boolean field. Suppressing data is popular on reports that have a lot of detail records. Being able to select whether or not to suppress detail records allows one to run the report and only see the summary information. Doing this means that one report can be a detail report or a summary report. The Suppress (No Drill-Down) option on the Section Expert requires a Boolean formula when it will be used conditionally.

Exercise 20.16: Conditional Section Suppression Using A Parameter Field

In this exercise you will modify a report so that it can be run as a detailed report or a summary only report.

Create The Suppression Parameter Field

1. Save the E10.2 report as E20.16 Suppress section parameter field.

2. Type Summary Report in the Name field.

3. Type Yes in the first Value row, then type No in the second Value row.

4. Change the following options, then click OK.
    Prompt Text Do you want to run a Summary Only report?
    Change the Allow custom values option to False.

Modify The Section Expert Options

1. Open the Section Expert and add another page header section. You need the additional page header section because the field headings also have to be suppressed if the report will be run as a summary report.

2. Click on the Formula button for the Suppress (No Drill-Down) option for the page header b section, then type the formula shown below. This formula checks to see if the Summary Report parameter field has the value Yes. If it does, the page header b and details sections will be suppressed.

    ```
    If {?Summary Report} = "Yes" Then True
    ```

3. Highlight the formula and press **CTRL+C**, then click the Save and close button. This will let you copy the formula.

4. Click on the details section in the Section Expert, then click the Formula button across from the Suppress (No Drill-Down) option. Paste (Press **CTRL+V**) the formula into the Formula Text section, then click the Save and close button. Click OK to close the Section Expert.

Modify The Report

As mentioned earlier, when the report is run in the summary only mode, the field headings should not be displayed or printed. This is why you created the second page header section and added the suppression formula to the second page header section.

1. Move the field headings to the page header b section and save the changes.

   Press the F5 key. You should see the dialog box shown in Figure 20-30.

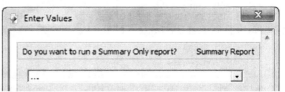

Figure 20-30 Summary only parameter field dialog box

2. Select Yes to run a summary only report. You should only see summary information on the report. Run the report again and select No.

Managing Data Entry In Parameter Fields

You have created several parameter fields in this chapter. While you took care and entered the data in the parameter fields correctly, it is unrealistic to think that people that run the reports will always enter information correctly in the parameter fields. If the reports are going to be part of an application, there are more options available for helping and guiding users to enter the data in parameter fields correctly in the development software then Crystal Reports provides. Crystal Reports does provide three types of options that you can use to help users enter data in the parameter fields correctly. These options are Min and Max field lengths, which use a range of values to limit the data. You have already used these options on date fields. The other options are Min/Max value and Edit Masks.

On string parameter fields the **MIN LENGTH** and **MAX LENGTH** options are used. The length refers to how many characters can be entered in the field. The number that you enter in the Max Length field should not be larger than the actual length of the corresponding field in the table. Any items in the Value column have to meet the min and max requirements.

The range limits **MIN VALUE** and **MAX VALUE** are primarily used for number and date fields. These options require that the data entered in the field be in a specific range. For example, if the min value is one and the max value is five, any number less than one or greater than five would not be accepted.

 If a number parameter field is populated with a static list of values and you do not want all of the values to be available, enter the min and max values for the range of data that you want to import before importing the values for the static list of values.

Edit Masks

In Chapter 14 you learned about masks. You learned that they are placeholders that determine how data will be displayed on a report. The Edit mask feature for parameter fields is similar. Edit masks are used to set the rules for how data has to be entered into a field. If an edit mask has 10 placeholders, that means that no more than 10 characters can be entered into the field. Each of the edit mask characters has its own rule. The characters can be combined in the same field as needed. For example, if you were going to use an edit mask for a country field, you may want to force the first character to be an upper case letter and the other characters could be a combination of upper and lower case letters.

Table 20-1 lists the mask characters that you can use. Edit masks provide a lot of flexibility for managing the data that is entered in parameter fields. An edit mask is a series of characters (placeholders) that control the type of data that can be entered in **STRING** parameter fields. The Edit Mask field is at the bottom of the Value Options list on the Create New Parameter dialog box.

The edit mask **>AA** could be used for a state field. AA forces two alphanumeric characters to be entered in the field. **>** forces the characters to be uppercase.

If the values entered are not correct, you will see an error message. Often, the error messages are cryptic and can confuse the person that is trying to run the report. If I use an edit mask on a parameter field, I put as much information in the Prompt Text field as possible to help the person enter the correct data.

Character	Rule
A	Requires that an alphanumeric character be entered.
a	Allows an alphanumeric character, but it is not required.
0 (zero)	Requires a numeric character to be entered.
9	Allows a numeric character, but it is not required.
#	Allows a digit, space, plus sign or minus sign, but it is not required.
L	Requires a letter to be entered.
?	Allows a letter, but it is not required.
&	Allows any character or space, but it is required.
C	Allows any character or space, but it is not required.
. , : ; - /	Allows separator characters, but it is not required.
<	Converts the characters in the field to lower case.
>	Converts the characters in the field to upper case.
\	Causes the character that follows the \ (back slash) to be taken as a literal.
Password	Does not display the actual characters that are entered. Instead, circles appear when text is entered into this field.

Table 20-1 Edit mask characters explained

Adding Parameter Field Criteria To A Report

In Chapter 10 you saw examples of selection criteria being displayed on the report by using a special field. [See Chapter 10, Displaying The Record Selection Formula Field] In addition to displaying selection formulas on a report, it would also be helpful to the person reading the report to be able to view the parameter criteria on the report.

You have learned how to create parameter fields that add a lot of interaction. The one thing that is missing is adding the parameter field criteria to a report. With all of the parameter field selection combinations that a report can have, including the selection criteria on the report would be helpful for the person running the report. Single value parameter fields can be dragged from the Field Explorer on to the report like other fields and will print as expected.

> Range value and multiple value parameter fields cannot be dragged onto the report and printed like single value parameter fields. If range value and multiple value parameter fields are added to the report, only the first value in the field will print. Printing solutions for these types of parameter fields are explained below.

Printing Parameter Range Fields

There are two functions, **MINIMUM** and **MAXIMUM** that can be used to print the range in a parameter field. These functions return the beginning and ending values. The formula below will print the date range on the report as long as the **NO LOWER VALUE** and **NO UPPER VALUE** options are not checked on the Enter Values dialog box. Replace the {?Date_Parameter} field shown in the formula below with the name of the parameter field that you want to print.

"Starting Date " & Minimum ({?Date_Parameter}) & " and Ending Date " & Maximum ({?Date_Parameter})

> You can use the Minimum and Maximum functions for any type of range parameter field data. It is not just for date ranges.

Exercise 20.17: Print Parameter Range Fields

1. Save the E20.13 report as E20.17 Print parameter range fields.

2. Create a formula field called Print Date Range. Type the formula shown below and save the formula. Type the formula all on one line.

   ```
   "Starting Date " & Minimum ({?Date Range}) & " and Ending Date "
   & Maximum ({?Date Range})
   ```

3. Add the Print Date Range formula field to the top of the page header section. Make the field at least four inches across the screen, then save the changes. Preview the report. You should see the date range at the top of the report, similar to the one shown in Figure 20-31. You will have different data on the report.

Starting Date 2/18/2010 12:00:00AM and Ending Date 2/7/2011 12:00:00AM						
Customer Name	Order Date	Ship Date	Order ID	Unit Price	Quantity	Order processing time
City Cyclists	12/02/2010	12/10/2010	1	$41.90	1	8
Deals on Wheels	12/02/2010	12/02/2010	1,002	$33.90	3	0

Figure 20-31 Parameter range field printed on the report

Printing Multi Value Parameter Fields Using The Join Function

If you drag a multi value parameter field to a report, the only value that will print will be the first one. All of the values that are selected in a multi value parameter field are stored in one field and are separated by a comma in the array. The **JOIN** function will print all of the values in the array.

The formula below is used to print all of the values in a multiple value parameter field. Replace the {?ShipVia} field with the name of the multi value parameter field that you want to print.

"Shipping Methods Selected: " + Join ({?ShipVia}, ", ")

Exercise 20.18: Print Multi Value Parameter Fields

1. Save the E20.6 report as E20.18 Print multi value parameter fields.

2. Create a formula field called Print Regions. Type the formula shown below and save the formula.

   "Regions Selected: " + Join ({?Region}, " , ")

3. Add the Print Regions formula field to the top of the page header section. Make the field longer, then save the changes.

4. Preview the report. Select two regions from the list, then type in other regions. The report should look similar to the one shown in Figure 20-32. You will have different data on the report.

Regions Selected: CA , WI , TX , FL			
Customer Name	Address1	Region	Country
Sporting Wheels Inc.	480 Grant Way	CA	USA
Rockshocks for Jocks	1984 Sydney Street	TX	USA
Trail Blazer's Place	6938 Beach Street	WI	USA

Figure 20-32 Multi value parameter field printed on the report

Deleting Parameter Fields From A Report

You may need to delete a parameter field from a report. If you do, follow the steps below.

1. Right-click on the parameter field in the Field Explorer that you want to delete and select **DELETE**.

   You will see the message shown in Figure 20-33. This message is letting you know that once you delete the field it cannot be undone.

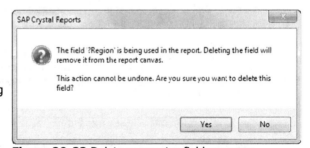

Figure 20-33 Delete parameter field message

2. Click Yes.

   You may see the message shown in Figure 20-34.

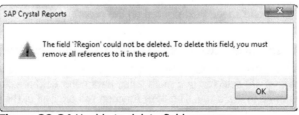

Figure 20-34 Unable to delete field message

This message is letting you know that the parameter field can't be deleted because it is being used in the report. Before you can delete a parameter field, you have to delete it from the places that it is being used in the report. In this example, it is being used on the Select Expert. If it was being used on the report to display the criteria that was used to run the report, you would have to delete it from there. The parameter field could also be used in a formula.

3. Click OK, then delete the parameter field from all of the places that it is being used in the report. Once you do that, repeat step 1 above and the parameter field will be deleted, then save the changes.

 If you close the report without saving the changes, then reopen the report, the parameter field will still be in the report.

Customizing The Enter Values Dialog Box

Attributes of the Enter Values dialog box can be modified. You need to have some web design experience to modify the Enter Values dialog box, in particular, HTML (Hypertext Markup Language) and CSS (Cascading Style Sheets). This is beyond the scope of this book, but I wanted to let you know that the dialog box can be modified.

The file that you would modify is promptengine_default.css. This file is in the folder listed below if you selected the default installation path when you installed Crystal Reports.

C:\Program Files(x86)\SAP Business Objects\Crystal Report 2011\crystalreportviewers\prompting\ css\

If you plan to modify this dialog box, keep in mind that any changes that you make will be applied to all Enter Values dialog boxes that point to the CSS file that you modify, not just one report. You should make a copy of this file before making any changes to it. Some of the features that you can customize are listed in Table 20-2.

Enter Values Dialog Box Changes	
Font	Background color
Font size	Prompt text box
Font color	Prompt button
Border	Size of text in a drop-down list

Table 20-2 Some of the Enter Values dialog box options that can be customized

CROSS-TAB REPORTS

 In this chapter you will learn how to create cross-tab reports, use the Cross-Tab wizard, use the Cross-Tab Expert and create charts from cross-tab data.

Overview

The cross-tab report takes the Select Expert one step further because it allows you to summarize the data that is in the detail section of a report and display it in a grid, which looks like a spreadsheet. This compact way of displaying data is possible because the data is grouped on two axes. The data is summarized horizontally and vertically. Cross-Tab reports are often used for comparison analysis. Examples of cross-tab reports are:

① Sales by sales rep by year.

② Sales by region.

③ Summarizing how many orders by year and by zip code, each sales rep has.

④ Sales of a specific product by sales rep, by month.

⑤ Summarizing how many customers by region purchased certain products by month or by year.

Cross-Tab reports often give new report designers difficulty. I suspect that this is because this type of report requires one to think in dimensions. Like spreadsheets, cross-tab reports have rows and columns. Each cell in a spreadsheet contains one piece of data. In a cross-tab object, the cell contains one piece of summary data (count, sum, average etc.) that is the equivalent of the sub totals that are usually in group footer sections of the report.

Cross-tab objects can be placed in a report or group section. If placed in a report section, it will summarize data for the entire report. If placed in a group section, it will summarize data for the records in the group.

Behind the scenes, cross-tab reports take the detail records that you are use to seeing, as well as, the groups and summarizes the detail data and places the result in a cell. Hopefully the following scenario will make the concept of cross-tab reports easier to understand.

Going From Standard Reports To Cross-Tab Reports

This scenario will use the first cross-tab example mentioned above; Sales by sales rep by year. The goal of this cross-tab report from a standard report perspective is to show sales for a year by sales rep.

The report shown in Figure 21-1 is a basic list report that sorts the sales, by sales rep and by year.

Sales By Rep By Year

Last Name	First Name	Order Date	Order Amount	Customer Name
Davolio	Nancy	02/19/2010	$789.51	Belgium Bike Co.
Davolio	Nancy	02/19/2010	$58.00	Spokes for Folks
Davolio	Nancy	02/26/2010	$68.90	Mountain Madmen Bicycles
Davolio	Nancy	02/27/2010	$1,529.70	Cycle City Rome
Davolio	Nancy	02/27/2010	$1,079.70	Mountain Madmen Bicycles
Davolio	Nancy	02/27/2010	$2,698.53	Pedals Inc.
Davolio	Nancy	12/02/2010	$41.90	City Cyclists

Last Name	First Name	Order Date	Order Amount	Customer Name
Suyama	Michael	02/06/2012	$5,879.70	Biking's It Industries
Suyama	Michael	02/08/2012	$863.74	Alley Cat Cycles
Suyama	Michael	02/09/2012	$5,219.55	Spokes
Suyama	Michael	02/10/2012	$659.70	Psycho-Cycle
Suyama	Michael	02/11/2012	$32.21	Whistler Rentals

Figure 21-1 Basic sorted report of sales by sales rep by year

The report shown above in Figure 21-1 contains all of the data one would need to determine sales by sales rep, by year. Because there aren't any totals for the groups, it would take a while to manually do the math, especially if there were hundreds of sales reps. Yes, I know what you are thinking, modify the report to group the data by sales rep, then by year. Figure 21-2 shows that report.

Can you tell me how many saddles Robert King sold in total? Or can you tell me who had the lowest number of sales in 2011? Okay, I'll wait while you open the report shown in Figure 21-2 and get a calculator to add up the totals for the sales reps. [See the Chapter 21 Cross-tab grouped report] I can wait. I have patience <smile>.

Like the report shown above in Figure 21-1, the report in Figure 21-2 has all of the information that you need to answer these questions.

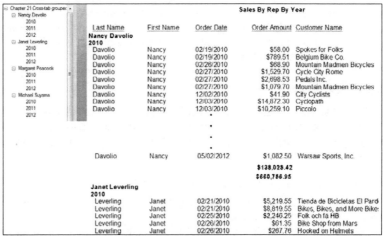

Figure 21-2 Data grouped by sales rep by year

The problem is that the data is spread out over several pages in the report which makes it difficult for comparison analysis. As you will see after completing Exercise 21.1, this same data in a cross-tab report will be in an easy to read format. With a cross-tab report you can quickly answer questions like how many sales Robert King had for three products and which sales rep had the lowest number of sales in 2011.

How To Create This Cross-Tab

Yes, I hear you grumbling and saying, "Great, I now see the advantages of creating a cross-tab report, but how do I get the data shown earlier in Figures 21-1 and 21-2 into cross-tab format?" Okay, here goes:

① Usually, the field down the left side of a cross-tab (that creates the rows) is the data element that there are more occurrences of. In this example, there are more sales reps than years. You can put the sales reps across the top of the cross-tab and still get the same results.

② The field that goes across the top (that creates the columns) represents the data element that there are less occurrences of.

③ The cells in the middle of the cross-tab are the sum (in this example, a count) of orders that the sales rep had for the year. This is the equivalent to grouping and sorting data.

④ The totals at the bottom of the cross-tab report display how many sales are for each year and a grand total number of sales for the entire report in the lower right corner of the cross-tab. These totals are automatically calculated in a cross-tab report.

⑤ I have saved the best for last; the placement of the fields on the Cross-Tab screen. The fields for the row and column were answered above. That leaves the field for the cells in the middle of the cross-tab report. Recall the original report criteria: Sales by sales rep, by year. You have already determined that the sales rep field (Employee Name field in the table), is what will be used for the rows. You have also determined that the Order Date will be used for the columns. The only field left is the sales (the orders). This is what goes in the Summary Fields section on the Cross-Tab screen. In this example, the cells represent a count of orders. The default calculation is Sum. You would change that to **DISTINCT COUNT** for the Order ID field.

Cross-Tab Wizard

The Cross-Tab wizard has two of the screens that the Cross-Tab Expert has. The screens on the wizard have less functionality. The Cross-Tab wizard also has many of the same screens as the Standard report wizard. The major differences between the Standard and Cross-Tab wizards are explained below.

① There are no detail records in a cross-tab report.
② The functionality of the wizard grouping and summary screens are combined on one Cross-Tab wizard screen.
③ Cross-Tab objects are most often placed in the report header or footer section, but they can be placed in other sections.

Cross-Tab Screen

Now that you have a foundation of cross-tab reports, the options on the Cross-Tab and Grid Style wizard screens will hopefully make sense. Figure 21-3 shows the Cross-Tab screen. Figure 21-4 shows the Grid Style screen.

The **AVAILABLE FIELDS** list is used to select the fields that are needed to create the report.

The **ROWS** section is used to select the fields that will be displayed down the left side of the report.

The **COLUMNS** section is used to select the fields that will be displayed across the top of the report.

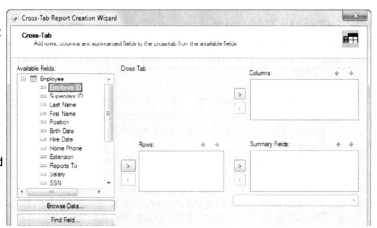

Figure 21-3 Cross-Tab screen

The **SUMMARY FIELDS** section is used to select the fields that will have the calculation (sum, count, average etc.). At least one field is required in the rows, columns and summary fields sections to create a cross-tab report.

 The actual data in text fields cannot be printed in the cells of a cross-tab without selecting a summary type that works with a text field like count, distinct count, minimum or maximum.

Grid Style Screen

The Grid Style screen is used to select the formatting for the cross-tab, which is similar to templates. Each style has formatting for fonts, totals and more.

Like other reports, you can format a cross-tab report manually.

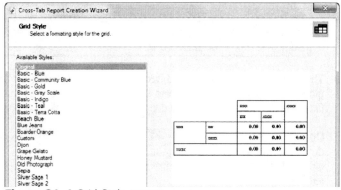

Figure 21-4 Grid Style screen

Exercise 21.1: Create A Cross-Tab Product Report

In this exercise you will create a cross-tab report that shows the number of sales for three classes of products: gloves, kids and saddles by sales rep.

1. Click on the Cross-tab report wizard link on the Start Page tab.

2. Add the Employee, Orders, Orders Detail, Product and Product Type tables, then click Next. Click Next on the Link screen.

3. Click on the Last Name field in the Employee table, then click the right arrow button next to the **ROWS** section.

4. Add the Product Type Name field in the Product Type table to the **COLUMNS** section.

 You can click on the field in the Available Fields list and drag it to the section on the Cross-Tab screen that you need.

5. Add the Quantity field in the Orders Detail table to the **SUMMARY FIELDS** section.

6. Select **COUNT** from the drop-down list under the Summary Fields section.

    The Cross-Tab screen should have the options selected that are shown in Figure 21-5.

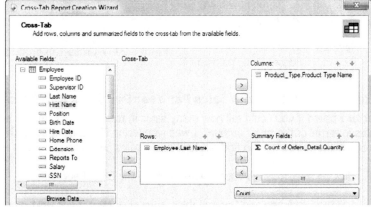

Figure 21-5 Cross-Tab screen options

7. Click Next, then select the **NO CHART** option, if it is not already selected and click Next.

 The reason that you added the Orders table and did not use any fields from the table is because it is the "link" between the Orders Detail table and the Employee table to get the Employee Name for each order.

8. This report needs to be filtered because you only want totals for three classes of products: gloves, kids and saddles. Add the Product Type Name field from the Product Type table to the Filter Fields list, then open the drop-down list and select **IS ONE OF**.

9. Open the next drop-down list and select gloves, kids and saddles.

   Figure 21-6 shows the options that should be selected.

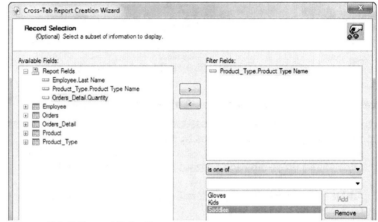

Figure 21-6 Record Selection options

10. Click Next. Click on the **ORIGINAL** grid style if it is not already selected, as shown earlier in Figure 21-4.

    Click Finish.

    The report should look like the one shown in Figure 21-7.

    Now can you tell me how many saddles Robert King sold in total?

    Save the report as E21.1 Cross-Tab product.

	Gloves	Kids	Saddles	Total
Davolio	85	18	49	152
Dodsworth	101	19	58	178
King	97	23	58	178
Leverling	84	25	56	165
Peacock	105	20	59	184
Suyama	84	25	56	165
Total	556	130	336	1,022

Figure 21-7 Cross-Tab product report

Exercise 21.2: Create A Sales Per Year Per Sales Rep Cross-Tab Report

Earlier I asked if you could tell how many sales in total Robert King had and who had the lowest total sales in terms of the order amount. I was wondering if you came up with the answer yet? If not, this exercise shows you how to find out how many sales per year each sales rep had.

1. Click on the Cross-tab report wizard link on the Start Page tab.

2. Add the Employee and Orders tables, then click Next. Click Next on the Link screen.

3. Click on the Last Name field in the Employee table, then click the right arrow button next to the **ROWS** section. Add the Order Date field to the **COLUMNS** section.

4. Open the drop-down list under the Columns section and select **FOR EACH YEAR**. This will create a column for each year that there are orders in the Orders table.

5. Add the Order Amount field to the Summary Fields section. Figure 21-8 shows the options that should be selected. This cross-tab report does not need to select (filter) any records.

Click Finish.

The report may look like the one shown in Figure 21-9.

Leave the report open to complete the next part of the exercise.

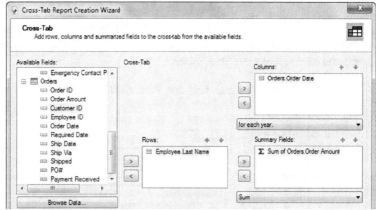

Figure 21-8 Cross-Tab screen options

 If the Orders table had 10 years worth of data and you only wanted to show some of the years on the report, you would select the Order Date field on the Record Selection screen and enter the date range for the years that you wanted to display on the report.

	2010	2011	2012	Total
Davolio	$71,862.70	##########	##########	##########
Dodsworth	$29,049.94	##########	##########	##########
King	$21,093.75	##########	##########	##########
Leverling	$44,121.64	##########	##########	##########
Peacock	$38,458.39	##########	##########	##########
Suyama	$54,804.22	##########	##########	##########
Total	##########	##########	##########	##########

Figure 21-9 Sales by year cross-tab report

6. If the column totals are on the top and to the left, right-click on the border of the cross-tab object and select Cross-Tab Expert. On the Customize Style tab, clear the **COLUMN TOTALS ON TOP** and **ROW TOTALS ON LEFT** options, then click OK.

Modify The Cross-Tab Report

As you can see, the grid is too small for the sales total amounts. This part of the exercise shows you how to modify the cross-tab report.

When you see fields cut off like they are in Figure 21-9 above, you should look at the **ALLOW FIELD CLIPPING** option on the Number tab on the Custom Style dialog box to make sure that the option is not checked. [See Chapter 7, Figure 7-24] If checked, the option causes the first digits in the field to be cut off until the remaining digits in the field can be displayed.

1. On the design tab, select all four of the Order Amount fields shown in Figure 21-10, then make the fields wider by dragging the right side border to the right.

   The border around the Cross-Tab will expand as you make the fields wider.

	Column #1	Total
Row #1 Name	rder Amount	rder Amount
Total	rder Amount	rder Amount

Figure 21-10 Order Amount fields selected

2. Center the Column #1 Name field and Total field headings.

3. The report should look like the one shown in Figure 21-11.

   Save the report as E21.2 Sales per year per sales rep cross-tab.

   Now you should be able to figure out who had the lowest sales amount each year.

	2010	2011	2012	Total
Davolio	$71,862.70	$450,865.83	$138,028.42	$660,756.95
Dodsworth	$29,049.94	$513,545.52	$140,253.75	$682,849.21
King	$21,093.75	$512,406.60	$215,255.59	$748,755.94
Leverling	$44,121.64	$447,235.19	$157,745.16	$649,101.99
Peacock	$38,458.39	$446,150.56	$147,190.82	$631,799.77
Suyama	$54,804.22	$496,881.48	$158,715.78	$710,401.48
Total	$259,390.64	$2,867,085.18	$957,189.52	$4,083,665.34

Figure 21-11 Sales Per Year Per Sales Rep Cross-Tab report

Exercise 21.3: Create Charts From Cross-Tab Data

Charts that are created from cross-tab data are often easier to create because the data has already been summarized. In this exercise you will create three charts and save them in the same report. Often, cross-tab data is stored in the report header. I find it easier to create additional report header sections and place each chart in its own section. This keeps the charts from overlapping when the report is viewed or printed. The Cross-Tab Data tab layout options on the Chart Expert were covered in Chapter 17.

Add More Report Header Sections

1. Save the E21.1 report as E21.3 Cross-Tab data charts.

2. Open the Section Expert and add three more report header sections.

Create The Quantity Sold By Product Type Chart

1. Add a chart object to the report header b section, then select the Side by side bar chart type, the Horizontal position and the Use depth effect options.

2. Make sure that the On Change Of option on the Cross-Tab layout screen has the Product Type Name field selected. The Subdivided By field should be set to None and the Show drop-down list should have the Quantity field selected.

3. Check the Show value option on the Options tab.

4. Change the Title to Qty Sold By Product Type.

Add the Footnote Report Header B.

Change the Group title to Product Type.

Change the Data title to Qty Sold.

Save the changes.

The chart should look like the one shown in Figure 21-12.

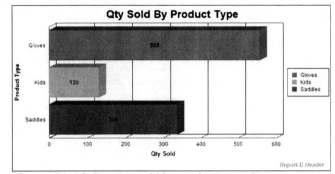

Figure 21-12 Quantity sold by product type chart (Report Header B)

Create The Quantity Sold By Product Type By Sales Rep Chart

The chart that you just created provides a high level overview of how many of each product type was sold. The numbers shown across the bottom of the cross-tab represent the totals. The chart that you will create in this part of the exercise will display how many of each product type was sold by each sales rep.

1. Add a chart object to the report header c section, then select the Stacked bar chart type, the Horizontal position and the Use depth effect options.

2. Select the Employee Last Name field from the Subdivided By drop-down list on the Cross-Tab data layout screen.

3. Add a major gridline to the Group axis option.

4. Check the Show value option on the Options tab.

5. Change the Title to Quantity Sold By Product Type By Sales Rep.
Add the Footnote Report Header C.
Change the Group title to Product Type.
Change the Data title to Qty Sold.
Save the changes. The chart should look like the one shown in Figure 21-13.

What you will notice is that each block on the chart is a running total, meaning that sales rep Dodsworth did not have 186 glove sales.

Instead, the sales rep sold the difference between 186 and 85 gloves.

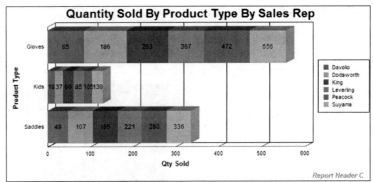

Figure 21-13 Quantity sold by product type by sales rep chart (Report Header C)

Create The Percent Of Quantity Sold Chart

The chart that you will create in this part of the exercise will display the total quantity of products each sales rep sold and what percent of the total product quantity their sales represent.

1. Add a chart object to the report header d section, then select the Pie chart type and the Use depth effect option.

2. Add the Employee Last Name field to the first list box on the Advanced layout screen. Add the Quantity field to the Show value(s) list, then change the summary type to Count.

3. Check the Show label and Show value options, then change the Legend layout option to Percentage. Explode the largest slice of the pie.

4. Change the Title to `Percent Of Qty Sold.`

   Add the Subtitle `The #'s on the chart represent the qty sold.`

   Add the Footnote `Report Header D.`

   Save the changes. The chart is on page 2 and should look like the one shown in Figure 21-14.

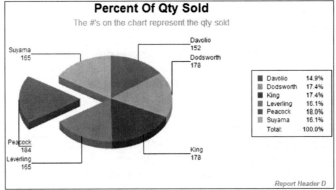

Figure 21-14 Percent of quantity sold chart (Report Header D)

Cross-Tab Expert

Earlier in this chapter you learned how to create a cross-tab report using a wizard. Now you will learn more about cross-tab reports by learning how to use the Cross-Tab Expert. Cross-Tab reports are often used to summarize large amounts of data in columnar format, in a relatively small amount of space. Cross-Tab reports do not have to be the only object on the report. You can add a cross-tab object to a report that has standard data. In addition to using the Cross-Tab wizard, there are three ways to add a Cross-Tab object to a report, as explained below.

① Right-click on a blank space on the report and select Insert Cross-Tab, then click in the report section that you want to place the cross-tab in.
② Click the Insert Cross-Tab button on the Insert Tools toolbar.
③ Insert ⇒ Cross-Tab.

The Cross-Tab Expert has three tabs: Cross-Tab, Style and Customize Style. Many of the options on the first two tabs are the same options that are on the Cross-Tab wizard.

Figure 21-15 shows the Cross-Tab tab.
Table 21-1 explains the buttons on the Cross-Tab tab.
Figure 21-18 shows the Style tab.
Figure 21-19 shows the Customize Style tab.
Tables 21-2 to 21-4 explain the options on the Customize Style tab.

Cross-Tab Tab

The options shown in Figure 21-15 are used to select the fields that will be used to create the cross-tab.

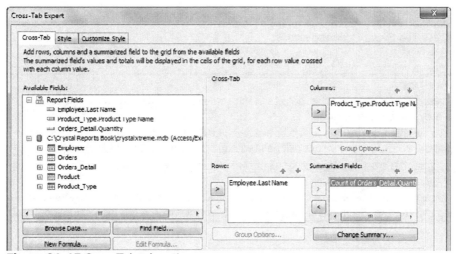

Figure 21-15 Cross-Tab tab options

Button	Opens The . . .
New Formula	Formula Workshop to create a formula for the cross-tab report. This means that you do not have to close the Cross-Tab Expert, if you need to create a formula for the Cross-Tab report.
Edit Formula	Formula Workshop to edit an existing formula. You can edit a formula that has been added to the cross-tab or a formula that is listed in the Available Fields list.
Group Options	Dialog box shown in Figure 21-16. It is similar to the Insert Group dialog box. After you click on a field in the Rows or Columns section, this button will be enabled, which will allow you to change the group options for the field.

Table 21-1 Buttons on the Cross-Tab tab explained

Button	Opens The . . .
Change Summary	Dialog box shown in Figure 21-17. It works the same way that the Insert Summary dialog box works and is used to change the summary type that was selected when the field was added to the Summarized Fields section. By default, numeric fields have the SUM summary type.

Table 21-1 Buttons on the Cross-Tab tab explained (Continued)

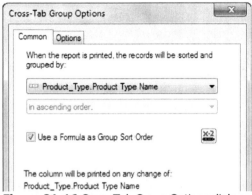

Figure 21-16 Cross-Tab Group Options dialog box

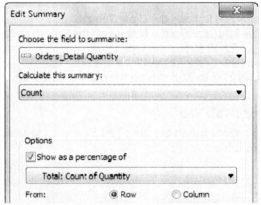

Figure 21-17 Edit Summary dialog box

 Cross-Tab Tips

① It is best not to place any other objects in the same report section as the cross-tab because they can be overwritten.

② When more than one field is added to the rows, columns or summarized fields sections on the Cross-Tab Expert, the values will be stacked in the same cell in the cross-tab.

③ If you want the cross-tab to capture all of the data in the report, place the Cross-tab object in the report header section.

④ It is better to position fields so that there are more rows than columns. Doing this will help keep the cross-tab from being forced to print horizontally on more than one page.

Style Tab

The options shown in Figure 21-18 are the templates that can be used to format the entire cross-tab object at one time.

These are the same styles that are on the Cross-Tab wizard.

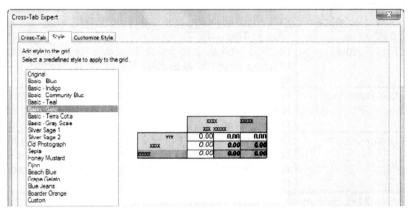

Figure 21-18 Style tab options

Customize Style Tab

The options shown in Figure 21-19 are used to apply formatting to a specific section of the cross-tab like a row or to the entire cross-tab object. Each field in the Rows and Columns sections represent a group. The options in the Grid Options section are applied to the entire cross-tab. The options in the Group Options section can be applied to each field.

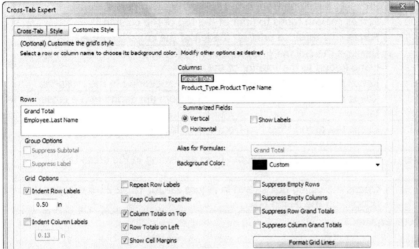

Figure 21-19 Customize Style tab options

Option	Description
Vertical/Horizontal	These options are used to select how the summarized fields will be displayed. There has to be at least two summarized fields to select one of these options. The **VERTICAL** option stacks the summarized fields in the same cell. You will see how this works later in this chapter. The **HORIZONTAL** option places the summarized fields side by side.
Show Labels	This option will display the summarized field name in the row or column header.

Table 21-2 Summarized Fields options explained

Option	Description
Suppress Subtotal	This option is only available if there are two or more fields in the Rows section or two or more fields in the Columns section. This option cannot be used on grand total fields. This option will suppress the subtotal for the row or column that is selected.
Suppress Label	This option is only available if the Suppress Subtotal option is checked. This option will suppress the Group By fields label.
Alias for Formulas	Is used to enter a different name for the field that is used on the cross-tab. The name entered in this field can be used in conditional formatting formulas instead of the field name in the table.
Background Color	This drop-down list box is used to select a background color for the row or column of data.

Table 21-3 Group Options explained

Option	Description
Indent Row Labels	Is used to select how much the row labels will be indented.
Indent Column Labels	Is used to select how much the column labels will be indented.
Repeat Row Labels	This option is only available if the Keep Columns together option is checked. This option will force the row labels to be repeated on other pages when the width of the cross-tab requires more than one page.
Keep Columns Together	Prevents a column from being split across two pages.
Column Totals on Top	Forces column totals to print at the top of the column.
Row Totals on Left	Forces row totals to print on the left of the cross-tab object.
Show Cell Margins	Displays the cell margins, which gives the appearance of white space being added to the interior of the cells.
Suppress Empty Rows	Keeps rows that do not have data from appearing in the cross-tab.
Suppress Empty Columns	Keeps columns that do not have data from appearing in the cross-tab.
Suppress Row Grand Totals	Keeps the grand total row from appearing in the cross-tab.
Suppress Column Grand Totals	Keeps the grand total column from appearing in the cross-tab.
Format Grid Lines button	Opens the dialog box shown in Figure 21-20. Table 21-5 explains the options on the dialog box.

Table 21-4 Grid Options explained

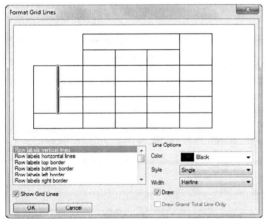

Figure 21-20 Format Grid Lines dialog box

Option	Description
Grid Line	Selects the grid line in the list box that you want to modify. The grid lines that you select will be highlighted in the grid at the top of the dialog box.
Show Grid Lines	Displays or hides the grid lines.
Color	Is used to select a color for the grid lines.
Style	Is used to select a style for the grid lines.
Width	Is used to select a width for the grid lines.
Draw	Is used to select a specific grid line to hide.
Draw Grand Total Line Only	If checked, this option will only display and print grid lines on grand total rows or columns.

Table 21-5 Format Grid Lines dialog box options explained

Cross-Tab Shortcut Menu

Like many features in Crystal Reports, the cross-tab object has its own shortcut menu, as shown in Figure 21-21.

The majority of the options were already covered in this chapter. The remaining options on the shortcut menu are explained in Table 21-6.

Figure 21-21 Cross-Tab object shortcut menu

Option	Description
Summarized Field Labels	The options shown in Figure 21-22 are used to select how the summary field labels are displayed.
Advanced Calculations	The options shown in Figure 21-23 are used to add more calculations to the cross-tab. Some of the calculations are to show trends in data and the difference between two groups.
Pivot Cross-Tab	[See Chapter 2, Table 2-11]

Table 21-6 Cross-Tab object shortcut menu options explained

The **SUMMARIZE HORIZONTALLY** option is used to display multiple summarized fields vertically in the same cell.

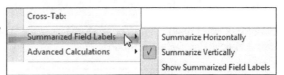

The **SUMMARIZE VERTICALLY** option is used to display multiple summarized fields horizontally in the same cell.

Figure 21-22 Summarized Field Labels options

The **SHOW SUMMARIZED FIELD LABELS** option is used to display the names of multiple summarized fields.

The **CALCULATED MEMBER** option opens the dialog box shown in Figure 21-24.

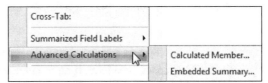

The **EMBEDDED SUMMARY** option is covered later in this chapter.

Figure 21-23 Advanced Calculations options

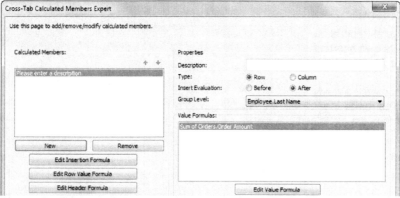

Figure 21-24 Cross-Tab Calculated Members Expert dialog box

Formatting Formulas

You can create conditional formatting formulas in a cross-tab using the Format Editor, similar to how conditional formatting formulas are created for other fields. In addition to being able to use the **CURRENTFIELDVALUE** and **DEFAULTATTRIBUTE** functions, cross-tabs can also use the **GRIDROWCOLUMNVALUE** function. This function is used to create a formula that depends on the value in a row that is related to the current cell. An advantage to using this function is that you can use the Alias field name instead of the real field name. The examples below demonstrate how these functions can be used in a cross-tab or OLAP grid.

Example #1 The formula below will set the current field (cell) to yellow if the value is greater than or equal to 25.

If CurrentFieldValue >= 25 Then crYellow Else DefaultAttribute

Example #2 The formula below will set the current field (cell) to yellow if the value is greater than or equal to 100 and the Product Name is "Gloves".

If GridRowColumnValue {Product.Product Name} = "Gloves" and CurrentFieldValue >= 100 Then crYellow Else DefaultAttribute

 You can use the **HIGHLIGHTING EXPERT** to format data fields in a cross-tab.

Exercise 21.4: Use The Cross-Tab Expert

In this exercise you will recreate the cross-tab report that you created earlier in Exercise 21.1. You will use the Cross-Tab Expert instead of the Cross-Tab wizard to create this report. You will enhance the report by completing the following tasks:

① Indenting the row labels.
② Modifying the grid lines.
③ Applying conditional formatting to change the background of cells that meet a specific condition.
④ Create a formula to calculate the total dollar amount of sales per product, per sales rep.

Create The Product Type Selection Criteria

The Cross-Tab wizard has a Record Selection screen that is used to create selection criteria. If you use the Cross-Tab Expert, you have different options. You can create a formula or create the selection criteria using the Select Expert.

1. Open a new report, then add the following tables to the report: Employee, Orders, Orders Detail, Product and Product Type.

2. Click Next to make sure that the tables are linked. If they are not linked, click the Link button, then click Finish. If they are linked, click Finish.

3. Open the Select Expert. Select the Product Type Name field in the Product Type table, then click OK. Select the "Is one of" operator, then add the gloves, kids and saddles options and click OK.

Create The Cross-Tab

1. Add a cross-tab object to the report header, then right-click on the border of the cross-tab object and select Cross-Tab Expert.

2. Move the Last Name field in the Employee table to the **ROWS** section.

3. Move the Product Type Name field in the Product Type table to the **COLUMNS** section.

4. Move the Quantity field in the Orders Detail table to the **SUMMARIZED FIELDS** section. Click the **CHANGE SUMMARY** button and change the summary type to Count, then click OK.

Customize The Cross-Tab

The Customize Style tab has several options that can be used to change the appearance of the cross-tab.

1. On the Customize Style tab, clear the **COLUMN TOTALS ON TOP** and **ROW TOTALS ON LEFT** options.

2. Check the Indent Row Labels option, then type .25 in the box below it.

3. Click the Format Grid Lines button. Select the **COLUMN LABEL BOTTOM BORDER** option in the list on the left, then select Dashed from the Style drop-down list. Click OK to close the Format Grid Lines dialog box, then click OK to close the Cross-Tab Expert.

4. Save the report as E21.4 Use the Cross-Tab Expert.

The report should look like the one shown in Figure 21-25.

Leave the report open to complete the next part of the exercise.

	Gloves	Kids	Saddles	Total
Davolio	85	18	49	152
Dodsworth	101	19	58	178
King	97	23	58	178
Leverling	84	25	56	165
Peacock	105	20	59	184
Suyama	84	25	56	165
Total	556	130	336	1,022

Figure 21-25 Use the Cross-Tab Expert report

Add Another Row Of Data To The Cross-Tab

In this part of the exercise you will create a formula that will calculate the total of each product that each sales rep sold.

1. Open the Cross-Tab Expert, then click the New Formula button.

2. Type Line Item as the formula name, then type the formula shown below.
    {Orders_Detail.Unit Price} * {Orders_Detail.Quantity}

3. Save the formula, then click on the formula field in the Available Fields list on the Cross-Tab Expert and add it to the Summarized Fields section.

    Click OK and save the changes.

    The cross-tab should look like the one shown in Figure 21-26.

	Gloves	Kids	Saddles	Total
Davolio	85 $2,735.59	18 $11,498.14	49 $1,929.29	152 $16,163.02
Dodsworth	101 $3,404.30	19 $11,625.66	58 $2,492.96	178 $17,522.92
King	97 $2,933.57	23 $15,069.70	58 $2,348.04	178 $20,351.31
Leverling	84 $2,668.06	25 $13,833.10	56 $2,235.63	165 $18,736.79
Peacock	105 $3,174.88	20 $10,830.79	59 $2,647.96	184 $16,653.63
Suyama	84 $2,486.31	25 $13,532.76	56 $2,026.98	165 $18,046.05
Total	556 $17,402.71	130 $76,390.15	336 $13,680.86	1,022 $107,473.72

Figure 21-26 Second row of data added to the cross-tab

If you are wondering why sales reps have the same quantity sold of a product but have different totals for the product, like the sales reps Leverling and Suyama do in the gloves column, it is because the products listed are categories of products, meaning that there are different types of gloves and each type of glove has a different price. I thought the same thing at first, that there was something wrong with the Line Item formula, so I created a detail report and looked at the raw data for the gloves and saw that there are different priced gloves. When you see data that does not look right or somehow catches your attention, you should take the time to look at the raw data to see if you can find out why the data looks the way that it does.

Creating And Using Embedded Summaries

In the previous exercise you created two formulas and placed both of them in the same cell using the Cross-Tab Expert. If you need to add more than one formula to the same cell in the cross-tab and do not want to use the Cross-Tab Expert, you can use the dialog box shown in Figure 21-27.

The options on this dialog box are used to change the order of formulas in a cell, create new formulas that will be added to the cross-tab or edit existing formulas in a cross-tab.

Right-click on the Cross-Tab border ⇒ Advanced Calculations ⇒ Embedded Summary, will open the dialog box.

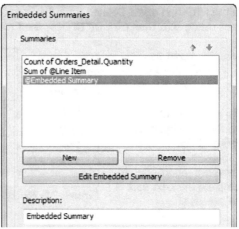

Figure 21-27 Embedded Summaries dialog box

Exercise 21.5: Add Percents To A Cross-Tab Report

In Exercise 21.2, the cross-tab shows yearly sales for each sales rep. In some cases it may be helpful to see what percent of sales each sales rep had. In Exercise 11.2 you learned how to create a percent calculation in a report that has groups. In this exercise you will learn how to add a percent calculation to a cross-tab report.

1. Save the E21.2 report as E21.5 Cross-Tab with percents.

2. Right-click on the border of the cross-tab and select Cross-Tab Expert.

3. On the Cross-Tab tab, add the Order Amount field to the Summarized Fields list, then click the Change Summary button.

4. On the Edit Summary dialog box, check the Show as a percentage of option. Select the Column option, as shown in Figure 21-28. The Row option will display the percent below the total sales amount in the cell.

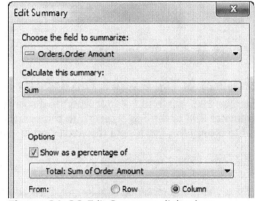

Figure 21-28 Edit Summary dialog box

5. Click OK to close the Edit Summary dialog box.

Add A Summary Label

The cross-tab would look better and be easier to understand if the percent field had a label.
The steps below show you how to add and customize a summary label.

1. On the Customize Style tab, select the Show Labels option, then click OK.

2. Select the first Order Amount label in the Row #1 and both Total row sections. Right-click and select Format Objects. Select the Suppress option on the Common tab on the Format Editor, then click OK.

3. Change the second order amount label in the Row # row to % of total.
   (**Hint:** Right-click on the label and select Edit Text.)

4. Save the changes, then preview the report. It should look like the one shown in Figure 21-29.

		2010	2011	2012	Total
Davolio		$71,862.70	$450,865.83	$138,028.42	$660,756.95
	% of total	10.88%	68.23%	20.89%	100.00%
Dodsworth		$29,049.94	$513,545.52	$140,253.75	$682,849.21
	% of total	4.25%	75.21%	20.54%	100.00%
King		$21,093.75	$512,406.60	$215,255.59	$748,755.94
	% of total	2.82%	68.43%	28.75%	100.00%
Leverling		$44,121.64	$447,235.19	$157,745.16	$649,101.99
	% of total	6.80%	68.90%	24.30%	100.00%
Peacock		$38,458.39	$446,150.56	$147,190.82	$631,799.77
	% of total	6.09%	70.62%	23.30%	100.00%
Suyama		$54,804.22	$496,881.48	$158,715.78	$710,401.48
	% of total	7.71%	69.94%	22.34%	100.00%
Total		$259,390.64	$2,867,085.18	$957,189.52	$4,083,665.34
		6.35%	70.21%	23.44%	100.00%

Figure 21-29 Cross-Tab report with percents

Exercise 21.6: Top N Cross-Tab Reports

In Exercise 12.5 you fixed a Top N report to display the correct data. In Exercise 20.12 you added a parameter field to the Top N report. In this exercise you will add a cross-tab grid to the E20.12 report to display the Top N data (for each day) in summary format.

1. Save the E20.12 report as `E21.6 Top N cross-tab`.

2. Make the group footer section longer, then add a cross-tab object to the section below the fields.

3. Open the Cross-Tab Expert. Add the Country field to the Rows list. Add the Order Date field to the Columns list.

4. Add the Order ID field to the Summarized Fields list, then click the Change Summary button. Select Distinct count from the second drop-down list.

5. Add the Order Amount field to the Summarized Fields list. You should have the options shown in Figure 21-30.

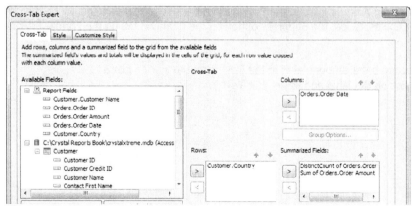

Figure 21-30 Cross-Tab tab options

6. Click on the Customize Style tab and make the following changes, then click OK.
    Clear the Column Totals on Top and Row Totals on Left options.
    Check the Suppress Row Grand Totals option.

Add Top N Functionality To The Cross-Tab

Adding Top N functionality to a cross-tab allows records to be used in the report, but not in a cross-tab.

1. Right-click on the border of the Cross-tab and select Group Sort Expert.

2. Open the Group Sort drop-down list and select Top N.

3. Click the Formula button. Add the Top N parameter field to the Formula Text section, as shown in Figure 21-31. Save and close the Formula Workshop.

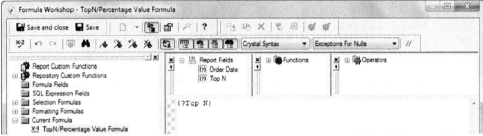

Figure 21-31 Top N formula

4. You should have the options selected that are shown in Figure 21-32.

    Click OK, then save the changes.

Figure 21-32 Cross-Tab Top N and Sort Expert dialog box

Test The Report

If you run the report with the following criteria, you will see the cross-tab shown in Figure 21-33 for the first order date. Date range 6/1/2011 to 6/30/2011, Top N value 12.

As you can see, the total order amount for the day matches the total on the cross-tab. The cross-tab displays the number of orders per country and the total dollar amount per country for each day.

6/20/2011		$49,011.39
	6/20/2011	
USA	7 $29,153.75	
China	6 $10,854.60	
Poland	2 $6,905.25	
Canada	3 $2,097.79	
Total	18 $49,011.39	

Figure 21-33 Top N Cross-Tab report

Exercise 21.7: Create Conditional Formatting In Cross-Tabs

Creating conditional formatting in cross-tabs is not that much different then creating conditional formatting in other types of reports. In this exercise you will create conditional formatting on the quantity cells in the gloves column to change the background color to yellow if the quantity is greater than or equal to 100. It would be helpful to quickly be able to see which sales reps sold the most of this particular product.

1. Save the E21.4 report as E21.7 Conditional formatting cross-tab.

2. In the first column of the cross-tab, right-click on the detail Quantity field and select Format Field.

3. On the Border tab, click the Formula button across from the Background option.

4. Type the formula shown below, then click the Save and close button.

    ```
    If GridRowColumnValue("Product_Type.Product Type Name") =
    "Gloves" and CurrentFieldValue >= 100 Then crYellow Else
    DefaultAttribute
    ```

5. Click OK and save the changes. Preview the report. The gloves quantity for two sales reps should have a yellow background.

Cross-Tab Printing Issues

Cross-Tab objects can have printing issues, in particular cross-tab objects that require more than one page to print horizontally. The Cross-Tab Expert has the Repeat Row Labels and Keep Columns Together options that you can use to resolve some printing issues. If there are horizontal printing issues, the options discussed below can help resolve them.

① **HORIZONTAL PAGE NUMBER** This special field counts the number of horizontal pages in a report. This field will not work if the cross-tab is in a section of the report that will not print page footers.

② **REPEAT HORIZONTAL PAGES** This option is on the Common tab on the Format Editor dialog box. It will force objects in the page header or page footer section to print on every horizontal page.

③ **RELATIVE POSITIONS** This option is on the Common tab on the Section Expert. Use it to control an object that is to the right of a cross-tab object. This option will cause the object next to the cross-tab to stay in the same relative position, regardless of how much the cross-tab grows.

ADDITIONAL CRYSTAL REPORTS FUNCTIONALITY

Overview

Believe it or not, this book only covers a little more than half of the functionality that Crystal Reports has to offer report designers. You may be thinking that you have learned enough in the first 21 chapters to create all of the reports that you need.

Some of the topics covered in this chapter, like the drill-down report builds on what you have already learned in previous chapters. Other topics are being introduced for the first time. Many of the reports that you learn how to create in this chapter are known as or referred to as non standard report types.

In this chapter you will learn how to:

☑ Create a barcode
☑ Add a Sort Control to a report
☑ Create Running Totals
☑ Create an Hierarchical Group report
☑ Use the Group Sort Expert
☑ Add a watermark to a report

Barcodes

Crystal Reports supports basic barcode creation and printing. Crystal Reports comes with the Code 39 barcode font, which has the two formats in the column on the left in Figure 22-1. This font does not print UPC or ISBN barcodes. You can buy other fonts from barcode vendors. [Click the Vendor button shown in Figure 22-1 to see what one vendor offers] To access the barcode utility, follow the steps below.

1. Open the report that has the field that you want to use to create the barcode from.

2. Right-click on the field that has the data that you want converted to a barcode and select **CHANGE TO BARCODE**.

    Only string and number fields can be converted to a barcode.

    You will see the dialog box shown in Figure 22-1.

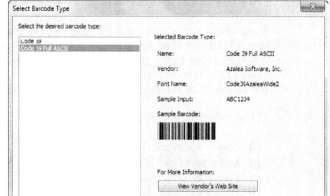

Figure 22-1 Select Barcode Type dialog box

3. Select the type of barcode that you want and click OK. The data in the field will be changed to a barcode, as shown in Figure 22-2.

Figure 22-2 Product ID field changed to a barcode

Formatting A Barcode
Just like you can format other objects on a report, barcodes can also be formatted. The steps below show you how to format a barcode.

1. Right-click on the barcode field that you want to format and select Format Field.
2. On the Format Editor, select the options needed to format the barcode field.

Sort Controls

This control will allow the person running the report to be able to sort the report on their own. In Chapter 10 you learned how to sort the records. The Sort control will handle a lot of the users requirements of needing a report sorted more than one way. You could create parameter fields that will allow the user to select a sort order, which you learned how to do in Exercise 20.14. The advantage of this control is that the data does not have to be refreshed.

Sort Control Tips
Keep the following in mind when using Sort Controls.
① They cannot be used in cross-tab objects, running total or summary fields, OLAP grids or subreports.
② They will sort all of the records.
③ They will automatically close any drill-down tabs that are open.

Exercise 22.1: Using Sort Controls

In this exercise you will add two sort controls to a report that will allow the user to sort the report in more than one way. Sort controls can only be used on fields in the details section that are sorted or fields that are grouped on in the report. The reason that fields that are grouped can be used is because all groups are sorted by default.

1. Save the E5.1 report as `E22.1 Sort Control.`

2. Sort the report on the Region and Postal Code fields.

3. Insert ⇒ Sort Control.

   You will see the dialog box
   shown in Figure 22-3.

Figure 22-3 Sort Control dialog box

4. Select the Region field, then click OK.

5. The mouse pointer will change to a cross-hair. Draw a box over the Region heading, then click on a blank space on the report. Resize the text object so that it is smaller.

6. Right-click on the Postal Code heading and select Bind Sort Control. Select the Postal Code option, then resize the control.

7. Save the changes. The report should look like the one shown in Figure 22-4.

Customer Name	Address1	Region	Country	Postal Code
UAE Cycle	Post Box: 278	Abu Dhabi	United Arab Emirates	3453
Psycho-Cycle	8287 Scott Road	AL	USA	35818
The Great Bike Shop	1922 Beach Crescent	AL	USA	35857

Figure 22-4 Sort controls added to the report

8. Click on the down arrow for the Region field. The report should be sorted in descending order by region. Click on the up arrow on the Postal Code field. The report should be sorted in ascending order by Postal Code.

It is not a requirement that the control be placed on a field heading. You can place the control any place on the report. The reason that I place them there is so that there are no extra fields on the report when it is printed.

If you placed the controls in the report header section, they would be visible on the first page of the report, as shown in Figure 22-5.

Figure 22-5 Sort controls in the report header section

An Easy Way To Add A Sort Control
To quickly add a Sort Control, right-click on the field heading in the report.
Select **BIND SORT CONTROL**, then select the field that you want to sort on.

Running Total Fields

Running total fields are similar to the summary fields that you have already learned how to create. While running total fields are similar to summary fields, they provide more options which adds more flexibility over the total (summary) fields that you can create. There are several differences between running total and summary fields, as explained below.

① Running total fields only calculate data that is displayed on the report.

② Running total fields can be placed in the details section of the report, which would display a total up to the current record.

③ Running total fields allow you to select when the values are calculated.

④ You can control when running total fields can be reset.

⑤ Running total fields are only evaluated/calculated during the **WHILE PRINTING RECORDS** pass of the report is taking place. Crystal Reports uses a multi pass system. This means that records in the "Others" group on a report will not be counted in grand totals.

⑥ Running total fields are calculated at the detail level (record by record) and summary fields are calculated at the group level. If a running total field is placed in the group header section, it will only include a total for the first record in the group because the other records in the group have not been processed at this point.

Top N reports do not have to include records that do not meet the Top N criteria. Records that do not meet the Top N criteria can be placed in the "Others" group on the report. It is important to note that records in the "Others" group will be included in any grand totals on the report, whether or not the records in the "Others" group are printed on the report.

The "Others" group is something that needs to be addressed during the report design phase. You have to find out if the people requesting the report want grand totals only for the records that meet the Top N requirements or for all records including those in the "Others" category. Figure 22-6 shows the Create Running Total Field dialog box. If you only want report or grand totals for the records that meet the Top N condition, you have to use a running total field instead of a summary field.

Running Total Field Performance
Using a lot of running total fields in a report will cause the report to take a performance hit. Manual running total fields will reduce the performance hit.

Create Running Total Field Dialog Box Options Explained

You have probably figured out that there are a lot of good reasons to use running total fields instead of summary fields. You have also probably realized that selecting the appropriate type of total field (summary or running total) requires some thought. The other item that you have to consider is where the running total field will be placed on the report. Table 22-1 explains what the running total field will calculate depending on which section of the report it is placed in. The output will change depending on the **EVALUATE** option that is selected.

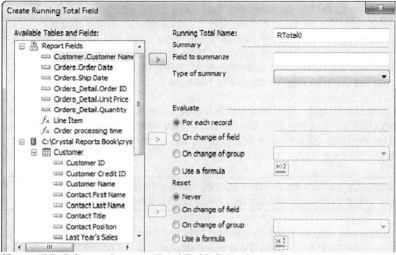

Figure 22-6 Create Running Total Field dialog box

Section	Which Records Will Be Calculated . . .
Report Header	The first record on the report.
Page Header	All records up to and including the first record that will be printed on the current page.
Group Header	All records up to and including the first record of the current group.
Details	All records up to and including the current detail record.
Group Footer	All records up to and including the last record in the current group.
Page Footer	All records up to the first record on the next page.
Report Footer	All records on the report.

Table 22-1 Running total field output options explained

Like other dialog boxes that you have used, the Available Tables and Fields list on the Create Running Total Field dialog box contains the fields and formulas that you can use to create running total fields. The options in the **SUMMARY** section on the right are used to enter a name for the running total field, select a field from the Available Tables and Fields list and select the type of summary.

The **FIELD TO SUMMARIZE** field may contain the name of a field that can be used to create summary information for. You can select a different field from the Available Tables and Fields list.

The options in the **TYPE OF SUMMARY** field drop-down list are the same as the ones for summary fields. The name of this field can be misleading because a running total field does more than create totals. Like summary fields, running total fields can provide counts, averages, percents and more.

Evaluate Section

The options in the Evaluate section are used to select when the running total field should be incremented. The options are used to select which records are included (evaluated) in the calculation. The options are explained below.

The **FOR EACH RECORD** option is most like a summary field calculation because the running total field is incremented after each detail record is processed.

The **ON CHANGE OF FIELD** option performs the running total field calculations when the value in the field is different then the value from the previous record. This is useful when the field that the running total field is using can have several records that have the same value and you only want to count the value once. This is like the Distinct Count summary type. If you are using a field like the Order ID field and the report uses the Orders and Orders Details tables, most of the time you should select the Order ID field from the parent table, which in this example is the Orders table.

When selecting this evaluation option, give some thought to the data that is in the field that you are using because records other then the first one that has the same data will not increment the running total field because this option excludes records. The key to using this option successfully is to select a field that has a lot of unique values in it.

 If you are going to use the **ON CHANGE OF FIELD** option, make sure that the records are sorted correctly, otherwise the report will display unexpected results.

The **ON CHANGE OF GROUP** option can only be used on a report that has a group. This option evaluates (increments) the running total field when the group changes.

If you need the running total field to be incremented based on a condition, select the **USE A FORMULA** option and click the Formula button next to the field. Then create a formula that the records must meet in order for the running total field to be incremented. An example of this would be if the report needed a total dollar amount of orders that were not processed in three days. The formula would check the Order processing time formula field. If it is greater than three, add the order total amount to the running total field. If you needed a count of how many orders were not processed that had an order processing time amount greater than three, you would create another running total field, use the count summary type and use the same formula for the running total field.

Reset Options

The options in the Reset section are used to select when the running total field should be reset to zero. The options are explained below.

Select **NEVER** if you want the running total field to be calculated for the entire report.

Select the **ON CHANGE OF FIELD** option when you want the running total field to be reset on a specific field.

If you were using the running total field to get group totals, you would select the **ON CHANGE OF GROUP** option, then select the field and select the group from the drop-down list. You could also create a formula that determined when to reset the running total field.

Select the **USE A FORMULA** option when the running total field can only be reset when specific criteria has been met.

 You should use a running total field on reports that suppress records if there is a group selection formula. Report grand totals are calculated **BEFORE** the group selection formulas that have suppression are calculated.

There are three ways to open the Create Running Total Field dialog box, as explained below.

   ① Right-click on the field in the details section that you want to create a running total for and select Insert ⇒ Running Total.

② Right-click on the Running Total Fields category in the Field Explorer, then select New.

③ Click on the Running Total Fields category in the Field Explorer, then click the New button on the Field Explorer toolbar.

Exercise 22.2: Create Two Order Processing Time Running Total Fields

In this exercise you will create two running total fields. You will create one to calculate an order total amount of orders that were not processed in three days. The second running total field will count the number of orders that were not processed in three days.

1. Save the E14.8 report as E22.2 Order processing time running totals.

2. Create the Line Item formula field shown below, then add it to the report after the Quantity field. Wrap the Order processing time field heading to two lines.

   {Orders_Detail.Unit Price} * {Orders_Detail.Quantity}

Create The Order Total Amount Running Total Field

In this part of the exercise you will create a running total field that will only count the Unit Price amount if the order processing time is greater than three days.

1. Right-click on the Line Item formula field in the detail section, then select Insert ⇒ Running Total.

2. Type Order total amount in the Running Total Name field, then select the Sum Type of summary, if it is not already selected.

3. Select the **USE A FORMULA** Evaluate option, then click the Formula button.

4. Double-click on the Order processing time formula field, then type > 3 as the criteria.

5. Highlight the formula and press the Ctrl+C keys. This will let you paste the formula into the next formula that you create. Click the Save and close button, then click OK.

6. Move the Order Total amount running total field and heading to the report footer section.

Create The Order Count Running Total Field

In this part of the exercise you will create a running total field to get a count of the number of orders that were not processed in three days.

If you preview the report you will see duplicate values in the Customer Name and Order ID fields. This means that some orders have more than one item. If this were live data, often the items that are in stock will ship immediately and the items that are not, will be delayed. Whatever the case is, you only want to count each order once. Therefore, using the Count summary option would not work. You would have to use the Distinct Count option on the Order ID field.

1. Open the Create Running Total Field dialog box and type Order count in the Running Total Name field.

2. Select the Order ID field as the Field to summarize, then select the distinct count Type of summary.

3.   Select the Use a formula Evaluate option, then click the Formula button.

4.   Paste the formula in by pressing the Ctrl+V keys. Click the Save and close button, then click OK.

5.   Move the Order count running total field and heading to the report footer section, then save the changes.

 You could get the same results without a formula if the report was sorted on the Order ID field and you selected the **ON CHANGE OF FIELD** Evaluate option.

Modify The Running Total Fields To The Report

1.   Format the Order total amount running total field to have a floating dollar sign.

2.   Rearrange the running total fields to look like the ones at the bottom of Figure 22-7. Save the changes. The totals on the last page of the report should look like the ones shown in the figure. As you can see, there is a rather large difference in count and amount of the orders that were not processed in three days versus the orders that are printed on the report.

Customer Name	Order Date	Ship Date	Order ID	Unit Price	Quantity	Line Item	Order processing time
Souzel Bike Rentals	12/12/2010	12/16/2010	3,189	$15.50	2	$31.00	4
Tom's Place for Bikes	12/12/2010	12/12/2010	3,190	$53.90	1	$53.90	0
Coastal Line Bikes	12/12/2010	12/13/2010	3,191	$33.90	3	$101.70	1
Hikers and Bikers	12/12/2010	12/12/2010	3,192	$479.85	2	$959.70	0
Mountain View Sport	12/12/2010	12/12/2010	3,193	$11.90	2	$23.80	0

Total # of orders >3 days processing 711   Total order amount >3 days processing$ 1,315,233.64

Figure 22-7 Order processing time running totals report

Exercise 22.3: Use Running Total Fields With Parameter Fields

Parameter fields are used instead of hard coding selection criteria. This makes the report much more flexible. The report that you created in Exercise 20.13 allows the user to select the date range and number of order processing days. In this exercise you will modify that report to include the running total fields that you created in Exercise 22.2. You will also create summary fields that provide totals for the entire report. These fields will demonstrate the difference between summary and running total fields.

1.   Save the E20.13 report as `E22.3 Running total and parameter fields`.

2.   Create the Line Item formula field, the Order total amount and Order count running total fields that you created in Exercise 22.2. Add the running total fields to the report footer section.

3.   Create two summary fields and headings. One for a count of orders and one for the total order amount of all records. Place these fields in the report footer section under the running total fields.

4.   Run the report for all of 2011, with an order processing time that is greater than or equal to four. Save the changes. The last page of the report should look like the one shown in Figure 22-8. There should be 2,616 records on the report.

Customer Name	Order Date	Ship Date	Order ID	Unit Price	Quantity	Line Item	Order processing time
Number of orders with a delay in shipping			529	Total order amount of delayed orders		$950,860.65	
	Total number of orders		1,562	Total order amount of all orders		$2,861,205.48	

Figure 22-8 Running total and parameter fields report

Running Total And Summary Field Limitation

The one limitation that both field types have is that they will not produce the correct result if the report suppresses data because by default, both fields will calculate the suppressed records that will not be printed on the report. This happens because both fields perform calculations without taking into account conditional formatting formulas that the suppress option may have.

In Exercise 16.7 you modified a report and added a formula to the Suppress (No Drill-Down) option on three sections of the report. This was done because the report requirement was to only display groups that met a condition. You have to follow the same process for a running total field. The reason that you have to do this is because you only want running total fields to include records that will actually appear on the report. To fix the E16.7 report, add the same formula to the running total fields.

Figure 22-9 shows the last page of the E16.7 report. This version of the report has summary fields and running totals in the report footer section. Notice that the amounts are different. The summary fields did not produce the amounts that you expected because it includes values not printed on the report. Running total fields only include values that are printed on the report. The reason that the totals in the summary fields section are larger is because they include records that are not printed on the report. As you read, summary fields are calculated in the first pass of the report. Filtering and suppression are done on the second pass.

Running Total Fields - Counts only for customers with an average order < 2500
# of customers with average order < 2500   202
# of orders with average order < 2500   1,017
$ amount of orders < 2500 $ 2,826,726.86
Average order amount for customers with order < 2500 $ 1,701.82

Summary Fields

Total # of customers on this report -   256

Grand Total # of orders - 1562

Grand Total $ amount of all orders - $ 5,830,030.25

Average order amount for all customers - $ 2,228.60

Figure 22-9 E16.7 report without suppression on the group header and footer sections

Running Total Field Limitations

The two limitations of running total fields are explained below.

① The calculation types are limited to the ones that summary fields use.
② Summary functions and shared variables cannot be used.

Hierarchical Group Reports

A hierarchical group is a special type of parent-child, one-to-many relationship. It shows the relationship between records that are in the same table. If it helps, think of the parent field as the field that is displayed in the group header section and the child fields will be displayed in the details section of the report. In Chapter 5 you learned about **RECURSIVE JOINS**. This type of join is required to create hierarchical reports.

Hierarchical groups are useful when you need to create a report where two fields in the same table are related to each other. This is what Crystal Reports refers to as a hierarchical group. This is how organizational charts are created. An Employee table lists the employees that work for the company. It also contains who each employee reports to. Remember that the person that has other people reporting to them is also an employee.

In this example, the people that have someone reporting to them are the "parent" portion of the relationship. Employees that do not have anyone reporting to them are the "child" portion of the relationship. The Hierarchical Group Options dialog box shown in Figure 22-10 is used to create a hierarchical group report.

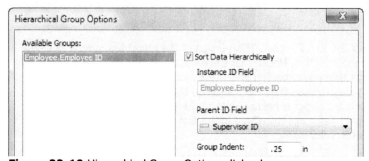

Figure 22-10 Hierarchical Group Options dialog box

The **AVAILABLE GROUPS** list contains all of the groups that the report has. The hierarchical report must be created using one of the groups that are listed in this section.

Once you select a group, check the **SORT DATA HIERARCHICALLY** option to indicate that you want to apply hierarchical sorting to the group that is selected.

The **INSTANCE ID FIELD** contains the field that will be used as the child field.

The **PARENT ID FIELD** contains the fields that can be used as the parent field. The parent record (in this example, the supervisor) will print first and then the employees that report to the supervisor will print below. All of the fields in this drop-down list are the same data type as the group field.

The **GROUP INDENT** option is used to select how much the child records should be indented. Using this feature is optional. If the columns do not contain a lot of data and the Group Indent option is greater than zero, it is possible that some data will not line up properly with the field headings. One way to fix this is to make the Group Indent number smaller. Another option is to resize some of the fields on the report. Leaving this option set to zero means that the child records will not be indented, which will make it difficult to see the hierarchical relationship.

Hierarchical Report Requirements

To create a hierarchical report, the following three requirements must be met.

① The table must have two fields that represent the same data. This allows the data in one field to point to another record in the same table.
② The parent and child fields must have the same data type.
③ The report must be grouped on the child field.

Exercise 22.4: Create A Hierarchical Group Report

In this exercise you will create an organizational report that shows who each employee reports to.

1. Create a new report and add the Employee table, but do not add any fields to the report.

2. Create a group on the Employee ID field. Use the Options tab to create a group name formula that combines the Employee first and last name fields.

3. Report ⇒ Hierarchical Grouping Options. You will see the Hierarchical Group Options dialog box. Check the Sort Data Hierarchically option, then select the Supervisor ID field from the Parent ID Field drop-down list.

4. Change the Group Indent option to .25. You should have the options shown earlier in Figure 22-10. Click OK.

5. Add the Position and Hire Date fields to the group header section, then format the Hire Date field so that the time is not displayed.

6. Save the report as E22.4 Hierarchical group report.

    The report should look like the one shown in Figure 22-11.

Andrew Fuller	Vice President, Sales	07/12/1991
Steven Buchanan	Sales Manager	09/13/1992
Nancy Davolio	Sales Representative	03/29/1991
Janet Leverling	Sales Representative	02/27/1991
Margaret Peacock	Sales Representative	03/30/1992
Michael Suyama	Sales Representative	09/13/1992
Robert King	Sales Representative	11/29/1992
Laura Callahan	Inside Sales Coordinator	01/30/1993
Anne Dodsworth	Sales Representative	10/12/1993
Albert Hellstern	Business Manager	03/01/1993
Tim Smith	Mail Clerk	01/15/1993

Figure 22-11 Hierarchical group report

Optional Hierarchical Report Options

If the Hierarchical report needs summary or grand totals, use the Insert Summary dialog box.

If you select the summary field and then open the Insert Summary dialog box, you will see the SUMMARIZE ACROSS HIERARCHY option illustrated in Figure 22-12.

This option creates a summary across hierarchical groups.

Figure 22-12 Hierarchy option illustrated

The Group Sort Expert

You have already used the Group Sort Expert to create and modify Top N reports. In addition to being able to create and modify Top N reports, the Group Sort Expert is used to sort groups in ways other than ascending or descending order.

You can sort groups based on values in a summary field in the group. For example, in Exercise 10.2, you created a report that grouped the orders by customer. You also created two summary fields for the customer group: One for the customers total dollar amount of orders and one for the total number of orders. If someone needed to see the orders in high to low or low to high order based on the total dollar amount of the customer, you could sort the customer group on the Order Amount summary field. If you sorted the Order Amount summary field in ascending order, the customers with the lowest total dollar amount would appear at the beginning of the group. Two of the ways to open the Group Sort Expert are explained below.

    ① Click the Group Sort Expert button on the Expert Tools toolbar.
    ② Report ⇒ Group Sort Expert.

In Exercise 11.2 you created a report that grouped the orders in 2011 by month. If you wanted to show the months with the highest monthly totals at the beginning of the report, you would sort the month group in descending order on the Order Amount summary field.

Figure 22-13 shows the Group Sort Expert dialog box. When you open the dialog box you will see a tab for each group that the report has. You can sort on as many of the summary values in the groups as needed. Keep in mind that the sorting starts with the first tab and works its way across the tabs.

In addition to the Top N, Bottom N, Top Percentage and Bottom Percentage options, the FOR THIS GROUP SORT drop-down list has the following options:

NO SORT, which is the default and will use the sort options that were set up when the group was created.

The **ALL** option will include all of the groups and not suppress any groups like the Top N, Bottom N, Top Percentage and Bottom Percentage options will.

The fields in the **BASED ON** drop-down list are the summary fields that are in a group section of the report.

Figure 22-13 Group Sort Expert dialog box

To create a Top or Bottom N report, the report must have the two items discussed below, before opening the Group Sort Expert.

    ①   The report must have at least one group.

    ②   The group that you want to use for the Top N report must have a summary field in it.

The way that you know that the report has both of the options discussed above is that you can open the Group Sort Expert. Reports that do not meet the criteria will not have the Group Sort Expert option enabled.

Exercise 22.5: Sort On The Customer Group By Order Amount Field

In this exercise you will change the sort order of the groups to show the groups that have customers with the lowest total order amounts at the top of this report. You will also sort the groups by the number of orders in descending order. This sort will happen within the order amount sort. This is helpful if two or more customers have the same order total amount.

1. Save the E10.2 report as E22.5 Group sorted on two fields.

2. Open the Group Sort Expert and select the All option from the drop-down list.

3. Select the Order Amount summary field, then select the ascending option.

4. Select the Order ID count field from the drop-down list on the right, then select descending and click OK. Save the changes. The report should look like the one shown in Figure 22-14. As you look through the report, you should see all customers with the lowest order amount totals at the beginning of the report.

	Order Date	Ship Date	Order Amount	Order #	Unit Price
Jakarta Sunrise Sports					
	06/06/2011	06/07/2011	$2,699.55	3086	$899.85
Total # of orders - 1		**Total $ amount of orders -**	**$ 2,699.55**		
Super Bike					
	06/24/2011	06/26/2011	$2,699.55	3166	$899.85
Total # of orders - 1		**Total $ amount of orders -**	**$ 2,699.55**		
Tel Aviv Outdoors					
	06/08/2011	06/18/2011	$2,699.55	3098	$899.85
Total # of orders - 1		**Total $ amount of orders -**	**$ 2,699.55**		
Bordeaux Sports					
	05/14/2011	05/14/2011	$2,939.85	3021	$2,939.85
Total # of orders - 1		**Total $ amount of orders -**	**$ 2,939.85**		

Figure 22-14 Group sorted on two fields report

As the report designer, it may be obvious to you how a report is sorted and grouped. Unlike the reports that you have created earlier in this book that have groups, reports that have groups that are sorted by a value in a summary field, may not be as easy for the reader to figure out how the report is grouped and sorted, just by looking at it.

If you look at the report shown above in Figure 22-14, you will see the group name (the company name field) in the group header section. Many people will think that this is how the report is sorted even though the report is sorted by the values in the order amount summary field. You should do something to make sure that the person reading the report is aware of how the report is sorted or grouped. There are three options that I select from to help clarify how a report presents data. You can use any of the options below or come up with a different solution.

① Add how the report is grouped and sorted as a subtitle on the report. For example, Grouped by (field name) and sorted by summary (field name), where you fill in the (field name).
② Add how the report is grouped and sorted to the page or report footer section.
③ Add the summary value to the group header section.

Creating Group Selection Formulas

Group selection formulas are used to filter groups that do not meet a condition. The formulas can be created by using the values in a group summary field or by using the values in the Group Name field. To use a Group Name field you have to use the Group Name function. The only time that you need to use this function is if the report has custom group names.

To create a group selection formula, select a summary field on the Select Expert instead of a detail field. In Exercise 22.5 you modified the report to sort the groups in ascending order. If you only wanted to see groups (in this example, customers) that have an order summary total amount less than $10,000 and are in the USA, you would create two selection criteria options: One on the Order summary total amount, which is a group summary field and one on the Country field.

Exercise 22.6: Create A Group Selection Formula

1. Save the E22.5 report as E22.6 Group selection formula.

2. Right-click on the Order Amount summary field in the group footer section and select the Select Expert Group option. Select the "Is less than" operator, then type 10000 in the next drop-down list. This is the group selection formula.

3. Click on the New tab, then select the Country field. Select the "Is equal to" operator, then select the USA region. Click OK.

4. Open the Select Expert for records and delete the Order Amount greater than 2499.99 criteria.

5. Click on the Order Amount tab, then click the Show Formula button. The group selection formula should look like the one shown in Figure 22-15. Click OK and save the changes. The report should look like the one shown in Figure 22-16.

Sum ({Orders.Order Amount}, {Customer.Customer Name}) < $10000.00 and {Customer.Country} = "USA"

Figure 22-15 Group selection formula

	Order Date	Ship Date	Order Amount	Order #	Unit Price
Ride Down A Mountain					
	05/23/2011	05/23/2011	$12.00	3041	$12.00
Total # of orders - 1		Total $ amount of orders - $ 12.00			
Colin's Bikes					
	05/21/2011	05/22/2011	$13.50	3038	$4.50
Total # of orders - 1		Total $ amount of orders - $ 13.50			
Tony's Better Bikes					
	05/22/2011	05/22/2011	$17.50	3040	$17.50
Total # of orders - 1		Total $ amount of orders - $ 17.50			

Figure 22-16 Group selection formula report

As you may expect, group selection formulas will suppress groups that do not meet the selection criteria. What I find interesting is that the summary field group totals are the same as if there were no suppressed groups. This is because there is a difference between suppressing groups and filtering records. Keep this in mind when creating group selection formulas.

Multi Column Reports

In Chapter 12 you used the Mailing Label wizard, which can be used to create multi column labels.

You can use the options on the Layout tab shown in Figure 22-17, on the Section Expert to create multi column reports.

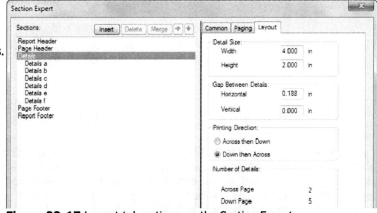

Figure 22-17 Layout tab options on the Section Expert

The options on the Layout tab are used to create columns like the Mailing Label wizard does. Unlike word processing software that often has a "Number of columns" option, the Layout tab does not. You create the columns by using the **DETAIL SIZE** and **GAP BETWEEN DETAILS** options.

The **FORMAT GROUPS WITH MULTIPLE COLUMN** option (On the Common tab, when the details section is selected) will cause the group header and footer sections to have the same width as the details section.

Exercise 22.7: Add A Watermark To A Report Using An Image

In this exercise you will use the Underlay option to add a watermark image to a report.

1. Save the E5.3 report as `E22.7 Image watermark`.

2. Create another page header section. Move the field headings to the new page header section.

3. Add the draft_watermark image file to the first page header a section.

   Place the image in the center of the section, then make it larger, as shown in Figure 22-18.

Figure 22-18 Image file added to the first page header section

4. Open the Section Expert for the page header a section. Select the Underlay Following Sections option, then click OK.

   Save the changes and preview the report. It should look like the one shown in Figure 22-19.

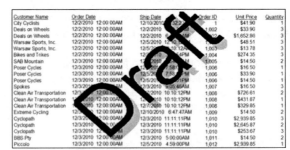

Figure 22-19 Watermark added to the report

The End!

If you are reading this paragraph, I hope it means that you have completed all of the exercises in this book. If so, congratulations because you have covered a lot of material. If some topics seem a little fuzzy right now, that is to be expected. Hopefully you have gained some valuable Crystal Reports skills and techniques. As you have probably figured out, unless you are creating a basic list report, there are a lot of options and features at your disposal to create reports that people will "like" to use. I hope that you enjoyed the book.

. . . .

INDEX

.bmp file type, 3-4, 7-17
.car file, 4-3
.csv export file, 13-19
.cub files, 3-2
.jpg file type, 3-4, 7-17
.pdf export file, 13-13
.png file type, 3-4, 7-17
.rpt file, 4-15
.rptr export file, 1-8, 13-9, 13-20
.rtf file, 3-3, 7-13, 13-10
.tiff file type, 3-4, 7-17
.wmf file type, 3-4
.xlsx export file, 1-8, 13-10, 13-16
3D chart customization options, 18-13
3D line chart, 17-4
3D riser chart, 17-4, 17-25
3D surface chart, 17-4
3D viewing angle, 18-13

A

absolute formatting, 15-2
Access/Excel (DAO) connection, 4-3
add background color (to a section), 8-3
add borders to fields, 8-3
add boxes, 8-5
Add Command To Report dialog box, 5-3
add image files, 7-5
add text object, 7-3
add to all group levels option, 10-10
add-ins menu, 2-6
adjust automatically option, 13-3
Adobe Acrobat (PDF) Export, 13-13
advanced calculations options
    (cross-tab), 21-15
advanced layout options (chart), 17-7
aged 0 to 30 days function, 9-4
aged 31 to 60 days function, 9-4
aged 61 to 90 days function, 9-4
alias table, 5-17
aligning objects horizontally, 6-5
aligning objects vertically, 6-4
all dates from today function, 9-4
all dates from tomorrow function, 9-4
all dates to today function, 9-4
all dates to yesterday function, 9-4
allow custom values, 20-9
allow discrete values, 19-6

allow field clipping option, 21-8
allow multiple values, 20-5, 20-9
allow range values, 19-6, 20-5
AND operator, 9-12
applied to group template, 18-3
applied to this instance, 18-3
area chart, 17-4, 17-22
array, 20-9
ascending (sort) order, 4-8, 10-4
auto arrange option (chart), 17-17, 18-12
auto complete, 14-11
auto range option (chart), 17-16
auto scale option, 17-16
automatic data refreshing, 4-14
automatic smart linking, 3-2, 5-14
Available data sources list shortcut menu, 4-5
average function, 10-9
Axes tab options (Chart Expert), 17-14

B

background color, 7-10
bar chart, 17-4, 17-20
barcodes, 22-2
basic syntax, 9-12, 14-5
blank report option, 1-9, 3-14
BLOB, 3-4
bookmarks, 13-13
boolean expressions, 15-18
boolean field formatting, 7-18
boolean field options, 10-4
boolean formulas, 15-18
boolean group #, 19-7
boolean parameter fields, 20-24
boolean text field, 7-19
border color, 7-10
Border tab options (Format Editor), 7-10
bottom 5 groups option, 12-6
Bottom N report, 12-6, 17-26
Box tab options (Format Editor), 8-5
browse data, 4-6
bubble chart, 17-4, 17-28
business views, 5-2

C

calendar 1st half function, 9-5
calendar 1st qtr function, 9-5

calendar 2nd half function, 9-5
calendar 2nd qtr function, 9-5
calendar 3rd qtr function, 9-5
calendar 4th qtr function, 9-5
calendar control, 19-12
call stack, 14-31
can grow option, 7-11
cascading list of values, 20-3
cascading prompts, 19-9, 20-3
case sensitive considerations, 9-17
center text across a page, 7-4
Change Group Options dialog
    box, 11-4, 11-12, 16-9
change group order, 11-2
Change in Record Selection Formula
    dialog box, 9-7
Character Map dialog box, 7-7
chart customizations, 18-14
Chart Expert, 17-2
chart menu options, 2-16
Chart Options dialog box, 18-9
Chart Sort Order dialog box, 17-10
chart templates, 18-20
chart trendlines, 18-6
chart types (more), 18-5
charts from cross-tab data, 21-8
Choose a Chart Type dialog box, 18-6
Choose a Pattern dialog box (chart), 18-18
Choose a Viewing Angle dialog box, 18-14
Choose Export File dialog box, 13-13
Choose Field dialog box, 9-6
ChrW(x) function, 14-27
clamp page footer option, 16-5
close border on page break option, 8-4
collapse button, 3-16
Color Highlight tab options
    (Chart Expert), 17-18
combine string fields, 14-22
combine text objects, 7-5
commands, 5-3
Common tab options (Format Editor), 7-9
Common tab options (Section Expert), 16-3
comparison conditional formatting, 15-14
concatenate (x&y) operator, 14-24, 14-26
conditional formatting, 15-2
conditional formatting (cross-tab), 21-22
connection options, 4-3
control structures, 14-5
convert database null values to
    default, 10-15, 15-9
copy a formula field, 3-23
correlation with function, 10-9
count function, 10-8, 10-14

covariance with function, 10-9
create bookmarks from group tree
    option, 13-13
Create New Connection folder, 4-4, 4-16
Create New Parameter dialog box, 19-3
Create Running Total Field dialog box, 22-5
crFloatingCurrencySymbol function, 15-17
Cross-Tab Calculated Members Expert
    dialog box, 21-16
Cross-Tab charts, 21-8
Cross-Tab Expert, 21-10
Cross-Tab Group Options dialog box, 21-12
Cross-Tab layout options
    (Chart Expert), 17-12
Cross-Tab reports, 21-2
Cross-Tab shortcut menu, 21-15
Cross-Tab Top N and Sort Export
    dialog box, 21-21
Cross-Tab Top N reports, 21-20
Cross-Tab wizard, 3-11, 21-4
Crystal Reports certification, 1-7
Crystal Reports menus, 2-7
Crystal Reports read-only export (.rptr), 13-20
Crystal Reports terminology, 3-4
Crystal Reports viewer, 13-21
Crystal Reports workspace, 3-13
crystal syntax, 9-12, 14-5
Current Parameter Values dialog box, 2-15
CurrentDate function, 14-27
CurrentFieldValue function, 21-16
custom colors, 8-15
custom function, 14-9
custom group names, 11-3, 11-9
custom grouping, 10-4, 11-3, 11-9
Custom Style dialog box, 7-15, 11-9
customize charts, 18-14
Customize Crystal Reports, 2-18

D

data dictionary, 3-2
data source options, 3-2, 4-3, 5-2
Data tab options (Chart Expert), 17-6
data types (database field), 3-3
data types (parameter fields), 19-5
database concepts, 3-2
Database Expert dialog box, 5-2
database menu options, 2-13
database server is case-insensitive, 9-17
Database tab options (Options dialog box),
    2-20
database terminology, 3-2
Date and Time Tab options, 7-16

date custom style options, 7-16
date field formatting, 7-16
date functions, 14-27
Date/Time field options, 10-4
DateAdd function, 14-27
DateDiff function, 14-27
day function, 14-27
default export options, 13-12
default formula language option, 2-20
default value for nulls option, 14-8
DefaultAttribute function, 15-8, 21-16
Define Named Group dialog box, 11-13
delete parameter field, 20-28
delete selection criteria, 9-13
deleting projects, 3-20
deleting reports, 3-20
deleting sections, 16-3
delivery method, 3-6
Dependency Checker, 3-20
Dependency Checker tab options (Options
    dialog box), 2-24
descending (sort) order, 4-8, 10-4
Design tab (workspace), 3-13, 3-17
detach pie slice, 17-24
direct driver, 4-3
displaying record selection formulas, 10-23
distinct count function, 10-8, 10-20
docking explorer windows, 3-26
Document Properties dialog
    box, 4-15, 8-9, 9-18
does not start with operator, 9-3
don't summarize option, 17-9
doughnut chart, 17-4, 17-24
drill down group tree option, 3-16
drop shadow, 7-11
Dual (X) Axis Settings dialog box, 18-17
dual axes option, 18-12
duplicating a formula field, 3-23
dynamic image location, 3-4
dynamic list of values, 20-2

E

edit formulas, 9-15
edit mask characters, 20-26
edit menu options, 2-8
Edit Summary dialog box, 11-7
edit text object, 7-2
edit x axis labels, 18-12
editing charts, 18-2
Embedded Summaries dialog box, 21-18
enable currency symbol option, 15-16
enforce join types, 5-15

Enter Values dialog box, 19-9, 20-29
evaluate section options (running total), 22-5
Excel 2007 export format, 1-8, 13-10, 13-16
Excel data only export, 13-16
Excel export format options, 13-15
Excel Format Options dialog
    box, 13-15, 13-17
exceptions for nulls option, 14-8
expand button, 3-16
Expert Tools toolbar, 2-5
explorer shortcut menu, 3-28
explorers, 3-21
export destination options, 13-11
Export dialog box, 13-9
export format options, 13-8
Export Options dialog box, 13-13
export to csv, 13-19
export to Excel, 13-14, 13-16
export to PDF, 13-13
Export To Text dialog box, 13-21
Exporting Records dialog box, 13-14
Expression Editor toolbar
    (Formula Workshop), 14-7
extend to bottom of section when
    printing, 8-5, 8-6
External Command toolbar, 2-6
extracting a custom function, 14-12

F

F5 key, 3-14
Field Explorer, 3-22
field type symbols, 3-24
Fields tab options (Options dialog box), 2-21
file menu options, 2-7
filtering records, 9-2
Find dialog box, 2-9, 14-8
find in field (explorer option), 5-6
find in formulas, 3-24, 14-8
find panel, 3-15
find results window, 14-8
font color conditional formatting, 15-15
Font dialog box, 2-23
Font tab options (Format Editor), 7-13
Fonts tab options (Options dialog box), 2-23
for each record option, 17-8
foreign key fields, 3-3
Format Background dialog box (chart), 18-15
format boolean fields, 7-18
Format Chart Frame dialog box, 18-16
Format Data Labels dialog box (chart), 18-16
format date fields, 7-16
Format Editor, 7-7

Format Grid Lines dialog box, 21-14
Format Gridlines dialog box (chart), 18-15
format lines (horizontal), 7-21
format lines (vertical), 7-22
format menu options, 2-12
Format Other Dimensions dialog box, 17-14
Format Painter, 7-19
Format Series Marker dialog box
   (chart), 18-16
Format Series Riser dialog box (chart), 18-14
format text object, 7-4, 7-10
format time fields, 7-16
formatting charts, 18-2
formatting numeric fields, 7-14
formatting string fields, 14-26
Formatting toolbar, 2-3
Formula Editor, 14-10
Formula Editor tab options
   (Options dialog box), 2-20
formula evaluation order, 14-14
Formula Expert, 14-12
formula fields, 3-4, 3-22, 14-9
formula naming conventions, 14-14
formula text section, 14-10
Formula Workshop, 14-6
formulas, 14-2
full outer join type, 5-12
functions, 9-4, 14-4
functions tree, 14-10
funnel chart, 17-5

G
gantt chart, 17-5, 17-31
gauge chart, 17-5, 17-31
general toolbar (Formula Workshop), 14-6
Go To dialog box, 2-9
gradient chart color options, 18-15, 18-18
grid (workspace), 6-9
grid options (cross-tab), 21-14
GridRowColumnValue function, 21-16
Group Expert, 11-11
group layout options, 17-10
group name field, 3-22, 10-18, 11-3, 11-9
group options (cross-tab), 21-13
group selection formula, 14-7, 22-14
Group Selection Formula Editor, 14-9
Group Sort Expert, 17-10, 22-12
group sort options, 10-4
group tree, 3-16
grouping data (with a parameter field), 20-22
grouping records, 10-2, 10-10
guidelines, 6-6, 6-8

H
help menu options, 2-17
hierarchical group report, 22-10
highlight data (with a parameter field), 20-18
Highlighting Expert, 15-3
histogram chart, 17-5, 17-32
horizontal alignment options, 6-5
horizontal lines, 7-21
Hyperlink tab options
   (Format Editor), 7-8, 7-14

I
If Then Else statement, 14-21, 15-7, 15-10
import static list of values, 19-18
import text from a file, 7-4
in ascending order, 4-8, 10-4
in descending order, 4-8, 10-4
in original order, 10-4
in specified order, 10-4, 11-12
include options, 17-10
include this value, 19-6, 20-6
include ties option, 17-10, 20-17
index field, 3-2
Index Legend, 4-18
indirect driver, 4-3
inner join type, 5-12
InRepeatedGroupHeader function, 16-10
insert detail field headings, 2-19, 6-8
insert flash object, 6-2
insert from file, 7-4
Insert Group dialog box, 10-3
insert group name with group option, 10-13
insert menu options, 2-11
insert picture, 7-5, 7-17
insert sort control, 6-2
Insert Summary dialog box, 10-8
insert to report option, 5-4
Insert Tools toolbar, 2-4
is any value operator, 9-4
is between operator, 9-3, 9-10
is equal to operator, 9-3, 9-6
is false operator, 9-4
is greater than operator, 9-3
is greater than or equal to operator, 9-3, 9-9
is in the period functions, 9-4
is in the period operator, 9-4
is less than operator, 9-3
is less than or equal to operator, 9-3
is like operator, 9-3
is not between operator, 9-3
is not equal to operator, 9-3
is not in the period operator, 9-4

is not like operator, 9-3
is not one of operator, 9-3
is one of operator, 9-3, 9-8
is true operator, 9-4
IsNull function, 14-21, 15-9
item editor options, 15-3, 15-4
item list options, 15-3, 15-4

J

join function, 20-27
join types, 5-12, 5-15

L

Label Aliasing dialog box, 18-12
last 4 weeks to sun function, 9-4
last 7 days function, 9-4
last full month function, 9-4
last full week function, 9-4
last year mtd function, 9-5
last year ytd function, 9-5
layering objects, 6-12
Layout tab options (Options dialog box), 2-19
Layout tab options (Section Expert), 16-5
LCase function, 14-21
left outer join type, 5-12
legend options, 17-18
length (field), 3-2
length (str) function, 14-21
line chart, 17-4, 17-21
line formatting (horizontal), 7-21
line formatting (vertical), 7-22
Line tab options (Format Editor), 7-22
Link Options dialog box, 17-29
link types, 5-16
linking tables, 4-17, 5-11, 5-14
list of values (cascading), 20-3
list of values (dynamic), 20-2
list of values (static), 19-15
Loaded Modules dialog box, 2-18
lock size and position, 16-3
long list of values options, 20-7
lowercase (str) function, 14-21

M

Mailing Label wizard, 3-11, 12-13
Manage XML Exporting Formats
    dialog box, 13-21
managed lists, 19-14
manual join types, 5-15
many-to-many relationship, 5-10
map menu options, 2-16

margins, 13-3
markers (chart), 17-17, 17-22
markers (guidelines), 6-7
mask options, 14-26
max length option, 20-25
max value option, 20-25
maximum function, 10-8, 20-27
maximum number of lines, 7-11
MaxNBrowseValues registry key, 4-7
median function, 10-9
menus, 2-7
merging sections, 16-3
min length option, 20-25
min value option, 20-25
minimum function, 10-8, 20-27
MOD function, 14-14, 16-14
mode function (numeric), 10-9
mode function (text), 10-8
modify selection criteria, 9-10
month function, 14-27
month to date function, 9-4
move to bottom of section when
    printing, 7-22
moving objects, 6-4, 6-8, 6-12
multi-axes options, 18-12
multi-column reports, 22-15
My Connections folder, 4-16
My Recent Reports, 1-9

N

Navigation Tools toolbar, 2-4, 3-15
nested if statement, 15-8, 15-11
new page after option, 16-4, 16-6
new page after visible groups, 16-9
new page before option, 16-4, 16-6
next 30 days function, 9-4
next 31 to 60 days function, 9-4
next 61 to 90 days function, 9-4
next 91 to 365 days function, 9-4
no lower value, 19-6, 20-6, 20-27
no upper value, 19-6, 20-6, 20-27
nocolor, 16-14
NotOnLastRecord function, 16-7
Nth largest, N is function, 10-8
Nth most frequent, N is function, 10-8
Nth smallest, N is function, 10-8
nudging objects, 6-12
null (values), 3-2, 10-15
Number tab options (Format Editor), 7-14
numeric axis chart, 17-5, 17-30
numeric field formatting, 7-14
numeric formulas, 14-15

numeric summary calculation options, 10-9

O

object layering, 6-12
Object Size and Position dialog box, 6-11
ODBC driver, 4-3
ODBC export format, 13-20
ODBC Formats dialog box, 13-20
odd/even page headers, 16-16
OLAP Cube wizard, 3-11
OLAP layout options (Chart Expert), 17-13
OLE DB (ADO) connection, 4-4
OLE DB driver, 4-3
on change of field option (running total), 22-6
on change of group option
    (running total), 22-6
on change of option, 17-7
one-to-many relationship, 5-10
one-to-one relationship, 5-10
OnFirstRecord function, 15-16
operators, 9-3
operators tree, 14-10
Options dialog box, 2-19
Options tab options (Chart Expert), 17-17
OR operator, 9-12
Order Links dialog box, 5-7
order of precedence, 14-14
other dimensions, 17-14
over 90 days function, 9-4

P

page breaks, 16-6
page indicator, 3-15
page margins, 13-3
Page N of M, 8-8
page orientation, 13-3
Page Setup dialog box, 13-2
paging tab options, 16-4
paint brush, 7-20
pan option (chart), 18-2
paper size options, 13-3
Paragraph tab options (Format Editor), 7-13
parameter fields, 3-22, 19-3, 22-7
Parameter Order dialog box, 20-14
parameter range fields, 20-27
parameters panel, 3-16, 19-10
PDF export options, 13-13
percent calculations, 11-6
Performance Information dialog box, 2-15
picture (str) function, 14-21, 14-25
Picture tab options (Format Editor), 7-17
pie chart, 17-4, 17-23

Pivot Cross-Tab option, 2-12
Pivot OLAP grid option, 2-12
population standard deviation function, 10-9
population variance function, 10-9
preferred viewing locale, 2-11
preview panel, 3-15
Preview Sample dialog box, 13-6
Preview tab (workspace), 3-13
primary key fields, 3-3, 5-9
print parameter fields, 20-27
printer options, 13-4
printing options, 13-2
projectexplorer.xml file, 3-20
projects, 3-18, 3-20
prototype, 3-8
Pth percentile, P is function, 10-9
push pin, 3-27

Q

query, 5-3
query panel option, 2-13
querying the database, 9-2

R

radar chart, 17-4, 17-27
read-only export format (.rptr), 1-8,
    13-9, 13-20
Record Selection Formula Editor, 14-9
record selection formula field, 10-23
record selection formula option, 14-7
Record Sort Expert, 10-6, 10-13
recordnumber special field, 16-14
recordset, 5-2
recursive join, 3-13, 5-14, 22-10
Refresh Report Data dialog box, 19-9
refreshing report data, 4-14
region & language options, 8-9
relational database, 3-2, 5-9
relationships, 3-2, 5-10
remove all horizontal guidelines, 6-2
remove all vertical guidelines, 6-2
remove toolbars, 2-6
repeat group header on each page, 16-9
report bursting indexes, 4-13, 4-16
report creation options, 3-10
report custom functions, 14-9
report design process, 3-4
Report Explorer, 8-12
Report Explorer section shortcut menu, 8-14
report fields tree, 14-10
report menu options, 2-14
Report Options dialog box, 13-7

report packages, 3-18
report processing model, 4-21
report prototype, 3-8
report sections, 3-8, 3-18
report summary information, 9-18
report viewer, 13-21
Report wizard, 3-11, 12-2
Reporting tab options (Options
    dialog box), 2-21
repository custom functions, 14-9
Repository Explorer, 3-25
reserve minimum page footer, 16-5
reset options (running total), 22-6
reset page numbers, 16-7
resize chart, 18-3
resize handles, 6-3
resize image, 7-6
resize objects, 6-9
right outer join type, 5-12
rotate text, 7-12
Rounding tab options (Format Editor), 8-6
row color formula, 16-14, 20-19
rulers, 3-18
running total field, 3-22, 10-16, 22-4
run-time errors, 14-31

S
sample standard deviation function, 10-9
sample variance function, 10-9
save preview picture, 9-18
Saved Data Indexes dialog box, 4-16
Saved Data Selection Formula Editor, 14-9
saved data selection formula option, 14-7
saving data options, 4-13, 9-5
Search Expert dialog box, 2-9
section bars, 3-18
Section Expert, 8-2, 16-2
section short names, 2-19, 3-8, 10-11
sections of a report, 3-8, 3-18
secure logon option, 4-4
Select Barcode Type dialog box, 22-2
select case statement, 14-5, 15-17
select distinct data for browsing, 4-6
Select Expert, 9-3, 9-5, 9-7
select expert button, 2-6
selecting fields and objects, 6-3
selecting records, 9-2
selection formulas, 14-9
Send Mail dialog box, 2-8
separated values (csv) export options, 13-19
Series Options dialog box, 18-17
set data source location, 2-13

Set Default Export Options dialog box, 13-12
set parameter order option, 19-9
Set Print Date and Time dialog box, 13-6
shortcut menus, 6-2
show as a percentage of option, 10-10, 11-6
show field names, 2-19, 7-16
show formula button, 9-7
show gridlines, 17-15
show hidden sections in design, 6-2
show last page button, 3-15
show on (viewer) panel, 19-5
Show SQL Query dialog box, 2-13
show value(s) option, 17-7
size options, 6-10
slice of pie chart, 17-24
smart linking, 3-2, 5-14
Smart Tag & HTML preview options
    (Options dialog box), 2-23
snap to grid, 6-9
software updates, 1-10
sort control, 22-2
sort detail records, 10-13
sorting data (with a parameter field), 20-21
sorting records, 10-6
special fields, 3-4, 3-22, 8-7
SQL, 5-3
SQL Expression Editor, 14-12
SQL expression field, 3-22
Standard Report wizard, 12-3
Standard toolbar, 2-2
start page tab, 1-8, 1-9
starts with operator, 9-3
statements, 14-5
static list of values, 19-15
Statistics tab options, 9-19
status bar, 3-14
stock chart, 17-5, 17-28
stored procedures, 5-3
string formulas, 14-21
string functions, 14-21
string operators, 14-21
string summary calculation options, 10-8
Structured Query Language, 5-3
subdivided by option, 17-12
Subreport Links dialog box, 2-10
subscript operator, 14-23
subsections, 8-2
sum function, 10-9
summarize across hierarchy
    option, 10-10, 22-12
summarized field labels options
    (cross-tab), 21-15

summary calculation options (numeric), 10-9
summary calculation options (string), 10-8
summary fields, 3-4
summary location option, 10-10
summary options, 10-10
Summary tab options, 9-18
Suppress (No Drill-Down) option, 16-11
suppress data (with a parameter field), 20-24
suppressing fields, 15-12
suppressing sections, 15-12, 16-10
swapping fields, 8-16
syntax language and editors, 14-4
syntax rules, 14-3
system tables, 5-4

T

table alias, 5-17
Template Expert dialog box, 2-15
Template screen, 12-7
templates (chart), 18-20
text export options, 13-21
text field (object) formatting, 7-4
text interpretation, 7-13
text object fields, 3-4
text rotation, 7-12
Text tab options (Chart Expert), 17-18
time field formatting, 7-16
Time tab options (Custom Style), 7-16
toolbar shortcut menu, 2-6
toolbars, 2-2
Toolbars dialog box, 2-6
top 5 groups option, 12-6
Top N report, 12-6, 12-10, 20-16, 21-20
ToText function, 14-21, 14-26, 14-27
trendlines, 18-6
trim (str) function, 14-22
truncate function, 14-30
Type tab options (Chart Expert), 17-3

U

UCase function, 14-22
underlay following sections option, 18-7
undock (Explorer) option, 3-28
union join type, 5-12
Universes, 4-4
unmanaged lists, 19-14
updates, 1-10
uppercase (str) function, 14-22
use a formula as group name, 16-9
use a formula as group sort order,
    10-4, 11-13
use current parameter values, 19-9

use depth effect, 17-4, 18-9
use indexes or server for speed, 9-17
use saved data, 9-8
user defined groups, 11-12
user defined sort order, 10-5

V

vertical alignment options, 6-4
vertical lines, 7-22
view menu options, 2-10
viewing formulas, 9-11
Visual Linking Editor dialog box, 5-15

W

watermark, 22-16
week to date from sun function, 9-4
weighted average with function, 10-9
while do/do while, 14-5
while printing records, 22-4
wildcard characters, 9-18, 20-15
window menu options, 2-17
wizards, 3-10
Workbench, 3-18, 3-20, 4-16
Workshop tree, 14-9
workspace, 3-13

X

X axis, 17-15
XML export format, 13-21
XML Export Options dialog box, 13-21
Xtreme database, 3-11
XY scatter chart, 17-4, 17-25

Y

Y axis, 17-15
year function, 14-27
year to date function, 9-4

Z

Z axis, 17-15
Zoom dialog box, 2-11
zoom options, 3-15
zooming in/out on charts, 18-2

No Stress Tech Guides

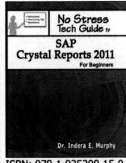

ISBN: 978-1-935208-15-0

ISBN: 978-1-935208-17-4

ISBN: 978-1-935208-16-7

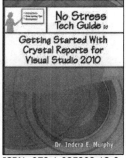

ISBN: 978-1-935208-12-9

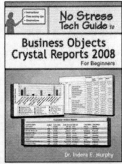

ISBN: 978-0-9773912-9-5

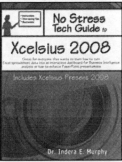

ISBN: 978-1-935208-05-1

ISBN: 978-1-935208-14-3

ISBN: 978-1-935208-00-6

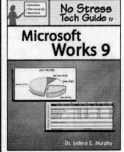

ISBN: 978-0-9773912-7-1

ISBN: 978-1-935208-08-2

ISBN: 978-1-935208-10-5

ISBN: 978-0-9773912-8-8

Visit us online to see the entire series www.tolanapublishing.com

Lightning Source UK Ltd.
Milton Keynes UK
UKOW021336310513

211564UK00004B/10/P